CCH/Advocis FPSC-approved Capstone Course

1st Edition

CCH Canadian Limited
300-90 Sheppard Avenue East
Toronto Ontario
M2N 6X1
1 800 268 4522
www.cch.ca

.CCH
a Wolters Kluwer business

Advocis®
The Financial Advisors Association of Canada

Published by CCH Canadian Limited

Edited by:
Jill Booker, Hon. B.Sc.

The right to use the marks CFP®, CERTIFIED FINANCIAL PLANNER® and CFP is granted under licence by FPSC to those persons who have met its educational standards, passed the FPSC CERTIFIED FINANCIAL PLANNER Examination, satisfied a work experience requirement and abide by FPSC Code of Ethics.

ISBN: 9781554961184

© 2009, CCH Canadian Limited
First Edition

Typeset by CCH Canadian Limited.
Printed in the United States of America.

Preface

CCH acknowledges Jamie Aldcorn, CA, CFP, MBA, M.Ed., for the revision of this course. Jamie would like to thank Sandra, his wife, and Jill Booker from CCH Canadian, for their patience and assistance during the preparation of this textbook.

This program was originally developed under the leadership and guidance of Deborah Kraft, BBA, CFP, CLU, CH.F.C., TEP. In addition to Deborah, other contributors to this program include James Kraft, CA, MTax, CFP, CLU, CH.F.C., TEP, John McIlroy, B.A. (Hons), M.A., MBA, MTax, and Mary Lawless, B.A.

About the CFP® Education Program

The CFP® is an internationally recognized designation held by more than 100,000 people in 19 countries around the world. Financial Planners Standards Council (FPSC), a member of the Financial Planning Standards Board (FPSB), has licensed more than 17,000 individuals in Canada.

Qualifying to take FPSC's CERTIFIED FINANCIAL PLANNER (CFP®) Examination is a demanding process. Yet the professional rewards for successful candidates are significant. On average, CFP professionals who have achieved this coveted certification report a substantial increase in gross income and preferred clients in comparison to non-designates.

This CFP® Education Program is an accredited qualifying course of study designed with the CFP certification requirements in mind. By successfully completing this course of study, you'll gain both the knowledge and confidence to help you succeed in obtaining the designation, and in building a thriving financial planning practice. Working with industry experts, we have created five comprehensive courses, containing 28 modules of current and relevant content. Topics covered closely match the CFP® Professional Competency Profile and Examination Blueprint. By focusing on the most important concepts and required skills, this program helps you optimize your study time.

The Competency Profile

FPSC has publicized its "CFP® Professional Competency Profile: FPSC's Standards of Competence for CFP® Professionals". The Competency Profile is based on a comprehensive analysis of the profession and establishes the complete set of financial planning competencies required of a CFP professional. As described by FPSC, the competencies:

- provide a description of what CFP professionals must be able to do in practice;

- offer a description of the abilities that professionals possess; and

- give a representation of the tasks, job-related skills, knowledge, attitudes and judgments required for competent performance by members of the profession.

The Competency Profile reflects current practice, but also considers the expectations of the profession over the next several years.

Impact on CFP Examination Candidates: You can use the Competency Profile to understand the scope of competence required for the CFP Examination. It is the foundation for the blueprint of what is tested on the CFP Examination. All registrants in our CFP® Education Program are strongly advised to visit the FPSC Web site (www.cfp-ca.org) to obtain detailed information pertaining to both The Competency Profile and the CFP® Examination Blueprint.

Impact on CCH Canadian and Advocis as a CFP Education Provider: The Competency Profile will be used to guide the development of our financial planning curriculum to support program registrants in acquiring the knowledge, skills and abilities needed to meet professional requirements. Anticipating the provision of The Competency Profile, our CFP® Education Program has an increased focus on application of knowledge by incorporating:

- study note application pieces that are mini-cases used throughout the program to expand upon or explain concepts;

- additional exercises, problems and/or case studies at the end of each module in each course to help you apply learning and retain knowledge; and

- comprehensive cases that help integrate concepts presented in individual modules.

Our CFP® Education Program will focus on further incorporating changes that meet the requirements of The Competency Profile and related development of Professional Skills and Technical Knowledge. Our commitment to continuous improvement enables us to adapt and evolve the program's study and testing materials to meet the evolving education needs of the CFP professional.

CCH/Advocis FPSC-approved Capstone Course — First Edition

This course begins with a profile of the Canadian financial planning industry and reviews the professional Code of Ethics and Practice Standards. A summary of key topics from the core curriculum is organized into the six areas of technical knowledge (Modules 20–26). The CFP® Professional Competency Profile and CFP Examination Blueprint are covered along with examination writing techniques in Module 27. The final section of the course provides the student with case studies and multiple-choice questions to practice and test their knowledge.

Module 20 The Financial Planning Industry

Module 21 Taxation Planning

Module 22 Risk Management and Insurance

Module 23 Asset Management

Module 24 Retirement Planning

Module 25 Estate Planning

Module 26 Financial Management

Module 27 Path to the CFP Certification and Examination Review

Module 28 FPSC Financial Plan and Case Studies

Features of this Course

This course textbook/online edition offers pedagogical features that have been developed to create enhanced learning opportunities.

Detailed Table of Contents — These provide students with a comprehensive summary for each module.

Study Note Application Piece (SNAP) — SNAPs are mini-cases used throughout the program to expand or explain concepts. SNAPs are important for building student confidence in dealing with cases.

Index — There is an index, which provides easy access for locating key terms, for each module, as well as a comprehensive index for the course text.

Self-Test Questions & Solutions — There is a section at the end of each module with questions and solutions based on the content of the module for self-testing your comprehension of the material.

End of Module Exercises and Case Studies — Additional self-review materials are included in this edition of the study text. You are encouraged to work through these self-test exercises and case studies because they provide further opportunity for you to review and reinforce the concepts learned, as well as prepare for the module tests and the course exam. Please note that the solutions to these additional review materials are not included in the study text.

How do you obtain the withheld solutions?

In-class students can obtain these solutions from your instructor who, in turn, will have received them from CCH. Self-study registrants taking the course online will find the solutions within the course content resident in the "My Courses" section of Training Sphere, the course Web site where you will take your module tests and course exams. Semester-based, self-study students may obtain these solutions from Advocis on request, if not received beforehand.

The Use of a Financial Calculator — A financial calculator is required for this course. For ease of learning, the Hewlett Packard 10BII is the recommended calculator as helpful hints and calculator instructions within the course material refer to specific features of the HP10BII calculator. The HP10B calculator is an older version of the HP10BII calculator and will work equally as well, although the key locations vary slightly.

Can you use another financial calculator? Definitely yes, provided that your financial calculator has the capability of calculating internal rates of return, the net present value of a stream of future cash flows, as well as time value of money problems. In addition, you should be familiar with the required keystrokes of your own calculator.

The financial calculator utilized for CFP Course One is suitable and meets all of the requirements.

GENDER REFERENCE

To avoid repetition with references to he/she or his/her, the program has been developed utilizing feminine references for even-numbered modules and masculine references for odd-numbered modules. The terms he and she are interchangeable throughout the course content unless otherwise noted.

STUDENT EDITION SOFTWARE

Your text includes CDs with educational versions of the following financial planning software products:

- oneSource: CCH Canadian's Financial Planning Research Library; and
- FP Solutions Advanced: CCH Canadian's Financial Planning Software.

Disc 1: CCH Canadian Financial Planning Research Library — This educational version of the extensive electronic research library gives you a wealth of planning information, including the basics of finance, insurance, investment planning, taxation, estate and retirement planning. The CCH library allows you to do key word and phrase searches and will direct you to the information you need. Hypertext links to the references in oneSource will guide you to legislation, commentary, government forms and checklists relevant to your practice or program of study. *Note:* The tests and course exam are based only on the content in the study text.

Disc 2: CCH Canadian Financial Planning Software — The educational version of CCH Canadian's array of financial planning software, which is available in four levels of complexity, includes a demo of *FP Solutions Advanced* software. *FP Solutions Advanced* allows advisors to analyze a client's entire financial situation, including cash flow analysis, and is considered the most appropriate level to accompany the course material. Students can become familiar with the program using the demo and then contact CCH Canadian to receive a free subscription for four months to the commercial version.

THE CFP® EDUCATION PROGRAM: AN OVERVIEW

Course 1 (Advocis 231) — *Financial Planning Fundamentals — Third Edition*

This course introduces the fundamentals important to the discipline of financial planning. Students will acquire an understanding of the concepts and applications associated with financial calculations and the analysis of financial statements. The basic concepts of contracting and family law are covered, followed by an analysis of government sponsored benefit programs.

Course 2 (Advocis 232) — *Contemporary Practices in Financial Planning — Seventh Edition*

This course introduces students to basic income tax laws, moving into a more advanced study as these laws relate to areas of financial planning. A review of the professional and ethical responsibilities associated with the role of a financial planner and an understanding of the structures and services within the financial industry are covered in the course. Different forms of business structures are explored in-depth, along with an understanding of trusts.

Course 3 (Advocis 233) — *Comprehensive Practices in Risk and Retirement Planning — Third Edition*

Designed to provide students with a comprehensive understanding of the principles and applications related to the concepts of managing risk and retirement planning, this course covers products, issues and practices in the area of insurance and retirement. Included is an understanding of the risk management process along with the retirement planning process moving through the wealth accumulation phase into retirement.

Course 4 (Advocis 234) — *Wealth Management and Estate Planning — Third Edition*

This course introduces the student to the fundamentals important to the topics of economics and investing as they relate to key areas of financial planning. It examines a broad array of investment products and explores the subject of personal financial management. The course concludes with estate planning fundamentals, concepts and applications.

Advocis 239 — *CCH/Advocis FPSC-approved Capstone Course — First Edition*

This course begins with a profile of the Canadian financial planning industry, and reviews the professional Code of Ethics, Practice Standards, and the six areas of technical knowledge. The CFP® Professional Competency Profile and CFP® Examination Blueprint are covered along with examination writing techniques. The final section of the course provides the student with case studies and multiple-choice questions to practice and test their knowledge.

PROGRAM COMPLETION REQUIREMENTS

Successful completion of the Capstone Course qualifies students to write the Financial Planners Standards Council's Financial Planning Examination Level 2 (FPE2).

ACADEMIC PARTNERS

For the Instructor

Instructors who have chosen this study guide for their program offering have access to test and exam content for use with the program. Contact us for more information on the implementation of student assessment. PowerPoint slides are available for each module. Instructors also receive complimentary study texts with CCH Canadian student edition software including access to technical support. More information on instructor support material is available from CCH.

For the In-Class Student

Please direct enquiries regarding course content to your instructor; however, you may contact CCH Canadian technical support for queries regarding the educational software in the accompanying CDs contained in the study guide. Identify the course taken and the specific software program when speaking to a CCH Canadian client service representative.

SELF-STUDY LEARNERS

For those who are working through the course on a self-study basis, the following information will be helpful to your success in learning and mastering the content within the program. Self-study learners will have online access to a qualified Study Leader through the Training Sphere Web site. Students will also have access to an online open forum.

Self-study learners may contact CCH Canadian technical support for queries regarding the educational software in the accompanying CDs contained in the study guide. Please identify the course taken and the specific software program when speaking to a CCH Canadian client service representative.

Overview

Course Five consists of nine modules. Upon the completion of the financial planning modules (Modules 20–26), students are required to complete two multiple-choice tests. After completion of the course, students write a course exam that covers material from all modules.

Students enrolled in the fifth course will submit two written tests, provided at registration, and write the course exam at one of the regularly scheduled exam sittings. Academic institutions will administer student tests and exams to in-class students.

These tests are mandatory and must be completed in sequential order. Students who have not completed all module tests will not be allowed to write the exam and, therefore, will not pass the course.

THE COURSE PROCESS

Step	Action	Module Number	Module Name
One	Study	20	The Financial Planning Industry
Two	Study	21	Taxation Planning
Three	Study	22	Risk Management and Insurance
Four	Study	23	Asset Management
Five	Study	24	Retirement Planning
Six	Study	25	Estate Planning
Seven	Study	26	Financial Management
Eight	Study	27	Path to the CFP Certification and Examination Review
Nine	Study	28	FPSC Financial Plan and Case Studies

Step Nine:

<u>Self-study students</u> must write two tests, as directed at registration, that cover Modules 20 to 22 and Modules 23 to 26. The final comprehensive course exam will be administered at a designated exam location. There are three semesters per year in which self-study students may enroll. The time and location of exams will be available on the program provider's Web site.

<u>Students in Academic Settings</u> will receive direction from their instructor.

Course Marks

Tests (combined)	40% of total mark
Exam	60% of total mark

To pass this course, the student must obtain a minimum overall grade of at least 60%.

Each test or exam may be written only once.

Self-study students who do not obtain a minimum overall grade of at least 60% may apply to write a paper-based supplemental exam for a fee. This option is available only once.

THE CFP
EDUCATION PROGRAM

CCH/ADVOCIS FPSC-APPROVED CAPSTONE COURSE

MODULE 20
THE FINANCIAL PLANNING INDUSTRY

Module 20
THE FINANCIAL PLANNING INDUSTRY

Module 20
The Financial Planning Industry

INTRODUCTION

"CCH/Advocis FPSC-approved Capstone Course" is the Capstone Course within the CCH/Advocis CFP qualifying education program. The course builds on the foundation of the technical knowledge and skills acquired from the first four core curriculum CCH/Advocis courses to assist the CFP student in integrating the information across all the elements of financial planning. The course uses a competency-based approach to review the technical and professional skills required of today's Certified Financial Planner® (CFP). The Capstone Course's focus is the financial planning practices, professional skills, and integration which are inherent in the Competency Profile and essential to the practice of financial planning. The Capstone Course integrates all of the components of financial planning and requires completion of a comprehensive financial plan.

This textbook begins with an overview of the financial planning industry, recent developments in the CFP professional standards and the Code of Ethics and Practice Standards. The second section focuses on the six financial planning components (financial, asset and risk management, and tax, retirement and estate planning). Each module covers the CFP Competency Profile Technical Knowledge in the same order as Appendix B of the CFP Competency Profile. The third section discusses the CFP Professional Competency Profile (Competency Profile), the structure of the CFP examination process and exam writing techniques. The final section allows the student to apply and practice what they have learned during the course using case studies and multiple choice questions to assess the student's comprehension of the technical and professional competencies. The course is essential for anyone preparing to write the national CFP® Financial Planning Examinations — FPE1 or FPE2.

FPSC-APPROVED CAPSTONE COURSE LEARNING OBJECTIVES[1]

Upon successful completion of the course, the student should be able to:

- Apply and integrate technical knowledge gained from core curriculum courses (prerequisite and co-requisite) in the identification and analysis of issues relating to personal financial planning.
- Collect all qualitative and quantitative information required to develop a financial plan.
- Evaluate client's objectives, needs and values that have financial implications.
- Analyze and synthesize personal financial situations.
- Identify potential opportunities and constraints, assess information to formulate strategies.
- Formulate and evaluate strategies to develop a financial plan.
- Prioritize and consolidate recommendations into a financial plan.
- Communicate information, ideas, and concepts to clients and others in a written and oral manner that is understandable.

In the process of completing the Capstone Course Learning Objectives listed above, the student should integrate the following objectives:

- Demonstrate ethical judgment in providing professional services.

---

[1] FPSC Capstone Course Guidelines, August 2009.

- Assess the impact of the economic, political and regulatory environments on financial situations.
- Demonstrate logic and reasoning to identify the strengths and weaknesses of alternatives or approaches to problems.
- Adhere to FPSC's CFP Code of Ethics and the CFP Financial Planning Practice Standards as they apply to the financial planning process.

In regards to the financial plan requirement, the student will be able to:

- Address issues across a wide range of financial planning components.
- Integrate the financial planning components and clearly prioritize the components that may be most relevant given the client's position in her life cycle.
- Demonstrate the fundamental financial planning competencies.
- Make recommendations, supported by appropriate analysis and synthesis.
- Demonstrate appropriate professionals skills when creating and presenting financial plans.
- Communicate a completed comprehensive financial plan clearly and professionally.

Unit 1

Financial Planning Overview

THE FINANCIAL PLANNING INDUSTRY

The financial services industry has undergone significant changes in the last ten years. As the traditional four pillars of the financial services industry — banks, trust companies, insurance companies and investment dealers — have been deregulated, it has lead to more choice in financial products and services for consumers. Financial planning is a small component of the larger financial services industry. Financial Planners Standards Council (FPSC) defines personal financial planning as the integrative process of developing strategies to help clients manage their financial affairs to meet life goals.[2] Key to the financial planning profession is the ability to identify and analyze interrelationships among sometimes conflicting objectives across a large breadth of financial planning activities. Based on the client's needs, a financial plan may deal with one or all of the six main financial planning components including financial management, asset management, risk management, taxation or retirement and estate planning.

The CFP® designation identifies individuals who adhere to internationally recognized professional standards in education, experience and ethics as established in Canada by the not-for-profit FPSC. There are more than 17,000 CFPs in Canada. A CFP professional is also guided by the Code of Ethics and Practice Standards. FPSC is supported by the following organizations: Advocis, the Canadian Institute of Chartered Accountants, The Canadian Institute of Financial Planning, Certified General Accountants of Canada, Certified Management Accountants of Canada, and the CUSOURCE Credit Union Knowledge Network.

The following provides a snapshot of CFP membership in 2008.[3] Fifty per cent of the members have been within the industry for less than sixteen years. The majority of CFPs work for financial planning, mutual fund, banks/trusts, or insurance companies. Over 86% have a post-secondary level of education, and many hold other professional designations. The members are mainly compensated based on commissions (49%) or salary and bonus (21%), and most have more than 200 clients each. The average income is over $75,000, with 32% of the members making over $150,000. Nearly 70% of the members are male.

---

[2] FPSC, "CFP Professional Competency Profile", page 1.

[3] FPSC, Annual report, 2007-2008.

In 2006, FPSC released the "CFP Professional Competency Profile" which outlines the set of financial planning competencies and technical knowledge, skills and abilities required of a CFP professional. The profile is based on financial planning being defined as "the process of creating strategies to help clients manage their financial affairs to meet life goals". There are three levels of activities: collection (gathering, calculating and determining facts), analysis (identifying potential opportunities and strategies), and synthesis (development and the evaluation of recommendations/strategies). Within each financial planning activity there are six financial planning components: financial management, asset management, risk management, tax planning, retirement planning and estate planning, and four sets of professional skills: ethical judgment, professional practice, written and oral communication. The six components are based on eleven technical areas covering taxation, insurance, investments, and related areas. Modules 21–26 address the six financial planning components. Additional information on the Competency Profile is located in Module 27 of the textbook.

NEW RULES FOR CFP CERTIFICATION

In November 2008, FPSC released new requirements for obtaining CFP certification effective July 1, 2010. These requirements will affect all candidates who have not passed the CFP Examination by June 2010. Candidates who qualify under the Approved Prior Credential policy (CA, CGA, CMA, CFA, CLU, FCIA, LL.B., or Ph.D. in Business, Finance, or Economics) must complete both exams and successfully complete an FPSC-approved Capstone Course.

Candidates applying to FPSC to meet or repeat the examination requirement of the CFP certification program on or after July 1, 2010 will be enrolled in the new program and must abide by the new requirements. The current six-hour CFP Examination will not be offered after June 2010 and will be fully replaced by a two-stage examination process, Financial Planning Examination Level 1 (FPE1) and Financial Planning Examination Level 2 (FPE2). The first FPE1 sitting will be in November 2010. The first FPE2 sitting will be held in June 2011. A candidate can only attempt each exam a maximum of four times.

In order to be eligible to write the FPE2, the candidate is required to successfully complete an FPSC-approved Capstone Course such as this CCH/Advocis course, in addition to successful completion of FPSC-approved core curriculum education (Courses 1 to 4 of the CCH/Advocis CFP Program), and obtaining at least one year of work experience. The Capstone Course requires the completion of a financial plan.

The work experience required has increased from two years to three years. One year of qualifying financial planning work experience must be completed prior to writing the FPE2. In additional, all candidates must adhere to the Code of Conduct established by the FPSC and maintain continuous registration with FPSC throughout the path to CFP certification.

Additional information is in Module 27 and available from the FPSC at http://www.fpsccanada.org/public/new_cfp_certification_guidelines. See Appendix Two for a summary of the key changes to CFP certification requirements.

SIX-STEP FINANCIAL PLANNING PROCESS

There are six steps which should be followed during the process of financial planning. The following provides a summary of the activities in each step (see Appendix One for further details).

Step #	Planning Step
One	Establishing the client-planner engagement.
Two	Gathering client data and determining goals and expectations.
Three	Clarifying and identifying: • financial status; • problem areas; and • opportunities.
Four	Developing strategies to meet the client's needs and goals, and presenting the financial plan.
Five	Implementing the financial plan.
Six	Monitoring the financial plan.

PROFESSIONAL SKILLS

Professional skills address the fundamental abilities and personal traits that define a financial planning professional. A CFP professional is expected to conduct themselves as a professional when dealing with clients and other colleagues. Professional skills are inherent in the performance of every competency. The nature of the Professional Skills in the CFP Professional Competency Matrix overlays the complete Competency Profile.

The Competency Profile identifies four sets of Professional Skills, each with specific indicators of performance, as follows:

- Ethical Judgment
- Practice
- Communication
- Cognitive

PS. 1. Ethical Judgment

PS. 101 Establishes client relationships based on trust

PS. 102 Offers and provides professional services with integrity

PS. 103 Demonstrates objectivity in providing professional services

PS. 104 Acts in the best interest of the client in providing professional services

PS. 105 Recognizes limits of competence and voluntarily seeks the counsel of and/or defers to other professionals when appropriate

PS. 106 Performs professional services in a manner that is fair and reasonable

PS. 107 Provides appropriate and timely disclosure of conflicts of interest to clients and others

PS. 108 Maintains confidentiality of all client information

PS. 109 Acts in order to reflect credit upon the profession

PS. 110 Acts diligently in providing professional services

PS. 2. Practice

PS. 201 Complies with relevant financial services laws and regulations

PS. 202 Adheres to professional code of ethics and standards of professional practice

PS. 203 Makes appropriate judgments in areas not addressed by existing ethical or practice standards

PS. 204 Maintains awareness of changes in the economic, political and regulatory environment

PS. 205 Engages in continuous learning to ensure currency of knowledge and skills

PS. 206 Conducts appropriate research when performing analysis and developing strategies

PS. 207 Exercises substantial autonomy and initiative in the performance of professional activities

PS. 208 Exercises responsibility for own and/or firm's ability to deliver services to a client for the duration of engagement

PS. 3. Communication

PS. 301 Gives attention to what clients and others are saying and takes time to understand the points being made

PS. 302 Establishes good rapport and relationships with clients and others

PS. 303 Communicates information and ideas orally in a manner understandable to clients and others

PS. 304 Communicates information and ideas in writing in a manner understandable to clients and others

PS. 305 Presents logical and persuasive rationales

PS. 306 Deals effectively with objections and complaints

PS. 4. Cognitive

PS. 401 Uses mathematical methods or formulas as appropriate

PS. 402 Gathers data and integrates information from a variety of sources to arrive at a solution

PS. 403 Uses logic and reasoning to identify the strengths and weaknesses of alternative solutions, conclusions or approaches to problems

PS. 404 Considers the relative costs and benefits of potential actions to choose the appropriate one

PS. 405 Makes informed professional decisions when faced with incomplete or inconsistent information

FPSC CODE OF ETHICS

The FPSC's Council Code of Ethics consists of two parts: *Part 1 — Principles* and *Part II — Rules*. Principles are statements expressing the ethical and professional ideals of CFP professionals. The seven principles are: Integrity, Objectivity, Competence, Fairness, Confidentiality, Professionalism, and Diligence. The Rules provide practical guidelines for the principles.

To help the candidate remember the principles, there is a phrase that can be derived from the first letter of each Principle: *I Owe Canada Five Cents Per Day* (Integrity, Objectivity, Competence, Fairness, Confidentiality, Professionalism, and Diligence).

A summary of the Code of Ethics follows. See http://www.fpsccanada.org/professionals/code_ethics for a complete version.

Principle 1: Integrity

A CFP professional shall always act with integrity.

Rule 101: Shall not associate with conduct involving false or misleading statements.

Rule 102: Responsibilities regarding funds/client property include: doing so with care required of a fiduciary, acting only in accordance with governing legal instrument, maintaining complete records of property, not commingle client funds and personal funds, and only using client funds or property for means intended and authorized by the client.

Rule 103: Shall not solicit clients through false/misleading communication about the size, scope, or areas of competence of the CFP of firm, nor give the impression she is representing the views of the FPSC or any other group unless authorized.

Principle 2: Objectivity

A CFP professional shall be objective in providing financial planning to clients.

Rule 201: Shall exercise reasonable and prudent professional judgment in providing financial planning.

Rule 202: Shall act in the interests of the client.

Principle 3: Competence

A CFP professional shall provide services to clients competently and maintain the necessary knowledge and skill to continue to do so in those areas in which the CFP professional is engaged.

Rule 301: Only offer advice on those areas in which CFP is competent. If not competent in an area, seek council of or refer clients to qualified individuals.

Rule 302: Do not intervene in the personal affairs of clients on matters outside the scope of the engagement.

Principle 4: Fairness

A CFP professional shall perform financial planning in a manner that is fair and reasonable to clients, principals, partners, and employers and shall disclose conflicts of interest in providing such services.

Rule 401: Timely disclosure of all material information/facts, i.e., how the CFP is paid, third party relationships, conflicts of interest, and compliance with all laws and regulations.

Rule 402: Tell client what services are within your scope as a CFP (versus broker).

Rule 403: Inform client of changes in conflicts of interest, business affiliations, compensation structure, new or changed agency relationships.

Rule 404: Disclose contingency fee based compensation arrangements in writing.

Rule 405: Do not violate applicable human rights legislation.

Principle 5: Confidentiality

A CFP professional shall maintain confidentiality of all client information.

Rule 501: Do not disclose confidential client information without client consent, unless in response to a proper legal or regulatory process.

Rule 502: Do not disclose confidential information gained by reason of your position unless required by law.

Rule 503: Do not use client information for personal benefit.

Rule 504: Maintain same level of confidentiality for an employee as for clients.

Rule 505: If acting as a Partner of a financial services firm, you owe a duty to act in good faith with the other partners.

Principle 6: Professionalism

A CFP professional's conduct in all matters shall reflect credit upon the profession.

Rule 601: Do not engage in any conduct that reflects adversely on the profession or the CFP Marks.

Rule 602: Use the Marks in compliance with FPSC rules.

Rule 603: Inform the FPSC if another CFP has violated the Code.

Rule 604: Do not criticize another CFP without notifying her first. May submit criticism directly to FPSC should the matter be of such a nature that proper notice is not appropriate.

Rule 605: Inform appropriate regulatory and/or professional body if you have knowledge that raises a substantial question of unprofessional, fraudulent, or illegal conduct by a CFP professional.

Rule 606: Inform supervisor/partners of your firm if you have reason to suspect illegal conduct within the firm.

Rule 607: Perform financial planning in accordance with laws, rules, and regulations.

Rule 608: Do not obtain clients in a way that lowers the dignity of the profession.

Rule 609: Only provide services that you are qualified/licensed or registered to provide.

Rule 610: Return client records on a timely basis.

Rule 611: Do not use the Code to harass, maliciously injure, embarrass, and/or unfairly burden another CFP professional.

Principle 7: Diligence

A CFP professional shall act diligently in providing financial planning.

Rule 701: Only enter into a client engagement after securing sufficient information that the relationship is warranted by the individual's needs and objectives and that the CFP has the ability to provide the services or supervise other professionals in providing the services.

Rule 702: Make/implement only those recommendations that are suitable for the client.

Rule 703: Do reasonable investigation of the financial products you recommend to your clients.

Rule 704: Give the client reasonable advanced notice of your intent to stop providing services to the client.

Rule 705: Properly supervise subordinates in their delivery of financial planning. Do not condone or accept conduct in violation of this Code.

CONTINUING EDUCATION (CE) REQUIREMENTS[4]

FPSC's CE Requirements

New Continuing Education requirements took effect January 1, 2009. In order to maintain FPSC's high standard of competence, CFP® professionals and successful CFP Examination candidates are obligated to complete at least 30 Continuing Education (CE) credits annually. This must be attested to each year upon renewal.

All CE credits must be related to the CFP Professional Competency Profile. Of the 30 CE credits required, a minimum of 20 CE credits must be in the verifiable category. A CFP professional may claim up to a maximum of 10 non-verifiable CE credits per year. CE credits are accumulated on a calendar year basis (between January 1 and December 31).

- **CE Activities must focus exclusively on the CFP Professional Competency Profile.** All CE activities undertaken in 2009 and thereafter must be directly related to the Competency Profile. They can be related to:
  — Elements of Competency
  — Professional Skills
  — Technical Knowledge
- **New classification of CE activities.** Activities will be classified as "verifiable" or "non-verifiable", determined by the supporting documentation submitted for that activity. "Technical" and "general" categories will no longer apply.
- **More CE credits allowed for approved courses.** Under the new policy, courses may be eligible for a maximum of 40 CE credits; this was previously limited to 30.

Reporting and Supporting Documentation

CFP professionals are required to attest to the completion of their CE requirements for the calendar year specified on the annual Application for FPSC License Renewal Form. No supporting documentation is required at the time of renewal.

Any verifiable excess credits carried over from the previous year may also be subject to audit; FPSC offers an online tool for CE tracking that all CFP professionals may use to help in logging accumulated CE credits. It is recommended that all CE supporting documentation be kept for at least three years.

Audit

A percentage of CFP professionals are chosen randomly for the CE audit each year. CFP professionals who renew late are more likely to be audited, and anyone who must be reinstated is automatically subject to audit. Additionally, to maintain the integrity of the

---

[4] *Note:* The Continuing Education information provided in this section is reproduced from FPSC's Web site (www.fpsccanada.org) with permission. While it is accurate at the time of printing, the reader is strongly advised to review FPSC's Web site for current requirements.

financial planning profession, FPSC reserves the right to audit any CFP professional for any reason. CFP professionals who are selected for audit will be requested to supply supporting documentation for their verifiable credits. Supporting documentation is not required for non-verifiable credits.

Failure to Comply

CFP professionals who fail to comply with the CE requirements or Audit requirements within the stipulated period will be suspended and may be subject to disciplinary action by FPSC. Misstated or fraudulent reporting of CE credits will be reported to the Enforcement Department as a violation of the FPSC's Code of Ethics.

Exemptions

A CFP professional can request an exemption from CE requirements for one calendar year due to extenuating circumstances. These requests are reviewed on a case-by-case basis, and may include such things as medical, disability, or parental leave.

Continuing Education Categories

Verifiable CE Credits

Of the 30 CE credits required, a minimum of 20 CE credits must be in the verifiable category. Verifiable CE activities can be supported by the following types of documentation:

- Certificate of attendance, which must include the following:
  — Participant's name
  — Date of the activity
  — Name of the activity
  — Signature and/or stamp of the Education Provider
- Personalized letter from Education Provider on letterhead, which must include the following:
  — Participant's name
  — Date of the activity
  — Duration for seminars/conferences/programs/presentation
  — Signature and/or stamped of Education Provider
  — Signatory's contact information

FPSC requests that course descriptions and/or agendas indicating the duration of the program are included with the submission. If this information is not provided, it may result in a delay and/or the activity may not be approved.

- Transcripts from the Education Provider, which must include the following:
  — Participant's/Student's name
  — Date of enrollment and/or date of completion
  — Name of the course

This must be an official transcript or photocopy. Course description/curriculum must be included upon submission.

- Contracts for Teaching, which must include the following:
  — Instructor/Presenter's name
  — Duration of the course
  — Year/semester of the course
- Supporting documentation for writing engagement:
  — Contract for Writing Assignment
  — Sample of the articles must be attached
  — The articles must have been written in the year they are reported

— Pay stubs/Receipt/Invoice

The above list of sufficient supporting documentation is not all-inclusive and FPSC will consider other documentation upon request.

Non-Verifiable CE Credits

A CFP professional may claim up to a maximum of 10 non-verifiable CE credits per year. A non-verifiable activity is an activity that:

- Cannot be verified by a third party with supporting documentation,

OR

- No proof of completion is provided by a third party.

Examples of non-verifiable activities are:

- Self-study — reviewing updates on Tax Rules
- Reading industry-related materials and/or professional trade publications such as: *The Bottom Line*, *Advisor's Edge*, *Investment Executive*, *The Financial Post* and Advisor.ca
- Listening to audio tapes, video tapes, CD-ROM related to topics applicable to the CFP Professional Competency Profile

Please note that lost or unattainable documentation will result in the activity being denoted as non-verifiable at audit.

- Fundamentals of Financial Planning
- Ethics
- Retirement Planning and Employee Benefits
- Investment Planning
- Tax Planning
- Estate Planning
- Risk Management (Insurance)

How to Calculate Credits

In general, one hour of qualifying activity = one CE credit.

In order to be a qualifying activity, the content of the activity must be related to the CFP Professional Competency Profile (the Elements of Competency, Professional Skills, and Technical Knowledge Listing).

Appendix One

Summary of the Six-Step Financial Planning Process

1. Establish the client–planner engagement

The planner should:

- Explain issues and concepts related to the overall financial planning process that are appropriate to you.
- Discuss the scope of the client/planner engagement.
- Explain the services she will provide and the process of planning and documentation.
- Clarify your responsibilities as a client.
- Clarify her responsibilities as your planner. This should include a discussion about how and by whom she will be compensated.

The client (you) and the planner should:

- Discuss the scope of the client/planner engagement.
- Agree on how decisions will be made.

2. Gather client data and determine your goals and expectations

The planner should:

- Obtain information about your financial resources and obligations through interviews or questionnaires.
- Gather all the necessary documents before giving you the advice you need.

The client and the planner should:

- Define your personal and financial goals, needs and priorities.
- Investigate your values, preferences, financial outlook and desired results as they relate to your financial goals, needs and priorities.

3. Clarify your present financial status and identify any problem areas and opportunities

The planner should:

- Analyze your information to assess your current situation (cash flow, net worth, tax projections, etc.).
- Identify any problem areas or opportunities with respect to your:
  - Capital needs
  - Risk management needs and coverage
  - Investments
  - Taxation
  - Retirement planning
  - Employee benefits
  - Estate planning
  - Special needs (i.e., adult-dependent needs, education needs, etc.)

4. Develop and present the financial plan

The planner should:

- Develop and prepare a financial plan tailored to meet your goals and objectives, values, temperament and risk tolerance, while providing projections and recommendations.
- Present the plan to you and establish an appropriate review cycle.

The client and the planner should:

- Work together to ensure that the plan meets your goals and objectives.

5. Implement your financial plan

The planner should:

- Assist you in implementing the recommendations discussed if you want. This may involve coordinating contacts with other professionals such as investment funds sales representatives, accountants, insurance agents and lawyers.

The client and the planner should:

- Ensure that the recommended plan is implemented.

6. Monitor the financial plan

The planner should:
- Agree on who will monitor and evaluate whether your plan is helping you progress toward your goals.

If the planner is in charge of the process, the planner should:
- Contact you to review the progress of the plan periodically and make adjustments to the recommendations required to help you achieve your goals.

This review should include:
- A discussion about changes in your personal circumstances and how they might affect your goals.
- A review and evaluation of the impact of changing tax laws and economic circumstances.
- A review of your life circumstances and an adjustment of the recommendations if needed as those circumstances change through life events such as birth, illness, marriage, retirement, etc.

Source: http://www.fpsccanada.org/fpsc/articles/financial_planning_process.

Appendix Two
Key Changes to CFP® Certification Requirements

KEY CHANGES TO CFP® CERTIFICATION REQUIREMENTS

	Current Policy	New Policy EFFECTIVE JULY 1, 2010
CERTIFICATION PROGRAM FOR ACCREDITED EDUCATION (AE) CANDIDATES	**FPSC-APPROVED CORE CURRICULUM PATH:** • Successful completion of FPSC-approved Core Curriculum program • Successful pass of CFP Examination • Two years of financial planning work experience • Agreement to adhere by the Code of Ethics; disclosure of past or pending litigation • Agreement to adhere by FPSC's Practice Standards	**FPSC-APPROVED CORE CURRICULUM PATH:** • Successful completion of FPSC-approved Core Curriculum program • Successful pass of Professional Competence Examination 1 (PCE1) • Successful completion of an FPSC-approved Capstone Course • Successful pass of Professional Competence Examination 2 (PCE2) • Three years of qualifying financial planning work experience • Agreement to adhere by the Code of Ethics; disclosure of past or pending litigation • Agreement to adhere by FPSC's Practice Standards
CERTIFICATION PROGRAM FOR APPROVED PRIOR CREDENTIAL (APC) CANDIDATES	**FPSC-APPROVED PRIOR CREDENTIAL PATH:** • Hold one of the following credentials: CA, CGA, CMA, CFA, CLU, FCIA, member of Provincial Law Society, PhD in Finance, Business, or Economics • Successful pass of CFP Examination • Three years of financial planning work experience • Agreement to adhere by the Code of Ethics; disclosure of past or pending litigation • Agreement to adhere by FPSC's Practice Standards	**FPSC-APPROVED PRIOR CREDENTIAL PATH:** • Hold one of the following credentials: CA, CGA, CMA, CFA, CLU, FCIA, member of Provincial Law Society, PhD in Finance, Business, or Economics • Successful pass of Professional Competence Examination 1 (PCE1) • Successful completion of an FPSC-approved Capstone Course • Successful pass of Professional Competence Examination 2 (PCE2) • Three years of qualifying financial planning work experience • Agreement to adhere by the Code of Ethics; disclosure of past or pending litigation • Agreement to adhere by FPSC's Practice Standards

KEY CHANGES TO CFP® CERTIFICATION REQUIREMENTS

	Current Policy	New Policy Effective July 1, 2010
CONTINUOUS REGISTRATION	There is no requirement to abide by a Code of Conduct while completing the CFP certification program.	To remain eligible for CFP certification, all candidates must adhere by a Code of Conduct and maintain continuous registration with FPSC from the first approval from FPSC to write the PCE1 until CFP certification.
CERTIFICATION PROGRAM TIME WINDOW	The number of years to complete CFP certification is unlimited.	The number of years to obtain CFP certification from completion of Core Curriculum program to CFP certification is no greater than 12 for the FPSC-approved Core Curriculum path. There can be no more than eight years from first attempt at PCE1 to CFP certification for APC (Approved Prior Credential) candidates.
EDUCATION REQUIREMENT	Candidates may qualify for the education requirement by successfully completing an FPSC-approved Core Curriculum program, or holding a professional designation under the Approved Prior Credential policy.	Candidates may qualify for PCE1 by successful completion of FPSC-approved Core Curriculum program, or holding a professional designation under the APC. While APC candidates are not required to complete an FPSC-approved Core Curriculum education program, all candidates must successfully complete an approved Capstone Course to be eligible for PCE2.
EDUCATION TIME WINDOW	Candidates must attempt the CFP Examination within five years of completing an FPSC-approved Core Curriculum program.	Candidates must attempt the PCE1 within four years of completing an FPSC-Approved Core Curriculum Program. Candidates must attempt the PCE2 within four years of successful completion of an FPSC-approved Capstone Course.
WORK EXPERIENCE REQUIREMENT	Approved Core Curriculum (ACC) candidates require completion of two years of qualifying work experience. Approved Prior Credential (APC) candidates require completion of three years of qualifying work experience.	All candidates require completion of three years of qualifying financial planning work experience. What is considered to qualify as financial planning work experience remains unchanged.

KEY CHANGES TO CFP® CERTIFICATION REQUIREMENTS

	Current Policy	New Policy EFFECTIVE JULY 1, 2010
TIMELINESS OF EXPERIENCE	ACC candidates must complete two years of qualifying work experience within a single five-year span. This span must occur within the five years on either side of successful completion of the CFP Examination. APC candidates must complete three years of work experience prior to qualifying for the CFP Examination. This experience must be completed within 10 years prior to writing the CFP Examination.	All candidates must complete three years of qualifying work experience within the eight years prior to obtaining CFP certification. All candidates must complete at least one year of the three years qualifying work experience prior to attempting PCE2. This one year of work experience must be within the previous four years.
EXAMINATION REQUIREMENT	All candidates must pass the single six-hour competency-based multiple choice CFP Examination.	The examination requirement will be met via a staged approach comprising two examinations: PCE1 and PCE2. Candidates must pass the PCE1 prior to registering for PCE2. PCE1 will be comprised of competency-based multiple choice questions. PCE2 will be comprised of a variety of competency-based question types.
EXAMINATION REWRITE POLICIES	ACC candidates are not limited in the number of times they can attempt the CFP Examination. APC candidates are limited to two attempts, after which they must complete a FPSC-approved Core Curriculum program.	The maximum number of attempts for all candidates is four for PCE1 and four for PCE2.
EXAMINATION TIME WINDOW	To maintain examination eligibility, candidates must re-attempt the CFP Examination within five years of their most recent attempt.	To maintain eligibility for either PCE1 or PCE2, candidates must re-attempt within four years of their most recent attempt.

THE CFP
EDUCATION PROGRAM

CCH/ADVOCIS FPSC-APPROVED CAPSTONE COURSE

MODULE 21
TAXATION PLANNING

Module 21
TAXATION PLANNING

Module 21
Taxation Planning

Unit 1

Tax Assessment and Personal Income Tax

101. ASSESSMENT RULES[1]

Residency

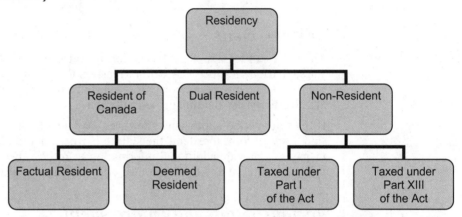

Income tax is imposed based on residency and income source. Canadians are taxed on worldwide income. Non-residents are taxed on income earned in Canada such as Canadian employment earnings, business income and gains on capital property.

A resident of Canada includes a person who normally resides in Canada (factual resident) or deemed resident. To become a non-resident, an individual must sever their residential ties to Canada (i.e., no bank accounts, health cards, driver's license, etc.). If a person sojourns or visits Canada for a total of 183 days or more, they are deemed to be a Canadian resident for tax purposes. They must pay tax on worldwide income for the whole year. If a person comes to Canada to establish residential ties to Canada, he is considered a resident of Canada when the ties are developed. He pays income tax on worldwide income from the day residency is established to the end of the year.

Dual residency occurs when an individual is a resident of more than one country. Residency for tax purposes is then based on location of permanent residence, citizenship, and habitual abode rules.

Requirement to Self-Assessment

Income Tax Filing

The Canadian tax system is based on individuals and businesses self-assessing the amount of tax to be remitted for income and Goods and Services tax (GST), if applicable. Canadians must only file an income tax return if they have income tax payable, sell capital property or are requested by the Canada Revenue Agency (the "CRA") to file a return.

For GST/HST returns, registered individuals and companies are required to compute the net difference between the amount of GST charged and the amount of GST they paid called input tax credits (ITCs). If the GST collected is greater than the ITCs, they must

---

[1] *Note:* Modules 21 to 26 cover topics in the same order as Appendix B of the CFP Competency Profile. "101 Assessment Rules" is the first section in Appendix B of the CFP Competency Profile.

remit it to the federal government on their GST return. If the ITCs are greater than the GST collected, they file a GST return to get a refund. The frequency (monthly, quarterly, and yearly) of how often the GST return needs to be filed is based on the amount of GST due for the year.

To apply for the personal GST tax credit, an individual taxpayer just has to tick the appropriate box on the income tax return. The GST credit is not taxable income.

The federal and provincial governments set their own income tax rates. Provincial income tax owing is a percentage of the actual income of the taxpayer, rather than as a percentage of the federal tax owed by the taxpayer (called the <u>t</u>ax <u>on</u> <u>i</u>ncome (TONI) system). Three departments run Canada's tax system: the Finance Department drafts and revises the *Income Tax Act* (the "Act"); the CRA administers the Act and collects taxes and the Department of Justice handles litigation.

Reassessment

The CRA can reassess a tax return for up to three years. After three years, the return is statute-barred and the CRA cannot reassess the file unless they allege that the taxpayer was guilty of some misconduct or gross negligence in preparing the return, in which case they are able to bypass the three-year limitation.

If the time period approaches the three year time limit, the CRA may request the taxpayer sign a waiver form to extend the statute bar period and allow for additional time for the taxpayer to provide additional information to resolve the dispute. Waivers can be revoked by the taxpayer at any time and take effect six months after the waiver is signed.

Administration and Enforcement

Deadlines for Returns and Balance Due

An individual's tax return and taxes owing are due April 30 of the year following the taxation year, unless they are a:

- **Self-Employed Taxpayer and Spouse.** Due June 15, with any amount owing due April 30;
- **Deceased Taxpayer.** Due the later of six months after the taxpayer's death or April 30 of the year following death.
  - If the taxpayer was self-employed or the spouse of a self-employed individual the tax return is due June 15 of the following year, if the death occurred between January 1 and December 15; or six months after death if the death occurred between December 16 and December 31.
  - The due date if taxes are owing on the final return is April 30 of the year following death if the taxpayer died between January 1 and October 31, or six months after death if the taxpayer died between November 1 and December 31.
- **Partner in a Partnership.** Due June 15, with any amount owing due April 30;
- **Corporation.** Within 6 months of their fiscal year end, the taxes owing are due 60 days after fiscal year-end and 90 days for corporations claiming the small business deduction; or
- **Trust.** Within 90 days after the year end of the trust.

Income Tax Installments

Installment payments are required when a taxpayer's income is not subject to withholding at the source like employees, or if net tax owing was $3,000 or more (2009) ($2,000 for 2008 and prior) in the two previous years and is expected to be again. Installments of one quarter of the estimated tax payable are made on 15th of March, June, September, and December.

Penalties

Interest must be paid on late installments. Interest can be offset on late payment(s) by making an early payment of the following installment amount.

Income Tax Penalties

Failure to File a Return

Failure to file a return results in a 5% penalty on unpaid tax. An additional 1% is imposed for every unpaid month (up to a maximum of 12%). A second failure to file is subject to a second-occurrence penalty (if it follows within three years of the first) of 10% of the unpaid amount, plus 2% per month up to 20 months.

Failure to Report Income

Failure to report income results in a 10% penalty on the unreported amount if there has been unreported income in any of the three previous three years.

Failure to Pay Tax

Interest is imposed on late or deficient taxes owed. Interest charges are set quarterly at the average rate of 90-day Government of Canada treasury bills during the first month of the preceding quarter, plus 4%.

Third-Party Civil Penalties

Third-party civil penalties were introduced by the Department of Finance in 1999 to deal with dishonest tax advisers and situations where a third-party furnishes a statement they know, or should have known, to be false or statements that are false because of an omission of fact. In large-dollar transactions, penalties can be as high as $100,000. The third-party can be guilty whether or not deception was intended; therefore, there are implications for financial advisors.

Tax Planning, Avoidance, and Evasion

Tax planning includes using legal activities to reduce or eliminate tax.

Tax avoidance occurs when taxpayers apply the law to reduce taxes payable, but in a way that may be abusive of the Act.

Tax evasion happens when a taxpayer knowingly tries to deceive the CRA by reporting less taxes payable than what they are required to pay. The taxpayer may be subject to criminal and civil prosecution.

The general anti-avoidance rule (GAAR) was developed in 1998 to help the CRA to deal with tax avoidance. GAAR imposes taxes on any financial gain that accrues as a result of trying to avoid taxes. The CRA may challenge any misuse of the Act under GAAR.

Objections and Appeals

After receiving a tax return, the CRA reviews the return and sends the taxpayer a Notice of Assessment. If the CRA agrees with the taxpayer's return, the tax return file is closed. The CRA has up to three years to reassess an original return, after which it is statute-barred.

If the CRA disagrees with a filed return, they will send a Notice of Assessment with more or less tax owing than the taxpayer reported. The taxpayer should review the Notice of Assessment carefully. If he does not agree with the Notice of Assessment, he should contact the CRA's district office to try to resolve any issues.

If the taxpayer and the CRA still do not agree, the taxpayer can file a Notice of Objection within the later of 90 days of when the assessment was mailed, or one year from the due date of the return to have the dispute formally reviewed by the CRA. The Notice of Objection is sent to the Chief of Appeals at the District Taxation Office. If the taxpayer still disputes the CRA assessment/reassessment, they may appeal to the Tax Court of Canada as a final step.

Income Tax Terminology

Terminology	Definition of spouse	Definition of Common-Law Partner
Spouse and Common-law partner	Legally married.	A person of the same or opposite sex, living in a conjugal relationship with the taxpayer: • for 12 continuous months;* or • who is the natural or adoptive parent of the taxpayer's child or has custody and control of your child aged <19 years, and the child is wholly dependent on that person for support.
Separated spouse and Separated common-law partner	A spouse who is separated due to marriage breakdown.	A common-law partner, separated from the taxpayer, for less than 90 days due to a conjugal relationship breakdown.
Former spouse and Former common-law partner	A spouse becomes a former spouse when the divorce becomes final.	A common-law partner becomes a former common-law partner on the first day after a 90-day separation. Reconciliation after the 90-day separation results in common-law partner status only after your current relationship with the person lasts at least 12 continuous months.*

Note: Separations of less than 90 days do not affect the 12-month period.

For income tax purposes, effective January 1, 2001, a common-law partner includes same-sex common-law partners.

102. EMPLOYMENT INCOME

Definitions and Remuneration

Employment income is income earned through effort, not passive activities, such as salary, bonuses, commission, directors' fees, severance payments, or retiring allowances. It includes taxable benefits (automobile benefits, employer-paid education, low-interest employee loans, RRSP contributions, etc.).

Self-employed income covers five types: business, professional, commission, farming, and fishing income.

Other income includes other types of income such as support payments, and retirement income.

After all income is included, the taxpayer may be able to deduct certain items from total income to arrive at net income, such as:

- RRSP and RPP contributions
- Office in the home
- Employment expenses
- Carrying charges and interest expense
- Professional, Association, Union Dues
- Allowable business investment losses

- Moving expenses
- Support payments
- CPP/QPP Contributions
- Attendant care expense
- Social benefit repayment
- Child care expenses

Commission Income

Commission sales agents may use the cash basis (versus the accrual method) if it accurately reflects their income.

Severance Payment

Severance payments are considered earned income for income tax purposes. They are paid in recognition of a long term of service by the employee upon termination of employment.

Retiring Allowance

A retiring allowance (also sometimes called severance pay) is an amount paid to officers or employees when or after they retire from an office or employment in recognition of long service or for the loss of office or employment. There are situations when a person can transfer all or part of a retiring allowance to a registered pension plan (RPP) or a registered retirement savings plan (RRSP).

The amount that is eligible for transfer under section 60(*j*.1) of the Act is limited to:

- $2,000 for each year or part of a year before 1996 that the retiree worked; plus
- $1,500 for each year or part of a year counted for the $2,000 limit before 1989 of employment in which the employee did not contribute to, or the contributions were not vested in, a RPP or DPSP. The number can be a fraction.

Benefits

Automobile Benefits (Standby Charge)

For employer-owned vehicle:

Standby charge = 2% × (number of months the vehicle is available for use) × (total original cost of the vehicle) - employee reimbursements attributable to the standby charge made no later than 45 days after the end of the year.

If the automobile is available 12 months of the year, then up to 24% of the cost of the automobile is included in the employee's income each year.

For leased vehicles:

Standby charge = ⅓ × ((monthly lease cost excluding insurance or other itemized charges) × (number of months the vehicle is available for use)) - employee reimbursements attributable to the standby charge made no later than 45 days after the end of the year.

Reduced Standby Charge

For 2003 and later years, the employer must specify that vehicle is required for business use and that it is used 50% or more for business purposes as measured by kilometres traveled.

Reduced standby charge = (basic standby charge) × ((average personal-use kilometres per month) ÷ 1,667).

Automobile Benefits (Operating Cost Benefit)

Alternative One

Operating cost benefit = 0.24 per km (for 2009) × Personal-use kilometres

Alternative Two

If business use > 50% or more:

Operating cost benefit = 50% × Standby charge

GRANT

Assume that Grant drove a $30,000 company-owned automobile a total of 20,000 kilometres in the year. During that time, 75% of the kilometres were for business purposes while the other 25% constituted personal driving. While Grant did not keep a detailed driving record, he had sufficient general records to approximate the 75%/25% split. The operating cost of the vehicle (gas, oil, maintenance, insurance, etc.) totalled $5,000 during the 12 months of the year that Grant drove the automobile. The company paid for all operating costs.

What is Grant's income inclusion?

The basic standby charge is (2% × (cost of vehicle) × (number of months driven)). In this case, the standby charge is $7,200, calculated as:

Standby Charge

$$= 2\% \times \$30,000 \times 12 \text{ months}$$
$$= \$7,200 \text{ for the year}$$

Calculation of Reduced Standby Charge

$$\$7,200 \times \left(\frac{(20,000 \times 25\%)}{12} \div 1,667 \right)$$
$$= \$1,800$$

Grant must also include an operating cost benefit in his income. Because Grant does not have detailed driving records, but can substantiate more than 50% business use, he can use the operating cost formula that designates the operating cost benefit to be 50% of the standby charge amount. Under this formula, Grant's operating cost benefit is $900, derived as follows:

Operating Cost Benefit

$$= 50\% \times \text{standby charge}$$
$$= 50\% \times \$1,800$$
$$= \$900$$

Note that the operating cost benefit charged to Grant is not related to the expenses incurred by his employer with respect to the automobile. Instead, the government prescribed formula must be applied.

The total income inclusion for Grant for the company owned automobile is:

Standby charge	$1,800
Operating benefit	900
Total	$2,700

Had Grant kept detailed driving records to support driving 5,000 kilometres of personal use, he could have used alternative one to calculate an operating cost benefit of $1,200 (20,000 kilometers × 25% × $0.24/km). There is no benefit to using alternative one for Grant in this case.

Insurance

Private Non-Group Wage Loss Replacement Plans

If the premium for individual (not group) sickness or accident insurance, disability plans or income maintenance plans is paid by the employer, the premium is a taxable benefit to the employee. If the employee becomes ill, any benefit payments are non-taxable to the employee since the premium was included in income as a taxable benefit.

Group Life Insurance Premium

Employer-paid premiums are a taxable benefit to the employee.

Provincial Hospitalization and Medical Insurance Premiums

Premiums paid by the employer are a taxable benefit to the employee, except where the province levies a provincial health tax to the employer, such as Ontario's Employer Health Tax.

See Appendix One, "Taxable and Non-Taxable Employee Benefits", for more information.

Stock Plans and Options

Employee Stock-Option Plans

The basic rule is that a taxable benefit arises when an option is exercised and the shares are purchased, not when the option is granted.

Taxable benefit = (Value of shares acquired) - (Cost to acquire the shares)

The employee's adjusted cost base (ACB) includes:

- Cost to acquire the shares;
- The amount of the taxable benefit; and
- The amount, if any, paid for the options.

There is an offsetting deduction available if the FMV of shares when the options were granted was equal to or greater than the exercise price of the shares plus any costs associated with acquiring the options. The employee can claim a deduction equal to 50% of the taxable benefit. To qualify for the deduction, the employee must deal at arm's length with the corporation, and the shares acquired must be common shares. The deduction does not affect the employee's ACB of the shares.

Employee Stock-Option Plans (CCPC Corporations)

CCPCs are Canadian-Controlled Private Corporations. The employment taxable benefit is the same amount, but the income inclusion is deferred until the shares are sold versus under the basic rules where income inclusion occurs when the shares are purchased.

There are two ways to qualify for the offsetting deduction: the shares when the option is exercised are held for a minimum of two years, or the exercise price is equal to or greater than the FMV of the shares when the options were granted. The double criteria allow an employer to grant options to an employee at an exercise price less than the FMV of the shares when the option is granted.

Employee Stock-Option Plans (Public Shares)

The employment taxable benefit is the same amount and occurs when the shares are purchased, not at the date the options were granted.

The income inclusion, up to a maximum of $100,000 per year, can be deferred until the shares are sold. To qualify, the employee must meet all the criteria under the basic rule, not be a specified shareholder (holds < 10% of all shares), and the total amount paid (exercise price) must not be less than the FMV of the shares when the option was granted. To claim the election, the employee files an election form with his employer within 15 days following the year he exercises his option.

Retirement Savings Plans

Registered Retirement Savings Plans Contributions to Employees

Employer contributions to an employee's RRSP or payment to cover RRSP administration fees, are a taxable benefit. An employee can claim a deduction for the RRSP contribution which offsets the income tax effect. Amounts withheld from an employee's remuneration at the employee's request for RRSP contributions are not taxable benefits.

For additional information, see section 404, "Registered Retirement Savings Plans", in Module 24.

Loans

Interest-Free, Low-Interest, Forgiven Loans, Home Loans to Employees

Interest-Free Loan

Interest benefit = Prescribed interest rate per quarter × Loan × Time period

Low Interest Loan

Interest benefit = (Prescribed interest rate per quarter × Loan amount × Time period) - (Interest actually paid during the year and 30 days after the end of the year)

Forgiven Loans

Benefit = Face value of the loan

Home Loans to Employees

Home Loan to Purchase a Home

The interest benefit calculation uses the lesser of the prescribed interest rate at the time of the loan and prescribed rate for each quarter.

If the term of the loan exceeds five years, the home loan's prescribed interest rate is reset every five years.

Interest benefit = Prescribed interest rate per quarter × Loan amount × Period of time

Home Relocation Loan

This is a loan to an employee that moves 40 kilometres closer to work. The employer reports the total interest benefit using the same interest benefit formula from above. The employee can claim a deduction equal to the taxable benefit charged on the first $25,000 for five years.

Other Benefits

Employer-Paid Education

If the training is primarily for the benefit of the employer, it is not taxable to the employee. If the training is primarily for the benefit of the employee, then it is a taxable benefit to the employee. The employee includes the employer-paid education cost as a taxable benefit and can claim non-refundable tuition and education tax credits, if applicable.

Financial Planning or Tax Planning

Financial planning or tax planning is not taxable to the employee if the employer pays for services in respect to re-employment or retirement. They are taxable benefits if the employer pays for regular financial or tax preparation/planning.

Other Taxable Benefits

Some other taxable benefits include the personal use of frequent flier points accumulated through business travel, employer-paid travel benefits for the spouse or the employee's family, and employer-paid parking.

Non-Taxable Benefits

The following are examples of non-taxable benefits:
- Reasonable auto allowances for employee using own car:
  — $0.52 per km for the first 5,000 km; $0.46 per km thereafter (2008 and 2009)
  — Additional $0.04 per km for NW Territories, Yukon, and Nunavut
- Registered Pension Plans (RPP)/Deferred Profit Sharing Plan (DPSP) contributions
- Counselling services for mental/physical health, re-employment or retirement

- Relocation expenses
- Private health services plans, such as dental or extended health
- Use of employer's recreational facilities
- Club dues if membership is for the benefit of the company
- Premiums for group wage-loss replacement programs
- Gifts and awards
  - The employee may receive up to two non-cash gifts per year valued at less than $500 in total. If the amount is greater than $500, the full amount is a taxable benefit.
  - The employee may receive up to two non-cash awards per year valued at less than $500 in total. Gift certificates, items readily convertible to cash, and cash do not qualify for these exceptions and are considered fully taxable to the employee.
- Awards for personal injury
- Structured settlements
- Lottery winnings
- Life insurance benefits due to the death of the life insured
- GST/HST credit
- Child Tax Benefits payments
- Allowance for newborn children from the Quebec family allowance
- Disability or death payments resulting from war service

Deductions

Automobile Expenses

Commission sales people can claim deductible automobile expenses. They can claim CCA and interest payments on an automobile used for employment purposes against all types of income, not just commission income.

Home Office Expenses

Criteria for the Deduction for Workspace in the Home

The workspace is the principle place of business *or* used exclusively to earn business income; **and** the workspace is used on a regular and continuous basis for meeting clients, customers, or patients.

A reasonable proportion of eligible expenses are deductible on pro-rata basis

- According to floor space; or
- According to number of rooms in the house.

Workspace in the Home Deductible Expenses

Proportionate share of:	Circumstances		
	Self-Employed	Employee (No Commission)	Employee (Commission Sales)
Home maintenance (i.e., fuel, electricity, minor repairs, etc.)	Yes	Yes	Yes
Home insurance	Yes	No	Yes
Property taxes	Yes	No	Yes
Mortgage interest	Yes	No	No
Mortgage principal	No	No	No
Capital Cost Allowance	Yes	No	No
Rent (if property is not owned personally)	Yes	Yes	Yes

Note: The chart assumes that the individual meets the global and other criteria, making him eligible to deduct qualifying expenses.

For self-employed individuals, the amount deductible is limited to the amount of net income earned from the business, prior to the deduction of home-office expenses. An individual cannot create a business loss through the use of at-home expenses. Any unused workspace expenses can be carried forward indefinitely.

Employees who qualify to claim a deduction for workplace in the home cannot use the deduction to create a loss from employment. Excess deductions can be carried forward and deducted against similar income in the future.

Meals and Entertainment, Promotion

Commission salespersons may deduct reasonable costs of earning employment income up to the amount of commission income earned, i.e., promotional items for gifts, entertainment expenses, supplies, business equipment. The total of eligible deductions (excluding capital cost allowance (CCA) on automobiles and interest on car loans) cannot exceed the individual's commission income (base salary is not included in the calculation).

Regular salary employees can not deduct meals and entertainment, or promotion expenses.

Legal Fees

If a taxpayer incurs legal fees to collect wages or other remuneration owed by a current or former employer, the legal fees are tax deductible from employment income.

103. BUSINESS INCOME

Definitions, Fiscal Year, and Accrual Accounting

A business is any activity, trade, calling, or profession whereby an individual carries out activities that makes a profit or have a reasonable expectation of making a profit. Losses incurred from hobbies, lifestyle or sports activities are not deductible unless the business has a reasonable expectation of profit. There are five categories of self-employed income: business, professional, commission, farming, and fishing income.

Sole proprietors and partnerships (other than where all partners are corporations), report their business activities for the calendar year ending December 31. Most business income must be reported on an accrual basis of accounting, which recognizes revenue and expenses when they occur, and not when the money is received or paid (the cash basis).

Deductibility of Business Expenses

To be deductible, expenses must be related to the business activity and be reasonable in the circumstances. Some of the more popular expenses businesses are allowed to deduct include: home office, promotion, office expenses, travel, 50% of business meals and entertainment, auto expenses, and interest.

Expenditures for capital items can be written off over time following the CCA rules. See the prior section on "Employment Income" for the deductibility of home office expenses.

104. PROPERTY INCOME

Income from property is considered to be a return received on an investment that requires little or no time or effort (passive versus active) to generate the return. It includes rent, royalties, interest, and dividends.

Interest Income

For individuals, interest income may be reported under the "cash method", "receivable method", and "annual accrual basis". Once a method is selected, the taxpayer must consistently follow the same method. Interest income earned as of every annual anniversary of an investment contract must be reported as accrued interest income in the taxation year in which the anniversary falls, except if the income has been accrued for tax purposes in the prior year. Interest income received or receivable during a calendar year must be reported as income for the calendar year to the extent it has not been accrued for income tax purposes. Corporations, trusts, partnerships must use the accrual method to report interest.

Dividend Income

Dividends from taxable Canadian corporations are eligible for a 25% or 45% dividend gross-up and dividend tax credit treatment depending on the type of dividend received. Eligible dividends from public Canadian corporations and certain private, resident corporations that must pay tax at the general corporate rate have a 45% gross-up and a 27.5% dividend tax credit. Dividends from CCPCs not subject to the general corporate tax rate (called other than eligible dividends) are subject to a 25% gross-up and a 16.67% dividend tax credit. These rules try to integrate the personal and corporate tax return systems.

The federal Dividend Tax Credit (DTC) is:

Other Than Eligible Dividends	**Eligible Dividends**
• 16.67% of actual dividend	• 27.5% of the actual dividend
• 13.33% of the taxable dividend	• 18.97% of the taxable dividend
• 66.67% of grossed up portion	• 61.1% of the grossed-up portion

(The grossed-up portion is 25% or 45% portion of the actual dividend)

Stock dividends are taxable and the gross-up and DTC rules apply. Stock splits are not taxable.

Foreign Source Dividend Income (Non-Resident Corporations)

Dividends from non-resident corporations are not eligible for dividend gross-up and dividend tax credit treatment. The dividends are added to income in the amount received (in Canadian dollars).

Dividend Income from Spouse or Common-Law Partner

A taxpayer may elect to include in his income all dividends received by his spouse from taxable Canadian corporations. The election benefits the taxpayer where the taxpayer's non-refundable tax credit for the "spouse or common-law partner amount" is reduced or eliminated because of the spouse's taxable dividends from Canadian corporations.

Dividends Allocated from a Trust

Dividends that are allocated to beneficiaries are taxed exactly as if they were received directly from a corporation.

Rental Income

The net income earned on rental properties is included in total income (on form T776). Income and expenses are recorded under the accrual method of accounting. There is the need to differentiate operating expenses from capital expenditures. A taxpayer can claim CCA for capital items.

Revenue is reported as gross rental income, including payments of any kind, such as cash and services.

RUDDIE

Since Ruddie agreed to mow the lawn, his landlord reduced his rent by $100 from $800 per month. Ruddie's landlord would record $9,600 as the total gross revenue and $1,200 as a gardening expense.

Current Operating versus Capital Expenses

Expenditures that have a lasting benefit of more than one year or improve a building beyond its original condition should be capitalized and amortized according to the CCA rules. Examples include replacement of a fence, a new garage, or new windows. All other expenditures that maintain the property are current expenses and can be deducted in full in the current year. Examples include property taxes, mortgage interest, utilities, advertising, property upkeep, painting, and repairs and maintenance. There are special rules that allow for the deduction of expenses related to the costs of modifying the building to accommodate disabled persons, regardless of whether the expense is capital in nature.

Personal Use of Rental Property

If a taxpayer rents out a portion of his home to earn rental income, he is entitled to deduct reasonable expenses against the gross rental income. Total expenses are prorated based on the number of rooms or square footage in the home. If CCA is claimed as part of the rental expenses, it may impair the ability to claim the principal-residence exemption when the home is sold.

If a taxpayer changes the use of the home from personal-use to income-producing (or vice versa), the taxpayer will be deemed to have sold the property at the fair market value (FMV), which will trigger any accrued capital gains or recapture of previously claimed CCA. An election is available to enable the taxpayer to defer payment of the capital gain until the property is actually sold. The principle residence exemption is not available for the years that the property was income-producing.

Capital Cost Allowance

CCA is the depreciation method prescribed by CRA. CCA is a deduction from net income that reflects wear-and-tear or declining utility on depreciable capital property.

There are three types of capital property. *Non-depreciable property* does not incur wear-and-tear or become depleted because of usage. *Depreciable property* is owned by the taxpayer and is entitled to apply CCA. *Eligible capital property* covers intangible assets, such as incorporation costs, goodwill, or patents.

Common CCA Classes

- **Class 1.** Buildings, 4% declining balance;
- **Class 8.** Equipment, 20% declining balance;
- **Class 10.** Automotive equipment, computer equipment, 30% declining balance; and
- **Class 10.1.** Cars that exceed $30,000 in value, 30% declining balance.

Basic CCA Formula

CCA = UCC (of the class) × Prescribed rate (for the class)

UCC is defined as:

Capital cost of each property

Add: Amount of any recapture in income

Deduct: Accumulated CCA previously deducted

Deduct: Lesser of net sale proceeds or capital cost for each disposition

Deduct: Investment tax credits or assistance received

First-Year Rule

In the first year that an asset is purchased, CCA may only be claimed on 50% of net additions to a particular class. Common names for the rule are the *first-year rule*, the *half-year rule*, and the *50% rule*.

Small tools (class 12), and leasehold improvements, (class 13) do not follow the 50% rule. Calculation of net additions equals the sum of capital cost of new additions into the class minus the proceeds of disposition from the same class.

Short Taxation Year

The Act limits the CCA deduction to a maximum based on a pro-rated number of days. The formula is CCA × (number of days in taxation year ÷ 365). The reduction in CCA due to a short taxation year is in addition to the first-year rule.

General Guidelines

A depreciable asset must be purchased for the purpose of gaining or producing income to be depreciated using the CCA rules. The 2009 maximum capital cost for passenger vehicles is $30,000, plus applicable GST/HST and PST. Passenger vehicles where the actual cost exceeds a maximum of $30,000 are grouped into a separate class and subject to CCA at 30%.

If an asset is used for both personal and business purposes, CCA is based on a proportion of total capital cost of personal to business usage ratio.

Deductibility of Interest

Interest paid on money borrowed to earn property income or improve the rental property is deductible assuming there is a reasonable expectation of profit.

105. OTHER INCOME

Taxable Income

Spousal and Child Support

Spousal support is taxable to the recipient and deductible by the payor. The criteria for payments being classified as spousal support include:

- The payment is subject to use at the recipient's discretion;
- It is payable on a periodic basis;
- It is for the maintenance of the recipient and/or the recipient's children; and
- It is paid either to a spouse or former spouse pursuant to a written agreement or order while the couple is living apart or by a person who is the natural parent of a child of the recipient made under an order.

Payments outside of the above definition are not tax deductible to the payer or taxable income to the recipient.

Child Support

Under the current rules, child support payments are not taxable to the receiving parent and not deductible by the payer. If the agreement was made prior to May 1, 1997, child support payments are treated as taxable income to the receiving parent and deductible by the paying parent.

Combined spousal and child support payments are deemed child support:

- If a court order or agreement does not specify a spousal support amount; or
- Until the child support obligations are fully met if support payments are not paid in full.

Royalties

Royalties are considered taxable income when accrued.

Disability Benefits

Premiums for non-group wage loss replacement plans paid by the employer for non-group or private plans are taxable to employees if they relate to an individual plan for sickness or accident, disability-insurance or income-maintenance. Although the premium is a taxable benefit, if the employee becomes ill, any benefit payments are treated as non-taxable income.

Grants

Certain grants, like the Canadian Home Insurance program, are considered to be taxable income and must be included in the income of the spouse with the higher income in some cases.

Pension Income

Private pension, Canada Pension Plan, and Old Age Security (but not the Guaranteed Income Supplement portion) income is taxable income.

Pension Income Splitting

If you or your spouse or common-law partner received pension income that is eligible for the pension income amount, you may be eligible to split it for income tax purposes.

Income Payments from a Trust

Generally, dividend, interest and capital payments received from a trust retain their properties. For example, dividend income received from a trust is eligible for the dividend gross-up and dividend tax credit.

Employment Insurance Benefits

Employment insurance benefit payments are taxable income.

Scholarships

If a student is not eligible to claim the education tax credit amount, then scholarships, bursaries, or study grants in excess of $500 must be included in income.

If the student is eligible to claim the education tax credit, these amounts are non-taxable.

Non-Taxable Income

Child Support

See section 105, "Other Income", in this module regarding child support.

Capital Dividends

Capital dividends are a non-taxable source of income. They are considered a return of the capital a taxpayer invested.

Life Insurance Benefits

Proceeds received as a beneficiary of a life insurance policy are non-taxable.

Premiums for Group Wage Loss Replacement Plans

Employer-paid premiums are non-taxable to employees if it relates to a group plan for sickness or accident, disability-insurance or income-maintenance. Although the premium is not a taxable benefit, if the employee becomes ill, any benefit payments are treated as taxable income. Generally, if the premiums were paid in after-tax dollars, the receipt of payments is non-taxable.

Government Assistance Payments

Payments received from some government assistance programs such as the Child Tax Benefits and the GST credit are non-taxable.

Private Health Services Plans

If an employer makes contributions on behalf of an employee for an extended health or dental plan, the contribution is not a taxable benefit to the employee.

Counselling Services

Counselling services are not a taxable benefit provided the counselling relates to the mental or physical health of the employee or person related to the employee, or the employee's re-employment or retirement.

Other Non-Taxable Income

Lottery winnings, structured settlements, and awards for personal injuries are non-taxable.

Unit 2
Capital Gains

106. CAPITAL GAINS AND LOSSES

The Act does not specifically define what constitutes a capital gain. Capital gains occur when the proceeds of disposition are greater than the carrying cost of the capital item sold. Capital gains/losses are only recorded when the property is actually disposed of, or when the Act deems the taxpayer to have disposed of the property. An apple tree metaphor is often used to illustrate capital versus income. If a taxpayer is an apple producer, the apples that the tree produces are considered income, but if the tree is sold, it is considered a capital transaction.

The capital gains system is considered tax-advantaged because of several reasons, which include that appreciation of capital property is only taxable when a gain is realized by sale or deemed disposition, and only a portion of the gain (currently 50%) on capital property must be included in income. There are some exceptions that allow the full capital gain to be excluded from income such as the $750,000 qualified small business shares deduction, and there are some deductions that offset the inclusion of a capital gain on income.

There are three different categories of capital property:

- **Personal-Use Property.** Automobiles, boats, recreational equipment, cottage, principal residence, and similar items.

- **Listed Personal Property.** Works of art, jewelry, rare folio, rare manuscript, rare book, stamps, and coins.

- **Other Property.** Bonds, shares, rental property, equipment, and other items.

Calculation of Taxable Capital Gains, Allowable Capital Losses, and Net Capital Losses

Taxable capital gains = Capital gain × Inclusion rate (currently 50%)

Allowable capital loss = Capital loss × Inclusion rate (currently 50%)

Allowable capital losses can only be offset against taxable capital gains and can not be claimed against any other type of income except in the taxpayer's year of death.

Unused allowable capital losses become net capital losses that may be carried back three years or carried forward indefinitely to be claimed against taxable capital gains. Where a capital loss is realized in the taxpayer's year of death or a capital loss is carried forward into the year of death, the allowable portion is deductible against any type of income realized in that year.

Proceeds of Disposition

The proceeds of disposition includes the sale price of the disposed property and any compensation the taxpayer receives for expropriated, stolen or lost property. It is the gross amount before selling expenses. Deemed proceeds of disposition is the amount the taxpayer is deemed to have received for property according to rules of the Act.

Adjusted Cost Base

ACB is the capital cost of depreciable property, the acquiring of, but not the keeping of the property. ACB for non-depreciable property is the taxpayer's cost of property with specified adjustments.

Capital Gain on Disposition of Property

Capital gain = Proceeds of disposition - (ACB + Expenses of disposition)

Taxable capital gain = Capital gain × 50% (the capital inclusion rate)

Valuation Day

Valuation day (V-Day) marks the beginning of capital gains in Canada. A procedure was established to segregate gains or losses on property purchased prior to 1972 and sold after 1971. All clients owning property on V-Day were required to acquire a valuation of all of their non-depreciable property. Values were established as December 22, 1971 for publicly traded securities and December 31, 1971 for all other capital property. Taxpayers can elect the V-Day value or median rule to determine the ACB.

Under the median rule, the ACB for non-depreciable capital property owned by a taxpayer before 1972 is deemed to be the middle or median of the actual cost of property, the valuation day amount, or the proceeds of disposition.

Spousal Rollover Provision

Generally, an individual is deemed to have disposed of all of his capital property at FMV immediately prior to his death. The individual who acquires the capital property is deemed to have received it at a cost equal to the FMV.

If property is transferred to a spouse or common-law partner or a trust created for the spouse or common-law partner, the deceased taxpayer's capital property is deemed to be disposed of at the ACB or UCC (depreciable property) and the spouse who acquires the property assumes the decreased taxpayer's ACB or UCC. The spousal rollover is automatic.

To qualify for a spousal rollover, the deceased and spouse must have been resident in Canada prior to death and the property must vest in the spouse or trust created within 36 months after death.

If the spouse elects out of the spousal rollover, the deceased's deemed disposition of property would occur at FMV and the ACB of the property would be set equal to the FMV for the receiving spouse.

1994 Capital Gains Election

Until its elimination in 1994, Canadian resident taxpayers were eligible for a lifetime capital gains exemption of $100,000 on dispositions of a wide range of capital property. However, taxpayers who had not fully utilized the $100,000 exemption and had accrued capital gains prior to February 22, 1994, had the option of making an election on their 1994 income tax return to access any unused balance of their exemption. Taxpayers who filed this election were deemed to dispose of, and then re-acquire, all properties that were specified in the election. The election increased the ACB of the property up to its FMV as of February 22, 1994. If a taxpayer disposes of a capital property that was the subject of the 1994 capital gains election, they should ensure that the increased cost basis is used to compute the capital gains.

Superficial Losses

If a taxpayer incurs a loss on disposition of capital property while an identical property is acquired by the taxpayer or an affiliate within period of 30 days before or after disposition, the superficial loss is added to the ACB of acquired property. When the acquired property is sold, the higher ACB shelters the capital gains.

The superficial loss rule does not apply to disposition from:

- Death;
- Emigration;
- Recognition of a bad debt;
- Expiry of an option; or
- Change of use of the property.

Fair Market Value

The FMV is the price at which a property would change hands between a willing buyer and a willing seller when both parties have reasonable knowledge of relevant facts.

Deemed Disposition

A deemed disposition is a change in the use of property or a change in ownership, without a change in economic ownership. Examples: death of the taxpayer, transfer of property as a gift or donation, or change in use of rental property from rental to principal residence.

Voluntary disposition is the sale, gift or transfer of property from the taxpayer to another individual or trust. Involuntary disposition is the destruction, theft, foreclosure, or expropriation of property.

Taxable Portion

Taxable portion is the capital gain or loss multiplied by the capital inclusion rate that is included in income. Capital gains inclusion rate is the percentage of gain/loss used to determine the taxable capital gain or allowable capital loss included in income (currently 50%).

Taxable capital gains = Capital gain on non-depreciable property × Inclusion rate

Allowable capital loss = Capital loss on non-depreciable property × Inclusion rate

Capital gain or loss = Proceed of disposition - ACB + Disposition expenses

Allowable Business Investment Losses

Business investment loss is a capital loss realized on the disposition of debt or equity of a CCPC.

ABIL = Business investment loss × Capital gains inclusion rate

ABIL can reduce all types of income in the year incurred, not just capital gains. ABIL in excess of that used to reduce income to zero can be carried back three years, carried forward 10 years if the loss occurred before 2006, and carried forward 20 years if the loss occurred after 2006. After the 20-year carryforward period, any unused ABIL reverts to net capital loss and can be carried forward indefinitely and used to reduce taxable capital gains.

The deductible amount of an individual's ABIL must first be reduced by any previously claimed capital gains deduction. If any allowable business loss is deducted from income, an equal amount of taxable capital gains must be realized and reported as income in subsequent years before the capital-gains deduction becomes available.

Depreciable Assets

Undepreciated capital costs (UCC) are defined as:

Capital cost of each property

Add: Amount of any recapture in income

Deduct: Accumulated CCA previously deducted

Deduct: Lesser of net sale proceeds or capital cost for each disposition

Deduct: Investment tax credits or assistance received

The UCC balance is updated each year:

UCC opening balance (closing balance from previous year)

Add: Capital cost acquisitions

Deduct: Dispositions during year

Deduct: Adjustments

Equals: UCC before CCA

Deduct: CCA (rate × UCC before CCA less ½ net additions)

Equals: UCC at end of tax year

Disposition Summary

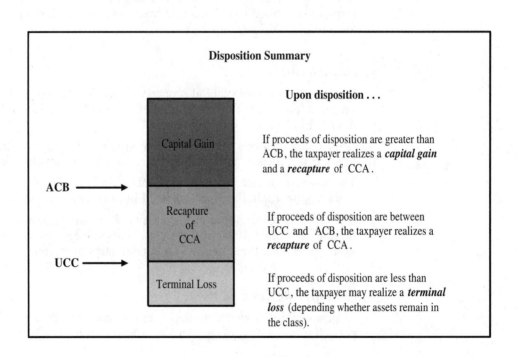

Disposition Summary

Upon disposition . . .

Capital Gain

If proceeds of disposition are greater than ACB, the taxpayer realizes a ***capital gain*** and a ***recapture*** of CCA.

ACB →

Recapture of CCA

If proceeds of disposition are between UCC and ACB, the taxpayer realizes a ***recapture*** of CCA.

UCC →

Terminal Loss

If proceeds of disposition are less than UCC, the taxpayer may realize a ***terminal loss*** (depending whether assets remain in the class).

After accounting for the disposition of disposable property, one of three situations will arise:

- **Positive UCC Balance with Assets Remaining in Class.** Continue CCA depreciation;
- **Positive UCC Balance with No Assets Remaining in Class.** Claim a terminal loss as an expense on the tax return; or
- **Negative UCC Balance.** A recapture of CCA depreciation is triggered. Recapture is treated as income.

Disposition of Land and Building

When building and land are purchased as a package, the purchase involves non-depreciable asset (land) and depreciable asset (building). The acquisition of the land and building will require an allocation of cost and later proceeds of disposition between the land and building in determining the tax result.

Eligible Capital Property

Eligible capital property refers to intangible items such as incorporation costs, goodwill or patents. Examples include: goodwill, trademarks, customer lists, Incorporation and reorganization costs, farm quotas, and government rights.

Cumulative Eligible Capital Account

A *cumulative eligible capital* (CEC) account is a single notional pool where 75% of acquisitions of eligible capital property are pooled. Seventy-five per cent represents the inclusion rate for a CEC account, and it is not tied to the capital gains inclusion rate of 50%. A taxpayer is entitled to a deduction from business income amortization equal up to 7% of any positive CEC account balance.

Disposition

Disposition of eligible capital property results in a credit to the CEC account of 75% of net proceeds (proceeds of disposition less the cost of disposition). The ACB of the property does not matter in the calculation.

If the credit creates a negative balance in the CEC account, the negative balance is brought into income. Income inclusion is separated into business income and capital.

The business income portion of the inclusion is the lesser of the credit balance or the sum of all eligible capital amounts claimed in prior years in excess of prior income inclusions.

The capital portion of the inclusion is $\frac{2}{3}$ of remaining negative balance after the business income adjustment (from the calculation above). The $\frac{2}{3}$ factor reduces the 75% CEC inclusion rate to 50%, the same rate for capital gains inclusion.

Principal Residence

As personal-use property, principal residence is exempted from capital gains tax. It is defined in section 54 of the Act as "ordinarily inhabited" in the year by:

- The taxpayer;
- The taxpayer's spouse/common-law partner;
- The taxpayer's former spouse/common-law partner; or
- A child of the taxpayer.

It may include any housing unit (house, condominium, cottage, mobile home, trailer, house boat), but only one residence can be claimed as principal residence. It is advantageous to claim the exemption on the property with the highest increase in value since it was purchased.

Principal residence exemption = Capital gain $\times$ ((1 + A) $\div$ B)

where:

A = Number of years designated as principal residence after 1971 while resident in Canada

B = Number of full or partial years of ownership after 1971

Second Residence

Prior to 1982, each spouse could claim a principal residence Effective in 1982, only one may be claimed per family. To claim the pre-1982 exemption each property must be owned solely by one spouse at the time of sale. For joint title properties, transfer of title to one spouse must occur prior to sale, capital gains on the transfer is avoided through the spousal rollover rules.

Change in Use

When personal-use property changes to income producing (and vice versa), the transfer creates disposition for tax purposes at the FMV of property. The new ACB of the property is raised to the FMV of the property.

There are two elections a taxpayer should consider when change of use occurs:

- The taxpayer may elect out of the change-in-use deemed disposition for personal-use to income-producing shift. The election defers the accrued gain until the property is disposed. The taxpayer cannot claim CCA on property during the income producing period of time, but must still report income from property.

- When changing from income-producing to principal residence, taxpayer may defer accrued gain until the property is disposed. The principle residence exemption is not available for those years that the property was income-producing.

Listed Personal Property

Listed personal property includes works of art, jewelry, rare folio, rare manuscript, rare book, stamps, and coins. The *de minimus* rule ($1,000 minimum) applies to listed personal property. The proceeds of disposition or the cost is set at the greater of actual proceeds or cost and $1,000 when calculating capital gains or losses. Net capital losses may only be claimed as offset against taxable capital gains on listed personal property and may be carried back three years or carried forward seven years.

To help remember the items, remember the phrase "CJARS", which is derived from taking the first letter of each item (coins, jewelry, art, rare books, and stamps).

Personal-Use Property

Personal-use property includes automobiles, boats, recreational equipment, cottage, principal residence, and similar items. Capital losses are not deductible but capital gains are taxable.

With the *de minimus* rule, proceeds of disposition and adjusted cost based on personal-use property are both set at a minimum of $1,000, and are applied as follows:

- Proceeds of disposition is the greater of actual proceeds and $1,000; and
- The ACB is the greater of actual cost and $1,000.

Use of Capital Losses

Allowable capital losses can only be offset against taxable capital gains and can not be claimed against any other type of income expected in the taxpayer's year of death. Unused allowable capital losses become net capital losses that may be carried back three years or carried forward indefinitely to be claimed against taxable capital gains. Where a capital loss is realized in the taxpayer's year of death or a capital loss is carried forward into the year of death, the allowable portion is deductible against any type of income realized in that year.

Capital Gains Deduction

There is a $750,000 capital gains exemption ($500,000 for dispositions occurring prior to March 19, 2007) on qualified farm property (QFP), qualified small business corporation shares (QSBCS), and qualified fishing property over a taxpayer's lifetime; this translates into a $375,000 capital gains deduction from net income in determining taxable income. The $100,000 capital gains deduction was abolished in 1994.

Capital gains deduction is the the least of:

- Unused lifetime deduction;
- Annual gains limit; or
- Cumulative gains limit.

Qualified Small Business Corporation Shares Criteria

The criteria is as follows: shares of CCPC where all or substantially all of the FMV of the assets is used to carry on active business, primarily in Canada; shares are owned for at least 24 months prior to disposition (some exceptions); and for the 24 months prior to the share disposition, more than 50% of the FMV of the corporation's assets was used to carry on active business, primarily in Canada.

Qualified Farm Property

Qualified farm property (QFP) includes:

- Real property used in a farming business in Canada by the taxpayer, the taxpayer's spouse or child, family farm corporation, or partnership;
- Shares in a family farm corporation;
- Shares in a family farm partnership; and
- Eligible capital property used in a farming business in Canada, such as a milk quota.

Cumulative Net Investment Loss

Cumulative net investment loss (CNIL) represent a taxpayer's net investment losses reported since 1984. The CNIL rules are designed to prevent claiming of a capital gains deduction as well as a deduction of investment expenses.

If cumulative investment income > cumulative investment expenses, then CNIL = zero

If cumulative investment expenses > cumulative investment losses, then CNIL carries a balance

Exclusions from Capital Gains Treatment

The disposition of a life insurance policy is excluded from capital gains treatment. Gain on disposition of life insurance is treated as an income gain and any loss on disposition of life insurance policy is not deductible.

Replacement Property Rules

These rules allow the capital gain and/or recapture on the sale of either former business property (FBP) or former property to be deferred until the sale of the replacement property, provided certain conditions are met. FBP is real property, held as capital property, and used by the taxpayer primarily for the purpose of gaining or producing income from a business. It does not generally include rental properties.

With *involuntary disposition*, a taxpayer must acquire a replacement property by the later of two taxation years or 24 months following the year of disposition.

With *voluntary dispositions*, the taxpayer must acquire a replacement property by the end of the first taxation year or 12 months following the year of disposition in order to be eligible for a deferral.

The following is the criteria:

- The property was acquired by the taxpayer to replace the FBP or former property;
- The property was acquired and used for the "same or similar use" as the former property; and
- The replacement property was acquired for the purpose of gaining or producing income from the same or similar business.

Capital Gains Reserve

If as part of the proceeds of a capital disposition, the taxpayer receives only a portion of the proceeds at the sale date and the remainder over several years, they may be able to claim an optional capital gains reserve. Example: a taxpayer sells a capital property for $50,000 and receives $10,000 each year for five years.

At least $\frac{1}{5}$ of the taxpayer's capital gain must be reported in the year of the sale, and each of the following four years, up to a maximum of five years (10 years for certain farm property or shares in a small business corporation). Reserves deducted in one year are added back to income the following year.

The maximum reserve amount is the lesser of:

- (Proceeds net yet due ÷ Total proceeds) × Gain; or
- ($\frac{1}{5}$ of gain) × (4 - number of preceding tax years ending after the disposition).

Unit 3

Deductions From Income

107. DEDUCTIONS FROM INCOME

Registered Contributions

RRSP or RPP contributions are deductible by the taxpayer, and subject to certain limitations based on an individual's net income from the prior year.

See section 404, "Registered Retirement Savings Plans", in Module 24 for further information.

Union and Professional Dues

Union and Professional Dues are tax deductible.

Child Care Costs

The deduction is usually claimed by the parent with the lower income. The spouse with the higher income can only claim the deduction when the lower income spouse is attending a designated education institute, infirm and unable to care for the children for at least two weeks, is confirmed to a prison for at least two weeks or living apart for at least 90 days due to martial breakdown.

It covers an eligible person providing child care services, nursery school or daycare, day camp or sports school, and boarding school or camp, and is calculated as the least of:

- The amount paid in the year;
- The sum of:
  - $4,000 for each child 7 years or older;
  - $7,000 for each child under 7 years of age; and
  - $10,000 for each child less than 17 years of age for whom anyone can claim a disability credit; or
- ⅔ of the earned income of the taxpayer.

Amounts for camps/boarding schools are limited to:

- $250 per week for each child for whom the disability credit can be claimed;
- $175 per week for each child < 7 years at the end of the year; and
- $100 per week for all other children.

Moving Expenses

Moves that qualify include starting new employment or a new business or attending post-secondary school that results in the taxpayer being 40 kilometres closer to the new location. A taxpayer can carry over excess moving expenses above the amount of income earned in the new location to the next tax year. Deductible expenses include: transportation cost to move household effects, traveling expenses between residences, temporary living expenses near the old or new residence, costs of selling and purchasing the old and new residences.

Interest and Carrying Costs

To be deductible, interest and carrying expenditures such as interest expense, guarantee fees, or safety deposit box must be reasonable. The business or property investment must have a reasonable expectation of earning income and that the borrowed funds must be clearly traceable to an income producing business or property.

Disability Support

The deduction is limited to the lesser of:

- The amount actually paid; or
- The taxpayer's earned income, plus, if taxpayer attended a designated educational institution, the least of:
  - Net income - earned income;
  - $375 × number of weeks in school; or
  - $15,000.

Support Payments

Spousal support payments are deductible. See section 105.

CPP/QPP Contributions

An employee's CPP/QPP contributions are tax deductible as non-refundable tax credits. For self-employed individuals who must pay both the employer and employee portion of CPP/QPP, the employee portion is deductible from net income as a non-refundable tax credit and the employer portion is deductible from total income in determining net income.

Legal Fees

If a taxpayer incurs legal fees to collect wages or other remuneration owed by a current or former employer, the legal fees are tax deductible from employment income.

Deductions From Net Income

Employee Home Relocation Loan

An *employee home relocation loan* is a loan given to an employee that moves 40 kilometres closer to work. The employer reports total interest benefit as a taxable benefit. The employee can claim a deduction equal to the taxable benefit charged on first $25,000 for five years.

Interest benefit = Prescribed interest rate per quarter × Loan amount × Period of time

Stock Option Deduction

A taxpayer can receive deductions in certain circumstances in the year the option is included in income (inclusion rate = 50% × the amount included in income). The primary criteria is that the strike price at the time the options were granted was equal to or greater than the FMV of the shares.

Also see section 117, "Employee Stock Options", in this module.

Losses of Other Years

Income and capital losses of other years may be claimed in the current taxation year.

Capital Gains Deduction

The Act allows Canadians to avoid tax on capital gains on QSBCS, qualified farm property, and fishermen up to $750,000. See the "Capital Gains" section for further details.

108. TAX CREDITS

Non-Refundable Tax Credits

If the non-refundable tax credits are not needed to reduce a taxpayer's taxes payable to zero, the credits are not refunded to the taxpayer. Tax credits (with the exception of charitable donations) are added together and multiplied by 15.0% (lowest federal tax bracket). If no tax is owed, most non-refundable tax credits are lost, with the exception of medical, charitable donations, and tuition/education credits; these have carry-forward provisions.

Amounts for 2009[2]

Basic Personal Amount — $10,320

Age Amount — $6,408

Spouse or Equivalent-to-Spouse Amount — $10,320

Eligible dependent — $10,320

Infirm dependents age 18 or older — $4,198

CPP — $2,118.60 (maximum)

Employment Insurance — $731.79 (maximum)

Canada employment amount — $1,044

Public transit passes — amount paid for monthly transit passes

Children's fitness tax credit — maximum $500 (An amount paid in 2009 for a prescribed program of physical activity for a child under 16 years of age at the beginning of the year.)

Adoption expenses — $10,909

Pension Amount — $2,000

Caregiver — $4,189

The criteria includes that at any time in 2009 the taxpayer maintained a dwelling where the taxpayer and one or more of their dependants lived. A "dependant" is defined as one of the taxpayer's or taxpayer's spouse or common-law partner's child or grandchild; or the taxpayer or the taxpayer's spouse or common-law partner's brother, sister, niece, nephew, aunt, uncle, parent, or grandparent who was resident in Canada. A dependant must meet **all** of the following conditions:

- was 18 years of age or over at the time he lived with the taxpayer;

- had a net income (line 236 of his return, or what line 236 would be if he filed a return) of less than $18,534; and

- was dependent on the taxpayer due to mental or physical impairment or, if he is the taxpayer or the taxpayer's spouse or common-law partner's parent or grandparent, born in 1943 or earlier.

Disability (for self) — $7,196

The taxpayer must have an impairment in physical or mental functions that is severe and prolonged. It lasted or is expected to last at least 12 months.

---

[2] Per January 27, 2009 Budget.

Eligibility and Transfer of Credit

The taxpayer may be able to claim all or part of his dependant's disability amount if he was resident in Canada at any time in 2009 and was dependent on the taxpayer for all or some of the basic necessities of life (food, shelter, or clothing), and one of the following situations applies:

- The taxpayer claimed an amount on line 305 for that dependant, or could have if there was no spouse or common-law partner and if the dependant did not have any income.

- The dependant was the taxpayer's or his spouse or common-law partner's parent, grandparent, child, grandchild, brother, sister, aunt, uncle, niece, or nephew, and the taxpayer claimed an amount on line 306 or 315 for that dependant, or could have if he had no income and had been 18 years of age or older in 2009.

Education Amount

Interest Paid on Student Loans

If a loan was made to the taxpayer under the *Canada Student Loans Act*, or similar provincial act, the taxpayer can claim the amount of interest paid on the loan in 2009 or in the prior five years if not claimed previously. Unclaimed interest may be carried forward for up to five years.

Tuition, Textbook, and Education

Tuition fees are more than $100 to attend a Canadian education institution. The education credit claim for a full-time student is $400 per month and for a part-time student is $120 per month.

For the textbook credit, the taxpayer can only claim it if he is eligible for the education amount. A full-time student can claim $65 for each month, and a part-time student can claim $20 for each month.

Transfer of Unused Amounts

The taxpayer has to claim his tuition, education, and textbook amounts first on his own return. He may be able to transfer the unused part of these amounts to his spouse or common-law partner, or his spouse or common-law partner's parent or grandparent.

The taxpayer can carry forward and claim in a future year the part of his tuition, education, and textbook amounts he cannot use (and does not transfer) for the year.

Amounts Transferred from Spouse or Common-Law Partner

The taxpayer may be able to claim all or part of the following amounts for which his spouse or common-law partner qualifies:

- The age amount (line 301) if the spouse or common-law partner was 65 or older;

- The amount for children born in 1991 or later;

- The pension income amount (line 314);

- The disability amount (line 316); and

- Tuition, education, and textbook amounts (line 323) that the spouse or common-law partner designates. The maximum amount that the taxpayer's spouse or common-law partner can transfer is $5,000 minus the amounts that he uses even if there is still an unused part.

Medical Expenses

Medical expenses are the lessor of 3% of net income, or $2,011. A taxpayer can claim medical expenses incurred by the taxpayer, the taxpayer's spouse or common-law partner, dependent child or grandchild, and the taxpayer's or taxpayer's spouse's or common-law partner's parent, grandparent, brother, sister, uncle, aunt, niece, or nephew who was dependent on the taxpayer for support. It is based on a 12-month period ending at any point in the current taxation year. Eligible expenses include payments for private or public hospitals, dentists, medical doctors, certain other medical practitioners, premiums for private health-services plans, prescription drugs and eyewear, hearing aids, attendant care, and guide dogs. Premiums for provincial hospitalization and provincial medical plans are not eligible.

Donations

Donations may be claimed up to a limit of 75% of net income. Cultural and ecological gift donations can be claimed for up to 100% of net income.

Donations are calculated as 15% on the first $200, and 29% thereafter. Donations of a couple may be claimed by either the taxpayer or the spouse or common-law partner of the taxpayer. It is more advantageous for the higher-income spouse to claim the deduction. A taxpayer can carry forward unused donations for five years.

Donations in kind (non-cash donations and capital property) are recorded at FMV. There is no capital gains tax on donations of ecologically sensitive land or publicly-listed securities. Donations must be to a registered charity to be deductible.

Refundable Tax Credits

Dividend Tax Credit

If the taxpayer received eligible dividends, the federal dividend tax credit is 18.9655% of the taxable amount of eligible dividends included on line 120. If the taxpayer received dividends (other than eligible), the federal dividend tax credit is 13.3333% of the taxable amount of dividends reported on line 180.

Overseas Employment

A taxpayer is able to claim this credit if they were a resident or deemed resident and were employed in specific areas outside of Canada such as natural resources, construction, engineering, or United Nations work for a period of six months or more.

Minimum Tax Carry-Over

If the taxpayer paid minimum tax on any of their 2002 to 2008 returns but does not have to pay minimum tax for 2009, they may be able to claim credits against the taxes for 2009 for all or part of the minimum tax they paid in those years.

Foreign Tax Credit

This credit is for foreign income or profit taxes a taxpayer paid. Foreign tax credit is usually the lower of the foreign taxes paid and the Canadian taxes due on the net income from the foreign country.

Political Contributions

The political contributions tax credit is for contributions to a registered federal political party or candidate. The credit amount varies from 75% to 33% is based on the total dollar value of the contributions.

Investment Tax Credit

The taxpayer may be eligible for this credit if **any** of the following apply. The taxpayer:

- bought certain new buildings, machinery, or equipment and they were used in certain areas of Canada in qualifying activities such as farming, fishing, logging, manufacturing, or processing;
- has unclaimed credits from the purchase of qualified property after 1996;
- has an amount in box 41 of the T3 slip, box 107 or 128 of the T5013 or T5013A slip, or box 128 of the T101 slip;
- has a partnership statement that allocates to the taxpayer an amount that qualifies for this credit;
- has an investment in a mining operation that allocates certain exploration expenditures to the taxpayer; or
- employed an eligible apprentice.

Labour-Sponsored Funds

Fifteen per cent of the investment amount is available as a credit up to a maximum investment of $5,000 (credit of $750) in the taxation year or previous year if the investment was made in January or February. Many provinces provide additional tax credits that match the 15%. If the investment is not held for 8 years, the tax credits must be repaid.

Under proposed legislation, a taxpayer will only be able to claim this credit if he can also claim a provincial credit.

109. TAX SHELTERS

Structure of Tax Shelters

A tax shelter is defined in the Act as any property for which a promoter represents that an investor can claim deductions or receive benefits which equal or exceed the amount invested within four years of its purchase. Types of tax shelters include: Rental Real Estate, Natural Resource Investments, E-Commerce Limited Partnerships, and Film Limited Partnerships and gifting arrangements. These tax shelters usually provide one of the following deductions: CCA, natural resources exploration and development deductions or scientific research and development deductions. A taxpayer may be able to claim a reasonable deduction up to the amount of the investment at risk.

110. TAXES PAYABLE

Tax Rates

Canada has a progressive income tax system. The taxation rate increases as a taxpayer's income increases. Marginal tax rate is the tax rate paid on the next dollar of income. The average tax rate is calculated as the total tax payable divided by the taxpayer's taxable income.

2009 Federal Personal Tax Brackets and Rates

Taxable Income	Tax Calculation
up to $40,726	15% of taxable income
from $40,726 to $81,452	$6,109 on $40,726 of taxable income *plus* 22% on the amount above $40,726
from $81,452 to $126,264	$15,069 on $81,452 of taxable income *plus* 26% on the amount above $81,452
over $126,264	$26,720 on $126,264 *plus* 29% on the amount above $126,264

PROVINCIAL TAX BRACKETS AND SURTAXES

Each province sets their own tax brackets and surtaxes. The Federal government collects all of the provincial taxes on behalf of the provinces, except for Quebec.

Alternative Minimum Tax

Alternative minimum tax (AMT) is a structure that provides for recalculation of an alternative amount of tax, based on removal of certain tax preferences when compared with the regular tax calculation. It is focused on removing tax shelters and credits.

The $40,000 income exemption results in AMT only applying to adjusted income in excess of $40,000.

Considerations

A taxpayer may owe AMT if he has taxable capital gains, dividends from a taxable Canadian corporation, claims any of the following tax credits (labour-sponsored fund tax credit, federal political contribution tax credit, investment tax credit, overseas employment tax credit, claims a deduction for employee home relocation loan or employee stock option), or claims a deduction for the following tax shelters:

- Losses created by deductions for Canadian exploration expenses, Canadian development expenses, or Canadian oil and gas property expenses;
- Losses created by deductions for CCA on film properties;
- Partnership losses incurred by a limited or passive partner;
- Losses deducted in respect of investments identified under tax shelter rules; and
- Carrying charges related to acquisitions of partnership interest.

Process

Tax liability is based on the higher of the calculation of federal tax and calculation of AMT. Calculation involves:

1. *Start:* With taxpayer's taxable income from T1 General
2. *Add back:* Certain tax preferences that lowered total income
3. *Deduct:* Gross-up portion of taxable Canadian dividends
4. *Deduct:* Basic AMT exemption of $40,000
5. *Multiply:* By the tax rate
6. *Deduct:* Certain personal tax credits
7. *Calculate:* Minimum tax payable (Step 5 - Step 6)

AMT Carryforward

For any year the taxpayer pays AMT, the amount by which AMT liability exceeds regular tax liability may be carried forward 7 years. If tax liability under the regular system exceeds AMT liability for that year during 7-year period, carryforward may be applied as tax payment against regular liability to reduce it to AMT amount for that year.

Deceased Taxpayer

AMT is not applicable in the year of the taxpayer's death. Any previous carryforward amount can be used to reduce the regular tax liability in excess of the minimum tax on a taxpayer's terminal return.

Unit 4
Tax Planning

111. INCOME SPLITTING

Attribution

Attribution rules restrict transfers and loans between designated persons. A *designated person* is the spouse/common-law partner, or related minor of the taxpayer.

Loans and Transfers

Spouse

Property transferred to a spouse results in income or loss from property being attributed to the taxpayer, and any net taxable capital gain or allowable capital loss resulting from disposition is attributed back to taxpayer. Attribution does not apply to property transferred from taxpayer to a spouse for consideration equal to FMV or loan at a reasonable rate of interest with the interest being paid during the year or within 30 days following the year-end.

Minor Children

Income on property transferred from a taxpayer to a minor who has not turned 18 by December 31 is attributed back to the taxpayer if the taxpayer does not deal at arm's length or if the minor is a niece or nephew. Attribution rules apply to a transfer to a child, grandchild, great-grandchild, niece or nephew. Attribution rules do not apply to capital gains on property or income earned on reinvestment of the original income.

Non-Arm's Length Individuals and Adult Children

This discussion does not include a spouse or partner, or a related minor. If property is loaned to an individual for the purposes of reducing taxes, any property income is attributed to the taxpayer. There is no attribution of property losses, capital gains, or capital losses.

Attribution rules do not apply to loans for value with a reasonable interest rate and repayment terms. Establishing a reasonable interest-rate charge can be proof that loan was not to reduce or avoid tax. Gifts between non-arm's length parties, who are not designated persons, are not subject to attribution.

Other Provisions

Both the transferor and transferee are joint and severally liable for any tax liability because of the attribution rules. With dividend income, the taxpayer must gross up the dividend and can claim the dividend tax credit. The capital gains exemption may be applicable.

Determining the type of income — property versus business income — is important in assessing attribution rules since rules do not apply to business income or losses. Income on income (called second generation income) is not attributed back to the transferor and is taxable to the transferee. Attribution rules may also apply to loans and transfers to a trust, borrowed funds, and loan guarantees.

Exemptions

Attribution rules do not apply in the following circumstances:

- Property transferred at FMV
- Loans bearing a reasonable interest rate
- Separation
- Death of the taxpayer
- Anti-avoidance rules

Kiddie Tax

Kiddie tax is imposed to discourage income splitting with minor children. A taxpayer who is a minor at the end of the taxation year is required to pay tax at highest rate on income from:

- Taxable dividends and other shareholder benefits from private corporations (Canadian and foreign companies) direct, through a partnership or through a trust; and
- Income from a partnership or trust where income is from goods or services to a business carried on by:
  — a related person;
  — a corporation in which the related person owns more than 10%; or
  — a professional corporation in which a related person is a shareholder.

Exceptions to Kiddie Tax

The kiddie tax is not applicable if the minor has no parent resident in Canada, private company shares were inherited from a parent, or if the inheritor attends post-secondary school on full-time basis or is eligible for the disability tax credit.

The kiddie tax does not apply to:

- Income from employment or personal services of the minor; and
- Dividends the minor receives on shares of a company listed on the stock exchange.

Methods of Income Splitting

Income splitting is considered one of the most effective ways to decrease taxes and maximize cash flow within a family unit. There are several methods to split income legally.

Attribution rules do not apply in the following circumstances:

- Property transferred at FMV
- Loans bearing a reasonable, prescribed interest rate
- Second generation income (income on initial income)
- Business income
- Reasonable wages paid to a spouse or related minor child
- Spousal RRSP contributions
- Capital gains realized by a related minor child
- Sale of non-income producing property
- Payment of family expenses by the higher-income spouse
- Gifts to adult children
- Splitting of the CPP and pension income

112. INTER VIVOS TRANSFERS

Inter vivos means between living persons. For example, an *inter vivos* trust is a trust that is between living people and *inter vivos* transfer is property that is transferred between living people.

Inter Vivos Transfer to a Spouse or Common-Law Partner

The Act provides for tax-free transfers of capital property between spouses. A spousal rollover of capital property is transferred tax-free when the transfer is from a taxpayer to his current spouse, former spouse in settlement of rights arising out of marriage/partnership, or a spousal or partner trust.

Tax Consequences

The transferor is deemed to have disposed of property at ACB or undepreciable capital cost in the case of depreciable property. The acquiring spouse assumes the transferor's ACB or undepreciable capital cost. The transferor incurs no capital gain or loss on the deemed disposition of property. The capital gain is not eliminated, but tax on the gain is deferred until the spouse disposes of the asset.

Inter Vivos Gifts

A deemed disposition occurs on property disposed of as a gift. The proceeds are equal to the FMV of the property. The FMV becomes the recipient's ACB.

Transfer of Farm Property

Inter vivos transfer of farm property and transfer upon death can occur on a tax-free rollover basis between parent and child if:

- The property is located in Canada and was used as a farm on a regular and continuous basis by the transferor, transferor's spouse, or children immediately prior to the transfer;
- The property is transferred from a taxpayer to a child as a consequence of death or *inter vivos*;
- The recipient child was resident in Canada; and
- The property becomes indefeasibly vested in the child within 36 months.

Transfer of Eligible Shares of a Qualified Small Business Corporation

This can occur on a tax-free rollover basis between a shareholder and corporation, following specific rules.

113. TRANSFER OF COMPANY SHARES

Transfer to a Corporation

The Act provides tax-free transfers of property into corporations to provide flexibility for shareholders and corporations in structuring their financial affairs. Normally, transfers of property (or shares) from a shareholder into a corporation are deemed to occur at FMV, accrued capital gains, or recapture is realized along with the associated income tax liability, although transfers can be completed under joint election on a tax-free rollover basis if the:

- Corporation receiving the property must be a taxable Canadian corporation;

- Consideration received by the shareholder on the transfer of property into a corporation must include a minimum of one share of the corporation;
- Property transferred must be eligible property; and
- The taxpayer and the corporation must jointly elect on form T2057.

Transfer Price to a Corporation

The taxpayer and the corporation can elect the transfer price of property based on:

Ranges for Transfer Price	Type of Property		
	Capital Property	Depreciable Property	Eligible Capital Property
Upper Limit	FMV	FMV	FMV
Lower Limit	Greater of: FMV of non-share consideration; and lesser of: 1. FMV of property, and 2. ACB of property.	Greater of: FMV of non-share consideration; and least of: 1. FMV of property, 2. UCC of class, and 3. ACB of property.	Greater of: FMV of non-share consideration; and least of: 1. FMV of property, 2. $\frac{4}{3}$ of CEC balance, and 3. ACB of property.

Transfer While the Owner is Alive

Gift or Sale

Transfers of property occurs at FMV. Capital gains and/or recapture are triggered on the transfer.

Estate Freeze

An *estate freeze* is a process by which an individual limits the growth of his estate and provides for the future growth to accrue to the benefit of his children or other family members. The individual transfers property (or common shares) into a corporation in exchange for preferred shares of the corporation valued equal to the FMV of the property transferred. Common shares are then given to the children. The individual has crystallized the amount of capital gains he or she will be required to pay upon disposition of the preferred shares at death.

Qualified Small Business Corporations

The amount of $750,000 in capital gains exemption is available to qualified small business corporations (QSBC). See section 106, "Capital Gains and Losses", in this module for further details.

QSBC shares criteria is as follows:

- Shares of CCPC where all or substantially all of the FMV of the assets are used to carry on active business, primarily in Canada;
- Shares are owned for at least 24 months prior to disposition (some exceptions); and
- For the 24 months prior to the share disposition, more than 50% of the FMV of the corporation's assets was used to carry on active business, primarily in Canada.

Capital Gains Deduction

For more information about the capital gains deduction, see section 106, "Capital Gains and Losses", in this module.

Use of a Holding Corporation

A taxpayer transfers his common shares in an operating corporation to a holding corporation and takes back preferred shares as consideration. The value of the preferred shares is usually equal to the value of the common shares transferred, therefore, there is no capital gains triggered.

Holding Companies

Opco is a term used to describe a company actively carrying on business. *Holdco* is a company whose primary purpose is to hold assets or investments.

Benefits of Using a Holding Company

Credit Protection

If Opco produces revenue greater than a shareholder needs, money can be transferred to Holdco as tax-free inter-corporate dividends.

Investment Opportunity

Earnings in excess of need for a closely held corporation can be left within the corporation so more assets are available for investment.

Differing Compensation Needs

If different shareholders of a closely held corporation have different compensation or cash flow objectives, using separate holding companies owned by each shareholder increases the compensation options for each shareholder. Operating companies can pay dividends to each holding company without immediate taxation. Each holding company can distribute income to the shareholders based on their specific needs.

Estate Planning

Holdco could be used to accumulate and diversify investments. When a shareholder dies, only the shares of Holdco must be dealt with. The individual investments are not affected. The assets in Holdco continue to exist separate from the taxpayer's estate, reducing the need to liquidate or transfer investment holdings. Upon the death of the taxpayer, the Holdco shares could pass through the taxpayer's estate in accordance with the will, or through intestate succession laws if no will exists.

Use of a Trust

For more information about the use of a trust, see section 503, "Power of Attorney for Property" and sections 508 to 510, "Trusts", in Module 25.

Family Law Issues

For more information about family law issues, see section 501, " Family Law", in Module 25.

Post Mortem Freeze

A *post mortem freeze* sets the current value of certain assets at their current FMV. The taxpayer receives fixed value preferred shares equal in value to the unrealized gain inherent in the frozen assets. This strategy freezes the capital gain at the current value upon the death of the taxpayer.

114. TAX CONSEQUENCES OF DEATH

Taxation Year

A final terminal tax return needs to be filed upon the death of a taxpayer. Three elective returns may also be filed, and these are rights and things, proprietor or partnership business income, and a testamentary trust return.

Filing Deadlines

The final tax return is due the later of:

- Six months after the date of the taxpayer's death; or

- April 30 of the year following the death.

If the taxpayer was self-employed or the spouse of a self-employed individual:

- If the death occurred between January 1 and December 15, the due date is June 15; or

- If the death occurred between December 16 to 31, the due date is six months after the date of death.

If testamentary debts are handled through a spousal or common-law partner trust, the due date for filing the final return is extended to 18 months after the date of death.

If a person dies after December 31, but on or prior to the filing due date for the previous taxation year, and he has not filed a return, the return and the balance owing is due within six months after the date of death.

If death occurred between January 1 and October 31, the balance of taxes is due by April 30 of the year following death. If death occurred between November 1 and December 31, balance of taxes owing is due six months after the date of death.

Rights or Things Tax Return

Income which was owed to the deceased, but not paid at the time of his death, can be reported on a *rights or things tax return*. If an election is made, all income that falls into the rights or things category must be reported on that return. The income can not be split between the terminal and rights or things returns. Items include: employment money owed (commissions, salary, vacation pay, or retirement allowance), uncashed matured bonds, bond interest earned up to the day of death but not yet paid or reported in a prior year, and declared any unpaid dividends if the ex-dividend date is prior to the date of death.

The return does not include RRSPs, RIF income, period accumulations such as bank interest, bond interest accumulated between the last payment date and date of death, or capital and eligible capital property.

Full personal tax credits, including medical expenses and charitable donations, may be claimed assuming the amounts have not been claimed on other tax returns.

Proprietor or Partnership Income

If the business operated on a fiscal year other than a calendar year, an optional return may be filed to capture the business income for the period between the fiscal year and the date of death (the stub period). If the separate return is not filed, all business income is reported on the final terminal tax return.

Testamentary Trust Income

If the deceased was an income beneficiary of a testamentary trust that operated on a fiscal year other than a calendar year, an optional return may be filed to capture the trust income for the period between the fiscal year and the date of death (the stub period). If the separate return is not filed, all income from the trust is reported on the final terminal tax return.

Estate Tax Return

Capital losses and terminal losses realized by the estate on the disposition of capital property and depreciable property, during the first taxation year of the estate, can be carried back and claimed on the terminal tax return for the deceased.

U.S. Estate Tax Return

If the taxpayer owned United States assets and had a worldwide estate valued at above $3.5 million (2009), they may have to file a U.S. Estate Tax return.

Accrued Income and Rights or Things

Accrued income which was owed to the decreased but not paid at the time of his death, must be reported on the terminal tax return or a right or things return.

Death Benefits

Benefit can be paid where the death benefit is in recognition of service in an office or employment. The first $10,000 of cumulative death benefit payments are exempt from income tax. Qualifying payments include lump sum or periodic payment in recognition of the employee's service or the deceased's settlement of accumulated sick-leave credits.

Non-qualifying payments include: retirement compensation arrangement payments, salary deferral program or pension funds, CPP/QPP death benefit, or accumulated vacation or overtime payable to the employee.

Deemed Disposition of Property

Generally, an individual is deemed to have disposed of all of his property at FMV immediately prior to death. The individual who acquires the capital property upon the taxpayer's death is deemed to have received the property at a cost equal to the FMV. Capital gains, capital losses, and CCA recapture may result.

Spousal rollover is an exception to the deemed disposition rule. The spousal rollover provision applies automatically. The capital property is transferred from the deceased to the spouse/common-law partner at the deceased's adjusted cost base or undepreciated capital cost.

See section 106, "Capital Gains and Losses", in this module for more information on capital and depreciable property.

Capital losses and terminal losses realized by the estate on the disposition of capital property and depreciable property, during the first taxation year of the estate, can be carried back and claimed on the terminal tax return for the deceased.

Non-Refundable Tax Credits

The following non-refundable tax credits may be claimed in full on each of the four tax returns:

- Basic personal amount
- Age amount
- Spouse or common-law partner amount
- Amount for eligible dependent
- Amount for infirm dependants age 18 or older
- Caregiver amount

The following non-refundable tax credits may be split across the four returns. The total claimed can not exceed the amount that would be allowed if only the final return was filed.

- Disability amount for deceased
- Disability amount transferred from a dependent
- Interest paid on certain student loans for deceased
- Tuition and education amounts (for deceased or transferred from a child)
- Charitable donations up to the net income reported on the return
- Cultural, ecological or Crown gifts
- Medical expenses, subject to the regular calculations

The following deductions and non-refundable tax credits may be claimed only if the return includes the related income:

- Employee relocation loan
- Stock options and share deductions
- CPP/QPP contributions
- Employment Insurance premiums
- Pension income amount
- Social benefits repayment

The following items, if applicable, may be claimed on the deceased's final terminal return but not on any of the elective returns:

- RRSP and RPP contributions
- Professional, association and union dues
- Child care expenses
- Attendant care expenses
- Allowable business investment losses
- Moving expenses
- Support payments

- Carrying charges and interest expense
- Losses from other years
- Capital gains deduction
- Amounts transferred from his spouse/common-law partner

Medical Expenses

The legal representatives of a deceased taxpayer may claim any medical expenses paid — for the year of death — by the taxpayer or his legal representative within any 24-month period that includes the date of death. The same expense may not be claimed more than once.

Charitable Donations

Charitable donations may be claimed up to 100% of the deceased taxpayer's net income. Excess amounts not claimed can be carried back one year and claimed as a credit, up to 100% of net income.

The completion of the income tax returns should be carefully managed to minimize the overall tax liability.

POST-MORTEM PLANNING

Spousal Rollover Provisions

If property is transferred to a spouse or common-law partner or a trust created for the spouse or common-law partner, the deceased taxpayer's capital property is deemed to be disposed of at the ACB or UCC (depreciable property) and the spouse who acquires the property assumes the decreased taxpayer's ACB or UCC.

To qualify for a spousal rollover:

- The deceased and the deceased's spouse must have been resident in Canada prior to death; and
- Property must vest in the spouse or the trust was created within 36 months after death.

Balance of Unused Capital Gains Exemption

If the deceased taxpayer had unclaimed capital gains exemption or unused capital losses, the trustee of the decreased estate may elect to opt out of the automatic spousal rollover provision and transfer the assets to a spouse at a value higher than the other's ACB to utilize the exemption or losses.

Treatment of Allowable Capital Loss

Where a capital loss is realized in the year of death or a capital loss is carried forward into the year of death, the allowable portion is deductible against any type of income realized in that year. Normally, allowable capital losses are only offset against taxable capital gains.

Registered Plans and Refunds of Premiums

Generally, if the assets of an unmatured RRSP pass to someone other than the spouse/common-law partner or qualified child or grandchild, the FMV of the assets must be included in the deceased's income in the year of death.

Refund of premiums is any amount paid out of, or under an RRSP to the spouse or common-law partner, dependent child or grandchild, prior to the plan's maturity.

If assets of an unmatured RRSP pass to spouse/common-law partner or qualified child or grandchild as a refund of premiums, there is no tax consequence to the deceased's estate and the responsibility for the tax liability passes to the recipient. The assets may be transferred directly into another qualified plan without creating an immediate tax consequence or, be received personally and subsequently contributed within the year or 60 days after the year end. If the funds are received personally and not contributed to a qualified plan, the refund of premium will be treated as taxable income.

RRSP Contributions after Death

Contributions can not be made to a deceased taxpayer's RRSP. Spousal RRSP contributions are allowed in the year of death or within 60 days after the end of the taxation year in which the taxpayer died.

Alternative Minimum Tax

AMT is not applicable in the year of a taxpayer's death, although any previous carryforward amount may be used to reduce a regular tax liability in excess of the minimum on the taxpayer's terminal return.

Attribution

Attribution rules no longer apply after the death of a taxpayer.

Transfers of Company Shares Upon Owner's Death

Shareholder agreements should address the succession of the business.

Buy-Sell Arrangements

A *buy-sell arrangement* is a subset of a shareholders' agreement and is a written document that outlines the terms relative to the succession of a business. A buy-sell arrangement is established during the business owners/partners' lifetimes.

There are three basic types of buy-sell arrangements:

- Cross Purchase Buy-Sell Arrangement
- Promissory Note Arrangement
- Share Redemption Arrangement

Cross Purchase Buy-Sell Arrangement

A *cross purchase arrangement* is built on the premise that each shareholder within the agreement agrees to purchase a specified percentage of the shares owned by the deceased shareholder at the time of death.

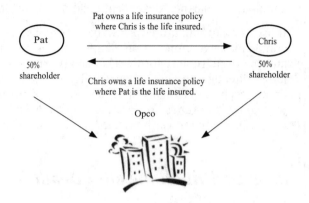

Pat owns a life insurance policy
where Chris is the life insured.

Chris owns a life insurance policy
where Pat is the life insured.

Insurance is owned on a criss-cross pattern.
Each policy owner pays the premium on the policy that she owns and names herself as beneficiary.
Proceeds from the life insurance are used to discharge the shareholder's obligation to purchase shares from the deceased's estate.

Promissory Note Arrangement

Under the *promissory note arrangement*, corporate owned life insurance is placed on the life of each shareholder, with the corporation named as the beneficiary. In the event that a shareholder dies, the surviving shareholder purchases the deceased's shares from his estate using a promissory note. When the surviving shareholder owns 100% of the company, the company collects the insurance proceeds on the corporate owned life insurance, and places the excess amount above the ACB of the policy in the capital dividend account (CDA).

Upon receipt of the life insurance proceeds, the company pays the surviving shareholder a capital dividend, which provides the surviving shareholder with the cash to pay off the promissory note to the deceased shareholder's estate.

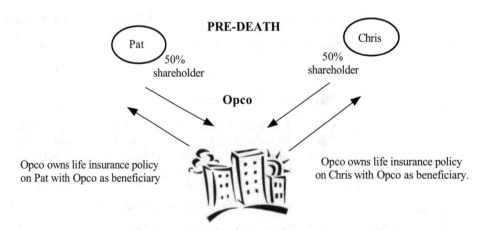

Opco purchases life insurance policies on each of the shareholders and designates the company
as beneficiary on each policy.
Premiums on the corporate owned life insurance policies are paid by the corporation.

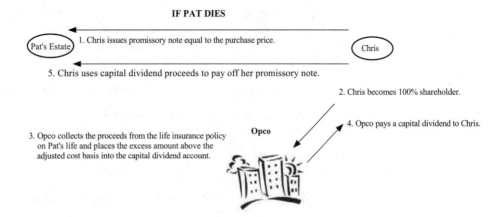

IF PAT DIES

Pat's Estate

1. Chris issues promissory note equal to the purchase price.

Chris

5. Chris uses capital dividend proceeds to pay off her promissory note.

2. Chris becomes 100% shareholder.

4. Opco pays a capital dividend to Chris.

Opco

3. Opco collects the proceeds from the life insurance policy on Pat's life and places the excess amount above the adjusted cost basis into the capital dividend account.

Share Redemption Arrangement

Under the *share redemption arrangement*, corporate-owned life insurance is placed on the life of each shareholder with the corporation named as the beneficiary. In the event that a shareholder dies, the company collects the insurance proceeds and places the excess amount above the adjusted cost basis of the policy in the CDA. The company uses the proceeds in the CDA to redeem the shares held by the deceased shareholder's estate. From an income tax point of view, the deceased will have a combination of capital and dividend treatment of the disposition of the shares depending on how the stop-loss rules affect the transaction.

For further details, see Module 10, "Life Insurance and Living Benefits", of CCH's "CFP Education Program" in Course 3.

115. TAXATION OF DIFFERENT LEGAL ENTITIES

For additional information on different entities, see section 506, "Business Ownership Structures", in Module 25.

Partnerships

There are two types of partnerships: general partnership and limited partnerships.

General Partnership

The provincial *Partnership Acts* define a partnership as a relationship between two or more parties carrying on an unincorporated business, with a view to profit. There are no legal formalities to create a general partnership.

Taxation of General Partnership

The partnership is treated as a separate person, including CCA, which takes place at the partnership, not partner, level. Taxation is based on the partnership's year end. Property and business income, taxable capital gains, and allowable capital losses are taxed at the partnership level. The partnership can choose their own fiscal year end.

Income flows through to the individual partner level when partnership allocations are made. Each partner includes his share of net income or loss from business on his personal income tax return. Non-calendar year-end partnership financial results must be reconciled to a

December 31 year end for individual partners. The partners can determine income allocation between partners, but the Act can override their allocations if (a) allocation was an attempt to reduce or postpone income for one partner; or (b) dealing was not at arm's length. Each partner tracks his contributions, allocations and draws in a capital account, representing his share of equity in the partnership.

Adjusted Cost Base of a Partnership Interest

For tax purposes, each individual's partnership interest is treated as capital property with an ACB. The partner's ACB is derived as follows:

Additions

- Contributions to capital
- Share of partnership income (including 100% of capital gain on disposition of partnership capital property)
- Share of capital dividends received by the partnership
- Share of government grants (for Canadian resource property) in excess of amounts repaid
- Share of life insurance proceeds received due to a partner's death

Deductions

- Share of partnership loss, including 100% of allowable capital losses
- Share of drawings or capital distributions
- Investment tax credits used by the partner
- Share of charitable gifts or political contributions

The Act excludes partnership interests from the rule that negative ACB be treated as an immediate capital gain.

Asset Transfer Into a Partnership

A provision in the Act allows for a rollover of property from partner to partnership if elected by taxpayer. The requirements are as follows:

- Must be a Canadian partnership;
- All partners resident in Canada; and
- Transferred property must be capital, Canadian or foreign resource property, eligible capital property, or inventory.

Disposition of a Partnership Interest

Disposition of a partnership interest will trigger a capital gain or allowable capital loss depending upon the situation. ACB of partnership interest is deducted from proceeds of disposition. Any negative ACB is added to the capital gain.

Limited Partnership

A limited partnership includes at least one general partner and one limited partner. Provinces usually have a Limited Partnership Act that allows the limited partner to contribute capital, but not be involved in business operations. The limited partner has limited liability. The managing partner is personally liable for debts and obligations.

Taxation of Limited Partner

Taxed the same as a general partnership, with two exceptions:

At-Risk Rules

The amount of allocated partnership losses that a limited partner can deduct is limited to the amount "at risk" less certain deductions. The at-risk amount has special calculation based on such elements as the limited partner's ACB of partnership interest; and the amount of the partner's share of current year's income and proceeds of disposition for resource property. Non-deductible losses can be carried forward for a limited partner.

Income Attribution

Attribution rules apply when a taxpayer loans, gifts or transfers funds to a spouse or related minor who uses the funds to invest in a limited partnership. Income from limited partnership is then treated as property, not business, income, and is attributed to the transferor.

Limited Liability Partnership

Limited liability partnerships are permitted in most provinces. They are similar to general partnership, but the personal liability of partners does not extend to negligent actions of the other partners, i.e., a partner cannot be sued personally for the negligence of another partner.

Actions can be taken against the partnership and the negligent partner personally, but the only amount at risk for other partners is the amount in their capital account. The amount of allocated partnership losses that limited partner can deduct is limited to the amount "at risk" less certain deductions. The at-risk amount has a special calculation based on such elements as the limited partner's ACB of partnership interest and the amount of partner's share of current year's income and proceeds of disposition for resource property.

CORPORATIONS

Corporation Definition

A structure that is created according to a prescribed set of rules and is recognized in the eyes of the law as a legal entity with rights and duties. It is a distinct and separate legal entity, not required to carry on active business. It can be an investment or holding company.

Corporate Taxation

Corporations pay different rates of flat tax on different types of income such as general active business income, active business income of a CCPC, and investment income.

Federal income tax rates, before any provincial taxes, are 19% for general active business income and 11% for CCPC on the first $500,000 (2009) of active business income.

Fiscal Year

Fiscal year is the taxation year for a corporation and it cannot extend past 53 weeks. It is not required to coincide with the calendar year, but if the corporation is a member of a partnership it may be required to report on a calendar year-end basis. It is common to select a slow period in business cycle as the year end and to select a year-end in the last six months of the year to allow for dividends to be paid to the owner–manager. This allows for tax-planning since dividends could be declared in one year by the corporation and paid the following calendar year. Dividends are only taxable for shareholders when received.

Dividend Income

Dividends received by a corporation do not qualify for the gross-up and dividend tax credit scheme. Dividends are deductible in calculating taxable income which results in no tax payable under Part I tax for recipient corporation if received from:

- A taxable Canadian corporation;

- Corporations resident in Canada and controlled by the receiving corporation; or

- Some non-resident corporations.

Private and subject corporations pay special Part IV refundable tax, used to discourage shareholders from postponing tax. Payment of Part IV tax is credited to the *refundable dividend tax on hand* (RDTOH) account. Dividend refund or Part IV tax is refunded at a rate of $1 for $3 of dividends paid. When a corporation pays the received dividends to the shareholders, the effect is that no taxes were paid by the corporation, and shareholders get taxed as though they received dividends directly from the original payer corporation.

Active Business Income and the Small Business Deduction

The small business deduction (SBD) allows capital to be provided to small businesses. Since small business corporations pay less tax, profits can be reinvested in the business. The SBD reduces taxes payable on up to $500,000 active business income.

The SBD is calculated as 17% (for 2009) of the lesser of:

- Active business income;

- Taxable income (net of income sheltered from foreign tax credits); or

- Business limit for year, currently $500,000.

Active business income is income from any business carried on by the corporation, other than specified investment business* or personal services business.** Includes adventure or concern in the nature of trade.

*A *specified investment business* (SIB) is defined as a corporation whose principal purpose is to derive income from property. If the corporation employs more than five full-time employees its income is considered active business income. SIB excludes credit unions and non-real property leasing businesses.

**A *personal service business* (PSB) is established when a person incorporates a company to provide services to an entity which he would have rendered as an employee of that entity. PSB exists to discourage individuals from incorporating to gain the tax advantages of corporations.

A *capital dividend account* (CDA) is a notional account available to private corporations to integrate corporate and personal income tax on receipt of items such as capital gains and proceeds of life insurance policies received by the corporation. If a private corporation incurs a capital gain, it pays tax on half; the remaining half (non-taxable portion) is added to the CDA. Funds can then be distributed to shareholders. The CDA allows for funds to be received personally tax-free. Public corporations do not have CDA or any similar type of account.

A CDA is comprised of five components:

Additions

- Non-taxable portion of net capital gains (cumulative)
- Capital dividends received from another corporation
- Non-taxable portion of dispositions of eligible capital property
- Proceeds of life insurance policies, where the corporation is the beneficiary, less ACB of the policy

Deductions

- Capital dividends paid

A negative balance in the non-taxable portion of cumulative capital gains does not reduce the CDA account in the above calculation.

Reporting

Corporations with a CDA must file a form T2054, along with a detailed schedule showing computation of the CDA, and a certified copy of corporate resolution authorizing information described in Regulation 2101 of the Act. Over-election of the CDA is subject to 75% tax on the difference. Credit in the CDA means the company received income that can be classified as capital dividend and can flow through tax-free to the shareholders.

Qualified Small Business Corporation Shares

Disposition of QSBCS may qualify for deduction of capital gain equal to $750,000.

The criteria is as follows:

- Shares of CCPC where all or substantially all of the FMV of the assets is used to carry on active business, primarily in Canada;
- Shares are owned for at least 24 months prior to disposition (some exceptions); and
- For the 24 months prior to the share disposition, more than 50% of the FMV of the corporation's assets was used to carry on active business, primarily in Canada.

116. TAX PLANNING FOR OWNER–MANAGERS

Transfer to a Corporation

The Act provides tax-free transfers of property into corporations to provide flexibility for shareholders and corporations structuring their affairs. Transfer from shareholder into corporation normally deemed to occur at the FMV, resulting in an accrued capital gain or recapture realized along with associated income tax liability unless a tax-free election is claimed.

Transfer can be completed under joint election on a tax-free rollover basis if:

- The corporation receiving the property must be a taxable Canadian corporation;
- Consideration is received by a shareholder on the transfer of property into a corporation must include a minimum of one share of the corporation;
- The property transferred must be eligible property; and
- The taxpayer and the corporation must jointly elect on form T2057.

Transfer Price to a Corporation

The taxpayer and the corporation can elect transfer price of property based on:

Ranges for Transfer Price	Type of Property		
	Capital Property	**Depreciable Property**	**Eligible Capital Property**
Upper Limit	FMV	FMV	FMV
Lower Limit	Greater of: FMV of non-share consideration; and lesser of: 1. FMV of property, and 2. ACB of property.	Greater of: FMV of non-share consideration; and least of: 1. FMV of property, 2. UCC of class, and 3. ACB of property.	Greater of: FMV of non-share consideration; and least of: 1. FMV of property, 2. $\frac{1}{3}$ of CEC balance, and 3. ACB of property.

Transfer To/From Partnership or Proprietor

Capital property transferred into a partnership is normally deemed to be disposed of at FMV, but the Act allows rollover of property from taxpayer to partnership where joint election is filed and the taxpayer receives interest in partnership.

Salary-Dividend Mix, Shareholder Benefits

Determining the optimal mix of remuneration for owner–managers between salary and dividends can provide tax planning opportunities. In many cases, salary is paid to an owner to get the taxable income below the $500,000 small business deduction limit.

Tax Deferral

When an owner–manager is paid a salary from the corporation, it is a deductible expense for the company. A company earns net profit when revenue is greater than expenses. The corporation may generate net income greater than the amount that the owner–manager needs personally as salary. The income that is not required by the owner can remain in the company and be taxed at the lower corporate income tax rates.

Dividends

The after-tax income of the corporation can be paid to the owner–manager as a dividend. To avoid double taxation, the dividends received by the owner–manager would qualify for the dividend gross-up and dividend tax credit system.

Capital Gains

The owner–manager may also retain profits in the company which increases the value of his equity investment in the corporation. When the owner–manager sells his shares, the income will be treated as a capital gain, and taxed at 50% only. The investment may also qualify for the $750,000 capital gains exemption.

Shareholder Taxation

Salary/Employment Income

A shareholder, who is a company employee, is paid a salary, the income is treated as regular employment income for the taxpayer. The corporation may accrue a bonus to the owner–manager, and claim the bonus as a business deduction in fiscal year that it is accrued. If the bonus is paid in the next calendar year, the owner–manager does not have to claim the income until the next calendar year. For the bonus to be deductible by the company, it must be paid within 180 days after the fiscal year end.

Regular dividends qualify for the dividend gross-up and dividend tax credit.

Capital Dividend Account

A shareholder is eligible to receive dividends from a private corporation's CDA tax-free. Dividends declared are treated as a return of capital and are not taxable to the shareholder when paid.

Shareholder Loan

If a *specified employee* (someone who owns more the 10% of the company) borrows money from the company, he will be subject to income tax on the loan if the loan is not repaid before the end of the next corporate year end. The loan cannot be part of a series of loans. A loan that does not fall within the above rules is treated as income to the shareholder in the year it is received. The corporation can not claim a tax deduction for the loan. A legitimate shareholder loan, to buy a personal residence or to acquire shares from the treasury of the corporation, for example, may be subject to an imputed interest benefit as a taxable benefit.

Purchase and Redemption of Shares

See section 106, "Capital Gains and Losses" and sections 112 and 113, "Transfer of Company Shares", for further details. Capital gains on the sale of a qualified small business corporation may be eligible for the $750,000 capital gains exemption.

117. EMPLOYEE STOCK OPTIONS

Employee Stock-Option Plans

Generally, a taxable benefit arises when an option is exercised and the shares are purchased, not when the option is granted.

Taxable benefit = (Value of shares acquired) - (Cost to acquire the shares)

An employee's ACB includes:

- Cost to acquire the shares;
- The amount of the taxable benefit; and
- The amount, if any, paid for the options.

Offsetting Deduction

If the option price is equal to or greater than the FMV of the share at the time the option is granted, the employee can claim a deduction equal to 50% of the taxable benefit. To qualify for the deduction, the employee must deal at arm's length with the corporation, and the shares acquired must be common shares. The deduction does not affect the employee's ACB of the shares.

Employee Stock-Option Plans (CCPC Corporations)

Employment taxable benefit is the same calculation, but the income inclusion is deferred until the shares are sold versus under the basic rules where income inclusion occurs when the shares are purchased.

There are two ways to qualify for the offsetting deduction:

- The shares when the option is exercised are held for a minimum of 2 years; or
- The exercise price is equal to or greater than the FMV of the shares when the options were granted.

The double criteria allows an employer to grant options to an employee at an exercise price less than the FMV of the shares when the option is granted.

Employee Stock-Option Plans (Public Shares)

The employment taxable benefit uses the same calculation, and occurs when the shares are purchased, not at the date the options were granted.

The income inclusion can be deferred until the shares are sold, up to a maximum of $100,000 per year versus under the basic rules where income inclusion occurs when the shares are purchased.

To qualify, an employee must:

- Meet all the criteria under the basic rule
- Must not be a specified shareholder (i.e., holds < 10% of all shares)
- Total amount paid (exercise price) must not be less than the FMV of the shares when the option was granted.
- File an election form with his employer within 15 days following the year he exercises his option

---

WAYNE

In 2002, Wayne is granted 2,000 options to buy shares of his employer (a publicly-traded company) for $25 each at a time when the fair market value of the shares is $25 each. Wayne's options vest in 2004. Wayne exercises his right to buy shares in 2006 at a time when the shares are worth $55 each. Finally in 2009, Wayne sells the shares for $100 each.

What are the income tax implications?

2002: nothing

2004: nothing

2006:

Wayne realizes a taxable benefit of $60,000, calculated as $55 (fair market value at the time of exercise) less $25 (exercise price) times 2,000 shares.

Taxable Benefit

$$= (\$55 - \$25) \times 2,000$$
$$= \$60,000$$

The value of Wayne's options is $50,000, calculated as $25 (value at the time when the options were granted) times 2,000 shares. Since this is less than the deferral provision of $100,000, Wayne can defer $60,000.

Summary

- Taxable benefit of $ 60,000
- Deferral $ 60,000
- Income inclusion   NIL

2009:

Wayne will realize a capital gain of $90,000, calculated as $100 (current fair market value) less $55 (cost of shares $25 plus taxable benefit of $30) × 2,000 shares.

Capital Gain

$$= (\$100 - (\$25 + \$30)) \times 2,000$$
$$= \$90,000$$

In addition, Wayne will have to recognize the deferral of $60,000 from 2006 as income, offset by claiming a security option deduction of $30,000 ($60,000 × ½) on line 249 of his 2009 return.

---

118. INTERNATIONAL TAX ISSUES

U.S. Estate Tax

Unlike Canada, the United States imposes an estate tax on the gross estate value less some deductions of U.S. property. U.S. real estate, shares of U.S. corporations, and U.S. corporate debt obligations form part of U.S. situs assets subject to U.S. estate tax. Only worldwide estates valued at over $3.5 million, which include U.S property are generally subject to estate tax.

Foreign Property Reporting

If a taxpayer owns or has an interest in foreign property valued over $100,000, he must report it on his tax return. Foreign property does not include: property in the taxpayer's RRSP, registered retirement income fund (RRIF), or RPP; mutual funds registered in Canada that contain foreign investments; property the taxpayer used or held exclusively in the course of carrying on his active business; or personal-use property.

Entering Canada

An individual who becomes a resident of Canada is deemed to have disposed of and re-acquired all property at FMV. Taxable Canadian property is treated as an exception to the deemed disposition rule.

Leaving Canada

If the taxpayer becomes a non-resident of Canada, he is deemed to have disposed of property upon crossing the border, and is deemed to have received proceeds equal to FMV. Exceptions to the rule are made for:

- Real property situated in Canada;
- Shares of a Canadian corporation not listed on a prescribed stock exchange;
- Shares in a Canadian public corporation if ownership is more than 25%; and
- A partnership or trust that has 50% of FMV assets in a taxable Canadian property, or Canadian resource property, and a life insurance policy in Canada.

In the case of taxable Canadian property, the disposition is deferred until the property is actually sold or another deemed disposition occurs. The taxpayer can elect to have property treated as taxable Canadian property rather than applying deemed disposition rules. The election requires the taxpayer to provide collateral upon leaving Canada for the potential tax payable. The taxpayer can also elect to have disposed of all of his taxable Canadian property at FMV to utilize current capital losses or net capital losses being carried forward.

Unit 5
Self-Test Questions

QUESTIONS

Question 1

The Act requires taxpayers to file income tax returns within prescribed time limits. Which of the following is/are correct?

1. In the case of a trust, within 180 days from the end of the year.

2. In the case of a corporation, within 6 months from their year-end.

3. In the case of an employed individual, on or before April 30th of the following year.

4. In some cases of deceased persons, within 6 months from the day of death.

     a. 3 and 4

     b. 1 and 3

     c. 1, 2, and 3

     d. 2, 3, and 4

Question 2

Your client was out of Canada for most of the previous year. She advises that she doesn't think she will bother to file a tax return. In responding, which of the following would you cite as a potential advantage of filing a return?

1. To take advantage of RRSP contribution room arising from earned income.

2. To establish oneself with the CRA as a cooperative citizen.

3. To receive federal or provincial credits (e.g., GST credit).

4. To obtain a refund of taxes withheld which are greater than required.

     a. 1 and 2

     b. 1 and 4

     c. 1, 3 and 4

     d. 2, 3 and 4

Question 3

Canada taxes non-residents on income earned in Canada, including:

1. rent

2. pension benefits

3. employment income

4. gains on the disposition of taxable Canadian property

5. gains on the disposition of foreign property

    a. 1, 2, 3 and 4 only

    b. 2, 3 and 5 only

    c. 3 only

    d. 4 only

Question 4

In which of the following situations must an individual file an income tax return for the applicable taxation year?

1. The taxes withheld by an employer on the taxpayer's behalf exceed taxes required.

2. The taxpayer has a taxable capital gain.

3. The taxpayer disposed of capital property.

4. The taxpayer owes tax for the year in excess of amounts already withheld on the taxpayer's behalf.

    a. 1 and 4 only

    b. 1, 2 and 3 only

    c. 2 and 3 only

    d. 2, 3 and 4 only

Question 5

Joan held 800 of the 220,000 outstanding shares of Ideal Corp., a taxable public Canadian corporation, when it decided to issue a stock dividend and capitalize $120,000 of its retained earnings. By how much will Joan's taxable income increase?

    a. $0

    b. $545

    c. $633

    d. $1,069

Question 6

During preliminary discussions, a prospective client tells you that he still owes tax on income earned three years ago, and he asks what the interest rate is on unpaid tax. Which of the following will apply?

   a. The interest rate on late tax payments is set quarterly, based on Treasury bill rates, plus 4%.

   b. A penalty of 5% of the unpaid tax is imposed, plus 1% per month for each month the tax remains unpaid.

   c. A penalty of 10% of the unpaid tax is imposed, plus 2% per month for each month the tax remains unpaid.

   d. A flat 10% penalty is imposed.

Question 7

Kevin receives a flat $100 per month from his employer for using his car for employment purposes. In addition, he receives $0.45 per kilometre. Which of the following best illustrates the tax treatment of these allowances?

   a. The $100 per month is not a taxable benefit, but the $0.45 per kilometre is a taxable benefit.

   b. The $100 per month is a taxable benefit, but the $0.45 per kilometre is not a taxable benefit.

   c. The total of the two amounts is taxable and must be included as income.

   d. Both amounts are considered to be reasonable and are not taxable.

Question 8

Which of the following is true, with regard to labour-sponsored venture capital corporations (LSVCC) and the labour-sponsored tax credit?

1. While the LSVCC concept was pioneered by provinces, the resulting tax credit is only available as a federal tax credit.

2. The federal credit is 15% of the investment amount up to $5,000.

3. Many provinces match the federal tax credit with an equal provincial tax credit.

4. To claim the credit one need only enter the amount on line 414 in Schedule I.

   a. 1 and 3

   b. 2 and 4

   c. 3 and 4

   d. 2 and 3

Question 9

Annie, Betty, Carly, and Dolly each borrowed $50,000 from their employer at 3% compounded annually. They have each agreed to repay the loan in full at the end of one year. During that time, the prescribed rate for each quarter was 5%, 5%, 5% and 6% respectively. Which of the following statements is incorrect?

    a. Annie, who used the money to purchase a new house, has a taxable benefit of $1,000.

    b. Betty, who used the money to purchase common shares, can deduct a total of $2,500 from her income.

    c. Carly, who used the money to buy a cottage, has a taxable benefit of $1,125.

    d. Dolly, who used the money to purchase a new car for personal use, has a taxable benefit of $1,125.

Question 10

Mary is 64 years of age and has withdrawn $1,000 per month from her RRSP holdings which she intends to use to qualify for the "pension income amount" on line 314 of her tax return. Which of the following statements is correct?

    a. The pension income amount is only available to those who have attained age 65.

    b. Withdrawals from Mary's RRSP will not qualify her to claim a pension income amount.

    c. Mary will be limited to a pension income amount of $2,000.

    d. As Mary is not 65, her pension income amount, as described above, may be claimed by her spouse, if he is age 65.

Question 11

Sandra's employer makes an automobile available for her exclusive use throughout the year. Her employer's monthly lease cost for the $30,000 automobile is $700. In addition, the employer pays the monthly insurance cost of $200. During the year, the employer paid gas and other operating expenses of $3,500. The automobile is important to Sandra as she travels extensively on work-related activities and considers the automobile a valuable benefit because she does not have to incur the personal expense of buying her own vehicle. Sandra's use of the vehicle for business purposes represented 75% of the total kilometres travelled. She averaged 900 personal kilometres per month. Calculate Sandra's standby charge.

    a. $1,512

    b. $3,203

    c. $5,600

    d. $8,400

Question 12

Sandra's employer makes an automobile available for her exclusive use throughout the year. Her employer's monthly lease cost for the $30,000 automobile is $700. In addition, the employer pays the monthly insurance cost of $200. During the year, the employer paid gas and other operating expenses of $3,500. The automobile is important to Sandra as she travels extensively on work-related activities and considers the automobile a valuable benefit because she does not have to incur the personal expense of buying her own vehicle. Sandra's use the vehicle for business purposes represented 75% of the total kilometres travelled. She averaged 900 personal kilometres per month. Calculate Sandra's operating cost benefit.

    a. 1,512

    b. 2,592

    c. 3,023

    d. 5,600

Question 13

Jinder works as an electrical engineer. She took a four-month electrical systems design software course that cost $600 in tuition and $100 in textbooks from an accredited local college. She enjoyed the course and learned a lot of information that was useful personally and for work. Her employer paid $700 for the course. Assuming Jinder's employer treated the course as a taxable benefit for Jinder, which of the following statements is/are true?

1. The course was primarily for the benefit of the employee.

2. Jinder can claim the tuition of $600 and textbooks costs of $100 if the course was part of a qualifying educational program at a designated educational institution.

3. Jinder is deemed to have paid the course costs of $700.

4. She can claim any applicable non-refundable education and tuition tax credits.

    a. 1 and 3

    b. 1, 2 and 3

    c. 2, 3 and 4

    d. 1, 3 and 4

Question 14

Ellen's employer paid the monthly group wage-loss insurance plan premium of $50 for three years. The employer withheld $300 from Ellen's pay cheque and charged her $300 as a taxable benefit each year. Ellen became ill and missed work starting in January of the following year. Because the illness caused Ellen to miss work, she qualified to receive a monthly benefit of $500. What impact, if any, does the employer's payment have on Ellen?

    a. Ellen incurred an annual taxable benefit of $600.

    b. Ellen incurred an annual taxable benefit but can claim $300 as medical expenses.

    c. The first $900 of benefits received is tax-free, after which any insurance receipts are treated as taxable income.

    d. No tax impact, because any payments received are non-taxable.

Question 15

Which of the following items are generally considered non-taxable transactions?

1. Employer-paid RPP contributions

2. A two-for-one dividend stock split.

3. Employer-paid premiums for individual wage-loss programs.

4. Transfer of investments between a parent and his son at FMV.

5. Tax planning seminars given to retiring employees.

      a. 1, 2 and 5 only

      b. 2 and 3 only

      c. 1 and 5 only

      d. 3 and 4 only

QUESTIONS & SOLUTIONS

Question 1

The Act requires taxpayers to file income tax returns within prescribed time limits. Which of the following is/are correct?

1. In the case of a trust, within 180 days from the end of the year.

2. In the case of a corporation, within 6 months from their year-end.

3. In the case of an employed individual, on or before April 30th of the following year.

4. In some cases of deceased persons, within 6 months from the day of death.

    a. 3 and 4

    b. 1 and 3

    c. 1, 2, and 3

    d. 2, 3, and 4

Answer: d

    ⇨   Statement 1 is incorrect since trusts must file within 90 days after the year end of the trust.

Question 2

Your client was out of Canada for most of the previous year. She advises that she doesn't think she will bother to file a tax return. In responding, which of the following would you cite as a potential advantage of filing a return?

1. To take advantage of RRSP contribution room arising from earned income.

2. To establish oneself with the CRA as a cooperative citizen.

3. To receive federal or provincial credits (e.g., GST credit).

4. To obtain a refund of taxes withheld which are greater than required.

    a. 1 and 2

    b. 1 and 4

    c. 1, 3 and 4

    d. 2, 3 and 4

Answer: c

    ⇨   All of the reasons are advantages of filing a tax return except statement 2.

Question 3

Canada taxes non-residents on income earned in Canada, including:

1. rent

2. pension benefits

3. employment income

4. gains on the disposition of taxable Canadian property

5. gains on the disposition of foreign property

     a. 1, 2, 3 and 4 only

     b. 2, 3 and 5 only

     c. 3 only

     d. 4 only

Answer: a

⇨ Non-residents are taxed on income from employment earnings, a business carried on the Canada and gains from the disposition of taxable Canadian property. They are not taxed on gains on foreign property.

Question 4

In which of the following situations must an individual file an income tax return for the applicable taxation year?

1. The taxes withheld by an employer on the taxpayer's behalf exceed taxes required.

2. The taxpayer has a taxable capital gain.

3. The taxpayer disposed of capital property.

4. The taxpayer owes tax for the year in excess of amounts already withheld on the taxpayer's behalf.

     a. 1 and 4 only

     b. 1, 2 and 3 only

     c. 2 and 3 only

     d. 2, 3 and 4 only

Answer: d

⇨ In statements 2, 3, and 4 the taxpayer must file a return. In statement 1, the taxpayer should, but is not required, to file a tax return to obtain a refund.

Question 5

Joan held 800 of the 220,000 outstanding shares of Ideal Corp., a taxable public Canadian corporation, when it decided to issue a stock dividend and capitalize $120,000 of its retained earnings. By how much will Joan's taxable income increase?

a. $0

b. $545

c. $633

d. $1,069

Answer: c

⇨ Joan's share of the dividend, grossed-up by 45%, is $633 (800 ÷ 220,000 × $120,000 × 1.45 = $633).

Question 6

During preliminary discussions, a prospective client tells you that he still owes tax on income earned three years ago, and he asks what the interest rate is on unpaid tax. Which of the following will apply?

a. The interest rate on late tax payments is set quarterly, based on Treasury bill rates, plus 4%.

b. A penalty of 5% of the unpaid tax is imposed, plus 1% per month for each month the tax remains unpaid.

c. A penalty of 10% of the unpaid tax is imposed, plus 2% per month for each month the tax remains unpaid.

d. A flat 10% penalty is imposed.

Answer: a

⇨ Statement (a) refers only to interest on declared but unpaid taxes. The other answers apply to failures to report income or to file a return, which may or may not also apply to a client who owes back taxes.

Question 7

Kevin receives a flat $100 per month from his employer for using his car for employment purposes. In addition, he receives $0.45 per kilometre. Which of the following best illustrates the tax treatment of these allowances?

a. The $100 per month is not a taxable benefit, but the $0.45 per kilometre is a taxable benefit.

b. The $100 per month is a taxable benefit, but the $0.45 per kilometre is not a taxable benefit.

c. The total of the two amounts is taxable and must be included as income.

d. Both amounts are considered to be reasonable and are not taxable.

Answer: c

⇨ The only allowance the CRA considers reasonable, and thus non-taxable, is one strictly based on a rate per-kilometre, based on actual kilometres driven for business purposes.

Question 8

Which of the following is true, with regard to labour-sponsored venture capital corporations (LSVCC) and the labour-sponsored tax credit?

1. While the LSVCC concept was pioneered by provinces, the resulting tax credit is only available as a federal tax credit.

2. The federal credit is 15% of the investment amount up to $5,000.

3. Many provinces match the federal tax credit with an equal provincial tax credit.

4. To claim the credit one need only enter the amount on line 414 in Schedule I.

    a. 1 and 3

    b. 2 and 4

    c. 3 and 4

    d. 2 and 3

Answer: d

⇨ The federal credit is limited to 15% of the investment to a maximum of $5,000 and many provinces match the 15% credit. Answer (d) is incorrect because applicants must also complete form T5006.

Question 9

Annie, Betty, Carly, and Dolly each borrowed $50,000 from their employer at 3% compounded annually. They have each agreed to repay the loan in full at the end of one year. During that time, the prescribed rate for each quarter was 5%, 5%, 5% and 6% respectively. Which of the following statements is incorrect?

    a. Annie, who used the money to purchase a new house, has a taxable benefit of $1,000.

    b. Betty, who used the money to purchase common shares, can deduct a total of $2,500 from her income.

    c. Carly, who used the money to buy a cottage, has a taxable benefit of $1,125.

    d. Dolly, who used the money to purchase a new car for personal use, has a taxable benefit of $1,125.

Answer: b

⇨ The interest deductible on money borrowed for Betty's investment would be the interest paid, 3% of $50,000, or $1,500. Annie's taxable benefit is based on the lesser of the prescribed rate and the quarterly rate (i.e., $50,000 × 5% × 1 year = $2,500 less 3% interest paid of $1,500 = $1,000). Carly and Dolly's taxable benefit is ($50,000 × 5% × $\frac{9}{12}$ + $50,000 × 6% × $\frac{3}{12}$) - (3% × $50,000) or $1,125.

Question 10

Mary is 64 years of age and has withdrawn $1,000 per month from her RRSP holdings which she intends to use to qualify for the "pension income amount" on line 314 of her tax return. Which of the following statements is correct?

  a. The pension income amount is only available to those who have attained age 65.

  b. Withdrawals from Mary's RRSP will not qualify her to claim a pension income amount.

  c. Mary will be limited to a pension income amount of $2,000.

  d. As Mary is not 65, her pension income amount, as described above, may be claimed by her spouse, if he is age 65.

Answer: b

  ⇨ Those not yet 65 by the end of the tax year may only claim the pension income amount of the lesser of $2,000 and the individual's qualified pension income, which does not include RRSP withdrawals. Even at age 65, the eligible pension income would only count life annuity payments out of an RRSP, not lump-sum withdrawals.

Question 11

Sandra's employer makes an automobile available for her exclusive use throughout the year. Her employer's monthly lease cost for the $30,000 automobile is $700. In addition, the employer pays the monthly insurance cost of $200. During the year, the employer paid gas and other operating expenses of $3,500. The automobile is important to Sandra as she travels extensively on work-related activities and considers the automobile a valuable benefit because she does not have to incur the personal expense of buying her own vehicle. Sandra's use of the vehicle for business purposes represented 75% of the total kilometres travelled. She averaged 900 personal kilometres per month. Calculate Sandra's standby charge.

  a. $1,512

  b. $3,203

  c. $5,600

  d. $8,400

Answer: b

  ⇨ The vehicle is leased not purchased. Answer (a) is the operating cost benefit of 50% of standby charge = 50% × 3,023 or $1,512. Answer (b) is the reduced standby charge of $5,600 × 900/1667 = $3,023. Sandra qualifies for the reduced standby charge since she drove the car for more than 50% for business purposes and the employer gave her the car for business use. Answer (c) is the basic standby charge of ⅔ × $700 × 12 = $5,600. Answer (d) is the income inclusion of $5,600 + 50% of standby charge of $5,600 = $8,400.

Question 12

Sandra's employer makes an automobile available for her exclusive use throughout the year. Her employer's monthly lease cost for the $30,000 automobile is $700. In addition, the employer pays the monthly insurance cost of $200. During the year, the employer paid gas and other operating expenses of $3,500. The automobile is important to Sandra as she travels extensively on work-related activities and considers the automobile a valuable benefit because she does not have to incur the personal expense of buying her own vehicle. Sandra's use the vehicle for business purposes represented 75% of the total kilometres travelled. She averaged 900 personal kilometres per month. Calculate Sandra's operating cost benefit.

   a. 1,512

   b. 2,592

   c. 3,023

   d. 5,600

Answer: a

> ⇨ Answer (a) ($1,512) is 50% of reduced standby charge of $3,023 calculated as (⅔ × $700 × 12 × 900 ÷ 1,667 km). Sandra also has the option of calculating the operating cost benefit as $0.24 per personal kilometre. In answer (b), $2,592 is the result (900 × 12 months × 0.24 = 2,592). She would not elect to use the per kilometre method since it results in a higher taxable benefit amount. Answer (c) is the reduced standby charge of $5,600 × 900 ÷ 1,667 = $3,023. Answer (d) is the basic standby charge of ⅔ × $700 × 12 = $5,600.

Question 13

Jinder works as an electrical engineer. She took a four-month electrical systems design software course that cost $600 in tuition and $100 in textbooks from an accredited local college. She enjoyed the course and learned a lot of information that was useful personally and for work. Her employer paid $700 for the course. Assuming Jinder's employer treated the course as a taxable benefit for Jinder, which of the following statements is/are true?

1. The course was primarily for the benefit of the employee.

2. Jinder can claim the tuition of $600 and textbooks costs of $100 if the course was part of a qualifying educational program at a designated educational institution.

3. Jinder is deemed to have paid the course costs of $700.

4. She can claim any applicable non-refundable education and tuition tax credits.

   a. 1 and 3

   b. 1, 2 and 3

   c. 2, 3 and 4

   d. 1, 3 and 4

Answer: d

> ⇨ If the employer considered the course as a taxable benefit, then the employer believed the course was primary for the benefit of Jinder and not the employer. As a result, Jinder is deemed to have paid the costs of $700 and is eligible to claim any applicable non-refundable tuition and education tax credits. Answer (b) is incorrect because she would be able to claim the tuition of $600, an education amount of $120 and textbook credit of $20 for each month she was a part-time student. If the course was primary for the benefit of the employer it is not a taxable benefit to the employee.

Question 14

Ellen's employer paid the monthly group wage-loss insurance plan premium of $50 for three years. The employer withheld $300 from Ellen's pay cheque and charged her $300 as a taxable benefit each year. Ellen became ill and missed work starting in January of the following year. Because the illness caused Ellen to miss work, she qualified to receive a monthly benefit of $500. What impact, if any, does the employer's payment have on Ellen?

    a. Ellen incurred an annual taxable benefit of $600.

    b. Ellen incurred an annual taxable benefit but can claim $300 as medical expenses.

    c. The first $900 of benefits received is tax-free, after which any insurance receipts are treated as taxable income.

    d. No tax impact, because any payments received are non-taxable.

Answer: d

    ⇨ If the employer and the employee both contributed to the premium and the employer charged its portion as a taxable benefit to the employee, benefit payments received are non-taxable.

Question 15

Which of the following items are generally considered non-taxable transactions?

1. Employer-paid RPP contributions

2. A two-for-one dividend stock split.

3. Employer-paid premiums for individual wage-loss programs.

4. Transfer of investments between a parent and his son at FMV.

5. Tax planning seminars given to retiring employees.

    a. 1, 2 and 5 only

    b. 2 and 3 only

    c. 1 and 5 only

    d. 3 and 4 only

Answer: a

    ⇨ Answers 1, 2, and 5 are non-taxable transactions. Answer 3 would result in a taxable benefit to the individual. Only employer-paid premiums for group wage-loss program are non-taxable benefits. A transfer between a parent and his son would result in capital gains or losses.

Appendix One
Taxable and Non-Taxable Employee Benefits

Allowance or benefit	Is it taxable?
Automobile allowances — reasonable per-kilometre reimbursement	No
Automobile allowances — fixed amount	Yes
Automobile standby charge and operating cost benefits	Yes
Club membership — employer-paid — membership benefits employer	No
Counselling services — tax and financial planning	Yes
Counselling services — health, re-employment or retirement planning	No
Discounts on merchandise — general employee population	No
Education expense — employer-paid — benefits employer	No
Education expense — employer-paid — no benefit to employer	Yes
Gifts and awards — in cash	Yes
Gifts and awards — non-monetary, within threshold	No
Gifts and awards — non-monetary, beyond threshold	Yes
Group term life insurance policies — employer-paid premiums	Yes
Interest-free and low-interest loans to employees	Yes
Moving expenses — specified employer-paid expenses	No
Parking — employer-paid	Yes
Premiums under provincial hospitalization and medical insurance plan — employer-paid	Yes
Premiums for group wage-loss replacement or income maintenance plans — employer-paid*	No
Premiums for non-group wage replacement or income maintenance plans — employer-paid	Yes
Professional fees — membership benefits employer	No
Recreational facilities — available to all employees at same cost	No
RRSP contributions — contribution paid by employer	Yes
RRSP administration fees — paid by employer	Yes
RPP contributions — contributions paid by employer	No
Spouse or common-law partner's travelling expenses — employer paid where spouse not engaged in supporting employer's business	Yes
Transportation costs (i.e., public transit) (other than for safety reasons)	Yes

Note: *Alternative structuring is possible.

**THE CFP
EDUCATION PROGRAM**

CCH/ADVOCIS FPSC-APPROVED CAPSTONE COURSE

MODULE 22

RISK MANAGEMENT AND INSURANCE

Module 22
RISK MANAGEMENT AND INSURANCE

Module 22
Risk Management and Insurance

INTRODUCTION

This section is intended to summarize the technical knowledge required of the risk management aspects of the CFP program. In order to assist with the identification of critical technical aspects and to support the application of those to client scenarios, the technical knowledge reviewed will be applied through the comprehensive case applications following the technical review section of this course.

Important technical knowledge required from the risk management program includes:

- The elements of the insurance contract;

- The characteristics of the various types of insurance contracts available to meet clients risk management planning needs; and

- The government-sponsored health and medical insurance programs plans and taxation.

Unit 1

Insurance

INSURANCE CONTRACT

Establishing an insurance contract requires specific elements for it to be an enforceable contract. An *offer and acceptance* for insurance is needed.

KATE

Kate meets with her certified financial planner, Tom, to explore the risk management part of her financial plan. Through a needs analysis, Kate is made aware of a need for insurance coverage. As an insurance licensed CFP, Tom recommends a product solution and helps Kate to complete an application for the coverage with ACB Insurance Company. The completion of the application is the *offer* and Kate is termed the *offeror*. The insurance carrier will be the one to give *acceptance* to the offer.

In addition to the offer and acceptance, additional requirements exist for the insurance contract to be enforceable by law:

- consideration;

- legal capacity to enter into such a contract;

- the capacity to contract; and

- legal intention by both parties to enter into a contract.

Consideration for an insurance contract would commonly be the payment of premiums by the policy owner.

An insurance contract is formed between two or more parties. There are specific roles needing to be fulfilled for the contract to take effect including the *applicant*, the *life insured*, who may be the same as the applicant, the *insurance carrier*, and the *beneficiary*. The applicant is the individual who completes the application and becomes the owner of the insurance contract.

At the time that the contract becomes effective, in most situations the policy owner must have an *insurable interest*, for the contract to be valid. In life insurance, insurable interest is defined by the *Insurance Act* to include parent, spouse, child, grandchild, employee, and potential other pecuniary interest. It is important to note that the insurable interest for life insurance only needs to be in place at the time the policy takes effect.

With property and casualty insurance, generally the only person(s) who can acquire insurance coverage is the person(s) who owns the property being insured.

TOM

Tom purchased a used car for his 18-year-old son, Adam, to drive to and from university. Adam has a part-time job so that he can pay for the cost of maintaining the car, including the mandatory insurance coverage. The owner of the policy is Tom because he is the owner of the vehicle despite Adam being the primary driver.

The insurance carrier goes through the process of underwriting the application submitted by the applicant to assess the risk before an acceptance can be offered. Full and truthful disclosure on the application is required for the contract to be valid. A number of factors affect the contract as follows:

- **Representation.** Involves the information on the application that is true to the best of the applicant's knowledge. A mistake in a representation can be corrected.

- **Warranty.** A guarantee and critical to the underwriting of the risk.

- **Material Fact.** A fact that has a definite influence on the decision of the parties of a contract. A mistake in material fact may affect the validity of the contract.

- **Material Misrepresentation.** The applicant's failure to disclose all pertinent information. An insurance contract is one taken in utmost good faith (*uberrimae fidei*). A material misrepresentation may void the insurance contract.

- **Mistake of Law.** When parties to a contract are mistaken with regard to the legal effect of some facts used in the underwriting of the contract. This will not generally affect the validity of the contract.

- **Concealment.** The conscious choice by one of the parties not to disclose, or skew, known facts material to the contract.

- **Incontestability Period.** Follows a two-year period where the insurance carrier could void the contract due to failure to disclose or misrepresentation. The two-year period is based on the time the contract has been in effect.

Once the application process is complete, a premium payment is necessary to put an issued policy into effect. When specific conditions are met, a carrier may provide interim insurance coverage known as a *conditional receipt* for the applicant.

The insurance contract once the application is accepted has three important characteristics as follows:

- **Aleatory.** Where one party to the contract offers a conditional promise to meet specific performance criteria should a specific event occur, and the other party to the contract offers something of value. In the case of an insurance contract, the insurance carrier promises to pay benefits should a specific event occur.

- **Adhesion.** When a contract is prepared by one party to the contract and requires the other party to the contract to accept or reject all of the conditions within the contract as a whole.

- **Unilateral.** When one party agrees to fulfill the conditions of the contract, and can be held accountable for the fulfillment of the contract. An insurance contract is a unilateral contract because all the conditions of the contract must be fulfilled by the insurance carrier.

ELEMENTS OF AN INSURANCE CONTRACT

The insurance contract may include one or more of the following depending on the coverage applied for by the applicant and the nature of the risk being underwritten.

- **Declarations.** Statements of fact by the policy owner relating to the risk, and forms the basis for decisions about the acceptability of the risk.

- **Rating.** The level of risk relative to a base-line risk.

- **Exclusions.** A loss for which the insurance carrier does not provide coverage.

- **Riders, Endorsements, and Floaters.** Amendments or additions that form part of the contract. Floaters are riders attached to property and fire insurance.

TYPES OF RISK

Insurance is an important tool for financial planners to use when developing the risk management aspect of a client's financial plan. However, it is only available to certain types of risks. Risks can be categorized into types of risk based on their impact and frequency.

- **Speculative Risk.** Involves the potential for a loss or a gain. This is not insurable.

- **Pure Risk.** Occurs when it is uncertain whether or not a loss will occur, and there is no potential for gain. This is insurable.

- **Dynamic Risk.** The broad risk associated with changes in the economy that affect society. This is not insurable, but may be supported by government programs at the time of an occurrence.

- **Static Risk.** The magnitude is predictable, quantifiable, and measurable. This is insurable.

- **Fundamental Risk.** The broad risk affecting large groups or segments of the population, and is a result of economic, political, or natural causes. This is not insurable, but may be supported by government programs at the time of an occurrence.

- **Particular Risks.** Single, isolated events with losses at an individual level, and are insurable.

When a risk is insurable, we need to differentiate between what is a peril and what is a hazard to that risk. The peril is what may cause a possible loss, while a hazard increases the possibility of a loss from a particular peril. A hazard may be either a "physical hazard", or a "moral hazard".

ADEL

Adel lives in an older home with an old furnace that has never been serviced. She is aware that the furnace should be cleaned regularly but doesn't bother. While doing some painting in her basement she leaves the paint thinner sitting next to the furnace. That day, a fire happens in her basement as a result of a spark from the furnace igniting the fumes of the paint thinner. In this scenario, the peril is the fire and the hazard is the un-cleaned furnace. Adel's choice to not clean the furnace and to leave the paint thinner next to the furnace are examples of moral hazards.

THE RISK MANAGEMENT PROCESS

Applying our knowledge about risk for the benefit of our financial planning clients is accomplished through the five-step risk management process.

- **Step One:** Setting risk management objectives.

- **Step Two:** Identifying and evaluating risks that may impose financial losses of dire, substantial, and minor consequences.

- **Step Three:** Selecting strategies.

  — *Risk control strategies* reduce the probability of a risk occurring and/or reduce the severity of the consequences that could result from a potential risk. These are classified as either *risk avoidance*, which is avoiding the risk completely, or *risk reduction*, which is reducing the level of risk.

  — *Risk financing strategies* involve strategies that assist in managing costs associated with a particular risk. These include *risk transfer/sharing* and *risk retention*.

- **Step Four:** Implementation.

- **Step Five:** Monitoring.

201. LIFE INSURANCE

Life insurance is a legal contract formed between the policy owner and the insurance carrier according to the elements required in a valid contract discussed above. The policy owner has the right to name a beneficiary, access the cash value, transfer ownership by an "absolute assignment", and may name a "successor" or "contingent owner" to assume ownership in the event of his/her pre-deceasing the life insured.

The *life insured* is the person whose life is insured. The assessment of the life insured forms part of the underwriting process of the risk being considered for the insurance contract. An insurance contract can be based on a single life insured or on a joint life of two or more lives. Typically, a joint life contract will be priced and pay benefits on one of the following:

- **Joint-Last-to-Die.** Pays a death benefit upon the last death. This type of policy is generally less expensive that the joint-first-to-die because it only becomes payable after the last death.

- **Joint-First-to-Die.** Pays a death benefit upon the first death.

It is important to make a beneficiary designation on the insurance contract to ensure that the benefits are paid to the intended recipient in the most efficient manner. In the event that a named beneficiary is not selected by the policy owner the proceeds of the insurance contract will be paid to the estate of the life insured. In other situations, it may make sense for the client to name the estate as the beneficiary depending on their financial plan. Important considerations for each option are noted in the table.

Named Beneficiary	Estate as Beneficiary
• Appears in policy • Benefit directly to beneficiary • Benefit does not form part of estate • Prompt payment • Privacy • Creditor protection for policy owner if spouse, child, grandchild, or parent of the life insured named irrevocably • Non-contested	• Liquid asset to estate • Estate may be easier to administer • Accessible to creditors • Probate fees

The designation of a named beneficiary may be either *revocable* or *irrevocable*.

- **Irrevocable.** The owner may not alter or revoke the designation without the prior consent of the beneficiary, and has limited control over the policy to alter or revoke designation or surrender policy.

- **Revocable.** The owner may alter or revoke the beneficiary designation.

While minors may be a beneficiary to a life insurance contract, they are not able to provide a valid discharge to the insurance company. Alternatively, it is possible for the named beneficiary to pre-decease the life insured. To ensure the benefits of the life insurance bypass the estate, a contingent beneficiary may be named who will receive the proceeds if the primary beneficiary pre-deceases the life insured.

Settlement options for the death benefit can include a lump-sum amount, deposit, or annuity, and may be selected by the policy owner or, if not, may be selected by the beneficiary at the time of claim.

Additional considerations for a client when considering a life insurance contract include:

- **Rescission Right.** Commonly termed the "10-day free look" for the policy owner to review the policy, and to cancel the policy if they choose. They will receive a full refund of any premiums paid.

- **Misstatement of Age.** An error where an age correction can be made to the policy allowing the coverage to remain in place, and the premiums will be adjusted to the correct age.

- **Grace Period.** The period of time, generally 30 days, after the premium due date. If the premium remains unpaid after the grace period, the policy has "lapsed".

- **Policy Reinstatement.** When a lapsed policy can be put back in force any time during the two-year period immediately following the date of the policy lapse. From the client, the carrier will require a request for reinstatement, payment of any outstanding premiums and any other indebtedness on the policy, and to provide evidence of insurability.

- **Suicide Clause.** The exclusion period for death by suicide up to 2 years from the issue date of the insurance contract.

PREMIUMS

The premium is the consideration paid by the policy owner for the insurance contract and is calculated as:

Premium = Mortality Cost + Operating Expenses - Investment Return

The mortality cost includes the mortality rate, which is the rate of death expected in the upcoming year measured by criteria including age, gender, or smoking status. The risk may be a standard risk or the carrier may impose a rating on the premium due to the nature of the risk. When a client exceeds the level of risk the insurance carrier is willing to accept, the risk is deemed uninsurable. Preferred rates, which are preferable to standard rates, apply when the risk is better than the standard for the insurance carrier.

To acquire an accurate understanding of a risk, the carrier underwrites the risk. This is a process of analyzing the information presented on the application. Included in the consideration are the life insured's health, physical condition, health history, family health history, occupation, and character. In addition, the addition of riders on the policy will impact the premium because riders increase the features of the plan design. Possible riders to a life insurance policy are listed in the following table.

Rider Name	Description
Waiver of Premium	If life insured becomes totally disabled, carrier will pay premiums on behalf of the individual
Accidental Death and Dismemberment	Death benefit increased if death is the result of an accident
Guaranteed Insurability	Guarantees the ability to purchase specified amount of additional insurance regardless of health
Cost of Living	Allows regular increases to the face amount of the coverage by the carrier to keep pace with inflation
Term Rider	Additional temporary insurance added to a permanent policy to increase the coverage for a temporary need

TYPES OF PLANS

Two main categories of life insurance exist: individual insurance and group life insurance. Each have unique characteristics and applications from a financial planning perspective for the client's risk management needs.

GROUP LIFE INSURANCE

Group insurance requires an individual to be actively at work or a member of a defined group or association for them to be enrolled for coverage in a plan. No additional evidence of insurability is usually required by the individual to receive the life insurance coverage.

The product generally offers a flat amount of benefit or a multiple of the individual's annual earnings for the benefit amount. Coverage will remain in place for as long as the individual is employed or until age 65 and is priced annually for the group based on one-year renewable term insurance pricing. Premium payment is the responsibility of the plan owner to remit to the insurance carrier and will be either paid for by the employer or through a deduction method.

While group insurance coverage can be an inexpensive source of life insurance protection for the client's needs, it is not guaranteed to be in place at the time it may be needed. Whether through termination of employment, retirement or cancellation of the plan by the employer, the financial planning client may find themselves without adequate life insurance coverage. To help address this feature of group life insurance, a conversion option may exist. *Conversion* allows the insured individual to convert their group life insurance coverage at employment termination, retirement or plan termination, into individually owned coverage with the carrier up to a maximum face amount at a premium rate reflective of the insured's age, coverage amount and product being converted into.

INDIVIDUAL LIFE INSURANCE

In contrast, individual life insurance is available to individuals outside of their employment. The individual is the owner of the product and may be the life insured. As a result, the individual determines the coverage and carrier for their life insurance. Premiums are paid by the individual themselves who are responsible for remitting the payment to the insurer as per the policy requirements.

The product will be either term or permanent in design. Term insurance is intended to provide protection for a set period of time. Term insurance provides pure insurance coverage for the client and will no longer provide coverage at the end of the term. Two important features exist on term insurance policies that need to be taken into consideration when planning: renewable and convertible options.

Term life insurance can be in increments of 1, 5, 10, or 20 years, or to a given age, such as 65 or 100.

Permanent life insurance is intended to provide coverage to a client for the whole of their life. Types of permanent policies include whole life insurance and universal life insurance.

FEATURES OF PLANS

Term Life

Term life insurance is the most simple, and generally has the lowest cost premium of the individual life insurance products. It is designed to provide life insurance coverage for a limited period of time. The coverage is usually designed to be in effect for periods ranging from one year through to terms extended for 5, 10, or 20 years of coverage with renewability through to a maximum coverage age. This maximum age is usually 65, 70, or 75 years old. At this age, the term insurance policy may expire.

If the insured feels a need for the life insurance coverage to remain in place beyond the term of the term insurance contract, a conversion option may be available that allows the client to convert their policy into a permanent type of product.

Term insurance provides for a benefit to be payable to the beneficiary in the event of the life insured's death during the term of the contract. The benefit will be selected at the time of purchasing the policy and will be either a level benefit for the period of the term or a decreasing level of coverage, such as with mortgage term insurance.

Whole Life

Whole life insurance is a permanent insurance coverage with a face amount and premium selected at the time of purchase. These remain fixed for the life of the policy.

Whole life is designed to provide permanent coverage for the life insured funded through the premiums paid and the interest earned on those dollars. In the early years of a policy, these dollars accumulate and form what is called the reserve. A portion of this reserve is what becomes the cash value of the policy and is available to the insured as a non-forfeiture right.

Reserve = Premiums paid to date + Interest earned - Mortality and plan expense charges

Cash surrender value is different from the cash value of the policy and is available to the policy owner when a whole life policy is terminated. The cash surrender value is the cash value less any surrender charges and policy indebtedness.

Dividends paid to a whole life policy owner are a division of the insurance carrier's surplus. Within a participating policy, dividends are considered as the equivalent of a refund of premium and so they enjoy a favourable tax treatment compared to dividends payable by a corporation.

Dividends are generally paid in one of five options as selected by the policy owner. Each option has its own unique tax considerations for the policy owner.

Dividend Option	Taxation
Cash Receipt	This is considered a partial disposition reducing the adjusted cost basis on the policy. If the adjusted cost base (ACB) is reduced below zero, the negative amount is a taxable income gain.
Automatic Premium Reduction	The dividend is used to reduce the amount of the annual policy premium. While the dividend reduces the ACB, the use of it as the premium increases the ACB by an equivalent amount and thereby has a net zero effect from an income tax perspective.
Paid-Up Additions	The dividend is used to purchase additional insurance coverage that does not require ongoing premium payments. This has the same tax impact as the automatic premium reduction option.
Accumulation	Dividends remain on deposit with the carrier to earn interest. The tax impact is the same as the cash receipt option plus the income earned on the dividends is taxable income to the policy owner.
Term Insurance	Dividends are used to purchase a term insurance rider on the base whole life policy. The tax consequences are the same as for paid-up additions and automatic premium reduction options.

Because whole life insurance does have a cash value, it is considered an asset to the policy owner. As an asset, it is available for policy loans and collateral assignment where the policy is used as security for a loan.

If the policy owner is no longer able or willing to pay the premiums for the life insurance policy, non-forfeiture options are built into the contract wording to keep the coverage in-force if a cash value has accumulated within the policy. The non-forfeiture options may include: cash surrender value, an automatic premium loan, purchase of an extended term insurance policy, or a reduced paid-up insurance policy.

Upon the death of the life insured, a death benefit is payable to the beneficiary and is calculated as the face amount plus any enhancements less indebtedness.

Universal Life

A universal life insurance policy is a very flexible type of permanent insurance. It is designed to address consumer's diverse needs through such features as a varying amount of coverage, premium payment flexibility, and interest-sensitive investments.

The pricing of a universal life policy is unique in that the three components of pricing are tracked separately to include: mortality charges, expenses charged for the policy and investment earnings within the policy. For pricing the policy, the carrier will consider the following:

Pricing = Mortality charges + Expenses - Investment earnings within the policy

Death benefit options are selected by the policy owner at the time of purchasing a universal life insurance policy. The death benefit options of the policy will generally be one of the following options:

- **Level Face Fixed.** The benefit remains level, and any accumulation within the policy reduces the carrier's cost of insurance (mortality cost).
- **Level Face Plus Deposits.** The face amount, plus gross amount of deposits.
- **Level Face Plus Account Value.** The face amount, plus policy account.
- **Indexed Death Benefit.** The death benefit indexed for inflation often based on the Consumer Price Index (CPI).

Non-forfeiture options and policy loans are available with universal life as with whole life insurance products.

Term 100

Term 100 is considered a permanent insurance product despite its name because it is designed to provide insurance coverage to the life insured's age 100. The premiums and coverage are selected by the policy owner at the time of purchase and remain level and guaranteed through the life of the contract.

With increasing life expectancy, it is important to note that the coverage may remain in force after the life insured reaches 100. At that time, no additional premium payments will be required. Contracts may offer a limited payment period of a set number of years or to a specified age.

TAXATION OF LIFE PLANS

Group Life Insurance

If the premium is employer paid the benefit is considered taxable to the insured and a tax deductible expense for the employer. As a result of the premiums being a taxable benefit, the death benefit is received by the beneficiary tax-free.

Individual Life Insurance

As of December 1, 1982, the status of exempt and non-exempt life insurance was established. This date is used to classify the tax treatment the policy is eligible to receive depending on its last acquired date relative to December 1, 1982. A policy issued before December 2, 1982 may qualify for grandparent status for tax treatment.

An "Exempt Policy" is one designed primarily to provide life insurance protection where the cash value within the policy does not exceed the cash value associated with a 20-pay endowment policy that endows at age 85. These policies only have income tax consequences at disposition.

A "Non-Exempt Policy" is one that does not meet the required definition of exempt, and is considered to be used primarily as an investment.

Last Acquired

Important transactions that could affect a policy's last acquired date include:

- Original issue of the policy;
- Transfer of policy to a new owner;
- The exercise of contractual rights; and
- A policy reinstatement.

Once the exempt and non-exempt status is identified, the amount of money subject to taxation is calculated using the ACB.

ACB = Sum of all premiums paid - Sum of the net cost of pure insurance

The annual taxation of an exempt policy is such that the income tax consequences only arise for the policy owner upon the disposition of the contract. The annual taxable amount is the amount of the policy's accumulated fund in excess of the policy's ACB and is added to the policy's ACB.

GORDON

Gordon owns a whole life insurance contract that he purchased from his cousin, Ed, who sells life insurance, to meet his final expense needs. The policy is considered non-exempt and has a death benefit of $50,000, with an accumulating fund worth $5,000. The ACB within the policy is $4,500. What might Gordon experience as tax consequences with the policy?

Because the policy is a non-exempt policy, Gordon will need to report income for his annual taxation. The amount that Gordon will need to report is the excess of the accumulation fund over the adjusted cost basis ($5,000 - $4,500 = $500). As a result of reporting the income, Gordon's insurance policy will have the ACB increased by the equal amount of $500.

Disposition of a life insurance policy can occur in a number of possible events. The table below identifies these events and summarizes the tax impact and ACB impacts of the disposition.

Disposition	Original Owner	New Owner
Death of life insured when non-exempt only	Taxable income = accumulating fund - ACB New ACB = increased by the amount reported in taxable income	
Ownership Transfer — Arm's length by filing an absolute assignment	Income gain = Proceeds - ACB Income loss = not recognized	New ACB = Proceeds of disposition
Ownership Transfer — Non-arm's length by filing an absolute assignment	Proceeds = Cash Surrender Value (CSV) Income Gain = CSV - ACB Income Loss = not recognized	New ACB = CSV
Full Surrender — to insurance carrier	Income gain = Proceeds - ACB Income Loss = not recognized	
Partial Surrender	Income Gain = Proceeds from partial surrender - (proceeds of partial surrender + total CSV) × (ACB))	
Shareholder Transactions	Income gain = FMV - ACB	New ACB = FMV
Rollovers — spousal or parent to child if policy on child	Income gain = 0	New ACB = Old ACB

202. DISABILITY INSURANCE

Disability insurance provides financial protection to an individual who becomes unable to work because of health impairment. The policy pays a benefit during the insured individual's lifetime in the form of a regular income stream to provide an income for a period of time until the individual can return to work.

Types of Plans

Disability insurance is available through group insurance packages and as individual coverage. The type of coverage is needed by a client will depend on their individual needs.

Features of Plans

Individual Disability Insurance

Individual disability insurance is underwritten based on a number of factors. The factors include: morbidity, occupational classification, age and sex, and current health of the individual to be insured.

The policy premium will be based on the underwriting factors above and the specific features of the coverage selected by the policy owner at the time of application. The *definition of disability* is a significant factor of pricing as it determines when benefits will be payable in a disability situation. The three standard definitions of disability generally used by carriers are *own occupation*, *regular occupation*, and *any occupation*.

Own Occupation

With an *own occupation* definition, the individual is unable to perform the substantial duties of her own occupation due to injury or sickness. This is the most costly and highest level of coverage available. In most situations, only very skilled professionals qualify for this definition of coverage.

Regular Occupation

With a *regular occupation* definition, the individual is unable to perform the substantial duties of the regular occupation in which she was engaged at the onset of disability due to injury or sickness. This definition is less costly than the own occupation.

Any Occupation

The *any occupation* definition requires that the individual be unable to perform any job for gainful employment for which she is reasonably qualified due to education, training or experience. This definition of disability is the least costly and the least attractive in terms of providing an individual with ongoing financial protection due to disability. An individual must be so incapacitated that she is unable to perform most any occupation.

Each of the three definitions outlined above provide the framework on which an individual's disability will be measured relative to her eligibility for benefits.

Some policies will provide a benefit in the event of a reduced disability. *Residual disability* is the loss of earned income of at least a defined per cent of prior earned income. In this situation, the monthly benefit will be reduced proportionate to the loss of income calculated as follows:

Proportionate monthly benefit = (Loss of earned income ÷ Prior earned income) × Monthly benefit

Partial disability is when the insured is still able to work either in her regular occupation, but is unable to perform one or more important duties, or is unable to spend more than half of the time usually spent in the occupation. A benefit as defined by the policy may be payable.

Once the risk has been assessed through the underwriting process and the definition of disability has been selected, the waiting or elimination period (when the benefits commence after a disability) and the benefit period (how long they will be payable) are final considerations for matching the individual disability insurance contract to the client's needs. The contract may contain additional contract guarantees relating to the cancellable or non-cancellable nature of the contract, and guarantees relating to the renewability of the contract. Riders for increasing coverage such as the automatic coverage enhancement rider and the cost of living adjustment will help the client keep coverage in proportion to their future needs. The premium refund rider will provide the policy owner with a refund of premiums paid in the situation where no benefit has been paid prior to a specific date in the policy as defined by the carrier.

Group Disability Insurance

Group disability insurance is provided on both a short-term disability and a long-term disability basis. The employer or association, as the policy owner, establishes the key parameters of the group contract with the carrier including the benefit amount payable to the employee. Usually this amount is a percentage of the employee's annual earnings to an overall maximum dollar amount of benefit. The premium for the group disability insurance is based on the profile of the group as a whole. This profile considers variables including age, sex and occupation.

Group disability insurance is renewable annually with premiums potentially being adjusted annually to reflect the updated profile of the group and the experience with the group prior to the renewal.

Taxation of Disability Plans

Group disability insurance plans have their disability benefits taxed differently depending on who pays the policy premium as follows:

- **Employer Paid.** The premium payments paid by the employer are taxable, while benefits, if disabled, are non-taxable.
- **Employer Paid With Employee Charged the Taxable Benefit.** The benefit payments are non-taxable.
- **Employer and Employee Paid.** The benefit payments received are taxable, but reduced by any amount the employee paid.

Individual disability insurance plans depend on who pays the premium as well. If the premiums are personally paid, then the benefits are received as non-taxable income to the recipient.

203. HEALTH INSURANCE

Health insurance provides coverage for the expenses associated with an individual's health expenses, whether routine or emergency care. As the costs to health care continue to increase, health care insurance is a critical part of a client's risk management planning in order to offset the impact these costs could have on their financial plan.

Types of Plans

The government provides a program of health insurance through the individual province's health insurance plans. In addition to this coverage, an individual may purchase private medical insurance often referred to as *extended health coverage*. The extended health coverage falls into one of two types of plans: supplemental health insurance coverage and dental insurance coverage.

Features of Plans

The government health insurance program has evolved out of the *Canada Health Act*. This federal health insurance legislation provides the criteria and conditions for the provinces/territories to follow in order to qualify for full federal contributions under the

Canada Health and Social Transfer (CHST) (federal dollars transferred to the provinces to support the cost of the provincial programs).

In order to receive the CHST funding, the provincial plans must meet specific criteria. The program criteria for funding include:

- **Public Administration.** The program must be operated on a non-profit basis by a public authority.
- **Comprehensiveness.** Requires that the program include coverage for all medically necessary hospital, physician, and surgical/dental health services.
- **Universality.** Requires that uniform terms and conditions exist for all insured residents.
- **Portability.** Accommodates for an individual who moves or travels outside his home jurisdiction, or travels outside Canada, within certain limits.
- **Accessibility.** Refers to an individual having reasonable access to health care services unimpeded by financial barriers.

Private Medical Insurance

Extended health coverage purchased privately may provide coverage for health insurance to supplement the benefits covered under the provincial health plans. Included in the coverage may be items such as prescription drugs, semi-private and private hospital accommodation, medical and hospital expenses incurred outside of Canada (within prescribed limits), paramedical services, and some vision care coverage.

In addition, dental insurance coverage may be purchased to cover services related to basic preventative services, major services, and orthodontic services.

Private medical insurance is priced based on many factors in addition to the services covered including the integration of deductibles, coinsurance, and plan maximums. These factors may be selected by the policy owner at the time of purchasing the coverage.

Taxation of Plans

When the provincial health plans require a "provincial health tax" be charged to employers to help cover the cost of providing provincial health insurance, there is no taxable benefit charged to the employee for this benefit.

Where the province charges a premium to individuals for coverage, the following is the financial impact depending on who the premium payer is:

- If the individual pays the premium on his own, there is no tax deduction available and no relief available through the non-refundable tax credits; and
- If an employer pays the premium on behalf of an employee, the employer's payment is charged as a taxable benefit to the employee.

Regardless of who pays the premium, the benefits are not taxable to the individual when received. When the private medical insurance is in a group insurance program and the premiums are paid by the employer, they are tax deductible by the employer as a business expense, and not taxable to the employee. As with the provincial plans, the benefits are not taxable to the individual when received.

204. CRITICAL ILLNESS

Critical illness insurance pays a lump-sum benefit to the policy owner during their life at the time of surviving a critical illness defined within the contract.

Features of Plans

The individual critical illness insurance policy will depend on the type of plan, plan design, and benefit amount selected at the time of purchase. In addition, the individual's age, health, and other medical and lifestyle information are used to establish the premium for the individual policy. The types of illnesses covered under a critical illness policy may vary by insurance carrier, but generally will include coverage for cancer, stroke, or heart conditions, in addition to others as identified by the carriers.

To make a claim for benefits, the individual must survive with the diagnosed illness for a specified period, often in the 30-day to 90-day range.

Taxation of Plans

There is some uncertainty regarding the Canada Revenue Agency's (CRA's) position relative to the taxation associated with a critical illness policy. Treatment of the premium payment and benefits depends on the structure of each policy.

205. LONG-TERM CARE INSURANCE

Long-term care insurance is an insurance product designed to pay a monthly benefit to help manage the costs associated with the long-term care of aging individuals. Plans are designed to commence payment of benefits when the insured reaches a defined level of incapacity related to the defined activities of daily living (ADLs). These activities normally include bathing, dressing, toileting, transferring, and eating.

Features of Plans

Long-term care insurance provides benefits based on one of three possible types of benefit payments:

- **Income Model.** Payment of an amount of monthly income, regardless of cost of care, selected at the time of establishing the insurance contract. The insured does not need to provide evidence where care was received to be paid.
- **Indemnity Model.** The insured must provide evidence that care has been received to receive the benefits. These policies pay the insured person a flat amount regardless of the amount of the insured person's expenses.
- **Reimbursement Model.** A benefit that requires receipts be submitted to the carrier for reimbursement for specific costs only.

Similar to disability insurance, both the elimination period and benefit amount and period are selected at the time of purchasing the contract. Within in the contract, some specific conditions such as self-inflicted injuries, alcoholism, some drug addictions, and mental and nervous conditions with no organic cause may be excluded.

To be eligible to claim benefits, each carrier's policy will define what is the trigger point for the payment of benefits to begin, usually defined by an individual no longer being able to perform two or more of the ADLs.

Taxation of Plans

From a taxation perspective, the premiums do not qualify as medical expenses so are not considered deductible from income. As a result, the benefit payments are non-taxable and are not treated as income by the insured when received.

206. PROPERTY AND CASUALTY INSURANCE

Property and casualty insurance includes all types of insurance, other than life and health insurance. The most common of these that clients need to be aware of within their personal risk management planning are their coverage options for automobile insurance and home insurance.

Types of Coverage

Automobile Insurance

Automobile insurance coverage is legislated for all owners of vehicles, and is legislated by each province/territory to their own minimum standards for the types and amounts of coverage required to legally operate a vehicle. Auto insurance coverage protects both the vehicle and the individuals through many coverage features.

Home Insurance

While home insurance is not a mandatory insurance coverage from a legislation perspective, it does build some important protection into the client's risk management plan for their home and the contents. Coverage ranges from comprehensive to basic coverage. *Comprehensive* will include the building and contents for all risks with the exception of any risks specifically excluded in the contract. *Broad coverage* provides all peril coverage for the building and named-peril coverage for the contents. As broad coverage includes only named-peril coverage for contents, its premium will be less than a comprehensive policy on the same property. Finally, a *basic/named perils* policy may be an option. This type of policy only includes perils that are specifically named for both the home and contents.

Features of Plans

Automobile insurance covers damage to people and property in many aspects including bodily injury, liability, and damages.

Bodily injury coverage includes benefits to compensate for injury to the insured and their passengers in the event of an automobile accident. Three specific types of coverage will be included in the policy wordings of an individual's auto insurance as follows:

- **Accident Benefits.** Provides compensation to the insured, to her passengers, and to pedestrians, for death or injury resulting from an accident.
- **Uninsured Motorist Coverage.** Provides coverage in the event that an accident occurs involving an uninsured motorist. That uninsured motorist still faces the possibility of criminal charges, and is liable for costs associated with at-fault accidents.
- **Family Protection.** A policy endorsement to cover an insured, her spouse, or a dependent relative, when they are injured by someone with no insurance or with a low limit of coverage.

Liability coverage for automobile insurance refers to third party liability coverage which is intended to compensate for injury or damage to property where the policy owner is found liable. If the resulting claim exceeds the amount of coverage, the motorist can be held personally liable for the shortfall.

Temporary substitute automobile coverage insures an individual when they drive another person's vehicle. In an accident, the insurance policy of the owner of the substitute vehicle is the first payer.

Collision coverage provides indemnity for the policy owner for losses when the owner's vehicle is damaged due to a collision.

Comprehensive coverage covers loss or damage to an insured's automobile resulting from a variety of perils, such as fire, theft, vandalism, or glass breakage, other than those covered under collision insurance.

Homeowners liability coverage does not normally include a deductible unlike auto insurance, and generally covers losses that arise through ownership of such things like boats and sailboats, and self-propelled lawnmowers or snow blowers.

Unit 2
Self-Test Questions

QUESTIONS

Question 1

Sam wants to purchase a life insurance policy where he is the policy owner and his spouse is the life insured. To be able to make such a purchase, Sam must have an insurable interest in his spouse. When must this insurable interest be present?

    a. At the time that the policy becomes effective and at the time of any claim.

    b. Indefinitely.

    c. Only at the time of any claim.

    d. Only at the time that the policy becomes effective.

Question 2

James, age 17, is the beneficiary of a life insurance policy where his father, Donald, is the owner and the life insured. If Donald were to die today, which of the following statements is true?

    a. James does not have the legal capacity to discharge the contract as a beneficiary.

    b. James has the legal capacity to discharge the contract as a beneficiary, provided both of his parents have predeceased him.

    c. James has the legal capacity to discharge the contract as a beneficiary, provided he purchases a term certain annuity with the funds from the policy.

    d. James has the legal capacity to discharge the contract as a beneficiary.

Question 3

Mahood's house was destroyed by a fire, which the fire department believe was caused by a poor connection between the furnace and the gas line. The hazard in this case is the:

    a. fact that the furnace uses gas

    b. poor quality connection between the furnace and the gas line

    c. the fire

    d. use of the furnace to heat Mahood's home

Question 4

Gord is an avid scuba diver and typically selects vacations where he can explore new areas. Gord recognizes the risk associated with scuba diving so has purchased life insurance where he has named his spouse as the beneficiary. Gord's purchase of life insurance is a strategy commonly referred to as:

    a. risk avoidance

    b. risk retention

    c. risk transfer

    d. segregation

Question 5

If the insured owner of a vehicle injures another party with his vehicle and is found liable, which of the following statements is true?

    a. If any resulting claim exceeds the insured's level of third party liability coverage, she can be held personally liable for any shortfall.

    b. If any resulting claim exceeds the insured's level of third party liability coverage, she cannot be held personally liable for any shortfall provided her amount of coverage met the minimum coverage amount established by the province.

    c. If any resulting claim exceeds the insured's level of third party liability coverage, she cannot be held personally liable if the injured third party has coverage for uninsured motorists.

    d. If the resulting claim exceeds the insured's level of third party liability coverage, she cannot be held personally liable if the injured third party has coverage for accident benefits.

Question 6

Which of the following factors would typically be a consideration when establishing the premium for an individual's automobile insurance policy?

1. Driving experience of any drivers of the vehicle

2. Life expectancy

3. Geographic region in which the insured vehicle will be driven

4. Total value of the insured vehicle

5. Age and sex of any drivers

6. Previous disability claims

    a. 1 and 6 only

    b. 1, 3, 4 and 5 only

    c. 2 and 4 only

    d. 2, 3, 5 and 6 only

Question 7

Place the following types of home insurance policies in the order of cost, beginning with the most expensive and ending with the least expensive.

1. Named perils.

2. Broad.

3. No-frills.

4. Comprehensive.

    a. 1, 2, 4 and 3

    b. 2, 4, 1 and 3

    c. 4, 1, 2 and 3

    d. 4, 2, 1 and 3

Question 8

When fire struck and destroyed a substantial portion of the contents of Connor's home, the insurance company explained that his policy would reimburse him for his loss based on the actual cash value of the items. With this type of policy, which of the following statements are true?

1. The claim settlement amount will not include a deduction for depreciation on each item.

2. The claim settlement amount will include a deduction for depreciation on each item.

3. Connor may use the funds from the settlement any way he wishes, and is under no obligation to actually replace the items.

4. Connor will receive reimbursement only if he repairs or replaces an item with another one of similar quality.

     a. 1 and 3 only

     b. 1 and 4 only

     c. 2 and 3 only

     d. 2 and 4 only

Question 9

In order to qualify for full federal cash contributions under the CHST program, the provinces must abide by the five criteria established by the federal government as they relate to provincial health services. The five criteria are:

1. Neutrality

2. Portability

3. Public administration

4. Comprehensiveness

5. Cohesiveness

6. Universality

7. Accessibility

8. Instantaneous

9. Assessment

10. Accountability

     a. 1, 4, 5, 7 and 8 only

     b. 1, 5, 8, 9 and 10 only

     c. 2, 3, 4, 6 and 7 only

     d. 2, 3, 6, 8 and 10 only

Question 10

While travelling in Italy, Steven consulted a plastic surgeon about a special type of cosmetic surgery he had read about in a news publication. Later, when in France, Steven visited the emergency ward at a local hospital after he injured his arm in a bicycle accident. Also, nearing the end of his trip, Steven stopped at an emergency medical clinic in England to have a doctor look at his leg because of severe swelling from a bug bite that he received that day. If Steven is a resident of ABC province in Canada, which of the medical visits will NOT be covered under his provincial health care plan?

1. Italy

2. France

3. England

     a. 1 only

     b. 1, 2 and 3

     c. 2 and 3 only

     d. 3 only

Question 11

Cathy is a member of her employer's extended health care plan, which has a $100 annual family deductible based on a calendar year, and provides for the employee to pay a 20% coinsurance. If Cathy's family has eligible health claims that total $2,555 this year, how much will Cathy receive as a reimbursement under the health care plan?

    a. $1,944
    b. $1,964
    c. $2,044
    d. $2,555

Question 12

Gord's employer pays the full premium, on Gord's behalf, for his participation in the company's group extended health insurance plan. Given this scenario, which of the following statements are true?

1. The premium payment is a tax deductible expense for the employer.
2. The premium payment is not a tax deductible expense for the employer.
3. The premium payment is a taxable benefit to Gord.
4. The premium payment is not a taxable benefit to Gord.

    a. 1 and 3 only
    b. 1 and 4 only
    c. 2 and 3 only
    d. 2 and 4 only

Question 13

Daniel owns a whole life insurance policy that has a face value of $300,000, a cash value of $19,000, an ACB of $5,000, and an annual premium of $2,200 due in July of each year. The insurance carrier declared a $900 dividend in June, which Daniel elected to leave on deposit to earn interest. With regard to this election, which of the following statements is true?

    a. By leaving the dividends on deposit, Daniel can defer the tax consequence into a future year.
    b. Daniel will have a new ACB of $6,300, after the payment of the July premium.
    c. Daniel will have a taxable income gain of $900.
    d. Daniel will have to gross up the dividend and include $1,125 in income.

Question 14

Ten years ago, John purchased a universal life insurance policy that has a face value of $1,000,000, and a current cash surrender value of $22,000. There is currently no policy loan outstanding. The annual minimum contribution for the policy is $3,000 per year. John does not want to continue making the annual contributions although he would like to maintain insurance coverage, of some amount, for the next few years. Which of the following options would allow John to address his needs?

1. He could stop making contributions into the plan and rely on the accumulating investments to cover the annual charges until there is no longer any value remaining.
2. He could stop making contributions, and reduce the face amount of the coverage, which will help to extend the period of insurance coverage.
3. He could stop making contributions and take out a policy loan equal to the cash value.

    a. 1 and 2 only
    b. 1 only
    c. 2 only
    d. 3 only

Question 15

Harvey owns a non-exempt life insurance policy with a death benefit of $500,000, an accumulating fund value of $47,000 and an ACB of $38,000. Given this scenario, what amount of income must Harvey report for the current policy year?

    a. $38,000
    b. $4,500
    c. $9,000
    d. None

Question 16

Donny is the policy owner and life insured of a life insurance policy with a death benefit of $250,000, a cash surrender value of $50,000 and an ACB of $42,000. Since Donny no longer has a personal need for the insurance, he has decided to transfer ownership of the policy to Sam, his adult son. What income tax consequence, if any, arises from this transfer?

    a. Donny must report a loss of $8,000.
    b. Donny must report an $8,000 income gain.
    c. Sam must report an income gain of $8,000.
    d. There is no immediate income tax consequence because the policy can roll from Donny to Sam on a rollover basis.

Question 17

At the bank's request, Ada has assigned her life insurance policy as collateral against a $1,000,000 loan that she has taken out at XYZ bank. Ada plans to use the funds to complete a major expansion to her recreational summer property. The face value of Ada's insurance policy is $2,000,000, the annual premium is $25,000 and the net cost of pure insurance is $19,750 for the current year. What amount of money can Ada reasonably deduct for income tax purposes?

    a. $12,500
    b. $19,750
    c. $9,875
    d. None

QUESTIONS & SOLUTIONS

Question 1

Sam wants to purchase a life insurance policy where he is the policy owner and his spouse is the life insured. To be able to make such a purchase, Sam must have an insurable interest in his spouse. When must this insurable interest be present?

    a. At the time that the policy becomes effective and at the time of any claim.

    b. Indefinitely.

    c. Only at the time of any claim.

    d. Only at the time that the policy becomes effective.

Answer: d

    ⇨ Insurance is intended to provide the policy owner with compensation for a financial loss. Therefore, insurable interest is required by law before a contract can be issued to ensure that the insurance is not being purchased for financial gain. Subsequent to the issuance of a policy, ownership of the policy can be transferred and is not subject to insurable interest requirements at that time.

Question 2

James, age 17, is the beneficiary of a life insurance policy where his father, Donald, is the owner and the life insured. If Donald were to die today, which of the following statements is true?

    a. James does not have the legal capacity to discharge the contract as a beneficiary.

    b. James has the legal capacity to discharge the contract as a beneficiary, provided both of his parents have predeceased him.

    c. James has the legal capacity to discharge the contract as a beneficiary, provided he purchases a term certain annuity with the funds from the policy.

    d. James has the legal capacity to discharge the contract as a beneficiary.

Answer: a

    ⇨ James cannot provide valid discharge of the insurance contract at this time as he is still considered a minor and cannot receive the proceeds directly. In the absence of a trustee appointment in the contract, the proceeds will be paid into court and James will be eligible to take control of the funds at his age of majority.

Question 3

Mahood's house was destroyed by a fire, which the fire department believe was caused by a poor connection between the furnace and the gas line. The hazard in this case is the:

    a. fact that the furnace uses gas

    b. poor quality connection between the furnace and the gas line

    c. the fire

    d. use of the furnace to heat Mahood's home

Answer: b

    ⇨ A hazard is a specific situation that increases the probability of a loss from a particular peril which in the above scenario would be the fire.

Question 4

Gord is an avid scuba diver and typically selects vacations where he can explore new areas. Gord recognizes the risk associated with scuba diving so has purchased life insurance where he has named his spouse as the beneficiary. Gord's purchase of life insurance is a strategy commonly referred to as:

    a. risk avoidance

    b. risk retention

    c. risk transfer

    d. segregation

Answer: c

    ⇨ Risk transfer is a tool used to manage risk where the individual either transfers the cost of a risk occurring to another party. In this situation, Gord has transferred the cost of his wife's financial loss at his death to the insurance carrier of his life insurance policy.

Question 5

If the insured owner of a vehicle injures another party with his vehicle and is found liable, which of the following statements is true?

    a. If any resulting claim exceeds the insured's level of third party liability coverage, she can be held personally liable for any shortfall.

    b. If any resulting claim exceeds the insured's level of third party liability coverage, she cannot be held personally liable for any shortfall provided her amount of coverage met the minimum coverage amount established by the province.

    c. If any resulting claim exceeds the insured's level of third party liability coverage, she cannot be held personally liable if the injured third party has coverage for uninsured motorists.

    d. If the resulting claim exceeds the insured's level of third party liability coverage, she cannot be held personally liable if the injured third party has coverage for accident benefits.

Answer: a

    ⇨ Third party liability coverage covers the policy owner if her vehicle injures another party or damages that person's property and the policy owner is found to be liable. If the claim exceeds the coverage, the policy owner can be held personally liable for the difference.

Question 6

Which of the following factors would typically be a consideration when establishing the premium for an individual's automobile insurance policy?

1. Driving experience of any drivers of the vehicle
2. Life expectancy
3. Geographic region in which the insured vehicle will be driven
4. Total value of the insured vehicle
5. Age and sex of any drivers
6. Previous disability claims

    a. 1 and 6 only

    b. 1, 3, 4 and 5 only

    c. 2 and 4 only

    d. 2, 3, 5 and 6 only

Answer: b

    ⇨ Automobile insurance premiums are established based on a series of factors including factors related to the driver and the vehicle. However, the health status, either current or previous, is not taken into consideration.

Question 7

Place the following types of home insurance policies in the order of cost, beginning with the most expensive and ending with the least expensive.

1. Named perils

2. Broad

3. No-frills

4. Comprehensive

    a. 1, 2, 4 and 3

    b. 2, 4, 1 and 3

    c. 4, 1, 2 and 3

    d. 4, 2, 1 and 3

Answer: d

> ⇨ Home insurance policies are generally bundled into packages based on what is or is not included in the coverage. Comprehensive coverage includes both the building and it's contents for all risks except named exclusions; broad coverage includes all perils for the building but only named perils for the contents; named perils coverage covers named perils only for building and contents; and no-frills coverage is a minimal coverage for properties not meeting normal underwriting requirements.

Question 8

When fire struck and destroyed a substantial portion of the contents of Connor's home, the insurance company explained that his policy would reimburse him for his loss based on the actual cash value of the items. With this type of policy, which of the following statements are true?

1. The claim settlement amount will not include a deduction for depreciation on each item.

2. The claim settlement amount will include a deduction for depreciation on each item.

3. Connor may use the funds from the settlement any way he wishes, and is under no obligation to actually replace the items.

4. Connor will receive reimbursement only if he repairs or replaces an item with another one of similar quality.

    a. 1 and 3 only

    b. 1 and 4 only

    c. 2 and 3 only

    d. 2 and 4 only

Answer: c

> ⇨ A home insurance policy allows the policy owner to select the basis for loss reimbursement when purchasing the policy. A policy may be selected as either replacement cost basis or actual cash value basis. The actual cash value basis reimburses the policy owner for the actual cost of replacement and takes into consideration the depreciation, age, wear-and-tear, and obsolescence of the insured item.

Question 9

In order to qualify for full federal cash contributions under the CHST program, the provinces must abide by the five criteria established by the federal government as they relate to provincial health services. The five criteria are:

1. Neutrality

2. Portability

3. Public administration

4. Comprehensiveness

5. Cohesiveness

6. Universality

7. Accessibility

8. Instantaneous

9. Assessment

10. Accountability

      a. 1, 4, 5, 7, and 8 only

      b. 1, 5, 8, 9, and 10 only

      c. 2, 3, 4, 6, and 7 only

      d. 2, 3, 6, 8, and 10 only

Answer: c

    ⇨   The *Canada Health Act* contains five criteria that the provinces and territories must meet in order to qualify for the full federal cash contribution under the CHST. The five criteria are: public administration, comprehensiveness, universality, portability, and accessibility.

Question 10

While travelling in Italy, Steven consulted a plastic surgeon about a special type of cosmetic surgery he had read about in a news publication. Later, when in France, Steven visited the emergency ward at a local hospital after he injured his arm in a bicycle accident. Also, nearing the end of his trip, Steven stopped at an emergency medical clinic in England to have a doctor look at his leg because of severe swelling from a bug bite that he received that day. If Steven is a resident of ABC province in Canada, which of the medical visits will NOT be covered under his provincial health care plan?

1. Italy

2. France

3. England

      a. 1 only

      b. 1, 2 and 3

      c. 2 and 3 only

      d. 3 only

Answer: a

    ⇨   Regardless of the province that Steven is from, for a medical visit to be considered under a provincial health care plan it must be deemed to be medically necessary.

Question 11

Cathy is a member of her employer's extended health care plan, which has a $100 annual family deductible based on a calendar year, and provides for the employee to pay a 20% coinsurance. If Cathy's family has eligible health claims that total $2,555 this year, how much will Cathy receive as a reimbursement under the health care plan?

    a. $1,944

    b. $1,964

    c. $2,044

    d. $2,555

Answer: b

> ⇨ A deductible is an amount of the eligible expense that the plan member must pay before the insurance coverage picks up the expense. The coinsurance is the percentage of the eligible expense remaining after the deductible that the plan member is responsible for. Therefore Cathy will be reimbursed for $2,555 less the deductible of $100 = $2,455 multiplied by the coinsurance of 20% = $491, which leaves a balance after coinsurance of $1,964.

Question 12

Gord's employer pays the full premium, on Gord's behalf, for his participation in the company's group extended health insurance plan. Given this scenario, which of the following statements are true?

1. The premium payment is a tax deductible expense for the employer.

2. The premium payment is not a tax deductible expense for the employer.

3. The premium payment is a taxable benefit to Gord.

4. The premium payment is not a taxable benefit to Gord.

    a. 1 and 3 only

    b. 1 and 4 only

    c. 2 and 3 only

    d. 2 and 4 only

Answer: b

> ⇨ The premiums paid by an employer on behalf of an employee for an extended health and/or dental plan are tax deductible by the employer as a business expense and is not considered a taxable benefit to the employee.

Question 13

Daniel owns a whole life insurance policy that has a face value of $300,000, a cash value of $19,000, an ACB of $5,000, and an annual premium of $2,200 due in July of each year. The insurance carrier declared a $900 dividend in June, which Daniel elected to leave on deposit to earn interest. With regard to this election, which of the following statements is true?

    a. By leaving the dividends on deposit, Daniel can defer the tax consequence into a future year.

    b. Daniel will have a new ACB of $6,300, after the payment of the July premium.

    c. Daniel will have a taxable income gain of $900.

    d. Daniel will have to gross up the dividend and include $1,125 in income.

Answer: b

> ⇨ The impact of receiving dividends and leaving them on deposit in a whole life policy is to decrease the amount of the ACB by the dividend payment and increase the ACB by the amount of any new premiums paid ($5,000 - $900 dividend + $2,200 of annual premium paid = new ACB of $6,300).

Question 14

Ten years ago, John purchased a universal life insurance policy that has a face value of $1,000,000, and a current cash surrender value of $22,000. There is currently no policy loan outstanding. The annual minimum contribution for the policy is $3,000 per year. John does not want to continue making the annual contributions although he would like to maintain insurance coverage, of some amount, for the next few years. Which of the following options would allow John to address his needs?

1. He could stop making contributions into the plan and rely on the accumulating investments to cover the annual charges until there is no longer any value remaining.
2. He could stop making contributions, and reduce the face amount of the coverage, which will help to extend the period of insurance coverage.
3. He could stop making contributions and take out a policy loan equal to the cash value.

    a. 1 and 2 only
    b. 1 only
    c. 2 only
    d. 3 only

Answer: a

    ⇨ Universal life includes non-forfeiture options for the policy owner who wants alternatives when they discontinue premium payments to allow the coverage to remain in force. Under a universal life policy, the mortality and expense charges must be covered annually for the policy to remain in force. These charges can be covered by the accumulating fund in the absence of premiums if there are sufficient funds in the account. If there is no cash value remaining in the plan, this could result in the loss of coverage.

Question 15

Harvey owns a non-exempt life insurance policy with a death benefit of $500,000, an accumulating fund value of $47,000 and an ACB of $38,000. Given this scenario, what amount of income must Harvey report for the current policy year?

    a. $38,000
    b. $4,500
    c. $9,000
    d. None

Answer: c

    ⇨ The annual taxable amount is the amount of the policy's accumulated fund in excess of the policy's adjusted cost basis. The taxable amount is subsequently added to the policy's adjusted cost basis. Therefore, for Harvey's policy the annual taxable amount is $47,000 less $38,000 = $9,000.

Question 16

Donny is the policy owner and life insured of a life insurance policy with a death benefit of $250,000, a cash surrender value of $50,000 and an ACB of $42,000. Since Donny no longer has a personal need for the insurance, he has decided to transfer ownership of the policy to Sam, his adult son. What income tax consequence, if any, arises from this transfer?

    a. Donny must report a loss of $8,000.
    b. Donny must report an $8,000 income gain.
    c. Sam must report an income gain of $8,000.
    d. There is no immediate income tax consequence because the policy can roll from Donny to Sam on a rollover basis.

Answer: b

    ⇨ A transfer of a policy ownership is considered a disposition within the life of the policy. The transfer of ownership to his son is considered a non-arm's length transfer. The income that must be reported in this situation is the amount of the cash surrender value in excess of the ACB. Therefore, for Donny that reportable income gain is $50,000 CSV - the $42,000 ACB = $8,000.

Question 17

At the bank's request, Ada has assigned her life insurance policy as collateral against a $1,000,000 loan that she has taken out at XYZ bank. Ada plans to use the funds to complete a major expansion to her recreational summer property. The face value of Ada's insurance policy is $2,000,000, the annual premium is $25,000 and the net cost of pure insurance is $19,750 for the current year. What amount of money can Ada reasonably deduct for income tax purposes?

    a. $12,500

    b. $19,750

    c. $9,875

    d. None

Answer: d

    ⇨ An income tax deduction is allowed when an insurance policy is assigned to a financial institution as collateral for a loan if certain criteria are met. To qualify, the assignment must be required by the lending institution, the lending institution must qualify as a restricted financial institution, and the interest payable on the money borrowed is or would be deductible in computing the taxpayer's income (i.e., loan used to generate business income). The last criteria does not apply since she plans to use the money for personal purposes.

**THE CFP
EDUCATION PROGRAM**

CCH/ADVOCIS FPSC-APPROVED CAPSTONE COURSE

MODULE 23
ASSET MANAGEMENT

Module 23
ASSET MANAGEMENT

Module 23
Asset Management

Unit 1

Investments

This module discusses the types and taxation of different types of investments, including fixed income, equity, mutual, and segregated funds. The second unit covers investment theories and strategies.

301. INVESTMENT VEHICLES

Cash Assets

Holding idle cash as an investment is usually considered a very conservative investment strategy since the cash could be invested to earn a higher return.

Money market mutual funds earn interest income, provide liquidity and safety of the principal. They earn slightly more interest than a bank account.

Treasury Bills

Treasury bills, also known as T-bills, are short-term debt instruments issued by the federal government, which are sold through the Bank of Canada to large financial institutions during a bi-weekly auction. Government of Canada T-bills are issued with maturities of approximately three, six, and twelve months. They are purchased at a discount and mature at face or par value. They are considered a very safe, low-risk investment, and provide investors with a highly liquid security.

- If a T-bill is held to maturity, returns are treated as interest income.

- If a T-bill is sold prior to maturity, the difference between the original price and proceeds of disposition usually results in both interest income and a possible capital gain or loss if interest rates have changed since the T-bill was purchased.

U.S. T-bills are treated the same as Canadian T-bills, except calculations are based on a 360-day year for U.S. T-bills, and 365 days for Canadian T-bills.

JESSE

Jesse bought a 92-day, $20,000 T-bill on June 1 for $19,750. He sold it on August 1 for $19,975. The quoted yield was 5.022%. What is the tax impact of selling the T-bill early?

$$\text{Interest} = \text{Purchase price} \times \text{Effective yield rate} \times \frac{\text{Number of days T-bill held}}{\text{Number of days in the year}}$$

$$= \$19,750 \times 5.022\% \times (61 \div 365)$$
$$= \$165.76$$

Or, using the number of days method: ($20,000 - $19,750) × 61 days ÷ 92 days = $165.76

Jesse calculates the capital gain as:

Proceeds of disposition	$19,975.00
Minus: interest	-165.76
Net proceeds	$19,809.24
Minus: adjusted cost base	-19,750.00
Capital gain	$ 59.24

Taxable capital gain ($59.24 × 50%) = $29.62.

Jesse's total income is $195.38 ($165.76 + 29.62).

Yield = (((Par value - Price) ÷ Price) × 365 ÷ Term).

A $1,000 par value, 90-day T-bill is purchased for $980.

$$\text{Yield} = \frac{(\$1{,}000 - \$980)}{980} \times \frac{365}{90}$$

$$= 8.3\%$$

The above is the simple yield. The effective yield can be calculated using a financial calculator.

HERMAN

Herman wanted to purchase a 180-day Canadian treasury bill with a quoted yield of 2.2554% and a maturity value of $100,000. What is the purchase price on Herman's T-bill?

The purchase price of Herman's T-bill is $98,899.98.

Market Price

= Face Value ÷ (1.0 + ((Quoted yield) × (Days to maturity) ÷ 365)

= $100,000 ÷ (1.0 + (2.2554% × 180 ÷ 365))

= $100,000 ÷ (1.0 + (0.022554 × 0.49315))

= $100,000 ÷ (1.0 + 0.0111225)

= $98,899.98

HANNAH

Hannah bought a 91-day T-bill, issued by the federal government, for $99,350. Calculate the effective annualized yield on Hannah's T-bill.

The quoted yield on Hannah's T-bill is 2.6242%.

Hannah's effective annualized return on this T-bill is 2.6502%, which is marginally higher than the quoted yield of 2.6242%.

We know the following information:

- P/YR = 1
- xP/YR = 0.249315068 [91 ÷ 365]
- PMT = 0
- FV = 100,000
- PV = -99,350

SOLVE FOR I/YR, which equals 2.6502

Fixed-Income Securities

Guaranteed Investment Certificate and Term Deposits

A guaranteed investment certificate (GIC) and term deposits are debt instruments that guarantee an investor a fixed rate of interest income for a set term. The investment period can be measured in days, months or years. GICs and term deposits generally pay a higher rate of interest than a bank savings account. Term deposits are short term (usually less than one year), low risk investments. Both investments can address investment objectives that include security of principal and income flow and they are covered up to $100,000 by the Canada Deposit Insurance Corporation (CIDC). The income earned on a GIC is treated as interest income. An investor must report accrued interest annually. GICs and term deposits are subject to inflation and reinvestment risk.

An index-linked guaranteed investment certificate (index-linked GIC) normally provides the investor with a guarantee that his principal will not be eroded. An index-linked GIC generally pays no interest throughout the term of the GIC, but instead the return is linked to a stock market index, typically a well-known index from Canadian or international markets. Returns from year to year will vary.

Gains on an index-linked GIC are taxed as interest income not capital gains. The interest income on an indexed-linked GIC is reported upon maturity. An index-linked GIC should not normally be considered for short-term investments; the market-related elements of an index-linked GIC suggest that a longer investment horizon is more appropriate, generally not less than three to five years.

EMILY

Three and a half years ago, Emily purchased a five-year, non-redeemable guaranteed investment certificate with a local financial institution. If she invested $10,000 on October 1, 2006 in a GIC that pays 5% interest, compounded annually, what is the income tax consequence?

We know that the maturity value of the GIC will be $12,762.82. However, what is the annual tax consequence?

Taxation Year	Interest Reported
2006 — 3 months	Nil
2007 — 12 months	$ 500.00
2008 — 12 months	525.00
2009 — 12 months	551.25
2010 — 12 months	578.81
2011 — 10 months	607.73
Total Interest Report	$ 2,762.79
Initial Investment	10,000.00
Maturity Value	$12,762.79

Bonds and Debentures

Bonds and debentures are debt instruments representing a loan from the investor to the issuer. The purpose of issuing bonds is to raise capital for the issuing institution.

In return, the issuer of the bond or debenture promises to pay the investor a specified rate of interest during the term of the security, and to repay the face value at maturity. With the exception of Government of Canada bonds, bonds are generally secured by physical assets owned by the issuing company. Debentures are not secured by assets.

The terms "face value", "par value", and "denomination" are interchangeable and refer to the monetary value of the bond at maturity.

A bond is normally issued at par, and is referred to as trading at par or face value when it is bought or sold at its par or face value. When a bond trades at a price in excess of its face value because the coupon rate is higher than the market rate, it trades at a premium. When a bond trades at a price below its face value because the coupon rate is lower than the market rate, it trades at a discount.

Bonds are generally classified by the length of time remaining until maturity, where: short-term bonds mature in the next few years, intermediate-term bonds come due within three to ten years and long-term bonds mature in more than ten years and up to thirty years.

The taxation of bonds occurs in three specific ways:

- Tax on the coupon payment (interest) is taxed in the year received;
- Capital gains or losses may arise if a bond is sold prior to maturity if there is a difference between the coupon rate and the current market interest rate; and
- If the bond was purchased at a discount or premium.

— If the bond were purchased at a discount, the discount would be viewed as a capital gain at maturity.

— If the bond were purchased at a premium, the premium would be viewed as a capital loss at maturity.

Factors affecting the value of bonds include the difference between the current market interest rate and the coupon rate, reinvestment risk, credit risk, and term to maturity of a bond.

BARBARA

On January 1, 2007 Barbara paid $15,000 for a bond issued by Keyboard Corporation. The bond had a face value of $15,000, and a coupon rate of 5.15%. On December 31, 2009, Barbara sold the bond for $17,500.

The annual coupon payments of $772.50 are taxed as ordinary income and are taxable on an annual basis. When she sold the bond, she incurred a capital gain of $2,500, or a taxable capital gain of $1,250 ($17,500 - $15,000) × 50%.

Types of Bonds

Government Bonds

The federal, provincial, and municipal governments all issue marketable bonds, which represent debt obligations of the issuing government. These bonds cannot normally be redeemed prior to maturity, but can be bought and sold in the open market.

Government of Canada real return bonds are marketable bonds that pay semi-annual interest based on a real interest rate; interest payments are adjusted by the CPI. These types of bonds provide the investor with protection against inflation over the long-term.

Canada Savings Bonds (CSBs) are non-marketable debt instruments issued by the Government of Canada, redeemable on demand by the registered owner at any time. Two types of bonds are available: interest bonds (R-series) and compound interest bonds (C-series).

Interest income on the regular interest bonds is paid annually and reported in the year it is received, whereas interest on the compound interest is reinvested until maturity and reported on an accrual basis.

Canada premium bonds (CPBs) are similar to CSBs in that they are issued and guaranteed by the Government of Canada and are available in the two types (C and R series), but unlike CSBs, CPBs can only be redeemed once each year. CPBs are eligible investments for an RRSP or RRIF. The taxation of CPBs is the same as for CSBs.

Corporate and Strip Bonds

Corporate bonds issued by a corporation differ from equity because the principal and interest on the bond issue is a debt obligation of the issuing corporation. The corporation's payment of interest to the bondholder is a deductible business expense for the corporation. The interest paid is higher than government bonds since the risk associated with a corporate bond is higher. They are attractive for inclusion in investment portfolios designed to fund long-term retirement and education costs.

HARRIETT

Harriett is considering the purchase of a Nomega Corp bond with a face value of $20,000 and 20 years remaining to maturity. The coupon on the Nomega bond is 5%, while the current market interest rate is 7%. What price should Harriett pay for the Nomega bond? (Disregard taxes.)

continued . . .

---

continued . . .

Based on these details, Harriett should be willing to pay $15,728.99 for the Nomega Corp bond.

We know the following information:

- P/YR = 2   [interest is paid 2 times each year]
- xP/YR = 20   [20 years to maturity]
- I/YR = 7   [use the current market rate]
- PMT = 500   [($20,000 × 0.05) ÷ 2]
- FV = 20,000   [at maturity Harriett will receive $20,000]
- MODE = END

SOLVE FOR PV, which equals -15,728.9855

The payment is derived by multiplying the face value of $20,000 by the coupon rate of 5%, and dividing the result by two to reflect the semi-annual nature of bond coupon payments. The I/YR is arrived at by using the prevailing market interest rate of 7%. The bond has 20 years left until maturity.

If Harriett pays $15,728.99 for this bond and the bond pays her $500 twice each year for 20 years, along with a return of the par value of $20,000 at the end of 20 years, the bond will have generated a 7% annual nominal return, which is the prevailing market rate.

The annual effective rate of return on this bond is 7.12%.

We know the following information:

- P/YR = 2
- I/YR = 7.0
- EFF% = 7.1225%

Strip bonds, or zero coupon bonds, are bonds that have the interest payments separated from the principal repayments. Strip bonds are sold at a discount to the face value and redeemed at face value. They are good investments for investors who do not require a regular cash flow of interest payments. For taxation purposes, although the bonds do not provide annual interest payments, taxpayers are required to include a notional amount of interest each year calculated as the difference between the bond purchase price and the face value at maturity.

Unless otherwise stated, when doing strip bond calculations, assume one compounding period per year (P/YR = 1).

CARL

On March 1, Year 1, Carl purchased a strip bond with a face value of $10,000, which matures in exactly five years. Carl purchased the bond for $7,700. What rate of return will Carl earn? What amount of interest will he report for the next five years?

- P/YR = 1
- XP/YR = 5
- PMT = 0
- PV = -7,700
- FV = 10,000

SOLVE FOR I/YR, which equals 5.3663

Taxation Year	Income Tax
Year 1	Zero
Year 2	$413.21 ($7,700 × 5.3663%)
Year 3	$435.38 ($7,700 + $413.21) × 5.3663%
Year 4	$458.74
Year 5	$483.36
Year 6	$509.31
TOTAL	$2,300.00

Convertible bonds and debentures permit the bondholder to exchange the bond for a predetermined number of common shares of the bond issuer's corporation at certain times during the life of the bond. The bonds tend to offer a lower rate of return due to the conversion benefit which provides the investor with the potential for appreciation in the company's common share value.

Mortgage-Backed Securities

When a pool of mortgages are packaged together, it creates what is referred to as a "mortgage-backed security" (MBS). Interest payments and principal repayments are made monthly into the pool. These funds are then paid to the investors. The majority of mortgage-backed securities in Canada are created through the NHA *National Housing Act*) Mortgage-Backed Securities Program (NHA-MBS).

There are four categories of mortgage pools that can be packaged into a NHA mortgage-backed security:

- Exclusive Homeowner;
- Multi-Family;
- Social Housing; or
- Any combination of the first three.

Mortgage-backed securities are considered high-quality investments and are fairly liquid, having an active secondary market where the security can be sold prior to maturity. Interest income on a mortgage-backed security is fully taxable but the capital receipts are not taxable. The capital portion of each receipt will lower the investor's ACB in the instrument.

An investor could also invest in mortgages on residential and commercial real estate. The mortgage is secured by the real estate and provides the investor with interest and principal payments.

Commercial Loans

If an investor invests in commercial or personal loans, they will receive interest income. The interest rate on the loans should be based on the risk characteristics of the party applying for the loan.

Equities

Every corporation must have share capital. A share is the shareholder's proportionate interest in the capital of the corporation. In comparison to bonds, common and preferred shares are considered tax advantaged investments because the dividend income is eligible for the gross-up and dividend tax credit.

Common Shares

Common shares represent equity or ownership in the corporation. They entitle the shareholder to vote for the board of directors, generate investment returns from the receipt of dividends and capital appreciation through increased share prices. Shareholders have limited liability and are not personally responsible for claims against the corporation.

Dividends are grossed up by 125% or 145% depending on the type of corporation and eligible for dividend tax credits. Stock dividends, the issuing of additional shares instead of cash, are taxed the same as regular dividends. Stock splits are not taxable to a shareholder.

Ex Dividend and Cum Dividend

If an investor purchases a stock after a dividend is declared but prior to the ex dividend (without dividend) date, the new owner is eligible to receive the declared dividend (called cum dividend, i.e., with dividend). After the date of record for the dividend, the price of the stock will normally fall in proportion to the amount of the declared dividend. Shares purchased after the date of record are known as ex dividend.

Share Purchase

There are several investment accounts that an investor can maintain with his stockbroker to facilitate the buying and selling of investment securities.

Cash Accounts

When stocks are purchased, the required money is deposited in the cash account and when stocks are sold, the net proceeds are deposited into the cash account.

Margin Accounts

Buying shares on margin is a means to buy shares for a combination of cash and a loan from the stockbroker. It is a form of leverage that will increase potential gains and losses. Investors can borrow up to 50% of the market value of the stocks being purchased.

The portion of the purchase price an investor must deposit is called the margin. If the value of the account drops below the required minimum, the investor will receive a margin call from the broker to deposit further funds into the account or the broker will sell enough of the stock to pay down the loan.

JAMES

James has $800 to invest in Alpha Inc. which is trading at $8 per share. He wants to leverage his funds, so he decides to borrow an additional 50% or $400 from his broker on margin and buys 150 shares instead of the 100 shares he could buy without buying on margin.

If the stock goes to $16, James could sell his 150 shares for $2,400, pay back the $400 loan (plus interest), and be left with $2,000 profit. He would have made a 150% return on his $800 investment. If he had just purchased the stock, he would have earned a 100% gain (($1,600 - $800) ÷ $800).

If the stock drops to $5, James would receive a margin call from the broker asking for him to put $25 in the account (the maximum loan value is 50% × 150 shares × $5 = $375, compared to the loan of $400). James decides to sell his 150 shares for $5 each and realizes $750. After paying back the $400 loan, he is left with $350, or a loss of 56% of his investment. If he had not margined, he would have only lost $300, or a 37.5% loss.

Short Selling

Short selling is a leveraged strategy to profit from dropping stock prices. The investor borrows shares from the broker, and sells them in the market. He later repurchases the shares, hopefully at a lower price, and returns the shares to the broker. If the shares drop in price, the investor will make a profit. If the shares increase in price, the investor will have a loss.

Preferred Shares

Preferred shares represent equity ownership in a corporation like common shares, but they do not provide the owner with voting rights. They carry preferential rights to dividends. Preferred shares are attractive to investors who have an interest in a regular income flow. The price of preferred shares moves in the opposite direction to interest rates.

From a corporation's perspective, preferred shares can be an attractive form of capitalization for a corporation because they do not commit the issuing company to the repayment of debt on a specific date and a missed dividend payment does not put the company into default.

Preferred shares can also be callable and retractable. With callable preferred shares, the issuing corporation has the right to call the shares for redemption. With a retractable feature, the preferred shareholder can force the issuing corporation to buy back the shares at a specified price on a specific date.

Convertible Shares

Convertible shares are preferred stock that include an option for the holder to convert the preferred shares into a fixed number of common shares, usually any time after a predetermined date.

Real Estate

Personal-use property includes automobiles, boats, recreational equipment, cottage, principal residence, and similar items. Capital losses are not deductible but capital gains are taxable. The *de minimus rules* apply such that proceeds of disposition and the adjusted cost base is set at a minimum of $1,000.

Income property, sometimes called rental property, may include residential, commercial or industrial real estate. Rental income is taxed as business income and changes in the capital value of property are taxed as capital gains or losses.

Land is usually vacant land. An investor may invest and hold the land anticipating the land to appreciate in value.

A *real estate investment trust* (REIT) is a trust that owns real estate properties and/or mortgages. When a REIT includes aspects of both real estate property ownership and mortgages, it may be referred to as a hybrid REIT, whereas an equity REIT involves only the ownership of real estate (no mortgages) and a mortgage REIT involves only real estate debt (mortgages).

DERIVATIVES

A *derivative* is a financial instrument whose value is dependent on the value and characteristics of an underlying security. The underlying security could be a currency, bond, stock, or commodity. Examples of common financial derivatives include put options, call options, futures, and swaps.

An option is the right, but not the obligation, to sell or buy an underlying security during a given period for a specified price, which is commonly referred to as the strike price.

Call Option

With a *call option*, the investor owns an option to buy a specific security. Call options are used by investors primarily for speculation, hedging, leverage, and as coverage against a short stock position. An investor pays a premium to the writer of the call option and hopes that the price of the underlying security will increase before the option expires. One option contract will cover 100 shares of the underlying stock.

Taxation

For the call buyer, if the option is exercised, the ACB is the strike price plus the premium paid. If the call expires, the premium becomes a capital loss subject to the 50% rule.

For the call writer, the premium is a capital gain, with an ACB equal to zero. If the option is exercised, the proceeds of disposition are equal to the strike price plus the premium received.

Put Option

A *put option* gives an investor an option to sell a specific security. They are used mainly to limit the downside with a particular investment while enjoying the full benefit of increases in the stock value. An investor pays a premium to the writer of the put option and hopes that the price of the underlying security will decrease before the option expires.

Taxation

If the put expires worthless, the buyer has a capital loss. If the option is exercised, the proceeds of disposition for the put buyer is the strike price less the premium paid.

Market Price Relative to Strike Price

If the market price is:	Call Option	Put Option
a. Above the strike price	in-the-money	out-of-the-money
b. At the strike price	at-the-money	at-the-money
c. Below the strike price	out-of-the-money	in-the-money

"In-the-money" is used to describe the position at which the option is worth money and the holder can exercise the option in order to generate a profit.

TOM

Tom purchased a call option one month ago that allowed him to purchase 100 shares of ABC stock at a strike price of $10 for a premium of $2.00 per option. The current market value of the stock is $15. Tom has the right, but not the obligation to force the writer of the call option to sell him the stock for $10. The option is "in-the-money" since the market value of $15 is higher than the $10 strike price. Tom will likely exercise the option resulting in a profit of $3 per option or $300 in total ($15 - $10 strike price less $2 premium) × 100 shares.

DONALD

Donald owns 10,000 shares of STU Company where the current market price is $25 per share. Donald could purchase a 100 put option contract on STU Company shares for a premium of $1.50 per share, which totals $15,000. The strike price of the put option is $20. Through the purchase of the put option contract, Donald is able to ensure that he can sell his 10,000 shares for $20 per share up until the put option contract expires.

If the price of the STU Company shares falls below the $20 strike price, Donald would likely exercise his put options. If the price of the stock falls to $15 per share, the put option acts as insurance that protects Donald so he will receive at least $20 per share. Donald also has another option. Rather than exercising the option, Donald could sell the put options on the open market, which should garner at least $5 per share (the difference between the strike price of $20 and the current market price of $15). This $5 per share represents a total of $50,000, which represents the intrinsic value of the option. There is also a time value associated with the intrinsic value. The $50,000 generated through the sale of the options compensates Donald for the loss he will incur in the value of the stock.

If the price of the STU Company shares increases above the current market price of $25, then Donald would not exercise the put options. If, for example, Donald decides to sell the shares when the market price is $40, he will incur a profit (excluding commissions) which equals the difference between his original purchase price and the price at which he sells the shares, in this case $40. His profit would be reduced by the $1.50 per share premium paid for the options.

The use of put options reduces Donald's risk of a price decline. Once purchased, the put options contract will either be exercised by Donald, expire, or can be traded on the options market.

Straddle

A *straddle* is an investment strategy whereby an investor holds a position in both a call and put option, on the same security, each with the same strike price. This type of strategy would be utilized if significant changes in the price of the underlying security are expected, but it is not clear as to the direction of the potential change. Straddles are used in a volatile market.

DONNA

Donna has followed the activities of Redo Inc., which is in the process of restructuring its finances. Donna anticipates that the market will respond either very positively to the restructuring efforts or very negatively. Although Donna is uncertain as to which way the market will react, she feels that there will be a strong response that will impact the value of the Redo Inc. shares.

Given Donna's strong feelings, she has decided to undertake a straddle position where she will purchase a put and call option on Redo Inc. shares, both for a six-month period, expiring in January. The details are as follows:
— January 25 call @ $1.50 premium
— January 25 put @ $2.00 premium

In the following discussion, disregard any commissions paid on any transactions.

Donna has purchased 1 call and 1 put option on the shares of Redo Inc. that expires in January (6 months from now) and each has a strike price of $25. This transaction gives Donna the right to:

- buy 100 shares of Redo Inc. at $25 per share. The call option becomes attractive when the market price of Redo Inc. rises above the $25 strike price.
- sell 100 shares of Redo Inc. at $25 per share. The put option becomes attractive if the market price of Redo Inc. falls below the $25 strike price.

The cost of this straddle is $350, calculated as:

$(100 \times \$1.50) + (100 \times \$2.00)$

As discussed previously, the underlying asset associated with an option is typically in standardized units of 100 and the premium applies to each unit of the underlying asset.

To determine the break-even price at which Donna will make a profit if the call or put is exercised:

Exercise Price of Call

(a) $25 + ($350 ÷ 100)

= $28.50

Exercise Price of Put

(b) $25 - ($350 ÷ 100)

= $21.50

If the price of Redo Inc. stock increases beyond $28.50, or decreases to a level below $21.50, Donna will make a profit on this transaction.

If the price of the security falls to $20, then she would exercise her put and sell 100 shares at $25. She will buy 100 shares at $20 and sell 100 shares for $25, making a $500 gain. Her cost to earn the $500 gain was $350.

If the price of the security rises to $30, then she would exercise her call option to buy 100 shares at $25. She will buy 100 shares for $25 and then immediately sell them for $30, making a $500 gain. Her cost to earn $500 was $350.

Right

A *right* provides the shareholder with the opportunity to purchase a prescribed number of newly authorized shares in order to maintain his proportional ownership of the existing corporation. This purchase opportunity takes place prior to the sale of the new shares to the general public and is quite often limited to a very specific, short period of time, which is a distinguishing feature between a right and a warrant. The value of rights trade on the stock market and their market value is based on the difference between the right's purchase price and the current market value of the stock.

Warrant

A *warrant* is a certificate issued by a corporation that entitles the holder to purchase a specified number of the corporation's common stock at a predetermined price, for an extended period of time. The purchase price of the security associated with the warrant is normally higher than the current market price of the underlying security. A warrant may be issued as an independent certificate. A warrant holds value and can be bought and sold on the secondary market. The value of a warrant depends on the current stock price. The higher the stock price, the higher the warrant value.

Forward Contract

A *forward contract* is a private contract where two parties agree to exchange an item in the future at a predetermined price. A financial future contract is a standardized forward contract, which is traded on an organized exchange. The exchange acts as an intermediary between the buyer and seller, with both the buyer and seller entering separate contracts with the exchange. The face value is the forward price multiplied by the quantity of items agreed to in the contract. The forward price is the price determined by the seller and buyer on a future date, and the spot price is the current actual cash price for immediate sale/exchange in the market. By selling the futures contract, the investor eliminates the risk of price fluctuations and establishes a final price.

Index Mutual Funds

Index mutual funds are a type of mutual fund with a portfolio constructed to match or track the components of a market index. It offers broad market exposure and lower management fees than regular mutual funds.

Exchange-Traded Funds

Exchange-traded funds (ETFs) are financial instruments that closely replicate various stock indexes or the returns of a basket of stocks or securities. They trade like individual stocks but are less risky, providing diversification over a range of holdings, and they offer lower management fees compared to mutual funds.

Commodities

Future contracts for *commodities* like wheat and gold are often used by producers as a hedge against adverse price fluctuations. Using a futures contract, a farmer could agree now to sell his corn in the future at a specific price.

The investor may also directly invest in the actual commodity such as precious metals like gold. Precious metals are used as a hedge against inflation during periods of economic uncertainty. They are generally considered liquid assets.

302. INVESTMENT STRUCTURES

Mutual Funds

Mutual funds are a large portfolio of securities purchased with a pool of funds contributed by many investors, and managed by investment professionals in accordance with the objectives of the fund. The pooling of funds allows the fund manager to buy many securities so that the fund's return is not heavily dependent on the ups and downs of a few investments.

Reasons for Investing in Mutual Funds

- **Professional Management.** Each mutual fund has an individual or team of professional money managers responsible for selecting and managing the portfolio of securities held within the fund.

- **Diversification.** Mutual funds provide smaller-size investors with the opportunity for diversification of assets across many securities, which reduces risk.

- **Liquidity.** Mutual funds are quite liquid since the investor can sell all or a portion of his units on any business day.

- **Disclosure.** The mutual fund industry is heavily regulated and subject to extensive disclosure requirements, placing significant accountability on the fund companies.

- **Scheduled Purchases.** Many mutual fund companies provide investors with access to scheduled purchase plans where an investor purchases mutual funds on a regular basis.

- **Transfers.** Mutual fund companies commonly allow investors to transfer assets between funds available within the same fund organization, at little or no charge.

"Net asset value per share" (NAVPS) refers to the price at which units of a mutual fund are purchased and sold. NAVPS = (Net asset value of fund) ÷ (Number of units outstanding).

Other Considerations

No Capital Guarantee — An investor does not receive any guarantees relative to the capital that is invested. Capital investment is subject to the volatilities of the marketplace, similar to common shares.

No Performance Guarantee — Past performance is no indication of future performance. Mutual funds carry risk and are subject to market volatility. An investor cannot select the price at which units are purchased or disposed of since prices are based on the NAVPS.

Closed-End Mutual Funds

A *closed-end mutual fund* is established as a corporation where a limited number of shares are issued by the corporation, and where the number of shares remains fixed. Closed-end mutual funds have the condition where the number of shares remains fixed and only changes if the corporation decides to raise additional capital by issuing additional shares. They often focus on a specialized type of investment such as bonds or precious metals and are considered to have low liquidity since the investor must have a willing buyer before the fund owner can dispose of his shares. The shares may trade at a premium or discount to the actual NAVPS of the investments.

Open-End Mutual Funds

Open-end mutual funds offer greater flexibility than closed-end funds because they continuously issue and redeem units directly from the fund itself. *Mutual fund* is used synonymously with the term open-ended investment fund. There two types of open-end mutual funds: mutual fund corporations and mutual fund trusts. The funds always trade at their NAVPS with any income earned passes through and is taxable to the investor.

Labour-Sponsored Venture Capital Corporations

Labour-sponsored venture capital corporations (LSVCCs) are investment corporations used to invest venture capital into Canadian businesses. Shares in an LSVCC are eligible for a non-refundable federal tax credit on the first $5,000 and may also qualify for a provincial tax credit. They may be purchased as non-registered funds, but are also qualified investments for a registered retirement savings plan (RRSP) and a registered retirement income fund (RRIF). They are high-risk investments. The funds must be held for eight years, or the tax credits need to be repaid.

The federal government introduced an amendment in 2008 that only allows the federal credit if the taxpayer is eligible for the provincial credit.

Types of Funds

There are hundreds of different mutual funds offered for sale throughout Canada; an important distinguishing factor is the grouping of mutual funds by their investment objectives and the types of securities held within the funds' portfolios. The three broad asset classifications are: income, growth, and growth and income.

Asset Classification

Income	**Growth**	**Growth & Income**
Money Market Fund	Equity Fund	Balanced Fund
Mortgage Fund	Global/International Fund	Asset Allocation Fund
Bond Fund	Speculative Fund	
Dividend Fund	Real Estate Fund	

Money Market Funds

Money market funds are comprised of low-risk short-term investments such as government T-bills, corporate papers, bankers' acceptances, and other short-term securities that provide interest income only. The funds NAVPS does not change (usually $10 per share). They are good for people who cannot tolerate a loss of capital and need access to their funds.

Mortgage Funds

A *mortgage fund* is one that is comprised of mortgages, generally on residential properties, and mortgage-based securities. They usually provide interest income and capital gains if mortgages are sold prior to maturity. The fund is low-risk and offers a low return.

Bond Funds

Bond funds invest in bonds. The types of bonds, such as government issued bonds or corporate bonds, will vary according to the objectives of the fund. They are seen as low-risk funds, but could be a bit riskier than mortgage funds due to the longer term of the bonds.

Dividend Funds

A *dividend fund* is comprised of preferred and common shares that demonstrate a regular pattern of dividend payments. They are relatively low risk and are designed to produce tax-preferred dividend income.

Real Estate Funds

The composition of investments within a *real estate fund* tend to be just that, real estate. Typically, the real estate is commercial and industrial in nature and includes properties such as shopping malls and office buildings. The funds, which are riskier due to the fluctuations in real estate values, may provide investors with rental income and capital cost allowance deductions. The funds are suitable for high risk, high net worth individuals.

Balanced Funds

A *balanced fund* is one that targets a range of securities, including bonds, preferred shares and common shares. They may provide interest, dividends and capital gains. Balanced funds are suitable for an investor that wants the security of fixed income investments and potential appreciation in stock markets.

Asset Allocation

The *asset allocation fund* can include a combination of bonds, preferred shares and common stocks, depending upon the fund manager's assessment of market conditions.

Equity Funds

An *equity fund* is comprised of stocks, which are mainly common shares. They provide capital gains and some dividends. They are considered higher risk given the fluctuations in the stock market and the lack of fixed income investments.

International and Global Funds

International and global funds are generally comprised of securities from a variety of countries, where the securities may include stocks and bonds.

Speculative and Venture Funds

Speculative and venture funds are comprised of shares of high-risk companies with high growth potential.

When assessing mutual fund performance, it is important to understand how the fund's performance compares with similar funds or relevant indexes. There are two main types of benchmark comparisons. The *Peer Group Average* assesses the returns of a select group of funds that have similar investment goals and policies, and the *Market Index* measures the return of the market or a key segment of the market. Quartile Rankings ranks mutual funds according to their asset class, where all funds of a similar class are grouped into a common segment.

The fund's annual return is reported after expenses, and incorporates the assumption that distributions have been reinvested in the fund.

Redemptions

Front-End Load

The fee associated with a front-end load is incorporated into the calculation of purchase price per unit. The purchase price per unit = (NAVPS) ÷ (1.0 - Sales charge).

ANDREW

Andrew has $15,000 he plans to use for the purchase of RT mutual funds. If Andrew purchases the funds when the NAVPS is $5 and he is charged a 2% front-end sales charge, how many units will Andrew purchase?

Purchase Price Per Unit

= (NAVPS) ÷ (1.0 - Sales charge)

= ($5) ÷ (1.0 - 0.02)

= $5.1020408

continued . . .

> *continued . . .*
>
> *Number of Units Purchased*
> = Total amount ÷ Purchase price per share
> = \$15,000 ÷ \$5.1020408
> = 2,940 shares
>
> The front-load commission for the transaction is \$300 (2% × \$5.1020408 × 2.940 shares). There is no redemption charge to the investor when units initially purchased with a front-load are eventually sold.

Deferred Sales Charge

While there is no direct charge to the investor upon the acquisition of many mutual funds, there may be a declining asset-value based redemption fee based on the length of time the mutual funds have been held prior to their redemption. The asset base against which the deferred sales charge (DSC) applies may be the original assets purchased or the current market value. Typically, the investor is allowed to move funds between the mutual fund family of funds and to redeem up a specified percentage of the funds annually (commonly 10%) without incurring redemption charges.

> *PARMINDER*
>
> In January 2007, Parminder purchased \$412,000 of PQR mutual funds on a DSC basis, when the NAVPS was \$8. The deferred sales charge schedule, which is based on the original assets, decreases from 6% in year one to 1% during the fourth year. In February 2010, when the NAVPS was \$12, she redeemed the mutual funds when a 1% DSC applied. How much did Parminder receive?
>
> Parminder received proceeds of \$17,880, and paid a DSC fee of \$120.
>
> Original purchase, she purchased 1,500 units (\$12,000 ÷ \$8).
>
> The current market value of 1,500 shares is \$18,000 (1,500 units × \$12).
>
> Applicable DSC redemption fee is \$120 ((1,500 units × \$8) × 0.01).
>
> Net proceeds are \$18,000 - 120 = \$17,880.

No-Load Mutual Funds

With a *no-load mutual fund*, the investor does not pay any up-front or DSC fees to purchase or redeem units.

Fees

The *management expense ratio* (MER) refers to the management fees charged directly to the fund, and is expressed as a percentage of the total assets held in the fund. MERs, which are listed in the fund's prospectus, will differ by type of fund and by company, and represent foregone earnings. MERs provide a way to compare management and other costs from one fund to another.

MER = (All fees and expenses payable during the year) ÷ (Average net asset value for the year).

The sale of mutual funds to investors can result in the payment of commissions to the dealer and advisor associated with the sale. Commissions are also commonly referred to as "loads" or "sales charges". Funds are commonly grouped according to their commission structure, which is defined as: front-end loads, deferred sales charges and no-load funds. In addition to any sales commission, the fund company typically pays an annual fee to the advisor/dealer to compensate the advisor/dealer for ongoing service and advice to the client, and is frequently referred to as a "service fee" or "trailer". Service fees are generally paid regardless of whether the fund was purchased as a front-end load or a deferred sales charge.

Segregated Funds

A *segregated fund* is a pool of investments that are held and managed separately from other assets of a life insurance company. Only life insurance companies offer segregated funds. According to the *Income Tax Act* (the "Act"), a segregated fund is deemed to be owned by a trust where the policy owner, also referred to as the unit holder, is deemed to be the beneficiary of the trust.

Benefits

Segregated fund contracts offer a guarantee of principal upon maturity or death. In many cases, the guarantee is more than the minimum 75%, and may be as high as 100%. Benefits include a beneficiary designation, successor owner and creditor protection. Investment income earned by a segregated fund policy retains its nature and flows through to the policy owner, allowing the policy owner to benefit from tax-advantaged investment income within the fund.

Segregated funds may be suitable in situations where creditor protection is important or as part of an investor's estate plan where the death benefit guarantee could be valuable. For individuals reaching retirement, the maturity and death benefit guarantee could be attractive. Conservative investors may find the maturity guarantees and re-set options attractive features. Aggressive investors may rely on the maturity guarantee as an offset against the risk associated with higher risk funds.

Comparison to Mutual Funds

Similarities

Segregated funds are a pool of investment assets where the securities held within the pool can be as diverse as with mutual funds. Segregated funds can include securities such as stocks, bonds or treasury bills. Investors purchase and sell segregated funds as a unit of the fund, with each unit having a defined price. Professional money managers who have strong investment knowledge and expertise are responsible for managing the fund's investment performance.

Differences

Beneficiary Designation

These funds provide the policy owner with the opportunity to protect the funds from the creditors of the policy owner, under specific conditions, by naming a beneficiary.

Life Insurance

They are considered insurance products and are regulated by the *Uniform Insurance Companies Act*, and not by any provincial securities act. Segregated fund products are sold only through individuals who are licensed to sell insurance products. A segregated fund policy has an owner and annuitant, where these two roles can be the same individual or different individuals.

Guarantees

Segregated fund contracts are required by law to guarantee that at least 75% of the invested principal, less any withdrawals, will be returned to the policy owner upon maturity of the contact or upon death. A segregated fund contract matures on the date set by the insurance carrier, and the maturity date cannot be less than 10 years after the contract was issued. The principal guarantee (deposit less withdrawals) cannot be less than 10 years after the date of each principal deposit.

Assuris Coverage

Assuris provides insurance protection to policy owners of segregated funds with guarantees.

Process

The process involves the insurance carrier's purchase and registration of the funds in the carrier's name, who then holds the funds for the sole benefit of the policy owner.

Other Considerations

Income Flow

The nature of segregated funds is that of an *inter vivos* trust, but where the Act requires that any taxable income earned by the trust must flow through to the beneficiaries of the trust. This allows the policy owner to benefit from tax-advantaged investment income within the fund.

Disposition

When a policy owner purchases a segregated fund contract, the units of the contract have an ACB attached to the contract. Acquisition fees for segregated funds are not deductible when the contract is first acquired and are not added to the contract's ACB.

Guarantee

In situations where the guarantee under a segregated fund policy is greater than the market value at the annuitant's death or maturity, the insurance company will make up the difference. The top-up amount is taxed as a capital gain. The investor will also incur a capital loss as the market value of the policy is less than the original capital invested.

Fees

Segregated funds may have different commission structures, including a front-end load, deferred sales charge and no-load. Segregated funds also have management expenses that are referred to as MERs. The MERs tend to be higher on segregated funds than on regular mutual funds. Most insurance companies restrict the sale of segregated fund policies to annuitant's under age 80, and sometimes even younger, because of the death benefit guarantee.

Hedge Funds

These are speculative funds which are allowed to use aggressive strategies that are unavailable to mutual funds, including selling short, leverage, program trading, swaps, arbitrage, and derivatives in an attempt to achieve above average returns. They utilize borrowed money to leverage their returns (and losses) and are not a very liquid investment. Investors in hedge funds pay a management fee as well as a percentage of the profits. Such funds are considered extremely risky and suitable for high-wealth investors only.

Partnerships

A *limited partnership* is a partnership that includes at least one general partner and one limited partner. The limited partner(s) contributes capital but is not involved in the ongoing business operations and they are not liable for the debts and obligations of the partnership. The general partner is responsible for managing the business operation and is personally liable for the debts and obligations of the partnership. A limited partner's risk is limited to the amount of their investment and the investment is not very liquid.

A limited partner is limited in the deduction of his allocation of partnership losses incurred by the partnership by the at-risk rules. Income attribution rules also apply when a taxpayer loans, gifts or transfers funds to a spouse, common-law partner or a related minor who uses the funds to invest in a limited partnership. Such income is treated as property, not business income.

Investment Trusts

There are three types of income trusts: resource royalty trusts, real estate investment trusts, and infrastructure or business trusts. Income and dividends flow through the trust and are taxed in the hands of the investor. The trusts tend to provide investors with high yield, stable income and they are considered very liquid and are attractive due to the flow through tax benefits. In 2006, the Canadian government passed legislation to tax trusts the same as other corporations and thus reduce some of the main tax benefits of trusts.

Unit 2
Investment Theories and Strategies

303. TYPES OF INVESTMENT RISK

- **Business Risk.** Operating risk of a company and volatility of earnings. An investor can diversify away business risk by investing in many different businesses.
- **Market Risk.** Sensitivity of an asset relative to changes in the overall market. An investor can not diversify away market risk.
- **Reinvestment Risk.** The ability to reinvest future proceeds in securities that have a similar risk-return profile, i.e., if interest rates fall, an investor must invest the coupon payment received on a bond at lower interest rates.
- **Interest Rate Risk.** The effect that increased interest rates have on the value of the investment. If interest rates rise, the market value of fixed income investments will drop.
- **Inflation Risk.** The probability that price increases will erode the value of an investment.
- **Marketability Risk.** The inability to sell the security due to the absence of an active market.
- **Liquidity Risk.** The risk that an investor can not turn their investment into cash quickly without incurring a loss.
- **Political Risk.** The political situation could change within a country.
- **Exchange Rate Risk.** The risk of fluctuations in foreign currency denominated investments.
- **Default Risk.** The risk of a company not being able to pay a debt.

304. MEASUREMENT OF INVESTMENT RISK

Investment Risk

A general principle of investment works on the premise that risk and return are inter-related: the greater the risk, the higher the return. *Investment risk* refers to the variability of investment returns.

Risk of return = Company specific risk + Market related risk

Unsystematic risk is company-specific risk that can be reduced through diversification of portfolio holdings. An investment may be subject to risk because of problems associated with the company's operation or profitability, which could be anything from labour strife, important patents being refused, to a major product liability suit being brought forward. Some estimates suggest that up to 60 or 70% of the risk in a given investment can be attributed to unsystematic risk.

Systematic risk is market-specific risk. It cannot be minimized through diversification. Some of the risk that is inherent in holding an equity investment in a specific company is general market related risk. Other factors that contribute to systematic risk include inflation and currency fluctuations.

The risk level associated with an investment during a specific period of time can be measured in two ways:

- The investment's total risk can be measured by its standard deviation; and
- The market risk (systematic) associated with the investment can be measured by its beta.

Standard deviation is the statistical measure of the distance a return is likely to be from the long-term average or mean. The greater the standard deviation, the greater the risk and the more uncertain an investor is of achieving the expected returns.

Normal Distribution Curve

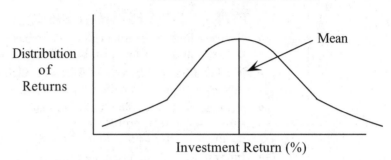

Beta measures the degree to which a stock's price fluctuates in relation to the overall market, and is calculated using regression analysis. The beta of the market is one. For example, if a stock has a beta of two and the market rose by 1%, the stock would increase if 2%. If the market dropped 1%, the stock would decrease by 2%. The stock is two times as volatile as the market.

Beta Value	Volatility
Beta = 0	Cash has a beta of 1, assuming no inflation, because there is no risk.
Beta between 0 and 1	Volatility is less than the market.
Beta = 1	Volatility is equal to the market.
Beta > 1	Volatility is greater than the market.

Impact of Diversification on Risk

Correlation is a measure of the relationship between two or more variables. The relationship between two securities is considered to have a:

- *Positive correlation* when the value of one security increases and so does the value of the other.

- *Negative correlation* when the value of one security increases while the value of the other decreases.

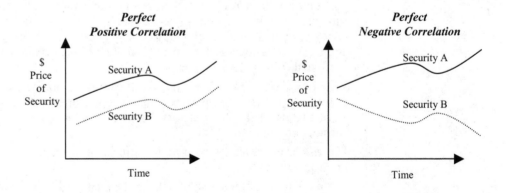

Systematic risk can be reduced by including negatively correlated securities in a portfolio.

305. PORTFOLIO MANAGEMENT TECHNIQUES

Diversification

The concept of diversification is built on the principle that diversification has a considerable impact on the composition and performance of an investor's portfolio. An investor can minimize portfolio risk by managing specific risk inherent to individual securities. The more investments in the portfolio, the more likely it is that random factors will cancel each other out and the expected return will be unaffected by random factors. The general principle of diversification is based on the premise that by combining securities into a portfolio, the risk associated with the total portfolio is reduced by an amount greater than the sum of the average risk of each security.

While it is very difficult to find investments with a perfectly negative correlation, portfolio managers will often look to a variety of diversifying principles to help build a portfolio of assets with as much negative correlation as possible.

Types of Diversification

There are several approaches to diversifying a portfolio.

Asset Classes

Asset classes refer to the grouping of securities by specific common characteristics unique to that specific set of securities such as income, growth or income and growth.

Industry

By having several industry sectors represented in a portfolio, diversification is enhanced.

Market Capitalization

Diversification can be enhanced by choosing stocks and bonds issued by companies of different sizes.

Domestic and Foreign

Geographical diversification would be effective to the extent that the risks that cause price volatility in one region would be unrelated to the risks that cause price volatility in another region.

Management Style

The management style of some investment managers can add to the diversification of a portfolio. For example, a contrarian investment style that focuses on buying when most are selling, and selling when most are buying, is designed to add diversification to the portfolio.

Fixed-Income Maturity Dates

Diversify by choosing investments with a variety of different maturity dates.

Credit Risk

Bonds are issued by organizations with different levels of creditworthiness. By creating a bond portfolio with bonds that have different credit risks, the diversification of the portfolio is enhanced.

Duration

Duration is used to predict expected changes in the price of a fixed-income security relative to an interest rate change. Duration is the weighted-average time to maturity for the cash flow on a fixed income security like a bond. If the portfolio's duration is above or below the target range, appropriate purchase or sale actions can be used to rebalance the portfolio.

Modern Portfolio Theory

Markowitz's Efficient Frontier

Markowitz's *efficient frontier* theory assumes that all individuals are risk averse, where risk is defined as the standard deviation of expected returns of investments. Each individual investment should be evaluated on the contribution to risk it makes to the portfolio. By looking at risk at the portfolio level, it is possible to use the covariance of stocks to reduce the risk of the portfolio without reducing the expected return of the portfolio. Efficient portfolios provide the maximum expected return for a given standard deviation (or level of risk). The theory is based on a risk-return approach where an investor must make a trade-off between the expected return on the portfolio and the amount of risk he is willing to assume.

If an investor invests in two stocks that each have an expected return of 12% but are perfectly negatively correlated, then the investor will have on average 12% return and limited risk because the covariance of the standard deviations will cancel each other out.

Capital Asset Pricing Model

The capital asset pricing model (CAPM) lays out a theory on the relationship between the risk of an asset and the expected return on that asset. The expected return on an asset is proportional to the systematic, non-diversifiable risk. The security market line (SML) represents the equilibrium relationship between the expected return and risk (standard deviation) of efficient portfolios comprised of combining no risk investments all the way to high risk investments achieved through buying securities on margin (borrowing).

$R = r_f + \beta \, (r_m - r_f)$

Where

R = Required rate of return (or just rate of return)

β = Beta

r_f = risk-free rate

r_m = expected return

CAPM assumes investors are risk-averse, favour a high expected rate of return, have the same investment time horizon (holding period), can borrow and lend at the risk-free rate, pay no taxes or transaction costs, and share the same view on the efficient set for all securities; it also assumes that securities markets are in equilibrium.

Arbitrage Pricing Theory

The major difference between Arbitrage Pricing Theory (APT) and CAPM centers on the number of factors that contribute to measuring risk. APT assumes that there are multiple ways to measure systematic risk in addition to beta, including interest rates, changes in inflation, investor confidence (risk premiums) and business related activities. APT investors search for unexpected events to buy and sell the same security on different markets or similar risk securities to benefit from perceived pricing differences. The main problem with APT is identifying the differences between expected and unexpected factors.

Post Modern Portfolio Theory

Post modern portfolio theory was formulated to overcome modern portfolio theories treating all uncertainty as returns around the mean measured by standard deviation. In this theory, downside risk is clearly distinguished from upside volatility. The theory suggests only volatility below the investor's expected return (called the minimum acceptable return (MAR)) translates into risk. Risk (volatility) is investor specific rather than being normally distributed (or the average return).

Efficient Market Hypothesis

The *Efficient market hypothesis* is a theory built on the premise that all known information is instantly reflected in the price of the stock. An efficient market will quickly determine the meaning of new information and adjust the stock price accordingly.

This hypothesis works on the assumption of three different degrees of efficiency:

- **Weak Form.** The current stock price reflects all historical information. An investor can not generate excess profits by trading on past trends.
- **Semi-Strong Form.** All historical and all publicly available information is included in the current stock price. An investor can not make excess profit based on analyzing all historical and publicly available information.
- **Strong Form.** All public and private information is included in the price of the stock, so it is not possible to make excessive profits. This form is not likely true given the number of people who have profited from insider information.

Investment Styles

Active Asset Allocation Strategies

Active investment refers to the process of buying stocks that are trading below their intrinsic value and selling stocks that are trading above their intrinsic value. For active investors to succeed, they must demonstrate a return that exceeds a benchmark portfolio, such as the S&P/TSX Composite Index or the S&P 500 Index.

Strategic Asset Allocation

Strategic asset allocation considers the division of the portfolio assets based on long-term forecasts for expected returns, variances and covariances. Strategic asset allocation is a method that establishes and adheres to a "base policy mix". This is a proportional combination of assets based on expected rates of return for each asset class such as bonds and stocks.

Dynamic Asset Allocation

With *dynamic asset allocation*, an investor constantly adjusts the mix of assets as markets rise and fall and the economy strengthens and weakens. With this strategy you sell assets that are declining and purchase assets that are increasing in value.

Tactical Asset Allocation

Tactical asset allocation is changing the portfolio's funds based on short-term forecasts using current market conditions. For example, using short sales affords investors the opportunity to exploit what they feel are overvalued stocks.

Insured Asset Allocation

With an *insured asset allocation*, investors try to design the investment portfolio in order to avoid large losses and secure minimum favourable returns. As the total value of assets held within the portfolio changes, the investor adjusts his exposure between the risk-free and riskier assets to rebalance back to a constant proportion.

For example, an investor establishes a base dollar amount of portfolio under which the portfolio should not drop. He may invest in risk-free assets up to the base dollar amount to ensure the portfolio does not decrease. As long as the portfolio achieves a return above this base, the investor tries to increase the portfolio value as much as possible thorough other active asset allocation strategies.

Integrated Asset Allocation

With *integrated asset allocation* the investor considers both his economic expectations and his risk in establishing an asset mix. It includes aspects of all of the above strategies, accounting not only for future market return expectations but also actual changes in capital markets and his risk tolerance.

Passive Investing

Passive investing is a financial strategy in which an investor makes as few portfolio decisions as possible, in order to minimize transactions costs including the incidence of capital gains tax. Passive investing gets its name from the fact that no active selection of stocks is undertaken. The investor attempts to construct a portfolio or invest in index mutual funds or exchange-traded funds that mirror the performance target, where the target is typically a well-diversified index such as the S&P 500.

Buy/Hold

In the *buy/hold* strategy, once investments are purchased, the investor holds them until the end of the investment period to reduce the fees he would pay with a more actively traded portfolio. The strategy ensures the investor is fully invested for the entire period, but does not guarantee the investor will achieve the market return on the portfolio.

Investment Product Analysis

Fundamental Analysis

With *fundamental analysis*, the investor measures the intrinsic value of a stock through studying the economy, the industry and the financial condition and management of a particular company to identify mispriced securities. The technique is built on the premise of a relationship between the price of a stock and the health of a company, the state of an industry and the economy as a whole. There are two main approaches: top-down and bottom-up. Under the top-down approach, forecasts begin at the economic level, move through to the industry level and conclude with company-specific forecasts. The bottom-up approach begins with forecasts for a specific company, which lead into industry forecasts and economic forecasts. Investors are driven to buy undervalued stock and sell overvalued stock based on the different intrinsic value estimates they have for a stock and its current market value.

Technical Analysis

Technical analysis is a process that is practiced by individuals known as technicians or chartists. Subscribers to this process believe that the price movement of stocks can best be explained through the mass psychology of investors and analyzing trends or patterns generated by market activity, such as past price or trading volume, as a means to evaluate a security, as opposed to the economic substance of the company issuing the security as utilized by the fundamental analysis approach. The 20 to 200-day moving average and the relative strength index that looks for patterns of closing stock prices being higher or lower, are two of the tools used by technical analysis.

306. SELLING AND BUYING TECHNIQUES

Style-Based Investing

The underlying premise of style-based investing is that certain categories of stocks have similar defining characteristics and performance trends. The two primary style types are value stocks, which targets stocks of companies where the stock is priced below average levels relative to historical prices, and growth stocks, which identifies stocks with a P/E ratio (price per earnings ratio) above the average, and where the earnings appear capable of continued, steady growth.

Leverage means acquiring investments using borrowed funds to increase the potential return on the investment. An example includes buying stock on margin. The advantage of leveraged investing is the magnification of the potential return. The exact opposite is also true in that a negative return is magnified and can substantially change the balance of risk compared to when no leverage is utilized.

Formula Investing

Formula investing is when an investor utilizes an investment strategy that is based on a specific set of rules, with no emotional implications.

Dollar-Cost Averaging

Dollar-cost averaging is an investment strategy in which a set dollar amount is invested on a regular basis in a particular investment, regardless of whether the market is moving up or down. It is also used to lower the overall cost per share, as it tends to remove volatility. The strategy is designed to take the guesswork out of trying to time the market. The minor downside is that the transaction fees associated with more frequent purchases can erode the overall returns realized by the investor.

BONITA

Bonita uses dollar cost averaging to purchase units in XYZ fund, on a DSC basis. Her monthly bank withdrawals and unit purchases, for the first six months of this year, are summarized below (disregard sales commissions):

Month	Bank Withdrawal	XYZ Unit Price	# of Units Purchased
Jan	$ 300	$5.00	60.0000
Feb	$ 300	$5.25	57.1429
Mar	$ 300	$5.19	57.8035
Apr	$ 300	$5.30	56.6038
May	$ 300	$4.90	61.2245
June	$ 300	$5.01	59.8802
Total	$1,800		352.6549

During the first six months, Bonita purchased 352.6549 units of XYZ fund. Her purchase price ranged from a low of $4.90 per unit to a high of $5.30. The average price of the units purchased during this time frame was $5.1041.

Using dollar cost average, Bonita was able to smooth out the purchase price of the units. If Bonita had used the $1,800 to make a single purchase, her unit cost may have been higher or lower than the average cost of $5.1041. Note that on three purchase dates, Jan, May and June, Bonita's unit cost was equal to or lower than the average, while in February, March and April the purchase price exceeded the average.

Dividend Re-Investment

Dividend re-investment is an investment strategy where any dividends are used to purchase additional shares. It is a passive investment strategy based on the dollar-cost averaging technique.

Systematic Withdrawal Plan

A *systematic withdrawal plan* (SWP) is a plan where the investor sets up, with the fund company, a pre-arranged schedule of withdrawals from the investor's mutual fund account. It can serve a variety of needs, such as minimum payment requirements out of a registered plan, such as a RRIF, a flow of funds needed to meet a debt obligation that entails a regular payment schedule or funds to provide an ongoing income or income supplement.

Buy and Hold

With a *buy and hold* strategy, once the stocks are purchased, the buy-and-hold investor holds them until the end of the investment period.

Short Selling

The *short selling* strategy involves the hope that the price of a security will fall in the future. The investor sells shares that he does not own, but anticipates that the price will drop in the future so that he can make a profit by buying the stock at a lower price in the future.

Unit 3
Self-Test Questions

QUESTIONS

Question 1

T-bills have which of the following characteristics?

1. Maturities of one year or less
2. High liquidity
3. Interest rates competitive with long term GICs
4. Redeemable only by the Bank of Canada

   a. 1 and 2 only
   b. 3 and 4 only
   c. 2 and 3 only
   d. 1 and 4 only

Question 2

Which of the following securities result in only interest income that must be accrued if they are held to maturity?

1. Treasury Bills
2. GICs
3. Index-linked GIC
4. Mortgage-backed securities

   a. 1, 2, and 3 only
   b. 2, 3, and 4 only
   c. 2 and 4 only
   d. 1 and 3 only

Question 3

James purchased a $1,000, 5 year, 5% bond two years ago when the prevailing interest rate was 6%. He wants to sell the bond this year. The current market rate is 4%. How much did James pay for the bond two years ago? (Rounded to the nearest dollar.)

   a. 1,171
   b. 1,000
   c. 957
   d. 853

Question 4

James purchased a $1,000, 5-year, 5% bond two years ago when the prevailing interest rate was 6%. He wants to sell the bond this year. The current market rate is 4%. Calculate the taxable capital gain when James sells the bond this year.

   a. 35.33
   b. 43.76
   c. 70.66
   d. 87.51

Question 5

Which of the following statements regarding the features of preferred shares is correct?

    a. They include voting rights.

    b. Preferred share dividends must be paid out before any common stock dividends can be distributed.

    c. Preferred shares cannot be callable.

    d. Most preferred shares have non-cumulative dividend rights.

Question 6

Andy has $25,000 to invest in a mutual fund. If Andy purchases the fund when the NAVPS is $15 and he is charged a 2% front-end load, how many units will Andy purchase?

    a. 1,667 units

    b. 1,633 units

    c. 3,060 units

    d. 1,500 units

Question 7

The major benefits of mutual fund investing include which of the following?

1. Professional management
2. Diversification
3. Liquidity
4. Safety of invested principal

    a. 1, 2 and 4 only

    b. 2, 3 and 4 only

    c. 1, 3 and 4 only

    d. 1, 2 and 3 only

Question 8

On a risk-return scale, place the following types of mutual funds in order starting with the safest alternative and ending with the riskiest:

1. Bond fund
2. Global fund
3. Money market fund
4. Equity fund

    a. 1, 2, 3, 4.

    b. 4, 3, 1, 2.

    c. 3, 1, 4, 2.

    d. 1, 3, 4, 2.

Question 9

Harry purchased a 180-day Canadian T-bill for $98,000 with a maturity value of $100,000. What is the quoted yield on Harry's T-bill?

    a. 2.77 %

    b. 3.25 %

    c. 4.14 %

    d. 4.78 %

Question 10

Which of the following statements regarding diversification is/are correct?

1. The principle of diversification has a considerable impact on the composition of an investor's portfolio.

2. The idea behind diversification is that as more securities are added to a portfolio, independent events will be good.

3. Simply put, it's about "not putting all our eggs in one basket".

4. The more investments in a portfolio, the less likely it is that random events will cancel each other out.

    a. 1 and 3 only

    b. 2 and 4 only

    c. 1 and 4 only

    d. 2 and 3 only

Question 11

Which of the following are considered as hedging strategies?

1. Index investing

2. Arbitrage

3. Event specific

4. Leveraged investing

    a. 2 and 3 only

    b. 1 and 2 only

    c. 3 and 4 only

    d. 1 and 4 only

Question 12

Which of the following statements are correct regarding dollar-cost-averaging?

1. A dollar-cost averaging strategy tends to raise a portfolio's volatility.

2. Dollar-cost averaging is a good way for an investor to maintain a regular investing regimen.

3. Dollar-cost averaging takes the guesswork out of trying to time the market.

4. In rising markets, dollar-cost averaging will produce a lower average cost per share than investing a lump sum.

    a. 1 and 3 only

    b. 2 and 3 only

    c. 1 and 4 only

    d. 2 and 4 only

Question 13

Inflation risk:

1. is not immediately obvious to an investor because purchasing power erodes rapidly.

2. is subtle and yet complex to manage.

3. can be dealt with through a direct reinvestment investment plan.

4. must be considered in developing retirement plans.

    a. 1 and 2 only

    b. 1 and 3 only

    c. 3 and 4 only

    d. 2 and 4 only

Question 14

Jason purchased a $40,000 T-bill on October 1 that was scheduled to mature 90 days after purchase. If Jason sells the T-bill on November 30, how will the investment earnings be taxed?

    a. As a capital gain or loss and interest income.

    b. As dividend income.

    c. As interest income.

    d. As a capital gain or loss and dividend income.

Question 15

Which of the following factors will normally influence the coupon rate that is initially established on a bond offering?

1. General interest rates in the market.

2. The type of asset pledged as security by the bond issuer, if any.

3. The market volatility of the bond issuer's common stock.

4. Credit rating of the bond issuer.

5. The beta of the bond issuer's stock.

    a. 1, 2 and 4 only

    b. 1, 3 and 5 only

    c. 2 and 4 only

    d. 3 and 5 only

QUESTIONS & SOLUTIONS

Question 1

T-bills have which of the following characteristics?

1. Maturities of one year or less

2. High liquidity

3. Interest rates competitive with long term GICs

4. Redeemable only by the Bank of Canada

    a. 1 and 2 only

    b. 3 and 4 only

    c. 2 and 3 only

    d. 1 and 4 only

Answer: a

    ⇨   T-bills are sold by the Bank of Canada with maturities of three, six and twelve months. T-bills are highly liquid and carry a low level of risk. They offer returns lower than GICs.

Question 2

Which of the following securities result in only interest income that must be accrued if they are held to maturity?

1. Treasury Bills

2. GICs

3. Index-linked GIC

4. Mortgage-backed securities

    a. 1, 2, and 3 only

    b. 2, 3, and 4 only

    c. 2 and 4 only

    d. 1 and 3 only

Answer: a

    ⇨   All of the securities expect for mortgage-backed securities result in interest income if held to maturity. Mortgage-backed security payments are comprised of interest income and capital receipts.

Question 3

James purchased a $1,000, 5-year, 5% bond two years ago when the prevailing interest rate was 6%. He wants to sell the bond this year. The current market rate is 4%. How much did James pay for the bond two years ago? (Rounded to the nearest dollar.)

     a. 1,171

     b. 1,000

     c. 957

     d. 853

Answer: c

     ⇨   The bond's present value is $957.35. Calculated based on

     ⇨   P/YR = 2

     ⇨   XP/YR = 5

     ⇨   PMT = $1,000 × 5% × ½

     ⇨   FV = 1,000

     ⇨   I/YR = 6%

SOLVE FOR PV, which equals $957.35

Question 4

James purchased a $1,000, 5-year, 5% bond two years ago when the prevailing interest rate was 6%. He wants to sell the bond this year. The current market rate is 4%. Calculate the taxable capital gain when James sells the bond this year.

     a. 35.33

     b. 43.76

     c. 70.66

     d. 87.51

Answer: a

     ⇨   The bond's value today is $1,028.01 based on

     ⇨   P/YR = 2

     ⇨   XP/YR = 3

     ⇨   PMT = $1,000 × 5% × ½

     ⇨   FV = 1,000

     ⇨   I/YR = 4%

SOLVE FOR PV, which equals $1,028.01

The capital gain is ($1,028.01 - $957.35) × 50% = $35.33

Question 5

Which of the following statements regarding the features of preferred shares is correct?

     a. They include voting rights.

     b. Preferred share dividends must be paid out before any common stock dividends can be distributed.

     c. Preferred shares cannot be callable.

     d. Most preferred shares have non-cumulative dividend rights.

Answer: b

Question 6

Andy has $25,000 to invest in a mutual fund. If Andy purchases the fund when the NAVPS is $15 and he is charged a 2% front-end load, how many units will Andy purchase?

    a. 1,667 units

    b. 1,633 units

    c. 3,060 units

    d. 1,500 units

Answer: b

    ⇨   The calculation is $15 ÷ (1.0 - 0.02) = $15.3061, $25,000 ÷ $15.3061/unit = 1,633 units.

Question 7

The major benefits of mutual fund investing include which of the following?

1. Professional management

2. Diversification

3. Liquidity

4. Safety of invested principal

    a. 1, 2 and 4 only

    b. 2, 3 and 4 only

    c. 1, 3 and 4 only

    d. 1, 2 and 3 only

Answer: d

    ⇨   All of the answers are benefits of investing in mutual funds except the safety of principal. Mutual funds do not guarantee the investor's principal amount.

Question 8

On a risk-return scale, place the following types of mutual funds in order starting with the safest alternative and ending with the riskiest:

1. Bond fund

2. Global fund

3. Money market fund

4. Equity fund

    a. 1, 2, 3, 4.

    b. 4, 3, 1, 2.

    c. 3, 1, 4, 2.

    d. 1, 3, 4, 2.

Answer: c

Question 9

Harry purchased a 180-day Canadian T-bill for $98,000 with a maturity value of $100,000. What is the quoted yield on Harry's T-bill?

    a. 2.77 %

    b. 3.25 %

    c. 4.14 %

    d. 4.78 %

Answer: c

    ⇨ Yield = (((Face value) - (Purchase price)) ÷ (Purchase price)) × 365 ÷ days to maturity) × 100

    ⇨ Yield = (((100,000) - (98,000)) ÷ (98,000)) × 365 ÷ 180) × 100

    ⇨ Yield = 4.14%

Question 10

Which of the following statements regarding diversification is/are correct?

1. The principle of diversification has a considerable impact on the composition of an investor's portfolio.

2. The idea behind diversification is that as more securities are added to a portfolio, independent events will be good.

3. Simply put, it's about "not putting all our eggs in one basket".

4. The more investments in a portfolio, the less likely it is that random events will cancel each other out.

    a. 1 and 3 only

    b. 2 and 4 only

    c. 1 and 4 only

    d. 2 and 3 only

Answer: a

    ⇨ Diversification can have an impact on the performance of a portfolio. With investment diversification as an investor adds more securities to the portfolio, the unsystematic risk is minimized as both good and bad independent events cancel each other out.

Question 11

Which of the following are considered as hedging strategies?

1. Index investing

2. Arbitrage

3. Event specific

4. Leveraged investing

    a. 2 and 3 only

    b. 1 and 2 only

    c. 3 and 4 only

    d. 1 and 4 only

Answer: a

Question 12

Which of the following statements are correct regarding dollar-cost-averaging?

1. A dollar-cost averaging strategy tends to raise a portfolio's volatility.

2. Dollar-cost averaging is a good way for an investor to maintain a regular investing regimen.

3. Dollar-cost averaging takes the guesswork out of trying to time the market.

4. In rising markets, dollar-cost averaging will produce a lower average cost per share than investing a lump sum.

    a. 1 and 3 only

    b. 2 and 3 only

    c. 1 and 4 only

    d. 2 and 4 only

Answer: b

    ⇨ Dollar-cost averaging (or constant dollar plan) is an investment strategy in which a set dollar amount is invested on a regular basis, regardless of whether the market is going up or down. The strategy eliminates trying to time the market and as a result reduces the volatility of the portfolio. In times of rising market price, the strategy would result in a higher, not lower, average cost per share compared to investing a lump sum.

Question 13

Inflation risk:

1. is not immediately obvious to an investor because purchasing power erodes rapidly.

2. is subtle and yet complex to manage.

3. can be dealt with through a direct reinvestment investment plan.

4. must be considered in developing retirement plans.

    a. 1 and 2 only

    b. 1 and 3 only

    c. 3 and 4 only

    d. 2 and 4 only

Answer: d

    ⇨ Inflation risk is the reduction in purchasing power due to inflation. It is complex to manage since it occurs slowly over a long period of time. Setting up a direct reinvestment plan is not effective in dealing with inflation. The greatest impact is the effect of inflation on retirement planning.

Question 14

Jason purchased a $40,000 T-bill on October 1 that was scheduled to mature 90 days after purchase. If Jason sells the T-bill on November 30, how will the investment earnings be taxed?

    a. As a capital gain or loss and interest income.

    b. As dividend income.

    c. As interest income.

    d. As a capital gain or loss and dividend income.

Answer: a

    ⇨ T-bills sold prior to maturity result in possible capital gains/losses and interest income.

Question 15

Which of the following factors will normally influence the coupon rate that is initially established on a bond offering?

1. General interest rates in the market.

2. The type of asset pledged as security by the bond issuer, if any.

3. The market volatility of the bond issuer's common stock.

4. Credit rating of the bond issuer.

5. The beta of the bond issuer's stock.

    a. 1, 2 and 4 only

    b. 1, 3 and 5 only

    c. 2 and 4 only

    d. 3 and 5 only

Answer: a

    ⇨ The main factors which affect the coupon rate on a bond offering are: the prevailing market interest rates, the collateral and the credit worthiness of the bond issuer.

**THE CFP
EDUCATION PROGRAM**

CCH/ADVOCIS FPSC-APPROVED CAPSTONE COURSE

MODULE 24
RETIREMENT PLANNING

Module 24
RETIREMENT PLANNING

Module 24
Retirement Planning

INTRODUCTION

The retirement income system in Canada is comprised of what is often referred to as the three pillars.

1. The first pillar refers to a minimum level of income during retirement that is provided through the social security benefits of Old Age Security (OAS), Guaranteed Income Supplement (GIS), and other supplements provided at the provincial level.

2. The second pillar refers to the public pension schemes of the Canada and Quebec Pension Plans, which provide retirement benefits to replace a portion of an individual's working income.

3. The third pillar of the Canadian retirement system is comprised of tax-assisted savings plans such as registered retirement savings plans (RRSPs), Tax-Free Savings Accounts (TFSAs), and employer-sponsored pension programs (RPPs), as well as general savings that have no special tax incentives.

Unit 1
Registered Pension and Profit Sharing Plans

401. REGISTERED PENSION PLANS

Consistent with trends in other industrialized nations, the length of time that Canadians spend in retirement is growing. The combination of the baby-boom effect and rising life expectancy will present significant financial challenges to Canadians, such as securing an independent retirement income.

Accumulation of funds and distribution of income from a registered pension plan is subject to rules under the *Income Tax Act* (the "Act") that are consistent across Canada; either a provincial or federal authority regulates the pension laws.

The federal government maintains jurisdiction over the federal pension legislation that covers pension plans organized and administered for the benefit of persons employed in connection with certain federal works, undertakings, and businesses.

Provincial law regulates the actual operation of the majority of pension plans across Canada. Federal and provincial pension legislation is intended to protect the rights of plan members and their dependants.

- The Canadian Association of Pension Supervisory Authorities (CAPSA) is a national inter-jurisdictional association of pension supervisory authorities, and its mission is to facilitate an efficient and effective pension regulatory system in Canada.

- The majority of pension plans are established as trusts, where the employer or a designated trust administers the pension plan on behalf of the plan member beneficiaries.

- Of the total number of individuals who participate in registered pension plans, about 85% are covered by a defined benefit plan, 13% by a money purchase plan, and 2% by a combination of defined benefit and defined contribution plans.

Plan Administration

Pension legislation requires that each registered pension plan have an administrator who is a body responsible for the pension fund and the plan operation. As well, the Canada Revenue Agency (the "CRA") has rules that dictate who can administer pension funds, which includes an insurance company or a trust, and the specific regulations as to acceptable trust arrangements.

Eligibility for membership in a pension plan is determined by the plan's design, although in most jurisdictions, the waiting period for participation in the pension plan cannot exceed 24 months for full-time employees.

Participation requirements may vary by different classes of employees, but there are restrictions that do not allow classes to be distinguished by the age or sex of the employees. In many pension plans, participation is not an option, but rather the plan is established with mandatory participation requirements where an employee must participate when first eligible.

Termination of a member's participation in a pension plan often aligns with termination of the individual's employment. This can differ in situations where the plan is a multi-employer plan.

Pensionable service refers to the plan member's employment period used in determining the amount of pension retirement benefit that accrues under a defined benefit type of plan. The design of the pension plan defines the formula for computing an individual's pensionable service, although pension regulations establish the minimum and maximum boundaries for calculating the time periods included in the service calculation.

Vesting refers to an employee's irrevocable entitlement to benefits from the pension plan.

At one time, when an individual's employment terminated, she lost all entitlement to any contributions an employer may have made to the company pension plan on her behalf. Now, most jurisdictions have a minimum vesting requirement that is usually a two-year vesting rule.

In the case of *locking-in provisions*, pension legislation in most jurisdictions requires that after a pension plan member meets certain criteria, any pension contributions or benefits cannot be withdrawn or forfeited, but rather are locked-in.

Depending upon the jurisdiction, the term *locked-in* is a provincial or federal pension benefits legislative requirement to ensure that pension contributions or benefits cannot be withdrawn. Where an active plan member terminates employment and transfers her locked-in entitlement to another plan, the locking-in provision requires that the funds be transferred to a locked-in RRSP or locked-in retirement account (LIRA).

The term *portability* refers to a plan member's ability to transfer credits or benefits accrued under the registered pension plan to another registered plan such as a registered pension plan or locked-in RRSP. Portability is generally a consideration when a plan member changes employment, but is also a consideration when the plan member dies, retires, or the plan terminates.

Normal Retirement Age. Every registered pension plan specifies an age at which plan members are normally expected or entitled to retire and receive a full, unreduced benefit. This is referred to as the normal retirement age (NRA). In many cases, individuals may retire from a plan prior to the NRA, but could be subject to a reduced retirement benefit.

Plan Amendments and Termination. Amendments to a private pension plan can usually be made at the employer's (plan sponsor's) discretion at any time; termination of a plan is also a discretionary decision that belongs with the plan sponsor.

In situations where a registered pension plan is amended or terminated, generally these actions cannot reduce a plan member's benefits earned to date. Some plans may also allow for the return of employer contributions if the plan is over-funded, whereby the plan has a surplus at the time that the plan is terminated.

Pension Plan Contributions

Contributory Plan. A pension plan that requires plan members to make contributions into the plan, through payroll deductions, is termed a *contributory plan*. The employee shares in the cost of providing the benefits that result from participation in the plan.

Non-Contributory Plan. A pension plan that does not require a plan member to make contributions into the plan is termed a *non-contributory plan*. The cost of providing the pension benefits under the plan is borne entirely by the employer.

Creditor Proof

Assets held in a pension plan are creditor proof in that they cannot be seized by a creditor of the plan member or by a creditor of the plan sponsor. This, of course, assumes that the pension plan was established in good faith, not simply because of a looming bankruptcy.

Multi-Employer Plan

This is a plan that provides coverage for employees of more than one employer and where no more than 95% of the active plan members are employed by a single employer or other participating employers who do not deal at arm's length.

Defined Benefit Pension Plans

A defined benefit pension plan provides pension benefits based on a defined formula where the benefit is known in advance of a participant's retirement. The formula for calculating the benefit is defined within the pension plan documents and provides the plan member with a good estimation of the level of retirement income that she can expect from the pension plan.

Benefit Formulas

There are three common types of formulas used in defined benefit pension plans:

- Final Earnings or Best Average;
- Career Average; and
- Flat Benefit.

Final Earnings/Best Average Earnings. The benefit is expressed as a percentage of the member's earnings multiplied by her years of participation in the plan, where the term "earnings" has a special calculation. The formula is typically 1% to 2% of the annual earnings per year of plan participation.

Final Earnings. The earnings used in the formula are based on the member's average final earnings for a prescribed period, usually between three and five years.

Best Average Earnings. The earnings in this case are based on the member's best earnings over a consecutive period, usually between three and five years, during the time in which the member participated in the plan. This type of formula allows an employee to begin retirement with a pension income closely aligned to her salary, just prior to retirement.

Career Average. This formula utilizes a member's pensionable earnings for each year of participation in the plan when calculating the total retirement benefit. It is easy to understand, and employers like it because the cost to provide the pension is easily determined and more predictable.

Flat Benefit. This type of plan uses a fixed amount in the pension benefit formula: a fixed dollar amount for each year of pensionable service. The formula does not generally take the individual's income into account but rather simply uses a pre-determined fixed amount for each plan member.

Contributions

Employer

The design of a defined benefit pension plan is such that there is a commitment on the part of the plan sponsor, usually the employer, to fund the cost of pension benefits. An employer's contribution to a defined-benefit plan is not calculated as simply a percentage of the employee's earnings, but rather is determined based on the results of the actuarial review.

- **Investment Return.** Specific assumptions are made regarding the potential investment return on the pool of assets within the pension fund. With a defined-benefit plan, because the plan sponsor is responsible for the solvency of the plan, investment decisions lie with the plan sponsor and, subsequently, the plan sponsor has full responsibility for the investment risk.

- **Expenses.** The cost of managing the plan is incorporated into the assumptions, but tends to be reasonably predictable.

- **Life Expectancy.** Assumptions are made regarding the life expectancy of the plan members as it relates to members reaching retirement age. If the actual life expectancies within the plan vary from the life-expectancy assumptions, it alters the results of the plan's expected performance.

- **Other Items.** With the commitment of establishing a registered pension plan comes a minimum employer contribution requirement in most jurisdictions, known as the "50% rule".

Employee

There are two types of employee contributions: *current service* and *past service*.

Current Service

By having employees contribute toward the cost of providing the benefit, the employer's cost is reduced, but the employer retains responsibility for the overall cost of the plan and for ensuring the plan remains funded to meet its liabilities.

An employee's contribution is normally established in the plan design as a percentage of pensionable or contributory earnings, where the term *contributory/pensionable earnings* has a specific definition. In some cases, the pension plan may be integrated with government benefits such as the Canada Pension Plan (CPP)/Quebec Pension Plan (QPP).

Past Service

Within some defined benefit pension plans there are specific circumstances where a plan member is given the opportunity to make additional contributions that are used to purchase pension benefits applicable to past service. When new pension plans are established, it is common for the plan to allow employees to purchase pension credits for periods of employment with the employer that were prior to the establishment of the pension plan.

Upgrades to a pension benefit, such as the purchase of periods of past service, have income tax implications that need to be considered, and affect an individual's level of RRSP contribution room.

Benefits

Entitlement

An individual's *benefit entitlement* in a defined benefit pension plan refers to accrued benefits that the individual has earned. There are some occasions where it is necessary to calculate a member's specific entitlement under a registered pension plan:

- on termination of employment;
- on retirement;
- at death; and
- on termination of the pension plan.

Calculation

Retirement income benefits from a defined benefit pension plan are based on a formula that the plan member knows in advance of retirement, and can be such formulas as *flat benefit* or *career average*.

Maximum Benefit Accrual Rate

The career average and final/best average benefit calculation formulas are based specifically on a member's earnings. In these situations where the formula is earnings based, the annual benefit accrual rate cannot exceed 2% of the member's remuneration.

Maximum Pension Rule

As of 2009, when a pension begins, the maximum annual entitlement is limited to a lifetime maximum based on the lesser of:

- $2,444 multiplied by the member's years of pensionable service; or
- 2% per year of service multiplied by the average of the best three years (three non-overlapping 12-month periods) of pensionable earnings.

The prescribed limit for the dollar maximum of $2,444 for 2009 will be indexed after 2009.

Integration With Government Benefits

Pension plans that provide for the integration of retirement benefits between the corporate pension plan and CPP/QPP generally use one of two methods for the integration:

- **Step Rate.** Where a lower benefit is paid on earnings up to the YMPE; or
- **Direct Offset.** Where a percentage of the CPP/QPP benefit is offset against the employer's pension plan.

Indexation

Inflation erodes the purchasing power of a fixed income. Inflation is often a matter of significant concern to pensioners because it reduces the purchasing power of a fixed pension income. The *Rule of 72* can be used to calculate the time it will take for inflation to reduce the purchasing power of a fixed pension to half.

To determine the point in time when purchasing power is cut in half, divide 72 by the rate of inflation (50% reduction in purchasing power = 72 ÷ rate of inflation).

Retirement

Normal Retirement

The majority of pension plans provide for a normal retirement date that ties into the date that the plan member reaches age 65. Upon reaching NRA, a plan member is generally offered a number of options relative to her benefit entitlement. The normal form of pension is an annuity type of payment, and may include:

- Life Income Pension
- Life Income with a Guarantee Period
- Joint and Survivor
- Joint and Survivor Option with a Guarantee Period

Early Retirement

It is common in most jurisdictions that registered pension plans provide the option for a plan member to retire with a life pension at any time within 10 years of NRA. *Actuarial reduction* refers to providing an early retirement benefit where the cost of the benefit is equivalent to the cost of the benefit if it had been taken at the normal retirement date.

- The plan member has made less contributions than if she had remained active in the plan until NRA;
- Investment earnings will be less on assets associated with the plan member who leaves prior to NRA; and
- There is the potential for a longer payout period, given that the benefit is being taken earlier than NRA.

Qualifying Factors

Registered pension plan members may qualify for an unreduced early pension under a defined-benefit plan, provided that the member meets one of the following criteria:

- has attained age 60 by the date that the pension commences;
- has at least 30 years of pensionable service; or
- the member's age plus years of qualifying service is 80 or more.

The third bullet is what is known as the *qualifying factor*; typically, 85 is common across many plans.

The standard criteria to qualify for an unreduced early pension is modified for employees in public-safety occupations, where the plan member must meet one of the following criteria:

- has attained age 55 by the date that the pension commences;

- has at least 25 years of pensionable service; or
- the member's age plus years of qualifying service is 75 or more.

When a plan incorporates a qualifying factor into the early retirement criteria, there is a specific formula that can be used to calculate the earliest age at which an individual may retire:

Earliest retirement age = (Member's age at time of joining plan + Qualifying factor) ÷ 2

Bridging Benefits

These are supplementary benefits that may be provided to a member who retires early to supplement her pension income until she reaches age 65, the point at which Old Age Security (OAS) and full CPP benefits are payable.

Postponed Retirement

Most jurisdictions and many registered defined benefit pension plans allow members to work beyond NRA and to continue to accrue additional pension credits.

Termination of Employment

Upon termination of employment before retirement, the member is entitled to specific benefits under pension standards legislation, usually:

- A lump-sum payment (unless the pension is vested or locked-in by law);
- Transfer of the value to another registered pension plan, if allowed by both the transferring and receiving plans;
- A deferred life annuity commencing before the end of the year the employee reaches age 69;
- A lump-sum transfer to a locked-in RRSP or LIRA;
- A lump-sum transfer to a life income fund (LIF) or, if allowed in the jurisdiction, a life retirement income fund (LRIF); or
- A combination of the above.

Death of a Plan Member

Pre-Retirement Death. There is no uniformity in the standards applied to pre-retirement death benefits across the various jurisdictions.

Post-Retirement Death. Where a plan member dies after having initiated her retirement pension, the form of pension originally selected at retirement will determine what benefits, if any, will be payable after the member's death.

Relationship Breakdown

Pre-Retirement

The division of pension assets upon marriage breakdown crosses pension and family law. All provinces, except Prince Edward Island, require that pensions be included as part of the divisible property upon marriage breakdown.

Direct Transfer Due to Relationship Breakdown

Payment from:	Transfer to:				Comments
	RPP	RRSP	RRIF	Annuity	
RPP lump sum	Yes	Yes	Yes	No	(1) Only a direct transfer is permitted; otherwise the amounts must be included in the recipient's income for the year in which it is received. (2) The payment must be made under a decree, court order, judgment of a court or under a written agreement relating to a division of property between two current or former spouses or common-law partners in settlement of rights arising out of a relationship breakdown. (3) To transfer to an RRSP, the individual to whom the funds are being transferred must be age 71 or younger at the end of the year in which the transfer occurs.

Post-Retirement

If a marriage breakdown occurs subsequent to retirement, when many retirement income decisions have already been made and cannot be adjusted, then the member's and her spouse's income rights would be taken into account in determining the level of support payments.

Income Tax Implications

The Act legislation and regulations that deal with retirement savings of all kinds are very complex. Registered pension plans must include specific, detailed, obligatory provisions in order to be registered with the Registered Plans Division of the CRA.

Contributions

An employer's contributions to a registered defined benefit pension plan are:

- Generally treated as a tax deductible business expense for the employer, provided that the contributions are based on the recommendations within the pension plan valuation report; and

- Not considered a taxable benefit to the employee so therefore are not included in an employee's taxable income.

Benefit Payout

Amounts paid into a registered pension plan as contributions have not yet been taxed. As such, amounts paid out to employees on a periodic basis are generally taxable to the recipient.

RRSP Contribution Room

The value of the benefits earned under a registered pension plan is approximated by the pension adjustment (PA), which is subtracted from the RRSP contribution room for the plan member. The formula is (9 × RPP benefit entitlement) - $600, up to a maximum of $21,400.

Past service pension adjustment (PSPA) is where a registered pension plan member becomes entitled to past service benefits or improvements to benefits for service after 1989 under a defined-benefit plan.

Pension adjustment reversal (PAR) is where a registered pension plan member does not eventually acquire a vested interest in a benefit under a plan.

Individual Pension Plans

An individual pension plan (IPP), commonly referred to as an "executive pension plan", is an employer-sponsored, defined benefit registered pension plan created for the benefit of qualifying individuals because of the unique constraints imposed by retirement savings legislation.

A "designated plan" is a defined benefit registered pension plan that is not maintained pursuant to a collective bargaining agreement and where more than 50% of the total pension credits or PA for plan members are for either connected individuals or persons whose income exceeds 2.5 times the YMPE.

Plan Fit

Designated plans are often established for the benefit of a top executive group or in owner–manager situations. IPPs offer successful, well-established entrepreneurs the opportunity to fund some of their retirement needs through contributions from the company.

Using an IPP, rather than the traditional RRSP savings route, an individual can maximize her personal pension benefits while meeting the rules prescribed by the CRA.

Generally, an IPP is most suited for executives or owner–managers of incorporated companies, who are forty or older, with regular annual earnings of at least $100,000.

Plan Design

The design of an IPP must assume a NRA of 65 and may utilize a career average earnings formula, but not a final/best earnings approach. The maximum annual benefit that may accrue to the plan member is the same as other defined benefit pension plans.

The plan is normally established as non-contributory, where the plan member is not required to make any contributions, and the employer assumes full responsibility for funding the required contributions to meet the accrued retirement income liability established by the plan design.

Past Service

For IPP members who are not considered connected individuals, the rules for making past service contributions are the same as for a regular defined benefit pension plan.

The CRA has established special rules relative to past service contributions for connected individuals where only post-1991 service can be recognized.

Plan Value

Tax Savings. Money contributed to an IPP is not considered salary, so it can be contributed to the IPP without attracting payroll taxes.

Creditor Protection. An IPP is entitled to all of the creditor protection measures afforded to any registered pension plan.

Savings Opportunity. An IPP is a registered pension plan and, once established, the employer has an obligation to make the required annual contributions. Therefore, in deciding between an IPP and an RRSP, it is important to consider both the short and longer-term cash flow projections.

Indexation. Indexing assumptions, up to a CRA prescribed limit, can be incorporated into the income projections for an IPP, which then translates into contributions required by the employer to fund the required income.

Target Income. While the CRA have rules dictating the liberties of the assumptions incorporated into IPP income projections, the fact that the employee knows the specifics of her projected retirement income formula gives him an advantage over an RRSP.

Market Risk. When volatile investment markets affect the investment performance of the IPP funds, responsibility lies with the employer to increase required contributions in order to fund the required level of retirement benefits provided in the plan.

Access to Funds. The rules for accessing funds within an IPP are the same as those established for a regular defined benefit pension plan. This differs from an RRSP, where there are tax consequences in doing so, but an individual can indeed withdraw funds from the RRSP.

Long-Range Planning. RRSPs provide the opportunity for long-range financial planning through the establishment of a spousal RRSP. IPPs do not have any equivalent to a spousal RRSP.

Asset Ownership. Under an IPP, the assets in the plan belong to the member; upon her death and the death of her spouse or partner, any remaining benefits are paid to the estate.

DEFINED CONTRIBUTION PENSION PLAN/MONEY PURCHASE PLANS

A *defined contribution pension plan* is one where contributions into the plan are based on a specific formula and the sum of accumulated contributions and earnings, credited to a plan member, is used to purchase a pension at retirement.

Contributions into a defined contribution plan include required employer contributions. If the plan is *contributory*, then employees also contribute on a regular basis. Contributions are allocated specifically to each plan member where the member's funds are held and earn an investment return.

Plan Fit

The term *defined contribution plan* is common terminology for any type of plan where contributions into the plan are a known quantity but the resulting benefits from the plan are dependent upon the total contributions and investment performance of the plan's assets.

Other types of defined contribution plans include a profit sharing pension plan (PSPP), a deferred profit sharing plan (DPSP), and an RRSP.

An inherent characteristic of a defined contribution plan lies in the fact that the plan member assumes responsibility for the investment risk.

Contributions

In a defined contribution pension plan, contributions may be based on a fixed percentage of pensionable earnings, a regular fixed dollar amount, or a specified amount based on years of service or hours worked. A defined contribution plan allows for contributions related to current service only.

Integration with Government Benefits

Some registered pension plans provide a level of integration, benefits and/or contributions with the CPP/QPP. For a defined contribution plan, integrated contributions often means reducing the pension plan's contribution rate by the CPP contribution rate on the pensionable earnings up to the YMPE.

Investment Selection

Contributions made into a defined contribution pension plan are invested and it is the sum of the contributions and investment earnings that will later be used for retirement.

Maximum Contributions

Within the structure of a defined contribution pension plan, the Act requires minimum annual contributions of 1% by the employer.

The limit for 2009 is the lesser of:

- 18% of earnings; or
- $22,000 (indexed after 2009).

Benefits

Entitlement

An individual's *benefit entitlement* in a defined contribution pension plan refers to the value of the funds accumulated within the pension plan to which one is legally entitled, under various circumstances.

There are a number of occasions when it is necessary to communicate a member's benefit entitlement under a registered pension plan:

- On termination of employment;
- On retirement;
- At death; and
- On termination of the pension plan.

In terms of benefit calculations, there is no restriction on the maximum pension that may arise under a defined contribution pension plan.

Benefit Comparison (Defined Benefit versus Defined Contribution)

In a *defined contribution plan*, investment earnings in the early years have the greatest effect on the eventual pension, since investments compounded over a long period of time directly impact the total asset accumulation under the plan.

Under a *defined contribution plan*, the individual knows the annual contributions, but the final pension on retirement is unknown. The pension amount is based on the investment returns on the annual contributions.

Under a *defined benefit plan*, the individual knows the amount of the annual pension at retirement.

Retirement

Normal Retirement

Upon reaching NRA (age 65), a plan member is generally offered a number of options relative to her benefit entitlement. In many jurisdictions, pension rules require that the resulting pension benefit at normal retirement incorporate a joint and survivor form of pension.

With spousal permission to opt out of the minimum requirement, the plan member is free to select an annuity, which may include:

- Life Income Annuity;
- Life Annuity with a Guaranteed Period;
- Joint and Survivor; and
- Joint and Survivor Option with a Guarantee Period.

Early Retirement

A defined contribution plan usually includes a minimum prescribed age at which a plan member may draw a pension from the plan, which is commonly set at age 55.

Bridging Benefits

The Act permits bridging benefits for money purchase plans; however, the benefit must cease by the end of the month following the month of the member's 65th birthday.

Postponed Retirement

Any postponed retirement must take into account that that the retirement pension must begin no later than the end of the calendar year in which the member reaches age 71.

Termination of Employment

Upon termination of employment before retirement, the member of a defined contribution plan is entitled to the current value of her own contributions.

As well, a plan member is usually entitled to the following options:

- A lump-sum payment of any funds that are not vested or locked-in by law;
- Transfer of the assets to another registered pension plan, if allowed by both the transferring and receiving plans;
- A deferred life annuity commencing before the end of the year the employee reaches age 71;
- A lump-sum transfer to a locked-in RRSP or LIRA;
- A lump-sum transfer to a LIF, or, if allowed in the jurisdiction, a LRIF; or
- A combination of the above.

Death of a Plan Member

Pre-Retirement Death

There is no uniformity in the standards applied to pre-retirement death benefits across the various jurisdictions; requirements vary significantly and are often dependent on whether the member was within the qualifying range for an early retirement pension.

Post-Retirement Death

Where a plan member dies after having initiated her retirement pension, the form of pension originally selected at retirement will determine what benefits, if any, will be payable subsequent to the member's death.

Relationship Breakdown

The notes on this subject under defined benefit plans also apply here.

Income Tax Implications

Registered pension plans must include specific, detailed, obligatory provisions in order to be registered with the Registered Plans Division of the CRA.

Contributions

An employer's contributions to a registered defined contribution pension plan are:

- Treated as a tax deductible business expense for the employer; and

- Not considered a taxable benefit to the employee and thus are not included in an employee's taxable income.

Benefit Payout

Amounts paid out to employees on a periodic basis are generally fully taxable to the recipient.

RRSP Contribution Room

Contributions made into a pension plan directly affect the pension plan member's RRSP contribution room.

402. SUPPLEMENTARY PENSION ARRANGEMENTS

Retirement Compensation Arrangement

Nature of a RCA

A *retirement compensation arrangement* (RCA) is a plan or arrangement under which an employer, former employer, or a non-arm's length person makes contributions to a custodian, who holds the funds in trust for the purpose of eventually distributing a benefit to the employee, on or after one of the following events:

- Retirement;

- The loss of an office or employment; or

- Any substantial change in services the employee provides.

Basically, a RCA is used to provide a supplemental pension, above the limits imposed on registered savings, for highly paid executives.

Taxation

An RCA trust is subject to a special tax regime: A RCA calculates income without any tax preferences. For example, the dividend gross-up and capital gains inclusion rate are not applicable in calculating a RCA's income. This means that dividends are included in the RCA's income without the gross-up, and capital gains are fully taxable in a RCA trust.

An RCA pays 50% tax on contributions into the RCA. Any tax that the RCA pays is refundable when the RCA makes distributions to its beneficiary.

The tax rate applicable to a RCA is 50%.

Distributions out of the Plan

Distributions, including periodic payments and lump-sum amounts made to a beneficiary out of the RCA trust, are taxable to the beneficiary; the RCA trustee is obligated to with-hold tax on distributions.

Distributions to a non-resident of Canada are subject to non-resident withholding tax. The Act prescribes a withholding rate of 25%, although this can be reduced.

When payments are made from the trust, the RCA trustee can claim a refund of the refundable taxes.

Deemed RCA

As an anti-avoidance measure, corporate-owned life insurance policies could be deemed a RCA. The deeming rules apply when three criteria are met:

- The corporation owns a life insurance policy;

- There is an obligation to pay post-retirement benefits to an employee; and

- It is reasonable to assume that the life insurance policy was purchased to fund the post-retirement benefit. If the deeming rules apply, the employer must also remit applicable withholding tax as if a RCA were in place.

Filings — Annual Information Return

In any year that contributions are made to a RCA, the contributing employer must com-plete and file an information return by the last day of February in the year following the calendar year in which the contributions were made to the custodian.

403. DEFERRED PROFIT SHARING PLANS

A *deferred profit sharing plan* (DPSP) is an employer-sponsored plan registered with the CRA in which an employer shares some of the profits of a business with employees. A DPSP is defined in section 147 of the Act, and is often viewed as a source of supplemen-tary retirement income for an employee.

A DPSP is not regulated as a pension plan under any legislation in Canada.

Contributions

A deferred profit sharing plan accumulates assets through two sources:

- Contributions made by an employer into the plan; and

- A lump-sum transfer of assets from another DPSP.

The maximum deductible limit is lesser of 18% of employee's compensation for year; or ½ of the money purchase limit for the year.

Year	Limit for Deduction of DPSP Contribution
2009	$11,000
2010	indexed

A pension adjustment (PA) from DPSP reduces the amount that the employee can contribute to a RRSP. The formula is the same as for a RPP, which is (9 × pension entitlement) - $600.

If an individual leaves an employer prior to retirement, a pension adjustment reversal may occur.

Withdrawals From a DPSP

All amounts vested in the participating plan member, who is a beneficiary of the DPSP, become payable not later than 90 days after the earliest of:

- The death of the employee;
- The day on which the employee terminates employment with the contributing employer;
- The day on which the employee turns age 71; or
- The termination of the plan.

Any amount taken as cash is fully taxable in the year of receipt. An amount may be transferred from a DPSP directly to another registered plan (and maintain the tax deferred status) if certain conditions are met. DPSP lump sum payments can be transferred tax-free to a RPP, RRSP, or RRIF.

Assessing Value

When assessing the value of a DPSP, that value depends upon the perspective from which the assessment is made.

The ability to participate in the profits of the employer can be attractive because it provides a reward for profitable performance of the corporation. An employer has the freedom to select participants in the DPSP.

A DPSP acts as a deferred form of remuneration, with the assets continuing to grow tax-sheltered until withdrawn from the plan. The ability to access funds within the plan, at any time, reduces the true value of a DPSP as a source of retirement income. An employee loses her right to any benefits under a plan if she leaves the plan (i.e., resigns or is terminated) before her entitlement to contributions made on her behalf becomes fully vested.

Death of the DPSP Plan Member

If an individual becomes entitled to assets of a DPSP because of the death of her spouse/common-law partner who was a member of a DPSP, any assets transferred directly to the following plans will retain the tax deferred status:

- A registered pension where the receiving spouse/common-law partner is a plan member;
- an RRSP where the receiving spouse/common-law partner is the annuitant and is under age 72 throughout the entire year in which the transfer is made; or
- Another DPSP where there are at least five beneficiaries throughout the year and where the receiving spouse is a participating member.

Any assets that are not transferred by the surviving spouse under the conditions outlined above are taxable to the surviving spouse.

Unit 2
Registered Retirement and Education Savings Plans

404. REGISTERED RETIREMENT SAVINGS PLANS

Registered retirement savings plans (RRSPs) were introduced in 1957 to encourage Canadians to extend their savings by specifically setting funds aside to provide income during their retirement years. An RRSP is a vehicle designed to address the *savings* or *wealth accumulation phase* of retirement plans. RRSPs have special tax advantages that allow for the deferral of income tax, which has the potential to greatly accelerate the accumulation of savings.

Establishing an RRSP

An RRSP is a plan registered with the CRA that is designed to allow the annuitant (plan owner) to accumulate savings specifically for retirement.

- "Unmatured RRSP." One that has not yet started to pay a retirement income to the annuitant and is still in a pure accumulation mode.

- "Matured RRSP." A plan that is paying retirement income to the annuitant.

Minimum Age

There is no minimum age at which an RRSP may be established; the requirement is based on earned income where earned income, as it relates to RRSP contributions, has a specific definition within the Act.

Maximum Age

An RRSP matures at the end of the calendar year in which the annuitant reaches age 71.

When funds move out of an RRSP, there are three choices available:

- Convert the RRSP to a RRIF;

- Purchase a registered annuity; or

- Cash in the RRSP.

Types of Plans

Individual RRSP

An individual RRSP is a personal savings plan established by way of a contract between the annuitant and the financial institution.

Self-Directed Individual RRSP

A self-directed RRSP, also considered an individual RRSP, allows a wider choice of investment options rather than one single investment type.

With a self-directed RRSP, an individual may hold multiple types of investments all within the same (single) RRSP, similar to a brokerage account for non-registered investments.

A few of the benefits of a self-directed account include:

- One RRSP account and therefore one statement with all investment information;

- The ability to better manage different types of investments under one single umbrella account; and

- The ability to move securities or other investment products already owned into the RRSP account (assuming the annuitant has the contribution room and that the investments are qualified investments).

Group RRSP

In the 1980s, an increasing number of financial institutions began to offer Group Registered Retirement Savings Plans (GRRSPs) as an additional retirement savings option.

A GRRSP is simply a series of individual RRSP accounts where contributions are generally made through payroll deductions.

The Act views a GRRSP as merely a collection of individual RRSPs; as such, a GRRSP is not subject to pension standards legislation, an attractive feature for many employers.

Contributions

Earned Income

Earned income generally includes:

- Income from office or employment;

- Royalties in respect of a work or invention;

- Net rental income from real property;

- Income from carrying on business as a proprietor or active partner;

- Receipt of taxable child and spousal support payments;

- Amounts received under a supplementary unemployment benefit plan (not including benefits received from the federal Employment Insurance program);

- Net research grants; and

- CPP/QPP disability pensions received in the year.

Earned income **does not** include:

- Investment income (i.e., dividend income or interest income);

- Taxable capital gains;

- Scholarships or bursaries received by the taxpayer;

- Business income earned as a limited partner;

- Employment Insurance benefits;

- Workers' Compensation benefits;

- CPP/QPP retirement benefits;

- OAS retirement benefits; and

- Retiring allowances.

The term *earned income* directly affects a taxpayer's contributions to an RRSP and for RRSP purposes it is a defined term found in subsection 146(1) of the Act.

Current Contribution Limit

The Act dictates a single limit on the total annual deductible contributions that can be made to all forms of tax-assisted retirement savings plans on behalf of an individual taxpayer, which applies to an employer sponsored RPP, a DPSP and an RRSP.

The prescribed formula is based on 18% of the taxpayer's earned income from the previous year up to a maximum dollar limit of $21,000 for 2009.

Pension Adjustment

A taxpayer's PA is the value of the benefits earned or accrued to a taxpayer because of her participation in a registered pension plan or DPSP. It is calculated as (9 × pension entitlement) - $600.

The prescribed formula has been developed on the basis that a taxpayer who accrues an annual pension benefit entitlement of 2% of earnings per year of plan participation will generally have a PA that uses up most of her RRSP deduction limit.

New Contribution Room

A taxpayer's *yearly contribution limit* is determined by three factors: earned income of the previous year, the maximum dollar limit established by the CRA, and whether or not she was a member of a RPP or DPSP in the previous year.

Pension Adjustment Reversal

Where a registered pension plan member does not eventually acquire a vested interest in a benefit under a pension plan, or receives a termination benefit which is less than the amount of the PA (including any PSPA) which has been previously reported to the government, a PAR is calculated, which restores some of the individual's RRSP contribution room.

Past Service Pension Adjustment

Where a registered pension plan member becomes entitled to a past service benefit or improvements to benefits for service after 1989 under a defined benefit plan, a PSPA may arise, requiring the recalculation of the (increased) benefit accrual for the previous year(s), and reducing the member's RRSP contribution room.

Total RRSP Contribution Room for 2009

EQUALS

Current contribution limit

(18% of earned income for 2008, to dollar maximum $21,000)

MINUS

2008 Pension Adjustment[a]

PLUS

2009 Pension Adjustment Reversal[b]

MINUS

2009 Net Past Service Pension Adjustment[c]

PLUS

Carry Forward of Unused RRSP Deduction Limit at the End of 2008

Notes:

(a) Applies to taxpayers who participate in a RPP or DPSP.

(b) May affect taxpayers who terminate participation in a RPP or DPSP.

(c) May affect taxpayers in a defined benefit plan (purchase of past service).

Types of Contributions

Contributions into an RRSP may be in the form of:

- cash;

- a deposit in-kind; or

- amounts transferred to an RRSP that are outside of RRSP deduction limits, such as retiring allowances, refunds of premiums received from the RRSP of a deceased annuitant and transfers from other deferred-income plans.

Timing

- Contributions made to an RRSP are deductible for income tax purposes within limits imposed by the CRA; and

- Eligible contributions made to an RRSP during the calendar year, also referred to as the taxation year, are deductible in the taxation year.

Taxation Year One — Timing of Deductible Contributions

- Contributions made between January and December of taxation year one

- *plus*

- Contributions made in first 60 days of taxation year two

Maximum Age Restrictions

Regular RRSP. A taxpayer may make contributions into an RRSP, where she is the annuitant, up to the end of the year in which she reaches age 71.

Spousal RRSP. A taxpayer (the contributing spouse) may make contributions into a "spousal RRSP", where the taxpayer's spouse is the annuitant, up to the end of the year in which the annuitant (the non-contributing spouse) reaches age 71.

Issuing Receipts

Financial institutions that hold the RRSP will provide an official tax receipt for amounts contributed to an RRSP.

Other Types of Contributions

The following types of transfers into an RRSP do not affect the taxpayer's deduction limit for the year:

- indirect transfers of a refund of premiums;

- indirect transfers of retiring allowances;

- indirect transfer of survivor's benefits from a RPP or DPSP by a spouse or common-law partner; and

- indirect transfer of benefits from unregistered pension plans for non-residents.

Excess RRSP Contributions

Cumulative excess amount is the amount by which an individual's undeducted RRSP contributions exceed the RRSP deduction room available to the individual. The CRA allows a lifetime over-contribution limit that is currently $2,000. The $2,000 is a cumulative amount consisting of undeducted contributions in excess of yearly RRSP deduction room.

Over-contributions must be calculated and reported on form T1-OVP, "Individual Income Tax Return of RRSP Excess Contributions". The penalty is 1% of the over contribution above $2,000 per month.

The government allows two concessions when calculating excess contribution room:

- Where a taxpayer participates in a mandatory Group RRSP, generally as part of her employment agreement, qualifying RRSP contributions are deemed to have been paid in the year following the actual year of contribution; and

- A PSPA is taken into account for penalty tax purposes only in the year following the year the PSPA is actually reported.

Retiring Allowance

Definition

A *retiring allowance* is a payment:

- on or after retirement from an office or employment in recognition of long service; or

- in respect of a loss of an office or employment of a taxpayer, whether or not received as, on account of, or in lieu of payment of, damages or pursuant to a court order

Calculation

An individual has the opportunity to shelter from tax some or all of the retiring allowance that she receives.

The formula to calculate the maximum amount of money that can be rolled over to an RRSP or RPP is:

- $2,000 times the number of years that the employee was employed with the employer or related employer, prior to 1996; and

- $1,500 for each year or part of a year counted for the $200 limit before 1989 of employment in which the employee did not contribute to, or the contributions were not vested in, a RPP or DPSP. The number can be a fraction.

Transfer

Eligible amounts that arise from a retiring allowance may be transferred to an RRSP or RPP either directly or indirectly.

These transfers can be done in the following ways:

- An employer can submit eligible rollover amounts directly to the individual's RRSP (a retiring allowance cannot be transferred to a spousal RRSP). If a direct transfer is utilized, then the taxpayer avoids withholding tax on the amount transferred; or

- The taxpayer may receive the funds personally, less withholding taxes, and later decide to make a transfer to an RRSP or RPP.

The rollover of a retiring allowance does not affect the taxpayer's normal RRSP limits and contributions.

Qualified Investments and Non-Qualified Investments

Qualified Investments

- Cash deposits and GICs with Canadian banks, trust companies and credit unions
- Shares of a corporation listed on a prescribed stock exchange in Canada
- Shares of corporations listed on a prescribed foreign stock exchange
- Shares or debt of a Canadian public corporation (other than a mortgage investment corporation)
- shares of a small business corporation or venture capital corporation
- Bonds, debentures, notes, mortgages, or similar debt obligations guaranteed by the Government of Canada (i.e., Canada Savings Bonds)
- Units in mutual fund trusts
- Foreign stock exchange index trusts
- Annuities, if purchased from a licensed annuities provider
- Warrants, rights or options that, if exercised, will result in the acquisition of a qualified investment
- Royalty units listed on a Canadian stock exchange and whose value is derived from Canadian resource properties
- Limited partnership units listed on a prescribed stock exchange in Canada
- A mortgage on Canadian property ((1) if the mortgage is for personal use by the annuitant, the mortgage must be administered by an approved lender and be insured by an approved insurer, under the *National Housing Act*; and (2) the terms of the mortgage must reflect normal business practice)
- Investment-grade gold and silver bullion, coins, bars, and certificates

Non-Qualified Investments

- Real estate
- Shares of private corporations, where the RRSP annuitant and her immediate family hold more than 10% of any class of shares
- Commodity futures
- Listed personal property, such as works of art and antiques
- Gems, other precious stones, and metals

Penalties for holding non-qualified investments in an RRSP can be costly. In the year an individual buys a non-qualified investment for her plan, her taxable income will be increased by the price that was paid for it. Income or capital gains earned by non-qualified investments while they're held in an RRSP will be subject to a special tax — the rate will be the same as that paid by a person in the top tax bracket. A penalty tax of 1% a month will be imposed on the FMV of non-qualified RRSP investments held at the end of every month.

Foreign Content Rule

The 2005 federal Budget eliminated the 30% foreign property rule limit effective January 1, 2005.

Income Tax Implications

Regular RRSP — Withdrawals During Annuitant's Lifetime

RRSP funds are accessible to the annuitant and may be withdrawn at any time; these cash withdrawals are included as income for the taxpayer in the year the withdrawal is made.

Withholding Tax

Amount Withdrawn	All provinces except Quebec (%)	Quebec (%)
Up to $5,000	10	21
$5,001 – $15,000	20	26
Over $15,001	30	31

Regular RRSP — At Maturity During Annuitant's Lifetime

An RRSP must mature by the end of the year in which the annuitant reaches age 71, and assets are often transferred to an income paying registered plan, such as a RRIF.

Transfer From an Unmatured RRSP

Assets from an unmatured RRSP may transfer directly to the following types of plans:

- another RRSP (annuitant must be age 70 or younger at the end of the year in which the transfer occurs);
- a RRIF; or
- a RPP.

Direct Transfer

Payment from:	Transfer to:				Comments
	RPP	**RRSP**	**RRIF**	**Annuity**	
Unmatured RRSP	Yes	Yes	Yes	Yes	(1) Only a direct transfer is permitted; otherwise the amounts must be included in the recipient's income for the year in which it is received. (2) To transfer to an RRSP, the annuitant to whom the funds are being transferred must be age 71 or younger at the end of the year in which the transfer occurs.

Direct Transfer Due to Relationship Breakdown

Payment from:	Transfer to:			Comments
	RPP	**RRSP**	**RRIF**	
Unmatured RRSP	No	Yes	Yes	(1) Only a direct transfer is permitted; otherwise the amounts must be included in the recipient's income for the year in which it is received. (2) The payment must be made under a decree, court order, judgment of a court or under a written agreement relating to a division of property between two current or former spouses or common-law partners in settlement of rights arising out of a relationship breakdown. (3) To transfer to an RRSP, the individual to whom the funds are being transferred must be age 71 or younger at the end of the year in which the transfer occurs. (4) Recipient and her spouse or common-law partner must be living separately and apart at the time of transfer due to a relationship breakdown.

Direct Transfers[1][2]

Payment from:	Transfer to: RRSP	Comments
RPP lump sum	Yes	This applies to lump-sum transfers an individual receives from her RPP and to an amount received from a current or former spouse or common-law partner's RPP because the current or former spouse or common-law partner died.
DPSP lump sum	Yes	This applies to lump-sum transfers an individual receives from her DPSP and to lump-sum transfers an individual receives from a current or former spouse or common-law partner's DPSP because the current or former spouse or common-law partner died.
Unmatured RRSP	Yes	
Matured RRSP	Yes	This applies only to a direct transfer of a commutation payment from the RRSP annuity only.
RRIF (property)	No	Property from one RRIF may be transferred to another RRIF but the transfer must take place directly between the two RRIFs.
RRIF (excess amount)	Yes	An excess amount refers to withdrawal amounts beyond the required minimum.

(1) Only a direct transfer is permitted; otherwise the amounts must be included in the recipient's income for the year in which they are received.

(2) To transfer to an RRSP, the individual to whom the funds are being transferred must be age 71 or younger at the end of the year in which the transfer occurs.

Death of an Annuitant

General Terms

Upon the death of the annuitant, if the assets of the unmatured RRSP pass to someone other than a spouse/common-law partner or a qualified child or grandchild, the fair market value (FMV) of the plan assets, immediately before her death, must be included in the annuitant's income for the year of death.

Refund of Premiums

A refund of premiums is defined as any amount paid out of or under an RRSP to the spouse or common-law partner of the deceased annuitant, prior to the plan's maturity.

Generally, a refund of premiums is terminology used to define assets from an unmatured RRSP resulting from the death of the RRSP annuitant and which are paid to a qualified beneficiary under specific conditions; qualified beneficiaries fall into three categories:

- The deceased annuitant's spouse or common-law spouse;

- The deceased annuitant's financially dependent child or grandchild; or

- The deceased annuitant's financially dependent child or grandchild who is mentally or physically disabled.

Spousal RRSP

Criteria

A spousal RRSP is one where a taxpayer may make eligible contributions to an RRSP that is held in her spouse/common-law partner's name. The taxpayer's spouse/common-law partner is the plan owner/annuitant, whereas the taxpayer is the plan's contributor and is often referred to as the contributing spouse.

Attribution

The CRA created *attribution rules* to prevent income splitting tax advantage abuse; this is also known as the *three year rule* or *current plus two year rule*.

Attribution rules are intended to discourage the use of spousal RRSPs for short-term income splitting and encourage the use of spousal RRSPs to accumulate assets for the purpose of providing retirement income. If a spouse withdraws funds from a spousal RRSP within three years of a contribution, the income is attributed back to the contributing spouse.

Contributing Spouse Over Age 71

A taxpayer can contribute to a spousal RRSP up to the end of the year in which her spouse or common-law partner reaches age 71, provided the contributing spouse has RRSP room.

Contributions after the Death of a Spouse

A taxpayer's legal representative can make contributions to a spousal RRSP on behalf of a deceased taxpayer in the year of the taxpayer's death or within 60 days after the end of the taxation year in which the taxpayer dies. Contributions cannot be made to a deceased taxpayer's RRSP after her death, but contributions to the spousal RRSP are permitted.

HOME BUYERS' PLAN

Initially introduced in 1992 as a temporary incentive program, the Home Buyers' Plan (HBP) became permanent in 1994.

The HBP is established as a program that effectively allows an individual to lend herself funds from her RRSP, free of tax, for the purpose of buying or building a qualifying home. HBP funds may be withdrawn from a spousal RRSP, but not a locked-in RRSP.

The annuitant of an RRSP may withdraw up to a cumulative maximum of $25,000 from one or more of her RRSPs to finance the purchase of a qualified home. Withdrawals from locked in RRSPs are not eligible.

Conditions for participating in the HBP

Situation 1 – You buy or build a qualifying home for yourself.
Situation 2 – You, a disabled person, buy or build a qualifying home for yourself.
Situation 3 – You buy or build a qualifying home for a related disabled person.
Situation 4 – You help a related disabled person buy or build a qualifying home.

Situation	1	2	3		4	
Person responsible for meeting the HBP conditions	You	You	You	Related disabled person	You	Related disabled person
Conditions you have to meet before applying to withdraw funds under the HBP						
You have to enter into a written agreement to buy or build a qualifying home.	✔	✔	✔	N/A	N/A	✔
You have to intend to occupy the qualifying home as your principal place of residence.	✔	✔	N/A	✔	N/A	✔
You have to be considered a first-time home buyer.	✔	N/A	N/A	N/A	N/A	N/A
Your HBP balance on January 1 of the year of withdrawal has to be zero.	✔	✔	✔	N/A	✔	N/A
Conditions you have to meet when a withdrawal is made						
Neither you nor your spouse can own the qualifying home more than 30 days before a withdrawal is made.	✔	✔	✔	N/A	N/A	✔
You have to be a resident of Canada.	✔	✔	✔	N/A	✔	N/A
You have to complete Form T1036.	✔	✔	✔	N/A	✔	N/A
You have to receive all withdrawals in the same year.	✔	✔	✔	N/A	✔	N/A
You cannot withdraw more than $25,000.	✔	✔	✔	N/A	✔	N/A
Condition you have to meet after all your withdrawals have been made						
You have to buy or build the qualifying home before October 1 of the year after the year of withdrawal.	✔	✔	✔	N/A	N/A	✔

Source: CRA, Home Buyers' Plan (HBP) Guide, RC4135.

Eligibility

To participate in the HBP, **ONE** of the following conditions must apply:

- You are withdrawing funds to buy or build a home for yourself as a first-time home buyer. You are **not** considered a first-time home buyer if you or your spouse or common-law partner owned a home that you occupied as your principal place of residence during the period beginning January 1 of the fourth year before the year of withdrawal and ending 31 days before your withdrawal.

or

- You are withdrawing funds to buy or build a home for a related person with a disability.

In addition, **ALL** of the following conditions must apply:

- You must enter into a written agreement (offer of purchase) to buy or build a qualifying home. The agreement may be with a builder or contractor, or with a realtor or private seller. Obtaining a pre-approved mortgage does not satisfy this condition.

- You intend to occupy the qualifying home as your principal place of residence.

- Your repayable HBP balance on January 1 of the year of the withdrawal is zero.

- Neither you nor your spouse or common-law partner owns the qualifying home more than 30 days before the withdrawal.

- You are a resident of Canada.

- You buy or build the qualifying home before October 1 of the year after the year of withdrawal.

Disabled Person's Assistance

Beginning in 1999, the HBP program was extended to provide assistance for disabled persons. An RRSP annuitant is permitted to withdraw funds for the purchase of a qualifying home for a disabled person, who may be the annuitant or who is related to the annuitant. *Related to* refers to an individual who is related to the annuitant by blood, marriage, or adoption.

The term "disabled" refers to an individual:

- Who is entitled to claim the disability amount on line 316 of the disabled individual's tax return for the year prior to the HBP withdrawal, and who continues to meet this criteria at the time of the withdrawal; or

- If the disabled person does not qualify for the disability amount on line 316 in any year prior to the HBP withdrawal, Form T2201, "Disability Tax Credit Certificate", may be certified by a medical practitioner and submitted for consideration.

Qualifying Home

The Act defines a *qualifying home* in section 146.01(1) as:

- A housing unit located in Canada; or

- A share of the capital stock of a cooperative housing corporation, the holder of which is entitled to possession of a housing unit located in Canada.

Single-family homes, semi-detached structures, apartment buildings (including duplexes and triplexes), condominium units, and mobile homes all qualify.

Withdrawals

Every time a taxpayer makes an eligible withdrawal under the HBP, she must complete the Home Buyers' Plan Form T1036, "Request to Withdraw Funds from an RRSP".

The maximum amount of all withdrawals from an RRSP under the HBP is $25,000 per taxpayer; where both spouses are eligible to participate in the HBP, each spouse may withdraw up to $25,000 for a combined total of $50,000.

Restriction on RRSP Deduction

A taxpayer's RRSP deduction limits will not be affected by participation in the HBP, provided the taxpayer does not:

- Contribute to her RRSP within 90 days prior to the HBP withdrawal; and

- Contribute to a spousal RRSP within 90 days prior to the spouse's HBP withdrawal.

Deduction for contributions made to an RRSP during the 90-day period prior to a withdrawal could be limited based on the FMV of the plan 90 days prior to the withdrawal, and the amount of the withdrawal.

HBP withdrawals do not affect the RRSP deduction except for the 90-day rule outlined above.

Repayment of Withdrawals

Schedule and Calculation

The HBP is established as a loan from an RRSP and, as such, a taxpayer who participates in the HBP has a 15-year period during which she must repay the RRSP amount.

The repayment period begins the **second** calendar year following the year in which the taxpayer made the withdrawal.

Designating a Repayment

To make a repayment, the taxpayer must make an RRSP contribution during the applicable repayment period and then must file a Schedule 7, "RRSP Unused Contributions, Transfers, and HBP or LLP Activities", as part of her Income Tax Return.

HBP Balance

When an HBP withdrawal is made from an RRSP, it creates an HBP balance. The balance at any time is:

- The total of all eligible HBP withdrawals made by the taxpayer

minus

- The total of all amounts designated as an HBP repayment

minus

- The total of all amounts included in the taxpayer's income because the required repayment was not made

Shortened Repayment Period

In the following situations, the repayment period may be shorter than 15 years:

- the HBP participant dies;
- the HBP participant becomes a non-resident; or
- the HBP participant is 72 years of age or over.

Cancelling Participation

A taxpayer can cancel her participation in the HBP if she meets all of the conditions required for participation, except that:

- She did not buy or build a qualifying home or replacement property; or
- She became a non-resident before buying or building a qualifying home or a replacement property.

A taxpayer who gave the HBP funds withdrawn to a related disabled person to acquire a home may cancel her participation in the HBP if she meets all of the conditions required for participation, except that:

- The disabled person did not buy or build a qualifying home or replacement property; or
- the disabled person became a non-resident before buying or building a qualifying home or a replacement property.

LIFELONG LEARNING PLAN

In 1999, the federal government introduced the *Lifelong Learning Plan* (LLP), which utilizes funds from within the RRSP as a loan to finance the annuitant's or the annuitant's spouse's education. It was established to effectively allow an individual to lend herself funds from her RRSP, free of tax, for the purpose of education. A taxpayer cannot use RRSP funds to finance her children's training or education.

Withdrawals from a locked-in plan are not permitted and, therefore, a locked-in RRSP is not an eligible source of funds for a LLP.

There is no limit to the number of times a taxpayer can participate in the program. Starting the year after the LLP balance is zero, she can participate again.

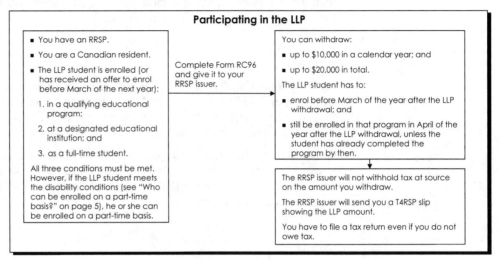

Participating in the LLP

- You have an RRSP.
- You are a Canadian resident.
- The LLP student is enrolled (or has received an offer to enrol before March of the next year):
  1. in a qualifying educational program;
  2. at a designated educational institution; and
  3. as a full-time student.

All three conditions must be met. However, if the LLP student meets the disability conditions (see "Who can be enrolled on a part-time basis?" on page 5), he or she can be enrolled on a part-time basis.

Complete Form RC96 and give it to your RRSP issuer.

You can withdraw:
- up to $10,000 in a calendar year; and
- up to $20,000 in total.

The LLP student has to:
- enrol before March of the year after the LLP withdrawal; and
- still be enrolled in that program in April of the year after the LLP withdrawal, unless the student has already completed the program by then.

The RRSP issuer will not withhold tax at source on the amount you withdraw.

The RRSP issuer will send you a T4RSP slip showing the LLP amount.

You have to file a tax return even if you do not owe tax.

Source: CRA, Lifelong Learning Plan Guide, RC4112.

Eligibility

Roles

Under the LLP program, there are two important roles:

- **LLP Participant.** The individual who withdraws funds from her RRSP under the LLP; and
- **LLP Student.** The individual whose education is being financed using the LLP.

A LLP student can be either the LLP participant herself or her spouse, but not the LLP participant's child.

Qualifying Educational Program

A *qualifying educational program* is an educational program that lasts three consecutive months or more, and all of the following conditions must apply:

- The student must be a full-time student (or a part-time student if she meets the disability conditions);
- The RRSP owner must be a resident of Canada;
- The student must enroll in a qualifying education program at a designated institution;
- Participation in the LLP must be done before the end of the year the student reaches 71 years old;
- The program must last three consecutive months or more; and
- The student spends at least 10 hours per week on courses or work in the program. Courses or work includes lectures, practical training or laboratory work as well as research time spent on a post-graduate thesis. It does not include study time.

Withdrawals

Use of the Funds

When all qualifying conditions have been met, there are no restrictions as to how the funds withdrawn under the LLP can be used.

Amounts

Under the *annual LLP limit*, the LLP participant may withdraw up to $10,000 in a single year from her RRSP. Any withdrawal in a single year that exceeds the annual LLP limit will create an excess (amount withdrawn less annual LLP limit), which is treated as income to the LLP participant in the year the funds are withdrawn.

The amount can be withdrawn from the RRSP until the January of the fourth year after the year of the first withdrawal, assuming the student continues to meet the LLP conditions. The maximum amount that can be withdrawn is $20,000. The RRSP issuer will not withhold tax on withdrawals.

Process

The individual needs to complete Form RC96, "Request to Withdraw Funds From an RRSP".

Restrictions on RRSP Deductions

A taxpayer's contributions to her RRSP are not affected after making a LLP withdrawal. However, deductions for contributions made to an RRSP during the 90-day period prior to a withdrawal could be limited.

Repayment of Withdrawals

The *repayment period* constitutes the 10-year period beginning no later than 60 days following the fifth year after the year in which the individual first received the funds.

Should the student fail to qualify for a full-time education credit for at least three months in two consecutive years that end before the fifth year, repayment is required to start within 60 days following the second of those years.

Repayment Schedule

- The fifth year after the first LLP withdrawal; or
- The first year after the last year in which the LLP student met the LLP qualifying conditions.

Any amount not repaid for a year as required is included in the recipient's income for the year.

LLP Balance

When a LLP withdrawal is made from an RRSP, it creates a LLP balance. The balance at any time is:

- The total of all eligible LLP withdrawals made by the taxpayer *minus*

- The total of all amounts designated as a LLP repayment

minus

- The total of all amounts included in the taxpayers' income because the required repayment was not made

Shortened Repayment Period

In the following situations, the repayment period may be shorter than 10 years:

- The LLP participant dies;
- The LLP participant becomes a non-resident; or
- The LLP participant is 70 years of age or over.

Cancelling Participation

A LLP participant can cancel her participation in the LLP if:

- The LLP student was not enrolled in the program when the withdrawal was made and does not subsequently enroll;
- The LLP student leaves the program before April of the year after the withdrawal, and 75% or more of the student's tuition is refundable; or
- The LLP participant becomes non-resident after the year in which a LLP withdrawal was made.

405. REGISTERED EDUCATION SAVINGS PLANS (RESPS)

Cost of Education

Tuition fees in Canada have increased dramatically due to higher costs and the growth of privatization. Bursaries, scholarships, student loans, and summer employment are a few of the ways to obtain needed financial support. Education costs are often categorized into three main areas: tuition, textbooks, and living expenses.

All expenses should be multiplied by the number of years associated with a program of study to get a full picture of the total costs.

Student Loans

Student loan programs through the federal and provincial governments are normally available to students who demonstrate a financial need. These programs typically involve an expectation that parents have a role to play in the cost of educating a child.

Some students find they do not qualify for student loans; others discover that loans are insufficient to cover actual expenses.

Recently, student loans are being viewed as a last resort because of the financial burden of repayment that looms into the future.

Income Tax

A non-refundable tax credit for interest paid on student loans during a taxation year is available to students or former students who are in the repayment phase of a loan. Only the interest portion of any payment is deductible, not the principal amount.

Other types of common income tax considerations for students:

Deductions

- Moving expenses

- Child care expenses

Non-Refundable Tax Credits

- Interest paid on student loans

- Tuition and education amounts

Introduction to RESPs

A registered education savings plan (RESP) is an educational savings program (ESP) registered with the CRA, and designed specifically to assist with saving for a child's post-secondary education.

The rules for RESP contracts have evolved over the years, and the government often permits existing plans to be administered on a "grandfathered" basis.

A RESP involves three key roles:

- **Subscriber.** The person who opens and makes contributions to the RESP; has authority to name beneficiary(ies).

- **Promoter.** The company that holds and manages the RESP, and receives contributions from the subscriber.

- **Plan Beneficiary.** The person who will benefit from the RESP.

Under the 2007 federal Budget, the $4,000 annual RESP contribution limit was eliminated, and the lifetime RESP contribution limit increased to $50,000 (from $42,000). If there is unused grant room because of contributions of less than the maximum in previous years, the maximum CESG for a year increased to $1,000 from $800. The lifetime CESG limit per child remains at $7,200.

Previously, students who pursued their post-secondary education on a part-time basis were not eligible to draw EAPs from their RESPs, because the RESP rules required that at least 10 hours per week be spent on courses or work. The 2007 federal budget relaxed the EAP requirement to accommodate qualifying part-time programs that do not meet the 10 hours per week requirement. Specifically, the government set a 12-hour per month requirement.

Types of Plans

There are three different types of RESP plans. These are:

- **Individual (Non-Family) Plan.** A plan where there is a single beneficiary under the plan.

- **Family Plan.** Involves more than one beneficiary, where each beneficiary is related by blood or adoption to each living subscriber under the plan, or to the deceased original subscriber.

- **Group Plan.** Typically available through a non-taxable entity such as a foundation, and is administered on an age-group basis.

Roles

Subscriber

The general criteria is no residency requirement, does need a Canadian social insurance number, and no age limit, but may need to be over 16 due to contract laws.

- **Joint Subscribers.** An individual and her spouse if they met the definition of "spouse" when the plan was established.
- **Changing Subscribers.** Can be done due to a relationship breakdown or death. The new subscriber is considered to have made all contributions into the plan, and tax issues due to excess contributions after 1997 are attributed to the new subscriber.

With multiple plans there is no limit to the number of plans a subscriber may establish, while with employer-sponsored plans, contributions are a taxable benefit to the subscriber.

Promoter

The organization with which a subscriber holds a RESP contract is referred to as the plan *promoter*, and is typically the company that holds and manages the RESP, and to whom the subscriber pays the RESP contributions.

Beneficiary

With multiple plans there can be a beneficiary under several RESPs, but annual and lifetime maximum contribution limits ($50,000) apply to each beneficiary.

The terms *blood relationship* and *adopted* applies to parents, children, grandchildren, and great-grandchildren, but does not extend to nieces, nephews, aunts, or uncles.

Contributions

Tax Implications

Contributions into a RESP plan are not tax deductible from the subscriber's income, but investment income is permitted to compound on a tax-sheltered basis.

Limits

RESP contributions are subject to a lifetime contribution limit that is applied at a beneficiary level. For each beneficiary, the lifetime limit is $50,000.

Contributions to a non-family plan can be made up to and including the 22nd year of the plan's existence, while contributions to a family plan cannot be made after the year in which the beneficiary reaches age 21.

Overcontributions

Overcontributions occur when total contributions made by all subscribers into all RESPs on behalf of a single beneficiary exceed the lifetime limit. The penalty is 1% per month of overcontribution at the end of each month, and tax on the overpayment is due no later than 90 days after the end of the taxation year.

Trustee Fees and Insurance Premiums

Payment for any insurance premium or trustee fees outside of the RESP does not affect contributions made into the plan. However, if any fees are charged within the plan and deducted from contributions made, the fees are considered contributions into the plan.

Transferring a RESP

When the assets of a RESP are transferred from one plan to another under the following conditions, there are no income tax implications if:

- The beneficiary under the transferring and receiving RESP is the same; or

- The beneficiary under the transferring RESP is a sister or brother of the beneficiary of the receiving RESP and the receiving beneficiary is less than age 21 when the transfer is made.

In any other transfer situation, the calculation of the lifetime maximum may result in an overcontribution situation

Qualified Investments

All property acquired by a RESP trust before October 28, 1998, is considered to be a qualified investment. Property acquired after October 27, 1998 must meet the criteria established for qualified RESP investments, which is specifically defined in the Act.

Examples of a few of the more common qualified investments for RESPs:

- Cash deposits and guaranteed investment certificate (GICs);

- Shares of a corporation listed on a prescribed stock exchange in Canada or in a foreign country;

- Units in mutual fund trusts; and

- Segregated funds.

Payments from a RESP

While the intention of a RESP is to help fund the beneficiary's cost of education, there are four types of payments that can be made from a RESP:

- Payment of contributions to the subscriber or beneficiary;

- Educational assistance payments (EAPs);

- Accumulated income payments (AIPs); and

- Payments to a designated educational institution in Canada.

Education Assistance Payments

Payment from a RESP of accumulated income from the RESP or Canada Education Savings Grant (CESG) amounts to a beneficiary under prescribed conditions. The beneficiary must be enrolled as a full-time or part-time student (or if full-time enrollment is not possible due to mental or physical impairment be enrolled as a student) in a qualifying education program (i.e., 10 hours or more per week for 3 weeks) at a post-secondary educational institution. The student can earn income from part-time work, but if the student is receiving income and the program of study is part of the student's employment, then the program is not considered as a qualifying program.

The maximum amount that can be paid to an individual before she has completed 13 consecutive weeks in a qualifying program is $5,000.

The *education assistance payment* (EAP) is taxable income to the receiving beneficiary.

Accumulated Income Payments

AIPs are an amount of income earned from the RESP that is paid out under the plan, often to the subscriber due to the RESP not being used by the beneficiary. It does not include earnings on contributions into a plan, earnings on the CESG, refund of payments, EAPs, payments to a school, RESP transfers, or repayment of the CESG.

Conditions:

- Payment made to or for a subscriber who is resident in Canada;
- payment made to one subscriber of the RESP; **and**

Any one of the following conditions must also apply:

- The plan has existed for 10 years and each individual who was a beneficiary has reached the age of 21, and is not currently eligible to receive an EAP;
- The plan has existed for 36 years (41 years under a special plan for disabled people); or
- All the beneficiaries under the plan are deceased.

AIP payments result in the plan being terminated by the end of February in the year following the first AIP. Payments are subject to regular income tax, plus an additional 20% (12% in Quebec). May be able to transfer the AIP to an RRSP to reduce taxes due in some cases.

Plan Termination

All funds must be withdrawn from the RESP, and the plan must collapse no later than the last day of the 36th year following the year in which the plan was established.

Assets from the collapsed RESP can be:

- Transferred to another RESP;
- Used to fund an EAP;
- Used to refund the CESG;
- Used to make an AIP; or
- Used to make a payment to a designated educational institution.

RESP Summary

The following provides a summary of RESPs:

- A *non-family RESP* may have only one beneficiary, and there are no restrictions as to who can be the beneficiary under the plan. A *family RESP* can have any number of beneficiaries, but requires that the beneficiaries meet relationship criteria relative to the subscriber.

- A maximum lifetime contribution of up to $50,000 may be made in relationship to any one beneficiary.

- Contributions are not tax deductible.

- Investment earnings accumulate tax-free and are typically paid out to the qualified beneficiary as an EAP

- The plan must be collapsed by the end of the 36th year in which it was established.

- To qualify for EAP payments under a plan, the beneficiary must meet specific qualifying criteria.

- If a beneficiary does not pursue post-secondary education, she may be replaced with a new beneficiary.

- If a beneficiary does not pursue post-secondary education and there is no replacement beneficiary, the contributor may withdraw the earnings under prescribed conditions.

Canada Education Savings Grant

The CESG is a grant paid by Human Resources Development Canada to the RESP trustee for deposit into an account on behalf of a specific beneficiary. Generally it is 20% of RESP contributions, up to a maximum from $500 to $600 on contributions up to $2,500 based on income levels.

The program involves a bonus payment from the federal government, designed as an incentive for Canadians to save for a child's post-secondary education.

Beginning January 1, 1998, each child resident in Canada accumulates CESG contribution room, which continues to accumulate and can be carried forward into the future. The maximum lifetime limit is $7,200.

Amount and Calculation

The CESG rate is increased on the first $500 contributed to a RESP in respect of a beneficiary who is a child under 18 years of age, and the family is receiving the Canada Child Tax Benefit (CCTB).

- 40% ($200) if the child's family has a qualifying net income for the year of $38,832 or less (for 2009); and

- 30% ($150) if the child's family has a qualifying net income for the year in excess of $38,832, but not exceeding $77,664 (for 2009). (*Note:* Limits change each year.)

The qualifying net income of the child's family for a year will generally be the same as the one used to determine eligibility for the CCTB.

Eligibility

A RESP beneficiary is eligible for the CESG up to the end of the calendar year in which she reaches age 17, provided she:

- is a resident of Canada at the time the RESP contribution is made; and

- has a valid social insurance number.

RESP beneficiaries aged 16 and 17 are only eligible for the grant, if:

- A minimum of $2,000 of RESP contributions were made with respect to the beneficiary before the year in which the beneficiary reached age 16; and

- A minimum of $100 annual RESP contributions were made with respect to the beneficiary in any four years prior to the year in which the beneficiary reached age 16.

Payments

When there have been grants from the CESG program paid into a RESP, a portion of each EAP is attributable to CESGs paid into the plan.

Grant Repayments

Repayment of the grant will be required in the following circumstances:

- The plan is collapsed, or registration of the RESP is revoked by the CRA;

- An AIP is made to the subscriber, or a payment is made to a designated educational institution directly;

- A beneficiary is replaced, except under certain circumstances; and

- An ineligible transfer is made from one RESP to another RESP.

406. REGISTERED DISABILITY SAVINGS PLANS

A *registered disability savings plan* (RDSP) helps parents and others save for the long-term financial security of a person with a severe disability. Contributions to RDSPs may be supplemented by a *Canada Disability Savings Grant* (CDSG) and a Canada Disability Savings Bond.

The lifetime contribution limit for an RDSP is $200,000, with no annual limit. Anyone can contribute to the RDSP with the written permission of the plan holder. Contributions are not tax-deductible and are not included in income when paid out of an RDSP. Investment income earned in the plan accumulates tax-free. However, grants, bonds, and investment income earned in the plan are included in the beneficiary's income for tax purposes when paid out of the RDSP.

A CDSG is a supplement that the government of Canada contributes to a RDSP.

Depending on the beneficiary's family income and contribution level, the government may grant up to $3 for every $1 in contributions received by a RDSP in a year, to a maximum of $3,500. The lifetime grant limit is $70,000. A CDSG can be paid into an RDSP on a contribution made to the beneficiary's RDSP by December 31 of the year the beneficiary turns 49 years old.

Beneficiary's Family Income	Grant	Maximum
$77,664* or less		
on the first $500	$3 for every $1 contributed	$1,500
on the next $1,000	$2 for every $1 contributed	$2,000
More than $77,664*		
on the first $1,000	$1 for every $1 contributed	$1,000

* *Note:* The beneficiary family income thresholds are indexed each year to inflation. The income thresholds shown are for 2009.

Canada Disability Savings Bond

A *Canada Disability Savings Bond* (CDSB) helps low-income families save for the long term financial security of an eligible person with a disability. The bond is paid into an RDSP by the Government of Canada, even if no contributions were made to the plan.

A CDSB is paid by the Government of Canada directly into a registered disability savings plan. Depending on the beneficiary's family income, the government may contribute up to $1,000 each year. The lifetime bond limit is $20,000. A CDSB can be paid into an RDSP until the year in which the beneficiary turns 49 years old.

Beneficiary's Family Income	Bond
$21,816* or less (or if the holder is a public institution)	$1,000
Between $21,816* and $38,832*	Part of the $1,000 based on the formula in the *Canada Disability Savings Act*
More than $38,832*	No bond is paid

* Note: The beneficiary family income thresholds are indexed each year to inflation. The income thresholds shown are for 2009.

407. TAX-FREE SAVING ACCOUNTS

The 2008 Budget introduced the *tax-free savings account* (TFSA). Starting January 1, 2009, Canadians aged 18 and older can save up to $5,000 every year in a TFSA. Contributions to a TFSA will not be deductible for income tax purposes, but investment income, including capital gains, earned in a TFSA will not be taxed, even when withdrawn. Unused TFSA contribution room can be carried forward to future years. The taxpayer can withdraw funds from the TFSA at any time for any purpose and the amount withdrawn can be put back in the TFSA at a later date without reducing the contribution room. Neither income earned in a TFSA nor withdrawals will affect the taxpayer's eligibility for federal income-tested benefits and credits, such as the Guaranteed Income Supplement and Canada Child Tax Benefit. Contributions to a spouse's TFSA are allowed and TFSA assets can be transferred to a spouse upon death.

While both the TFSA and RRSP plans offer tax advantages, there are key differences. Contributions to an RRSP are deductible and reduce the taxpayer's income for tax purposes. In contrast, the taxpayer's TFSA savings are not tax deductible. Withdrawals from an RRSP are added to income and taxed at current rates. A taxpayer's TFSA withdrawals and growth within his account is not — they grow tax-free.

Unit 3

Retirement Income

LIFE INCOME FUNDS, LOCKED-IN RETIREMENT INCOME FUNDS, AND PRESCRIBED REGISTERED RETIREMENT INCOME FUNDS

Life income funds and locked-in retirement income funds are retirement plans for locked-in money originating from registered pension plans.

Whether a registered pension plan falls under federal guidelines (*Pension Benefits Standard Act*, (PBSA)) or provincial pension legislation depends on the province of employment of the individual or the nature of the business establishing the pension. Most pension assets are locked in.

Unlocking Locked-In Funds

Special Circumstances

In some jurisdictions, there are circumstances where the following are applicable:

- Access to a cash payment or series of payments may be possible where the annuitant is certified to have a significantly shortened life expectancy because of a medical disability;
- Access to a lump-sum cash payment may be possible where the total value of the plan assets is quite low, based on specific criteria in the jurisdiction; and
- Access to a lump-sum cash payment for the entire LIRA/locked-in RRSP account balance where the annuitant is no longer a resident of Canada under the Act.

Prescribed RRIF

As of April 1, 2002, the establishment of a prescribed RRIF under Saskatchewan pension legislation increases the options available for some individuals and in many senses "unlocks" pension assets for some individuals.

408. LIFE INCOME FUNDS

A *life income fund* (LIF) is a restricted form of a RRIF designed to hold and distribute locked-in funds, and is subject to all of the rules of the Act that apply to RRIFs.

Establishing a LIF

LIFs can only be established with funds transferred from specific registered plans, which can include:

- Another LIF;
- A registered pension plan (subject to restrictions under the Act, and applicable pension benefits legislation);
- LIRA or locked-in RRSP; or
- Eligible life annuity.

Types of LIFs

Qualifying LIF

A qualifying LIF is one that was purchased before January 1, 1993 to which no property has been transferred after 1992, and to which property has been transferred after 1992 but the transferred property was from another qualifying LIF.

Non-Qualifying LIF

A non-qualifying LIF is one that was established after December 31, 1992, or, a LIF that was originally established prior to 1993 and to which assets have been transferred from a source other than from a qualifying LIF, at some point since the beginning of 1993.

Withdrawals from a LIF

Payments from a LIF are established within a prescribed range of a minimum and maximum amount. Minimum withdrawals must be made from a LIF each year, beginning in the year following its establishment.

Beginning in 1998, some provinces have allowed the use of a younger spouse or common-law partner's age for calculation of minimum payments.

Maximum = V/P, where

- **Maximum** is the maximum payment for the year;
- **V** is the value of the LIF on January 1; and
- **P** is the value of a projected annual pension of $1 beginning on January 1 of the year and continuing for the period ending December 31 of the year in which the annuitant turns age 90.

Investments

Financial institutions must register investment products offered for LIF plans with the CRA and adhere to regulations specified in pension standards legislation.

Asset Transfers

Prior to the Annuitant's Death

Before the annuitant turns 80, LIF assets may be transferred to other plans owned by the annuitant, including:

- LIF;
- LRIF (Alberta, Manitoba, Newfoundland, Saskatchewan, and Ontario);
- LIRA or locked-in RRSP (if age 71 or younger throughout the year of transfer); and
- Life annuity.

Income Tax Implications

Payments. Similar to RRIF, minimum LIF payments do not attract withholding tax. Payments above the minimum are subject to withholding taxes. All LIF payments are fully taxable income in the year the withholding is made.

Death of a LIF Annuitant. The same rules regarding a designated benefit and qualified beneficiaries (spouse, common-law spouse, dependent children and dependent grandchildren) apply to the LIF as described in the RRIF section. If there is a surviving spouse, provincial pension legislation may override the LIF beneficiary designation. If there is no surviving spouse, the assets will be unlocked and paid out to the beneficiary.

Relationship Breakdown

Upon the breakdown of a relationship, assets of the LIF are subject to division in accordance with legislative requirements; spouse's rights to benefits under a LIF account are terminated by separation or divorce.

Conversion to a Life Annuity

In jurisdictions where a LIF annuitant must use the balance in the LIF account to purchase a life annuity prior to the end of the year in which she reaches age 80 (or sooner if chosen), the annuity must adhere to a minimum prescribed plan design.

409. LOCKED-IN RETIREMENT INCOME FUNDS

A LRIF is a restricted form of a RRIF designed to hold and distribute locked-in funds, and is subject to all of the rules of the Act that apply to RRIFs.

Establishing a LRIF

Pension benefits legislation governs the minimum age at which pension benefits may begin, unless a younger age is permitted.

LRIFs can only be established with funds transferred from specific registered plans. Transfers are acceptable from the following registered plans:

- Another LRIF

- A registered pension plan (subject to restrictions under the Act, and applicable pension benefits legislation)

- LIRA or locked-in RRSP

- An eligible annuity

Withdrawals from a LRIF

LRIFs are subject to the same minimum payment rules as RRIFs and LIFs. The maximum payment for each year is equal to the greater of:

- The LRIF minimum prescribed payment;

- Net investment income, which means the total income earned since the plan began less withdrawals for the same period (if funds were transferred into the plan during the prior year, then the net income from the prior year on the other plan is added to this criteria);

- The investment income earned during the immediately preceding fiscal year; or

- For the first two fiscal years, 6% of the market value of the fund at the beginning of each year.

Asset Transfers

With the exception of the minimum payment, the annuitant may transfer LRIF assets to:

- Another LRIF

- A LIRA (provided the annuitant is age 71 or less throughout the year in which the transfer occurs)

- An eligible annuity

Income Tax Implications

Similar to a RRIF, minimum LRIF payments do not attract withholding tax, but all LRIF payments are fully taxable as income to the annuitant in the year the withdrawal is made.

Death of a LRIF Annuitant

The same rules regarding a designated benefit and qualified beneficiaries (spouse, common-law spouse, dependent children, and dependent grandchildren) apply to the LRIF.

Relationship Breakdown

Upon the breakdown of a relationship, the assets of the LIF are subject to division in accordance with legislative requirements; spouses' rights to benefits under a LRIF account are terminated by separation or divorce.

Selection of a LIF, LRIF, or PRRIF

The LIF and LRIF provide for regular income withdrawals within the prescribed limits, but otherwise the capital is inaccessible. This reduces the risk of quick depletion of the capital, but alternatively may create a financial hardship.

Similar to a RRIF, the risk associated with LIF and LRIF investment decisions lies with the plan annuitant.

Plan Comparison

	RRIF	LIF	LRIF	PRRIF
Minimum annual withdrawal	Yes	Yes	Yes	Yes
Maximum annual withdrawal	Yes	Yes	Yes	No
Access to plan assets other than for required annual withdrawals	Completely accessible	Access restricted by locking-in provisions	Access restricted by locking-in provisions	Completely accessible
Governing legislation	*Income Tax Act*	*Income Tax Act* **and** applicable provincial or federal pension benefits legislation	*Income Tax Act* **and** applicable pension benefits legislation	*Income Tax Act* **and** Saskatchewan pension benefits legislation
Spousal consent required to establish plan	No	Yes	Yes	Yes

Locked-In RRSPs and Locked-In Retirement Accounts

The locked-in RRSP was developed in the mid-1980s to provide terminating employees with an option other than leaving pension funds in the pension plan.

The term "locked-in retirement account" was introduced as a new name for a locked-in RRSP where the objective was to make it easier for financial institutions and plan members to distinguish between a locked-in RRSP and a non-locked-in RRSP.

The federal government and the provinces of Alberta, Saskatchewan, Manitoba, Ontario, Quebec, New Brunswick, and Newfoundland have introduced the LIRA, while British Columbia and Nova Scotia continue to refer to their plans as locked-in RRSPs.

Integration With an RRSP

All registered retirement plans, including locked-in plans, are registered under the Act.

A locked-in RRSP and LIRA may:

- Be established as a regular or self-directed plan; and
- Follow similar rules as a regular RRSP for qualified and non-qualified investments.

Establishing a Locked-In RRSP or LIRA

Although transfer options vary by jurisdiction, a locked-in RRSP/LIRA is one of the options to which locked-in pension funds may be transferred from a registered pension plan.

With a LIF and LRIF, minimum and maximum annual limits are imposed on the income taken from the plan.

A locked-in RRSP/LIRA does not allow for the withdrawal of funds under the LLP or the HBP.

Asset Transfers

Assets of a locked-in RRSP/LIRA may be transferred directly to the following types of plans, prior to the end of the year in which the annuitant turns age 71:

- Another locked-in RRSP/LIRA;
- A life annuity purchased through an insurance company;
- A LIF;
- A LRIF, if available within the jurisdiction; or
- A registered pension plan if the plan administrator agrees to administer the funds on a locked-in basis in accordance with pension legislation.

It is important to determine whether locked-in funds are governed by the federal PBSA, or by provincial legislation.

Plan Maturity

A locked-in RRSP/LIRA must mature by the end of the year during which the annuitant reaches age 71.

The types of plans to which locked-in RRSP/LIRA may be transferred at maturity are:

- A LIF; or
- The purchase of a life annuity.

LIRAs have the additional choice of transferring the assets to:

- A LRIF (Alberta, Manitoba, Newfoundland, and Ontario); or
- PRIF (Saskatchewan only).

Death of an Annuitant

A locked-in RRSP and LIRA follow the normal tax provisions associated with regular RRSP plans, including the provisions that prevail in the event of the annuitant's death.

Additionally, pension legislation in some jurisdictions requires that assets from a locked-in RRSP/LIRA must remain locked-in when the annuitant dies and the assets are transferred to a spouse.

If the deceased did not have a spouse at the date of death, generally the locked-in provision is removed.

410. REGISTERED RETIREMENT INCOME FUNDS

RRSPs were introduced in 1957 to encourage Canadians to extend their savings by specifically setting funds aside that would pay for their retirement years, while *registered retirement income funds* (RRIFs) were introduced in 1978 to increase the retirement income options of RRSP owners.

Establishing a RRIF

The establishment of a RRIF begins with the transfer of funds from another registered vehicle. Property can be transferred from:

- An RRSP;
- Another RRIF; and
- A registered pension plan.

The CRA refers to the owner of a RRIF as an "annuitant", and there is no limit to the number of RRIFs an individual may own. Using a RRIF, it is possible to establish a perpetual income from a RRIF over an individual's remaining lifetime or that of her spouse.

Transfer from an RRSP

There are several ways in which the transfer from an RRSP may occur:

- A transfer may occur from a "matured RRSP" to a RRIF where the annuitant of the RRSP is the same as the annuitant of the RRIF, and the payment is a direct transfer of a commutation payment from the RRSP annuity;
- A transfer may occur from an "unmatured RRSP" to a RRIF where the annuitant of the RRSP is the same as the annuitant of the RRIF;
- A transfer may occur from an "unmatured RRSP" to a RRIF where the annuitant of the RRSP is the current or former spouse or common-law partner of the RRIF annuitant; and
- A transfer of assets into a RRIF may occur from a refund of premiums.

Transfer from a RRIF

There are several ways in which the funds can be transferred between RRIF:

- A transfer may occur from one RRIF to another RRIF where the annuitant is the same under each of the two RRIFs;
- A transfer may occur between two RRIFs where the annuitant of the transferring RRIF is the current or former spouse or common-law partner of the receiving RRIF; and
- A transfer of assets into a RRIF may occur from funds labeled as a designated benefit.

Transfer from a RPP

Registered pension plan assets are normally transferred to locked-in registered plans; however, lump-sum amounts may be transferred to a RRIF depending on the provisions of the registered pension plan.

Types of RRIFs

The Act establishes a prescribed schedule of minimum payments that must be made from a RRIF, beginning the year after a RRIF is established. The prescribed schedule of payments from a RRIF is based on two different types of RRIFs: a *qualifying RRIF* and a *non-qualifying RRIF*.

Qualifying RRIF

A *qualifying RRIF* is one that was purchased before January 1, 1993, to which no property has been transferred after 1992; or to which property has been transferred after 1992, but the property is from other RRIF.

Non-Qualifying RRIF

A *non-qualifying RRIF* is one that was established after December 31, 1992.

Minimum Withdrawal Calculation

When a RRIF is first established, the annuitant has the option of electing to have the annual minimum withdrawal calculation based on either her age or the age of her spouse.

The calculation of the minimum withdrawal for a specific year utilizes two key pieces of information:

- The market value of assets in the plan as of January 1 of that year; and

- The age of the annuitant as of January 1 of that year (or the age of the annuitant's spouse or common-law partner if this election was made).

Minimum Payment Calculation for a Qualifying RRIF

If the RRIF annuitant is **under age 79** as of January 1, the minimum payment calculation for that year is:

Minimum payment = (Market value of plan assets on January 1) ÷ (90 - age*)

Note: *Age refers to the age of the annuitant as of January 1 (or the age of the annuitant's spouse or common-law partner if this election was made).

If the RRIF annuitant is **age 79 or older** as of January 1, the minimum payment calculation for that year is:

Minimum payment = (Market value of plan assets on January 1) × (CRA age* factor)

Note: *Age refers to the age of the annuitant as of January 1 (or the age of the annuitant's spouse or common-law partner if this election was made).

Minimum Payment Calculation for a Non-Qualifying RRIF

If the RRIF annuitant is **under age 71** as of January 1, the minimum payment calculation for that year is:

Minimum payment = (Market value of plan assets on January 1) ÷ (90 - age*)

Note: *Age refers to the age of the annuitant as of January 1 (or the age of the annuitant's spouse or common-law partner if this election was made).

If the RRIF annuitant is **age 71 or older** as of January 1, the minimum payment calculation for that year is:

Minimum payment = (Market value of plan assets on January 1) $\times$ (CRA age* factor)

Note: *Age refers to the age of the annuitant as of January 1 (or the age of the annuitant's spouse or common-law partner if this election was made).

Qualifying and Non-Qualifying Plan Issues

A qualifying RRIF has a lower minimum calculation for annual payments for ages 71 through age 77 than a non-qualifying RRIF.

When transferring money from an RRSP to a RRIF or between RRIFs, care should be taken to preserve the status of a qualifying RRIF. When transferring a RRIF between institutions, the relinquishing trustee must state whether the RRIF is a qualifying or non-qualifying RRIF and is required to pay out the remaining minimum amount. If property from a non-qualifying RRIF, or from an RRSP, is transferred to a qualifying RRIF, the RRIF becomes a non-qualifying RRIF where the minimum prescribed payment is re-calculated based on non-qualifying RRIF rules. If property from a qualifying RRIF is moved from one financial institution to another, the plan continues to be classified as a qualifying RRIF for minimum payout calculations.

Withdrawals From a RRIF

Ongoing Withdrawal by Annuitant

Starting in the year after a RRIF is established, minimum withdrawals must be made from a RRIF each year. A withdrawal based on only the minimum amount is not subject to withholding tax.

Frequency

Payments from a RRIF must be regular, and as long as the minimum income requirement is satisfied, an individual may withdraw as much as she wishes from the RRIF at any time. Individuals not relying on RRIF income usually only withdraw the minimum required.

Excess Amounts

Common choices for designing an income flow from the RRIF are minimum income, interest only, and a level income (i.e., $500 per month).

Transferring Assets

When assets of a RRIF are transferred from one RRIF to another, the relinquishing institution must pay out the minimum amount for the year.

Care should be taken in planning for such transfers, with particular attention to the payment schedules associated with the old and new RRIF and the actual amount of assets that will be transferred; while the old institution must complete the minimum payment for that year, the new institution could begin payments, if requested by the annuitant, but the annuitant would have to select a specific dollar amount or percentage because the minimum is not an option.

Spousal RRIF

Criteria

A "spousal RRIF" is established with assets transferred from a spousal RRSP or from another spousal RRIF. The benefit of a spousal RRIF is to potentially reduce income tax payable on retirement income by splitting assets used to provide future income.

Income Attribution

The CRA recognizes that income splitting creates tax advantages and has implemented "attribution rules" to prevent abuse, also known as the "current plus two year" rule.

Attribution may arise when the annuitant withdraws an amount from a spousal RRIF that is in excess of the minimum amount, and is the lesser of: the excess RRIF withdrawal; and contributions made to the spousal RRSP in the current or previous two taxation years that have not already been attributed.

Investments

A financial institution must register with the CRA to sell RRIF plans and must adhere to detailed regulations for the plan's administration. Assets accumulate tax free in an RRSP, and continue to accumulate tax free when transferred to a RRIF.

Similar to a self-directed RRSP, a self-directed RRIF allows the annuitant to hold a variety of qualified investments under one RRIF umbrella.

Qualified Investments

The general rules for RRIF investments are in essence the same as for RRSPs.

The 2005 Budget eliminated the foreign content limit of 30%.

Non-Qualified Investments

The following is a list of possible non-qualified investments:

- Shares of private corporations, where the RRIF annuitant and her or her immediate family hold more than 10% of any class of shares;
- Commodity futures;
- Listed personal property, such as works of art and antiques; and
- Gems and other precious stones.

When a RRIF acquires a non-qualified investment, it results in three consequences:

- The FMV of non-qualified investment at the time of investment is included in the annuitant's income;
- The RRIF trust is subject to a 1% penalty on the FMV of the non-qualified investment; and
- The RRIF trust is subject to income tax on the investment income earned on the non-qualifying investment.

Transfers Out of RRIF

This includes the transfer from a RRIF to a RRIF, or a transfer from a RRIF to an RRSP.

All property from a RRIF cannot be transferred directly to an RRSP, but the excess amount from a RRIF can be transferred, provided that the transfer occurs directly between the plans

Transfer from a RRIF to a Qualified Annuity

All property from a RRIF cannot be transferred directly to a qualified annuity, but the excess amount from a RRIF can be transferred.

Income Tax Implications

Regular RRIF — Payments to Annuitant

All payments out of a regular RRIF are fully taxable as income to the RRIF annuitant.

Minimum payments from the RRIF do not attract withholding tax; however, the payments are fully taxable in the year received and must be included as income for the recipient.

Withholding Tax

Amount Withdrawn	All provinces except Quebec (%)	Quebec[1] (%)
Up to $5,000	10	21
$5,001 – $15,000	20	26
Over $15,001	30	31

Note: (1) For 2006 and later.

Spousal RRIF — Payments

Spousal RRIF — Tax Liability for Income Payments

			Tax liability for income received from the spousal RRIF lies with:	
			Annuitant (non-contributing spouse)	Annuitant's Spouse (contributing spouse)
If no contributions have been made by the annuitant's spouse to any spousal RRSP in current or previous two years:			X	
If contributions have been made by the annuitant's spouse to any spousal RRSP in current or previous two years:	Annuitant withdraws only the minimum income required from the plan		X	
	Annuitant withdraws more income than the minimum required from the plan	(a) Minimum amount	X	
		(b) Excess amount		Subject to attribution rules

Pension Income Tax Credit

Payments from a RRIF qualify as eligible pension income for the pension income tax credit.

Death of the RRIF Annuitant

General Terms

Upon the death of the annuitant, if the assets of the RRIF pass to someone other than a spouse/common-law partner or a qualified child or grandchild, the FMV of the plan's assets, immediately before death, must be included in the annuitant's income for the year of death.

Designated Benefit

A *designated benefit* is defined as any amount paid out of a RRIF to the spouse or common-law partner of the deceased annuitant, or an amount paid to a financially dependent (or disabled) child or grandchild of the deceased annuitant.

General Summary — Designated Benefit

Designated Benefit Distribution

Designated benefit paid to:		Designated benefit may be transferred to:		
		RRSP(1)	RRIF	Annuity
Surviving spouse or common-law partner		X	X	X
Annuitant's financially dependent child or grandchild	dependent because of physical or mental infirmity	X	X	X
	dependent but not because of physical or mental infirmity			X(2)

(1) The qualified beneficiary must be younger than age 72 at the end of the year the transfer is made (to be eligible to make contributions to an RRSP).

(2) The annuity may provide payments based on a period of not more than 18 years minus the child or grandchild's age at the time the annuity is purchased. The payments from the annuity must begin no later than one year after the purchase.

Beneficiary Designation

There are two types of beneficiary designations: revocable and irrevocable. A *revocable beneficiary* designation may be changed by the owner of the plan at any time, and allows the owner to make any desired changes to the plan. An *irrevocable designation* prevents the owner of the plan from changing the beneficiary designation without the consent of the irrevocable beneficiary.

Individuals should seek professional advice to assess the effectiveness of a beneficiary designation under the laws applicable in their province.

Relationship Breakdown

Transfers to or from a RRIF may occur as the result of a relationship breakdown.

**Relationship Breakdown
Rollover Summary**

Situation	Type of Plan			
	RRSP	RRIF	RPP	Annuity
Transfer **from a RRIF to:**	X	X		
Transferred **to a RRIF from:**	X	X	X	

CCRS form *T2220, Transfer from an RRSP or a RRIF to Another RRSP or RRIF on Marriage Breakdown,* is used to request transfers from one registered plan to another upon breakdown of a relationship.

Selection of a RRIF

The selection of a RRIF as a retirement income vehicle brings with it considerations that must be carefully analyzed relative to the facts of a retiree's particular situation.

RRIF Payout Scenarios

	Scenario A	Scenario B	Scenario C	Scenario D
PV ($)	200,000	200,000	200,000	200,000
PMT ($)	1,500	1,500	2,000	1,166.67
I (%)	5	7	5	5
xP/YR	193.78 months or 16.15 year	255.14 months or 21.26 years	128.92 months or 10.74 years	298.81 months or 24.9 years

For simplicity, the calculations disregard minimum RRIF payments. However, the amounts shown above were in excess of the minimum amount at the starting point.

411. ANNUITIES

An annuity is the simplest retirement income option. In exchange for a sum of money, a financial institution will provide a series of regular payments for a period of time, like a mortgage payment in reverse.

In simple terms, there are two types of annuities:

1. **Life Annuities.** These guarantee a series of payments for an individual's lifetime (sometimes referred to as the measuring life).

2. **Term Certain Annuities.** These guarantee a series of payments for a defined period of time.

Registered Annuities

A *registered annuity* is purchased with assets from a plan that contains registered money, including a:

- RRSP

- LIRA or Locked-in RRSP
- DPSP
- Registered pension plan
- RRIF, LIF, LRIF, or PRRIF
- Refund of premiums
- Designated benefit

All registered annuities must be immediate annuities and must be designed to provide for a full year of payments in the year following purchase.

Non-Registered Annuities

A *non-registered annuity* is an annuity that is purchased with assets that are not from a registered plan. The funds used to purchase the annuity are regular savings, and are considered to be after-tax dollars because tax has already been paid on the savings.

The distinction between a registered and non-registered annuity is very important because the taxation differs. With a non-registered annuity, the plan owner and the annuitant do not always have to be the same person.

Income Tax Implications

Registered Annuities

Payments from a registered annuity are fully taxable to the recipient in the year that the payment is received.

Non-Registered Annuities

There is no tax sheltering associated with the accumulation of the funds used to purchase the annuity.

Non-Prescribed Taxation

With a non-prescribed annuity, the interest portion of the annuity is much higher in the early years of the annuity, and because tax is based on the interest component only, normal taxation is subsequently higher in the early years of the annuity.

Prescribed Taxation

To address the unattractive front-end tax situation inherent with non-registered annuities, in 1981, the federal government offered a new tax treatment whereby annuitants could opt to have the annuity treated as prescribed. With a prescribed annuity, less tax is paid in the early years of the contract than what would normally be paid based on the actual interest earnings of the annuity; a prescribed annuity reports a level amount of interest over the entire length of the annuity, resulting in:

- Tax deferral
- Lower tax in early years and higher tax in later years than would otherwise occur
- Level after-tax income
- Enhanced after-tax income

Calculating Capital and Interest Elements

- *Step One:* Capital Element
- *Step Two:* Number of Annuity Payments
- *Step Three:* Capital Proportion of Each Payment
- *Step Four:* Capital Element of Each Payment

Other Tax Issues

Non-registered annuity payments received after the age of 65 qualify for the pension amount federal tax credit. There are also special circumstances where non-registered annuity payments qualify for the pension amount federal tax credit for individuals under age 65.

Features of Annuities

The concept of an annuity is built on a series of payments, and the type of funds used to purchase the annuity determines if the annuity is a registered or non-registered annuity.

Immediate versus Deferred Annuity

- **Immediate Annuity.** One where the payments begin any time within one year of purchase.
- **Deferred Annuity.** Where the annuity payments are scheduled to begin at some date later than one year in the future.

Term of the Annuity

The term of the annuity is the period during which the payments will be made.

Term Certain Annuity

Term certain annuities provide guaranteed income for a specified period of time, chosen at the time of purchase. Once the last contractual payment is made, the annuity terminates.

Life Annuities

The different types of life annuities include:

- Straight life annuity
- Joint life annuity
- Life annuity with guarantee periods
  - Single life
  - Joint life

Indexed Annuity

An indexed annuity provides for an annual increase to the regular payment schedule, as selected by the annuitant at the time of purchase, up to a maximum percentage. The addition of indexation to an annuity is a very costly feature because the financial institution is providing a guarantee that the annual payment amount will increase steadily over the period of the annuity contract.

Temporary Annuities

These provide payments for a specified period, provided that the client remains alive.

Impaired Annuities

An *impaired annuity* is designed to pay a higher income amount than a regular annuity to an annuitant who has been diagnosed with an illness or disability that may reduce her life expectancy. Examples of illnesses that may reduce an individual's life expectancy and, therefore, would generally be considered in the evaluation of an impaired annuity, include:

- Cancer
- Diabetes
- Stroke
- Parkinson's
- Alzheimer's
- Chronic heart disease
- Severe hypertension
- Multiple sclerosis
- Congestive cardiac failure
- Renal, liver, or respiratory failure

Fixed versus Variable Annuity

- **Fixed Annuity.** The most common type of annuity, this provides a guaranteed amount of payment throughout the term of the annuity.
- **Variable Annuity.** Where the investment risk is shifted to the annuitant, similar to a RRIF.

Death

The surviving spouse receives the periodic payments if:

- The annuitant had purchased a life annuity with a guaranteed period that was not exhausted before death, and the surviving spouse elects to continue to receive these payments, rather than accept the commuted value of the RRSP; and
- The annuitant had purchased a term-certain annuity to age 90 and the term was not exhausted before death, and the surviving spouse elects to continue to receive these payments.

Selection of an Annuity

While the variety of annuity features available allows for flexibility, there is a cost associated with each feature, as well as risk. For example, with a life annuity, the retiree may die prior to her life expectancy and all payments would cease.

It is important to consider the features of an annuity relative to the retiree's specific situation.

Unit 4
Self-Test Questions

QUESTIONS

Question 1

Andy joined her employer's defined contribution pension plan on January 1, 2007, when she was first eligible. The plan, which had a two-year vesting schedule, required employee and employer contributions. Andy terminated employment with her employer on June 30, 2009. During the time that she participated in the company pension plan, Andy contributed $3,750 while her employer also contributed $3,750 on Andy's behalf. Which of the following statements is true with regard to Andy's financial entitlement upon termination from the plan?

    a. Andy is entitled to $7,500, the sum of her and the employer's contributions.

    b. Andy is entitled to the return of her $3,750 of contributions plus interest, as well as $2,812.50 in employer contributions.

    c. Andy's only entitlement is the current value of her $3,750 of contributions.

    d. Andy's termination prior to the end of the vesting period results in the loss of her and her employer's contributions.

Question 2

At the end of 2009, Bill is retiring after 30 years of participation in her employer's pension plan. The pension plan provides a benefit based on 1.8% of her best earnings over four consecutive years. Bill's career has progressed steadily with his promotion six years ago having caused a substantial jump in his earnings. Given the following earnings history, calculate Bill's annual pension.

Year	Amount
2004	$60,000
2005	$65,000
2006	$70,000
2007	$75,000
2008	$71,000
2009	$60,000

    a. $32,400

    b. $37,260

    c. $37,935

    d. $42,150

Question 3

With regard to contributions into a defined benefit pension plan, which of the following statements is/are true?

1. The employer's contribution amount is calculated as a percentage of the plan member's earnings.

2. The employer is responsible for the plan's solvency.

3. Employer contributions into the plan are a tax deductible business expense, if the contribution calculation adheres to CRA's prescribed guidelines.

4. Any shortfall in funding for the pension plan is the employer's responsibility.

     a. 1 and 4 only

     b. 1 only

     c. 2 and 3 only

     d. 2, 3 and 4 only

Question 4

When a pension jurisdiction requires that the pension benefit incorporate a "joint and survivor" form of pension, which of the following statements is/are true?

1. The intention is to have the actual pension benefit amount based on the combined life expectancies of the member and the member's spouse.

2. In most jurisdictions, the only action required for a plan member to opt out of this provision is to personally sign a pre-printed form in which she personally declines the provision.

3. A pension that incorporates a joint and survivor form of pension will provide a member with a higher benefit amount than when the pension is based on the member's life only (assuming all other features and guarantees are the same).

4. If a member pre-deceases her spouse and her pension incorporates a joint and survivor form of benefit, a predetermined percentage of the member's pension will continue to be paid to the surviving spouse for her remaining lifetime.

5. By electing a joint and survivor form of pension, the plan member is able to income split with her spouse by sharing her monthly pension income during the member's lifetime.

     a. 1 and 4 only

     b. 2 and 5 only

     c. 3 only

     d. 3, 4 and 5 only

Question 5

Danny is retiring this month and needs to make a decision regarding the features and design of her retirement benefit. Danny knows she wants to elect a joint and survivor form of pension but she is not sure if she wants a 70% survivor benefit or a 100% survivor benefit and what guarantee period, if any. With regard to Danny's decision, which of the following statements are true?

1. If Danny opts for the 100% survivor benefit, her pension income will be lower than if she opts for the 70% survivor benefit.

2. If Danny opts for the 100% survivor benefit, her pension income will be higher than if she opts for the 70% survivor benefit.

3. If Danny opts for a guarantee period on her pension benefit, her income will be lower than if she opts for no guarantee period.

4. If Danny opts for a guarantee period on her pension benefit, her income will be higher than if she opts for no guarantee period.

    a. 1 and 3 only

    b. 1 and 4 only

    c. 2 and 3 only

    d. 2 and 4 only

Question 6

Frank, the owner of Smart Stop Inc., would like to establish an IPP for himself. Frank established Smart Stop Inc. twelve years ago, at age thirty-nine. With an annual T4 income that exceeds $200,000, Frank has consistently earned substantial income from Smart Stop and sees continued growth in her regular earnings. Which of the following items is not permitted in the design of Frank's IPP?

    a. Contributions will be based on the maximum pensionable earnings permitted under a defined benefit plan.

    b. The NRA will be set as age 65.

    c. The benefit formula will be structured on a best earnings approach.

    d. The plan will be established as a non-contributory pension plan.

Question 7

Fanny is the owner of a long-established manufacturing business. Which of the following are important issues that she should consider when comparing an IPP to an RRSP?

1. The company assumes responsibility for the investment decisions associated with the IPP and must ensure that it remains solvent, whereas investment performance in an RRSP does not create any financial responsibility for the company.

2. If the company establishes an IPP, it has a legal obligation to make required annual contributions, whereas there is no legislated contribution requirement for an RRSP.

3. Once established, Fanny cannot easily access the funds in an IPP if an important need or emergency arises, whereas she could in an RRSP.

4. The contribution formula for an RRSP can incorporate an indexation feature that increases the amount of tax-deductible contributions a company can make into an RRSP, whereas this is not possible for an IPP.

     a. 1 and 4 only

     b. 1, 2 and 3 only

     c. 2 and 3 only

     d. 4 only

Question 8

When comparing a defined benefit pension plan and a defined contribution pension plan, which of the following statements is/are true?

1. A defined contribution plan allows an employer to readily predict pension costs, whereas this is a more complex task for a defined benefit plan.

2. A defined contribution plan is more complex to administer than a defined benefit plan.

3. Employees typically participate in the investment decisions associated with a defined contribution plan, but not with a defined benefit plan.

4. An employee's retirement pension is directly dependent upon the investment performance of a defined contribution plan, but this is not the case with a defined benefit plan.

     a. 1 and 4 only

     b. 1, 3 and 4 only

     c. 2 and 3 only

     d. 2 only

Question 9

Ina, a single woman, joined Mastertech Inc.'s defined contribution pension plan on January 1, 1979. On December 31, 2009, Ina plans to retire and expects that her pension accumulation will be valued at $243,750. If Ina uses the assets to purchase a single life annuity that begins immediately with payments at the beginning of each month, what monthly income will the pension assets purchase? Assume an annual nominal return of 6%, compounded monthly, and a life expectancy of 30 years.

   a. $1,454.13

   b. $1,461.40

   c. $1,562.67

   d. $1,570.48

Question 10

When an amendment is made to a pension plan, which of the following statements is/are typically true?

1. Amendments must be registered with CRA.

2. Amendments must be registered with the appropriate jurisdiction before any change becomes effective.

3. Amendments may not reduce a plan member's benefits earned to date.

4. Amendments may not reduce a plan member's benefits to be earned in the future.

5. In most jurisdictions, plan members are entitled to notice when a plan amendment may adversely affect the members' rights.

   a. 1 and 5 only

   b. 1, 2, 3 and 5 only

   c. 2 only

   d. 2, 3 and 4 only

Question 11

Lilly participates in Backspace Inc.'s defined benefit pension plan, which she joined eight years ago. The plan provides benefits of 2% for each year of service, based on the member's best three consecutive years of pensionable earnings. Lilly's best three consecutive years of earnings were the most recent three, with annual pensionable earnings of $43,000, $48,000 and $51,000. If Lilly has eight years of service, calculate the amount of annual pension benefit accrued to date.

   a. $3,786.67

   b. $7,573.33

   c. $8,160.00

   d. $946.00

Question 12

Ruth, a widow, joined her employer's defined contribution pension plan 28 years ago, and is now reaching age 65. Ruth would like to use her pension assets of $167,432 to purchase a life annuity with monthly payments beginning at the end of her first month of retirement. Assuming an annual nominal return of 5%, compounded monthly, and a life expectancy of 25 years, what monthly income will Ruth receive from her current pension assets?

    a. $923.01

    b. $926.86

    c. $974.73

    d. $978.79

Question 13

Tom, age 60, is ready to retire but is unclear as to how much pension his accumulation of assets will purchase. During the past eight years, Tom has accumulated $53,725 in total assets within his employer's defined contribution plan. If Tom purchases a single life annuity with monthly payments at the beginning of each month, what total monthly pension will the assets purchase? Assume a 30-year life expectancy and a 6.1% annual nominal return, compounded monthly.

    a. $323.92

    b. $325.57

    c. $705.64

    d. $708.64

Question 14

Vickie and Victor are discussing the differences between an IPP and an RRSP. Together they have made the following conclusions:

1. If an emergency arises, participants in either type of plan may withdraw funds as needed.

2. Once established, an employer is obligated to make annual contributions in order to maintain the solvency of both plans.

3. An RRSP allows income splitting, whereas an IPP does not.

4. The plan member assumes responsibility for investment risk associated with an RRSP but this is not the case with an IPP.

5. An IPP allows the member to count on a guaranteed level of income, whereas the RRSP provides no guarantee.

From the above list, which of the statements are true?

    a. 1 and 4 only

    b. 1, 2 and 3 only

    c. 2 and 5 only

    d. 3, 4 and 5 only

Question 15

Sandra had $250,000 of pensionable earnings in 2009 at her employer, Maxmoney Inc. She is a member of the defined contribution pension plan at Maxmoney and the plan requires contributions of 5% from her employer and 5% from Sandra as the employee (based on pensionable earnings). Based on the pension plan's contribution formula, what is the maximum dollar amount that may be contributed to the pension plan on Sandra's behalf?

    a. $12,500

    b. $19,000

    c. $22,000

    d. $25,000

QUESTIONS & SOLUTIONS

Question 1

Andy joined her employer's defined contribution pension plan on January 1, 2007, when she was first eligible. The plan, which had a two-year vesting schedule, required employee and employer contributions. Andy terminated employment with her employer on June 30, 2009. During the time that she participated in the company pension plan, Andy contributed $3,750 while her employer also contributed $3,750 on Andy's behalf. Which of the following statements is true with regard to Andy's financial entitlement upon termination from the plan?

    a. Andy is entitled to $7,500, the sum of her and the employer's contributions.

    b. Andy is entitled to the return of her $3,750 of contributions plus interest, as well as $2,812.50 in employer contributions.

    c. Andy's only entitlement is the current value of her $3,750 of contributions.

    d. Andy's termination prior to the end of the vesting period results in the loss of her and her employer's contributions.

Answer: c

⇨ Vesting refers to the employee's irrevocable entitlement to benefits from a pension plan. With the two-year vesting schedule, Andy will become entitled to the employer's contributions or resulting benefits after two years of pensionable service. However, Andy terminated her employment prior to the completion of the two years, so she is only entitled to the current value of her contributions.

Question 2

At the end of 2009, Bill is retiring after 30 years of participation in her employer's pension plan. The pension plan provides a benefit based on 1.8% of her best earnings over four consecutive years. Bill's career has progressed steadily with his promotion six years ago having caused a substantial jump in his earnings. Given the following earnings history, calculate Bill's annual pension.

Year	Amount
2004	$60,000
2005	$65,000
2006	$70,000
2007	$75,000
2008	$71,000
2009	$60,000

    a. $32,400

    b. $37,260

    c. $37,935

    d. $42,150

Answer: c

    ⇨   A pension based on a best earnings formula allows an employee to begin their retirement with a pension closely aligned to their salary just prior to retirement. The average earnings of Bill's best four consecutive years is $70,250 (($65,000 + $70,000 + $75,000 + $71,000) ÷ 4) representing her earnings from 2005 through 2008. Therefore Bill's pension formula is established as:

    ⇨   1.8% × $70,250 × 30 = $37,935.

Question 3

With regard to contributions into a defined benefit pension plan, which of the following statements is/are true?

1. The employer's contribution amount is calculated as a percentage of the plan member's earnings.

2. The employer is responsible for the plan's solvency.

3. Employer contributions into the plan are a tax deductible business expense, if the contribution calculation adheres to CRA's prescribed guidelines.

4. Any shortfall in funding for the pension plan is the employer's responsibility.

    a. 1 and 4 only

    b. 1 only

    c. 2 and 3 only

    d. 2, 3 and 4 only

Answer: d

    ⇨   The employer's contribution to a defined benefit plan is determined based on the results of an actuarial review. This review considers a broad range of elements to assess the plan's liabilities and the resulting required employer contribution.

Question 4

When a pension jurisdiction requires that the pension benefit incorporate a "joint and survivor" form of pension, which of the following statements is/are true?

1. The intention is to have the actual pension benefit amount based on the combined life expectancies of the member and the member's spouse.

2. In most jurisdictions, the only action required for a plan member to opt out of this provision is to personally sign a pre-printed form in which she personally declines the provision.

3. A pension that incorporates a joint and survivor form of pension will provide a member with a higher benefit amount than when the pension is based on the member's life only (assuming all other features and guarantees are the same).

4. If a member pre-deceases her spouse and her pension incorporates a joint and survivor form of benefit, a predetermined percentage of the member's pension will continue to be paid to the surviving spouse for her remaining lifetime.

5. By electing a joint and survivor form of pension, the plan member is able to income split with her spouse by sharing her monthly pension income during the member's lifetime.

    a. 1 and 4 only

    b. 2 and 5 only

    c. 3 only

    d. 3, 4 and 5 only

Answer: a

⇨ Pension rules may require that the pension benefit at a NRA include a joint and survivor form of benefit. This calculates the benefit based on the combined life expectancies of both the member and their spouse in the event of the member pre-deceasing their spouse. This form of pension allows the benefit to continue in full or at a set percentage to the surviving spouse if the plan member pre-deceases them. Because the benefit will continue for a potentially longer duration than the single life, the benefit is slightly reduced from a benefit based on a single life. This spousal option can be opted out of, provided the spouse gives written permission on the prescribed forms.

Question 5

Danny is retiring this month and needs to make a decision regarding the features and design of her retirement benefit. Danny knows she wants to elect a joint and survivor form of pension but she is not sure if she wants a 70% survivor benefit or a 100% survivor benefit and what guarantee period, if any. With regard to Danny's decision, which of the following statements are true?

1. If Danny opts for the 100% survivor benefit, her pension income will be lower than if she opts for the 70% survivor benefit.

2. If Danny opts for the 100% survivor benefit, her pension income will be higher than if she opts for the 70% survivor benefit.

3. If Danny opts for a guarantee period on her pension benefit, her income will be lower than if she opts for no guarantee period.

4. If Danny opts for a guarantee period on her pension benefit, her income will be higher than if she opts for no guarantee period.

     a. 1 and 3 only

     b. 1 and 4 only

     c. 2 and 3 only

     d. 2 and 4 only

Answer: a

     ⇨   The cost of providing a pension is directly related to how much of the benefit continues to the surviving spouse and the guarantee period for the benefit. Therefore, the longer the benefit is guaranteed the greater the cost to the plan and the less the pension income will be. Similarly, the larger the percentage of the survivor benefit, the greater the cost to the plan and the less the pension income will be.

Question 6

Frank, the owner of Smart Stop Inc., would like to establish an IPP for himself. Frank established Smart Stop Inc. twelve years ago, at age thirty-nine. With an annual T4 income that exceeds $200,000, Frank has consistently earned substantial income from Smart Stop and sees continued growth in her regular earnings. Which of the following items is **not** permitted in the design of Frank's IPP?

     a. Contributions will be based on the maximum pensionable earnings permitted under a defined benefit plan.

     b. The NRA will be set as age 65.

     c. The benefit formula will be structured on a best earnings approach.

     d. The plan will be established as a non-contributory pension plan.

Answer: c

     ⇨   An IPP has specific design requirements imposed by retirement savings legislation to a designated plan. The benefit formula for an IPP may utilize a career average earnings formula, but not a final/best earnings approach.

Question 7

Fanny is the owner of a long-established manufacturing business. Which of the following are important issues that she should consider when comparing an IPP to an RRSP?

1. The company assumes responsibility for the investment decisions associated with the IPP and must ensure that it remains solvent, whereas investment performance in an RRSP does not create any financial responsibility for the company.

2. If the company establishes an IPP, it has a legal obligation to make required annual contributions, whereas there is no legislated contribution requirement for an RRSP.

3. Once established, Fanny cannot easily access the funds in an IPP if an important need or emergency arises, whereas she could in an RRSP.

4. The contribution formula for an RRSP can incorporate an indexation feature that increases the amount of tax-deductible contributions a company can make into an RRSP, whereas this is not possible for an IPP.

    a. 1 and 4 only

    b. 1, 2 and 3 only

    c. 2 and 3 only

    d. 4 only

Answer: b

    ⇨   Indexing assumptions can be incorporated into the income projections for an IPP up to a CRA prescribed limit. As a result, the employer's contributions to the IPP will increase and be considered a tax-deductible contribution for the business.

Question 8

When comparing a defined benefit pension plan and a defined contribution pension plan, which of the following statements is/are true?

1. A defined contribution plan allows an employer to readily predict pension costs, whereas this is a more complex task for a defined benefit plan.

2. A defined contribution plan is more complex to administer than a defined benefit plan.

3. Employees typically participate in the investment decisions associated with a defined contribution plan, but not with a defined benefit plan.

4. An employee's retirement pension is directly dependent upon the investment performance of a defined contribution plan, but this is not the case with a defined benefit plan.

    a. 1 and 4 only

    b. 1, 3 and 4 only

    c. 2 and 3 only

    d. 2 only

Answer: b

    ⇨   A defined contribution plan is easy to administer and does not require an actuarial valuation at any point because the employer's liability is clearly established through a contribution formula.

Question 9

Ina, a single woman, joined Mastertech Inc.'s defined contribution pension plan on January 1, 1979. On December 31, 2009, Ina plans to retire and expects that her pension accumulation will be valued at $243,750. If Ina uses the assets to purchase a single life annuity that begins immediately with payments at the beginning of each month, what monthly income will the pension assets purchase? Assume an annual nominal return of 6%, compounded monthly, and a life expectancy of 30 years.

    a. $1,454.13

    b. $1,461.40

    c. $1,562.67

    d. $1,570.48

Answer: a

    ⇨ P/YR = 12

    ⇨ XP/YR = 30

    ⇨ I/YR = 6

    ⇨ PV = -243,750

    ⇨ FV = 0

    ⇨ MODE = BEG

SOLVE FOR PMT, which equals $1,454.13

Using the assumptions outlined in the question, Ina's $243,750 of pension accumulation would fund a monthly income of $1,454.13 for the remainder of her life.

Question 10

When an amendment is made to a pension plan, which of the following statements is/are typically true?

1. Amendments must be registered with CRA.

2. Amendments must be registered with the appropriate jurisdiction before any change becomes effective.

3. Amendments may not reduce a plan member's benefits earned to date.

4. Amendments may not reduce a plan member's benefits to be earned in the future.

5. In most jurisdictions, plan members are entitled to notice when a plan amendment may adversely affect the members' rights.

    a. 1 and 5 only

    b. 1, 2, 3 and 5 only

    c. 2 only

    d. 2, 3 and 4 only

Answer: b

    ⇨ Where a registered pension plan is amended or terminated, generally these actions cannot reduce a plan member's benefits earned to date. All amendments to pension plans must be registered with the CRA and any adverse impact of the change to a plan member's plan must be provided in a written notice to the member.

Question 11

Lilly participates in Backspace Inc.'s defined benefit pension plan, which she joined eight years ago. The plan provides benefits of 2% for each year of service, based on the member's best three consecutive years of pensionable earnings. Lilly's best three consecutive years of earnings were the most recent three, with annual pensionable earnings of $43,000, $48,000 and $51,000. If Lilly has eight years of service, calculate the amount of annual pension benefit accrued to date.

    a. $3,786.67

    b. $7,573.33

    c. $8,160.00

    d. $946.00

Answer: b

    ⇨ The average earnings of Lilly's best three consecutive years is $47,333.33 (($43,000 + $48,000 + $51,000) ÷ 3) representing her earnings. Therefore, Lilly's pension formula is established as:

    ⇨ 2% × $47,333.33 × 8 = $7,573.33

Question 12

Ruth, a widow, joined her employer's defined contribution pension plan 28 years ago, and is now reaching age 65. Ruth would like to use her pension assets of $167,432 to purchase a life annuity with monthly payments beginning at the end of her first month of retirement. Assuming an annual nominal return of 5%, compounded monthly, and a life expectancy of 25 years, what monthly income will Ruth receive from her current pension assets?

    a. $923.01

    b. $926.86

    c. $974.73

    d. $978.79

Answer: d

    ⇨ P/YR = 12

    ⇨ XP/YR = 25

    ⇨ I/YR = 5

    ⇨ PV = -167,432

    ⇨ FV = 0

    ⇨ MODE = END

SOLVE FOR PMT, which equals $978.79

Using the assumptions outlined in the question, Ruth's $167,432 of pension accumulation would fund a monthly income of $978.79 for the remainder of her life.

Question 13

Tom, age 60, is ready to retire but is unclear as to how much pension his accumulation of assets will purchase. During the past eight years, Tom has accumulated $53,725 in total assets within his employer's defined contribution plan. If Tom purchases a single life annuity with monthly payments at the beginning of each month, what total monthly pension will the assets purchase? Assume a 30-year life expectancy and a 6.1% annual nominal return, compounded monthly.

    a. $323.92

    b. $325.57

    c. $705.64

    d. $708.64

Answer: a

    ⇨ P/YR = 12

    ⇨ XP/YR = 30

    ⇨ I/YR = 6.1

    ⇨ PV = -53,725

    ⇨ FV = 0

    ⇨ MODE = BEG

SOLVE FOR PMT, which equals $323.92

Using the assumptions outlined in the question, Tom's $53,725 of pension accumulation would fund a monthly income of $323.92 for the remainder of his life.

Question 14

Vickie and Victor are discussing the differences between an IPP and an RRSP. Together they have made the following conclusions:

1. If an emergency arises, participants in either type of plan may withdraw funds as needed.

2. Once established, an employer is obligated to make annual contributions in order to maintain the solvency of both plans.

3. An RRSP allows income splitting, whereas an IPP does not.

4. The plan member assumes responsibility for investment risk associated with an RRSP but this is not the case with an IPP.

5. An IPP allows the member to count on a guaranteed level of income, whereas the RRSP provides no guarantee.

From the above list, which of the statements are true?

    a. 1 and 4 only

    b. 1, 2 and 3 only

    c. 2 and 5 only

    d. 3, 4 and 5 only

Answer: d

> ⇨ Once an IPP is established, the employer is required to contribute the necessary funds to maintain the plan's solvency and neither the employer nor the employee can easily access the funds should an emergency arise. Alternatively, an employer is not required to make annual contributions to an RRSP.

Question 15

Sandra had $250,000 of pensionable earnings in 2009 at her employer, Maxmoney Inc. She is a member of the defined contribution pension plan at Maxmoney and the plan requires contributions of 5% from her employer and 5% from Sandra as the employee (based on pensionable earnings). Based on the pension plan's contribution formula, what is the maximum dollar amount that may be contributed to the pension plan on Sandra's behalf?

    a. $12,500

    b. $19,000

    c. $22,000

    d. $25,000

Answer: c

⇨   The following schedule of contributions was made on Sandra's behalf:

Maxmoney Inc.:	$12,500
Sandra:	$12,500
Total contribution:	$25,000

⇨   Based on the pension plan's contribution formula, a total of $25,000 will be considered for contribution on Sandra's behalf, however this exceeds the maximum dollar amount allowed under the Act. Contributions on Sandra's behalf must not exceed the lesser of 18% of $250,000 and $22,000. In Sandra's case, 18% of $250,000 is $45,000, so the $22,000 maximum applies. The pension plan formula exceeds the maximum amount.

**THE CFP
EDUCATION PROGRAM**

CCH/ADVOCIS FPSC-APPROVED CAPSTONE COURSE

MODULE 25
ESTATE PLANNING

Module 25
ESTATE PLANNING

Module 25
Estate Planning

INTRODUCTION

Estate planning is a comprehensive process undertaken to ensure that:

- Loved ones are well cared for after the death of an individual.

- The transfer of assets to intended beneficiaries takes place according to the deceased's wishes.

- Income taxes are minimized without compromising the deceased's intentions.

Not just for the wealthy or those with significant assets, estate planning provides an individual with the opportunity to align the distribution of his estate with his intended wishes.

THE ESTATE PLANNING PROCESS

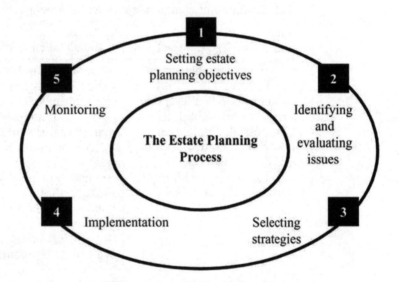

Estate Planning Checklist

- Incapacity
- *Inter Vivos* Trusts
- Rollover Rules/Deferred Tax Liability
- Liquidity
- Beneficiary Designation
- Ownership Structure of Assets
- Will
- Probate

Unit 1
Family Law

501. FAMILY LAW

Financial Planning Implications

Family law is a shared constitutional responsibility between the federal government and the provinces/territories. The federal *Divorce Act* governs divorce, spousal, and child support, while the province and territories govern custody and access.

Common-Law Relationships

The term *common-law partner* is defined as two people cohabiting in a conjugal relationship.

Matrimonial property legislation and intestacy legislation does not recognize common-law relationships in many provinces. Most provincial family law legislation (relating to spousal support obligations) recognizes common-law relationships.

The definition of common-law varies by province.

Marriage Contract	Cohabitation Agreement	Separation Agreement
— used to establish rights and obligations for both spouses during a legal marriage; or to establish terms for possible future events; — can be drafted prior to or during marriage; — cannot deal with child custody or access issues	— for common-law couples to specify rights and obligations during relationship; — if a common-law couple marries, agreement comes to force as marriage contract — most provincial legislation specifies that agreement applies between man and woman — same-sex couples often use private law contracts	— occurs when a couple choose to live apart permanently; — three methods to establish agreement: 1. Often negotiated between spouses 2. Court can establish custody, support and property arrangements 3. Spouses can create informal agreement (if agreement not honoured no legal protection for parties).

Divorce

Divorce is federally governed. Under the *Divorce Act*, there are three criteria to satisfy in order to obtain a divorce due to marriage breakdown:

- Separate living spaces for one year
- Adultery
- Mental or physical cruelty

Uncontested versus Contested

The term *uncontested divorce* describes a divorce under which both spouses agree to all issues. A *contested divorce*, on the other hand, is one where there is disagreement between the two spouses as to the terms of the divorce.

Corollary Relief Claim for Child Support, Spousal Support, or Custody

This generally requires preparation of financial statements demonstrating monthly expenses.

Joint Custody

Joint custody occurs when spouses share equal responsibility as parents. Both parents share in the decision-making as it relates to the child. The actual living arrangements of the child need not reflect equal time with each parent.

Access

The right to spend time with and receive information about the child for the non-custody holding parent.

Marital Property

The division of property and debts is a provincial, not federal, responsibility. In terms of marital property, *net family property* is the property that was valued (assets - liabilities) at the beginning and end of the the marriage. The spouse with the lesser amount of gain receives *equalization payments* from the other.

The reason for the divorce has no impact on the financial obligations of either spouse.

Proceeds from a life insurance policy, damages or the right to damages for personal injury, and gifts or inheritances received after the marriage, except for the matrimonial home, are **excluded** from the net family property calculation.

Division of Pension Assets

Division of pension assets crosses pension and family law. With the exception of P.E.I., pension assets are included as part of divisible property upon marriage breakdown.

There are four methods to divide pension assets:

- **Deferred Benefit Split.** The pension is divided at the "source" when it is actually paid. The member spouse and non-member spouse share in the pension payments in proportion to the amount earned during the marriage.

- **Transfer to Spouse's Plan.** A division of the actual pension assets can occur by transferring the appropriate proportion of assets from the member spouse's pension to the pension vehicle maintained by the non-member spouse.

- **Pension Trust.** This option involves the creation of a trust whereby the nominal owner (spouse in whose name the pension is held) of the pension is required to pay a portion of the pension income to the non-member spouse.

- **Valuation.** The pension assets subject to "sharing" are valued and accounted for in the overall distribution of property. This option allows the member spouse to retain the full pension amount by taking a reduction in other asset entitlements at the time of a property settlement.

Child Support

The Federal Child Support Guidelines were introduced in 1997. The purpose of the guidelines are as follows:

- Establish a fair standard of support so that children continue to benefit from both spouses

- Add objectivity to child support orders

- Provide guidelines to courts and spouses

- Ensure consistent treatment of spouses and children in similar circumstances

Financial Arrangements

- Child Support Guidelines (established by the federal government) determine support payments

- Appropriate financial arrangement for child is required before a divorce is granted
- Where no marriage occurred, or where a separation is sought and no divorce, provincial laws establishes rules for child support

Factors for Child Support Calculations

There are a number of factors that determine the calculations for child support. They include:

- The number of children
- Custody arrangement (sole, split, or shared custody)
- The payor's province of residence
- The payor's income, adjusted for "special expenses"

Enforcement

The provinces enforce child support payments by:

- Suspending driver's licenses
- Garnishing wages
- Seizure of assets

Separating partners are encouraged to resolve child support arrangements on their own, not through the court system.

Bankruptcy will not normally absolve the payor of his obligation under a support order.

Child Support Rules

Current	Pre May 1, 1997
• Not tax deductible by paying parent; • Non-taxable for receiving parent.	• Tax deductible for paying parent • Taxable income for receiving parent

Agreements established before May 1, 1997 remain under the old rules, unless a motion was made to change to new rules. Under new rules, the amount of pre May 1, 1997 payments can be different due to changes in tax rules.

Distinguishing Between Child and Spousal Support

Payments are deemed as child support if the following conditions are met:

- Court order does not identify the amount as spousal support; or
- Payment is paid directly to the third party within an agreement that does not identify that the amount is for the spouse.

If the payor falls short of the specified amounts, child support will be assumed to be paid before spousal support.

Spousal Support

Spousal support is taxable income to the receiving spouse, and deductible income for the payor.

To qualify for tax treatment, payment must be:

- Subject to use at recipient's discretion
- Payable on a periodic basis
- For maintenance of recipient or children
- Paid:
  - to a spouse (or former), while couple is living apart
  - by the natural parent of a child of the recipient, made under provincial order

Other Considerations

Items to be considered for tax purposes:

- Spousal credit
- Equivalent-to-spouse credit
- Child care deduction
- Capital property transfer
- Principal residence exemption
- Registered pension plan
- RRSP or RRIF
- Spousal RRSP
- Legal fees (incurred to establish child or spousal support)

Unit 2
Wills and Intestacy

502. WILLS

Terminology

- **Estate.** Includes all real and personal property.

- **Net Value of the Estate.** The value of the estate after payment of any charges to the estate, debts, and expenses.

In broad terms, all real estate and personal property owned wholly by an individual normally forms part of the individual's estate, except for select assets that are structured to pass outside of the estate to a named beneficiary, such as insurance proceeds.

Basics of a Will

Nature

A person who makes a will or dies leaving a will is referred to as a "testator", if male, or a "testatrix", if female.

Some provinces require that an individual be at least the age of majority to create a will, while other provinces allow younger persons to do so. However, in all cases the individual must be mentally competent.

A *will* is a legal document completed as a means to legally communicate a testator's directions relative to the distribution of his estate after his death. Jurisdiction over wills is a provincial matter. A will must comply with the respective provincial Wills act, and is effective from the date of the testator's death.

Purpose

A will communicates the testator's directions relative to issues, such as:

- How the testator's assets are to be divided;

- Appointment of an executor;

- Recommendation for the preferred guardian of any minor children; and

- Specific powers entrusted to the executor or any trustees.

A will is fundamental to estate planning as it minimizes expense and delay in the transfer of assets upon the testator's death.

Creation

If a testator makes a valid will while residing in one province and later relocates to a new province, normally the laws of the new province will govern the rules applicable to the testator's will, intestacy, dependant responsibility, and family law.

Administrative Issues

Updating a Will

A will should be reviewed and updated, where appropriate, at least every two to three years, or when there is a major life change, such as:

- Birth or adoption of a child
- Marriage
- Common-law partnership
- Separation from a spouse or common-law partner
- Inheritance receipt
- Illness or death of the executor/trustee/beneficiary
- Death of a child
- Relocation to a new province
- Provincial legislation change

Codicil

Used for a single item or several minor items, a *codicil* amends the will without having to create a new will.

Cancelling a Will

There are a number of circumstances that can cancel a will. These include:

- When a new legal will is created it automatically cancels a previous will.
- Destroying the original version (copies should be destroyed as well).
- If a testator marries or remarries after the date the will is signed (in all provinces except Quebec).

Retention of a Will

The original copy of a will is often retained at the lawyer's office once a will is created. Copies should also be maintained in a safe, secure location, such as a safety deposit box.

Estate Fundamentals

Note: The discussion from this point forward will focus on issues specific to the English form of will, unless otherwise specified.

Duties of Executor

Selection of an Executor

An *executor* is the person named within the will to carry out the instructions described in the testator's will. An executor can be a single individual, multiple individuals, or even a trust company.

The selection of the executor should consider the complexity of the estate and the type of skills the executor might have to demonstrate. Other things should also be considered such as the proximity of the executor to the testator, or to the estate.

The role of the executor includes:

- Gathering and accounting for assets of the estate;

- Payment of outstanding debts, including any income taxes triggered by the death of the deceased;

- Distribution of estate assets; and

- Completion of the personal and estate income tax returns.

Trustee Powers

An executor acts as a trustee for the beneficiaries of the estate and, in most situations, takes legal title to the property that is to be ultimately moved from the deceased to the beneficiaries.

Provincial laws dictate the powers of the executor.

Releases and Passing of Accounts

It is the estate executor or administrator's responsibility to bring closure to the estate through one of two methodologies.

Releases. To provide closure, beneficiaries or their representatives must have the appropriate authority to do so. When all of the beneficiaries are competent adults over the age of majority, they are typically considered in a position to provide a valid release.

Passing of Accounts. Involves the executor/administrator's presentation of the estate's accounts to the courts with a request for approval. While the passing of accounts is not typically a necessity, an executor often chooses this method because it is viewed as a more prudent approach.

Types of Wills

There are several types of wills, and these include:

- **English Form Will.** The most common type of will in Canada, it must be a written document, signed by the testator and have two witnesses.

- **Notarial Will.** This type is drawn up by a notary; it is commonly used in Quebec.

- **International Will.** This type is one prepared in a form that meets specific standards that are valid in jurisdictions that are party to the 1973 Convention Providing a Uniform Law of an International Will.

- **Holograph Will.** This will is written solely in the personal handwriting of the individual whose signature it bears.

- **Mirror Wills.** This is where two wills are drafted, quite often for spouses, and each testator is the beneficiary of the other's residuary estate.

- **Joint Will.** This one is where two or more people execute one will intended to serve as the will for any or all of the parties.

- **Mutual Will.** This type of will is commonly used with two spouses who execute separate but related wills. Where two documents are prepared as mutual wills, the two wills will mirror each other.

Clauses of a Will

Can include the introduction, identification, and revocation of previous wills, appointment of an executor, registered money rollover, payment of debts, bequests, trustee powers, trustee for minor beneficiaries, releases on behalf of minor beneficiaries, qualification of beneficiary, special provisions, guardianship, date and signatures, and other clauses.

Legacy/Bequest

The terms *legacy* and *bequest* are used interchangeably to describe a gift passed through a will. There are four classifications of a legacy, which is also referred to as a testamentary disposition under a will, including:

- **Specific.** This is an explicit and identifiable asset(s) of the estate, i.e., the cottage.

- **Demonstrative.** This is a monetary legacy where there is direction that the bequest be satisfied from the proceeds of a specific asset or property, i.e., $5,000 from GICs held at bank XYZ.

- **General.** This is monetary value paid out of the general assets of the estate.

- **Residual.** This is based on the assets remaining in the estate after all other bequests have been satisfied.

Ademption

The term *ademption* refers to the removal of a bequest within the will because the asset is no longer in the estate at the time of the testator's death. If the particular asset is already disposed of:

- The testator may well intend that the beneficiary receive nothing; or

- The testator may want to provide a substitute item.

Abatement

The term *abatement* applies to the situation where a bequest is made, but there are not sufficient assets available to satisfy the full bequest, so the amount is lowered or adjusted to reflect a reduced amount. Only the assets specifically named can be used to fulfill the request; it can not be fulfilled through other assets held in the estate.

Lapse

A *lapse* is where a gift cannot be made under a will because the intended beneficiary has predeceased the testator, and where there is no contingent beneficiary relative to the specific gift.

Exoneration

With *exoneration*, if any outstanding debts against a specific asset are not addressed, the asset's debt must be paid by the testator's estate when it passes to the beneficiary. Wills should address the handling of debts against specific gifts.

Residue

Residue, or the residual estate, is the remainder of the estate after debts, expenses, taxes, and legacy distributions.

Distribution of Estate

The priority of items differs by province, but of higher priority are:

- Funeral expenses
- Income taxes
- Taxes payable under provincial estate/probate legislation
- Solicitor's costs
- Liabilities incurred by the personal representative
- Commissions/fees payable to the personal representative
- Payment of other debts

Creditors

Creditors of the deceased must be paid before any distributions can be made to the beneficiaries of the estate.

Heirs

The testator has the sole authority to decide on the size of the bequest left to each beneficiary.

Timing

The timing of payments can differ — where the amount of money is sizeable, payments may be made in multiple installments.

Per Stirpes versus Per Capita

Per stirpes is a system where the children of a deceased parent share in the inheritance that their parent would have received had he survived the recently deceased descendant.

Per capita is an alternative system of inheritance where named descendants of the deceased share equally in the size of the share that each inherits regardless of degree of kinship.

Other Considerations

A second marriage or a common-law relationship creates the situation where two parties may bring separate estates into the relationship. Another consideration is if the heir has poor money skills.

Special Needs Beneficiaries

Minor Children

Minor children may inherit property, but the law requires that someone over the age of majority act as the trustee.

Educational Costs

Educational costs are a significant expense that should be dealt with in a will if applicable.

Disabled Child

Since government programs frequently pull back on services or financial support when a disabled individual's income or assets exceed prescribed limits, a bequest could affect qualification. A possible solution is an absolute discretionary, or Henson, trust.

Dependants' Relief

The definition of *dependant* varies by provincial jurisdiction. An individual's right to distribute his estate as he wishes does not remove his responsibility to provide adequately for his dependants. This falls under provincial jurisdiction, and each province establishes its own parameters.

Most provinces have legislation, often in the area of dependents' relief, succession or family law, that allows a spouse, common-law partner or children to make a claim against the estate if adequate provisions have not been taken to meet the deceased's financial obligations.

Spousal Rights

In some jurisdictions, such as Ontario, the surviving spouse has options that could circumvent the outcome of the testator's original intentions, and marriage is treated as an economic partnership. Upon the cessation of the partnership, there is an entitlement to an equalization payment from the deceased spouse to the surviving spouse.

As such, spouses in such jurisdictions have the opportunity to choose between taking an equalization payment or receiving the inheritance set out in the deceased's will.

Multiple Wills

Multiple wills are commonly used as a convenience for individuals who maintain assets in different jurisdictions. This type of arrangement may be undertaken to reduce the probate fees.

Types of Issues Needing Careful Management

The assets included in each will should be clearly identified so that the will deals only with those assets within the specific jurisdiction.

One will should not inadvertently revoke another will. Each will should be drafted to meet the unique rules of the specific jurisdiction, including powers of the trustee. Appropriate wording should be used in each of the wills relative to the payment of debts.

If a legacy is dealt with in only one will, there should be sufficient liquid assets available to address the legacy.

Probate

Probate, a provincial jurisdiction, is the legal process undertaken following the testator's death in order to have the will of the testator declared as valid and effective by the court, and to have the executor named in the will formally appointed to the role.

Letters of Administration

Administration is the term used to describe the process undertaken to appoint a legal representative of the deceased person when an individual dies without a valid will, when the will fails to appoint an executor or when the executor named in the will is not available to fulfill the role either by choice or because he is deceased.

Legal representative is the phrase commonly used to describe the roles of the estate executor and administrator.

Documentation

The process of probate involves the completion of an extensive series of forms and preparation of documents, and a complete inventory of the deceased's assets is prepared. Probate may involve the payment of fees, and these fees differ by provincial jurisdiction.

There is a loss of privacy since a probated will becomes open to public view.

Assets Subject to Probate

The structure under which an asset is owned plays a significant role in determining whether an asset is subject to probate. Assets that were wholly owned by the deceased, or that were owned as a tenant in common, are typically subject to the probate process.

Probate legislation in each province identifies the assets that are subject to probate, as well as the formula for calculating the value of the applicable estate subject to probate.

Fees

There may be a fee levied on the estate by the provincial court that grants the letters of probate. Each provincial jurisdiction establishes:

- Their applicable fee schedule; and
- The rules as to how the estate assets are valued relative to the application of any applicable probate fees.

Probate Planning

Confidentiality

The process of probate exposes the deceased's will to public view, resulting in the loss of personal and family privacy. Probate planning techniques that achieve a greater degree of confidentiality include:

- The use of an *inter vivos* trust because the assets do not form part of the deceased's estate;
- Select use of named beneficiary designations; and
- Appropriate use of joint title with the right of survivorship for asset ownership.

Cost versus Benefit

Avoiding probate fees should be only one of a number of factors considered when structuring any estate plan.

Developing the Plan

The organization of an individual's estate plan should reflect important issues, including wishes, objectives, asset control considerations, disposition, and testamentary intentions.

Influence of Residency

If an individual's sole objective is to minimize probate fees, one strategy is to relocate to a province with a modest probate schedule.

Non-Probate Assets

Assets that do not form part of the deceased's estate are not subject to probate and, thus, not open to public view. Non-probate assets include assets held in joint tenancy, assets with named beneficiaries (insurance contracts, RRSPs), successive owners for life insurance, and segregated fund policies.

Intestacy

Overview of Intestacy

Intestate is the term used when the deceased did not leave a legal will. When a person dies intestate, provincial legislation determines the distribution of the estate.

The *rules of intestacy* are the rules that the government uses to dictate who becomes a beneficiary of the estate. Each province develops and administers its own intestate legislation.

Recent legislative changes in various provinces have been made to incorporate common-law and same-sex relationships.

Appointment of an Administrator

When an individual dies without a will, an application is made to the courts for the appointment of an *estate administrator*. The administrator becomes responsible for the distribution of the deceased's property according to provincial intestate laws.

The order of preference followed by the courts when appointing the estate administrator often follows an established norm, and is:

- Spouse
- Children
- Grandchildren
- Parents
- Siblings
- Grandparents
- Great-grandchildren

Relationships

Descendant. A person whose lineage can be traced to a particular individual.

Ascendant. The person from whom one is descended.

Consanguinity. A relationship connection, by blood.

Lineal Consanguinity. This exists between descendants where one is directly descended from another.

Collateral Consanguinity. This describes individuals who have a common ancestor but have descended from a different line.

Distribution of the Estate

The estate is distributed according to the provincial laws of intestacy. *Issue* is a legislative term, and includes all lineal descendants, born inside and outside of marriage, as well as adoptees.

Preferential Share

Many provinces use this notion, and the amount differs by province.

If Net value of the estate < Pre-established preferential share amount *then* Full amount of the estate passes to the surviving spouse.

If Net value of the estate > Preferential share amount *then* Surviving spouse receives the preferential share amount and then shares in the residue with the intestate's children.

Beyond Preferential Share

The net value of the estate that exceeds the preferential share is shared between the surviving spouse and the intestate's issue. Typically, the distribution between the spouse and the child(ren) is based on simple criteria, such as where there is a spouse and one child, or where there is a spouse and more than one child.

No Preferential Share

Some provinces do not have a preferential share for the surviving spouse. In these cases, there are sharing arrangements in place, but without the spouse being allocated a favored amount.

Other Heirs

Provincial intestate legislation dictates that the estate is distributed to ascendants and collateral heirs according to a prescribed schedule unique to each provincial jurisdiction, when the deceased does not have a surviving spouse or children.

When the estate is distributed to the next of kin, kindred is computed by counting upward from the intestate to the nearest common ancestor and then downward to the relative.

Escheat

Escheat is the process, determined by provincial legislation, through which the estate passes to the Crown if a person dies intestate and without an heir.

Partial Estate

Partial estate may arise when an individual who has a valid will dies, but for some reason his will does not deal with the whole estate or a segment of the will is considered invalid. In this case, the provincial *Intestacy Act* will determine the distribution of the estate not dealt with in the will.

Will Substitutes

There are a variety of estate planning strategies that can serve as a substitute to a will, allowing an individual to do much of what he wants without the asset having to pass through his estate.

Through advance planning, an individual has the opportunity to assess the pros and cons of the various strategies relative to his personal circumstances and estate objectives.

Joint Tenancy Ownership

Ownership as joint tenants is unique because of the right of survivorship. The death of one of the joint tenants causes the deceased tenant's share to pass immediately upon death to the surviving tenant. As such, a joint tenant cannot sever his share of a piece of property through his will because property held as joint tenants passes automatically to the surviving joint tenant(s). A surviving tenant has full control of the property and is under no obligation to provide for the heirs of the deceased tenant.

When property is owned as joint tenants, it is subject to the creditors of any of the joint tenants.

Beneficiary Designations

Using a named beneficiary designation can be a useful strategy to:

- Eliminate issues that can arise due to probate;
- Ensure that the deceased's testamentary wishes are fulfilled; and
- Minimize the possibility of substantial assets becoming caught in lengthy delays brought about by challenges to the will.

When using a named beneficiary strategy, the asset owner needs to be aware of any changes that could impact the designation or circumvent the owner's intended wishes.

Inter Vivos Trusts

Inter vivos trusts can be established in advance of a parent's death in anticipation of providing for the maintenance and financial well-being of children in a wide variety of circumstances. They can be established for the benefit of a spouse or common-law partner, or ex-spouse or ex-common-law partner, and provide for the maintenance and financial well-being of elderly family members.

Inter vivos trusts are valuable for retaining control of business interests, or to maintain and administer a cottage or vacation property for the benefit of future generations.

The only reporting requirement for an *inter vivos* trust is with the Canada Revenue Agency (the "CRA"), so there is a significant element of privacy associated with the use of a trust.

In some circumstances, trusts can enhance the creditor protection of assets.

Donatio Mortis Causa

Donatio mortis causa occurs when a very ill person, anticipating that death is near or pending, gives a gift to an individual, conditional upon the ill person's death.

To constitute a valid *donatio mortis causa*, the gift must be:

- Of personal property, and not real property such as real estate;
- Made by the donor in peril of death; and
- Is only complete if death should occur as a result of an impending illness.

A *donatio mortis causa* gift does not form part of the deceased's estate, so is not subject to probate fees.

Taxation

See the income tax section of section 114, "Tax Consequences of Death", in Module 21 for the tax consequences of death and estate planning issues regarding the following items:

- Income
- Property Transfers
- Deemed Disposition
- Income Attribution

- Special Trusts (*alter ego* trusts, joint partner trusts, taxation of *alter ego* or joint partner trusts, spousal or common-law partner trust, living or family trust)

Holding Companies

A *holding company* can be a valuable place to accumulate and diversify investments so that when the shareholder/taxpayer dies, only the shares of the holding company are to be dealt with in his will. The assets within the holding company continue uninterrupted, reducing the need to liquidate or transfer many different investment holdings.

Upon the death of the taxpayer, the shares of the holding company can pass through the shareholder's estate in accordance with the provisions of the shareholder's will or can pass through the intestate succession laws if there is no will.

Estate Freeze

An *estate freeze* is a planning technique that allows the owner of an operating company to freeze the growth of his interest in an operating company in order to avoid further capital gains on his shares that would be triggered at his death.

Implementing an estate freeze is common when a shareholder has accumulated sufficient long-term wealth, and would like future growth of the corporation to accumulate for the benefit of his intended heirs.

A *section 85 rollover* is a tax-free rollover where the transfer of common shares into the holding company is permitted without triggering a disposition or realization of capital gains to the original shareholder.

Insurance

Estate Planning

Life insurance is commonly used to fund bequests to family members or other beneficiaries, and the use of life insurance is an excellent way to ensure outstanding expenses at death do not detract from inheritances established through an individual's estate.

Buy-Sell Arrangements

This is a subset of a shareholders' agreement and is a written document that outlines the terms relative to the succession of a business. It is established during the business owners/partners' lifetimes, and can address a variety of situations.

Insured Annuity/Back-to-Back

This is a unique financial plan that utilizes the purchase of an annuity and life insurance policy into an integrated plan. Through the use of these two products, an individual may be able to provide a higher guaranteed level of income throughout his retirement years versus other interest-bearing investments.

Funding a Trust With Insurance

If the proceeds of insurance are intended for placement in a testamentary trust, the insurance passes through the estate and become exposed to creditors. One solution is for insurance proceeds to be paid into a trust settled by the estate.

POWER OF ATTORNEY

An individual does not automatically have the right to handle his spouse's legal and financial affairs in the event that the spouse is not able to because of illness or unavailability (i.e., being out of the country).

A power of attorney addresses the issue of who has decision-making authority (known as an *attorney* or *agent*) on another individual's behalf (referred to as a *grantor* or *donor*), under specific circumstances, while the grantor is alive. This is subject to provincial jurisdiction.

There are two primary types of power of attorney, and they relate to a *person's property* or a *person's health*.

503. POWER OF ATTORNEY FOR PROPERTY

A *limited power of attorney* can be drafted where the grantor authorizes the attorney to make decisions and commitments on the grantor's behalf, relative to a specific or defined task.

A *general power of attorney* for property typically provides the appointed attorney with the power to make any decision or commitments that an individual can make on his own, with the exception of making a will or a power of attorney.

General power of attorney terminates if:

- The grantor dies;
- The attorney dies; or
- The grantor becomes incapacitated.

A *continuing* or *enduring power of attorney for property* is commonly used as a legal means to provide an individual with the authority to act on the grantor's behalf, in the event that the grantor becomes incapacitated. The two types of enduring powers of attorney incorporate the continuing or enduring clause, or becomes effective when triggered by a specific event.

504. POWER OF ATTORNEY FOR PERSONAL CARE

A *power of attorney for personal care* is a legal document through which the grantor appoints an attorney (name of the role can vary by jurisdiction) to make binding decisions regarding the grantor's medical or personal care during the grantor's lifetime, but only when the grantor is unable to do so because he is incapacitated.

The key issue relates to the fact that the power of attorney for personal care is relevant only during the grantor's lifetime, and only when he is incapacitated and unable to make decisions for himself. The two different types of powers of attorney, property and health care, normally each require separate documents.

505. PERSONAL PROPERTY OWNERSHIP AND TRANSFER RULES

Joint Tenancy versus Tenants in Common

In both forms of ownership, all owners share equally in the right to possess and use the property, and each co-owner has the right to dispose of his share of the property during his lifetime in any manner, subject to provincial matrimonial property legislation.

The primary difference is the disposition of the property at the death of a co-owner. With *joint tenancy*, the title automatically passes to the surviving co-owner, while with *tenants in common*, the title to the property does not automatically pass to the co-owner, but is transferred to the heirs of the deceased tenant.

A valid joint tenancy requires the four unities.

- **Unity of Interest.** Each joint tenant must have equal interest in the property.
- **Unity of Title.** The interests of all joint tenants originate from the same document.
- **Unity of Possession.** Each joint tenant must have equal rights to the entire property.
- **Unity of Time.** The interest of all joint tenants must originate at the same time.

While it may be the parties' intentions to own an asset as joint tenants, if one of the four unities is not satisfied, the property is treated as tenants in common.

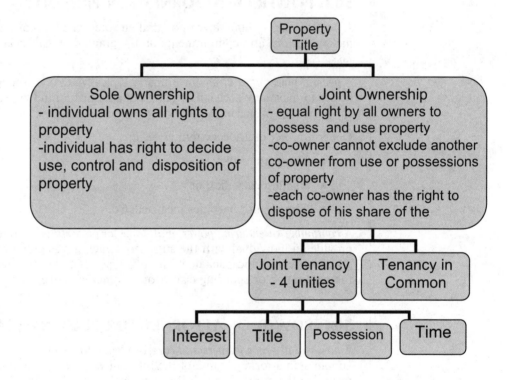

Unit 3
Business Ownership Structures

506. BUSINESS OWNERSHIP STRUCTURES

Proprietorships

Sole proprietorship is the simplest form of business organization. It is an unincorporated business owned by one individual. Sole proprietors must actively carry on business.

Unlimited Liability

All income, losses, liabilities and assets of business are the personal responsibility of the proprietor. Sole proprietorship is not a separate legal entity. The proprietor's personal property is exposed to creditors. Business assets are exposed to liability against the proprietor's personal debts. Many professionals, such as lawyers and accountants, operate as a sole proprietorship or partnership because some provinces prohibit incorporation of a professional practice.

Taxation

Financial results of the proprietorship affect personal income tax because business assets are personal assets. For example, capital gain/loss on the disposition of a business asset is treated as a personal gain/loss for tax purposes. The net income earned by the business is taxable to the proprietor in the year it is earned. The proprietor can employ staff and can pay family for work done, thereby reducing income. Income taken out of the company is considered a draw and treated differently than the net income the business earns each year.

Sole Proprietorship — Advantages and Disadvantages

Advantages	Disadvantages
• Simplicity of formation relative to other business structures • Business is extension of owner, no legal costs to create separate legal entity • Business is established quickly, at little cost • Working capital minimal, financed through personal assets • No corporate structure, minimal legal restrictions • Owner retains full control	• Low working capital can limit expansion • Owner makes all decisions, not good for those who want to share decisions • Continuity: owner must be solvent, legally competent and alive for the business to continue • Proprietor is personally liable for obligations and liabilities • Personal debts can be satisfied with business assets

Year End

The selection of a fiscal year end, other than December 31, can provide a tax planning opportunity to shift income between taxation years. Sole proprietorships are restricted to a December 31 year end. The restriction of a December 31 year end is viewed as a disadvantage.

Partnership

General Partnership

The provincial *Partnership Acts* define a partnership as "a relationship between two or more parties carrying on an unincorporated business, with a view to profit".

Characteristics of General Partnership

Fiduciary Responsibility

Each partner is considered to have full authority to act on behalf of the partnership.

Active Business

The partnership must actively carry on business and cannot passively invest. There must be a reasonable expectation of profit to deduct expenses from revenue, but there is no requirement that the partnership earn a profit each year.

Employee Relationship

Partners cannot be employees of the partnership.

Joint and Several Liability

Partners are responsible for the actions of other partners acting on behalf of the partnership. There is no limit to responsibility unless it is clear that the partner acted outside normal business activities.

Taxation of General Partnership

The partnership is treated as a separate person, including CCA, which takes place at the partnership, not the partner, level. Property and business income, taxable capital gains, and allowable capital losses are taxed at the partnership level.

The partnership can choose its own fiscal year end. Taxation is based on the partnership's year end, and income flows through to the partner level when partnership allocations are made.

Each partner includes his share of the net income or loss from the business on his personal income tax return. Partners can determine income allocation between partners, but the Act can override their allocations if the allocation was an attempt to reduce or postpone income for one partner, or the partners were not dealing at arm's length.

Each partner tracks his contributions and allocations, and draws in a capital account, representing his share equity in the partnership.

Partnership Interest

The individual's partnership interest is treated as capital property with the adjusted cost base (ACB). See section 115, "Taxation of Different Legal Entities", in Module 21 for further details.

General Partnership Review

Consideration	Advantage	Disadvantage
Ease of formation	x	
Start-up costs — minimal	x	
Working capital required — minimal	x	
Working capital — for expansion		x
Regulation — minimal	x	
Legal restriction — none	x	
Owner's ability to retain control — shared with partners (dividend authority)	x	
Business continuity — if addressed in partnership agreement	x	
Business continuity — if not addressed in partnership agreement		x
Liability — unlimited		x

Limited Partnership

A limited partnership includes at least one general partner and one limited partner. Provinces usually have a *Limited Partnership Act* that allows the limited partner to contribute capital, but not be involved in the business operations. The limited partner has limited liability. The managing partner is personally liable for all debts and obligations.

Taxation of Limited Partnership

A partner of a limited partnership is taxed the same as a general partnership, with two exceptions:

At-Risk Rules

The amount of allocated partnership losses that the limited partner can deduct is limited to the amount *at risk*, less certain deductions. The at-risk amount has a special calculation based on such elements as a limited partner's ACB of partnership interest and the amount of the partner's share of the current year's income and proceeds of disposition for resource property. Non-deductible losses can be carried forward for a limited partner.

Income Attribution

Attribution rules apply when taxpayer loans, gifts or transfers funds to spouse or related minor who uses the funds to invest in a limited partnership. Income from limited partnership is then treated as property, not business, income and is attributed to the transferor.

Limited Liability Partnership

Limited liability partnerships are permitted in most provinces. They are similar to general partnerships, but the personal liability of partners does not extend to the negligent actions of other partners. For example, a partner cannot be sued personally for the negligence of another partner. Legal action can be taken against the partnership and negligent partner personally, but the only amount at risk for other partners is the amount in their capital account.

Corporation

Corporation Definition

A structure that is created according to a prescribed set of rules and is recognized in the eyes of the law as a legal entity with rights and duties. It is a distinct and separate legal entity, not required to carry on active business (can be an investment or holding company).

Characteristics of a Corporation

Limited Liability

The owners, referred to as shareholders, are distinct from the corporation and therefore not liable for its debts. A shareholder's financial risk is limited to the cost of his investment.

Separation of Ownership and Management

The investor can be passive, or may play an active role in management. The active share-holder is referred to as an *owner–manager.*

Ease of Ownership Transfer

The shareholder may transfer ownership by transferring his shares to another person or another company.

Perpetual Existence

A corporation exists independent of its shareholders so it continues perpetually. Exceptions occur if the shareholders or a court order dissolves the corporation, or it loses its corporate status due to failure to comply with regulations.

Types of Corporations

Private Corporation

A private corporation is not controlled directly or indirectly by one or more public or Crown corporations.

Canadian-Controlled Private Corporation

A Canadian-controlled private corporation (CCPC) is either incorporated in Canada or resident since June 18, 1971, *and*:

- It is a private corporation (see definition above).
- It is not controlled directly or indirectly by one or more foreign individuals, trusts, partnerships, or corporations.

Public Corporation

A corporation resident in Canada with a class of shares listed on a prescribed stock exchange in Canada; or resident in Canada and has elected to be a public corporation and has otherwise complied with requirements for the number of shareholders and the dispersion of ownership.

Director's Responsibilities and Liabilities

The board of directors supervises and directs the business affairs of the corporation. The board's stewardship of the corporation will typically include identifying the principal risks of the corporation's business, and ensuring the implementation of systems to manage these risks, such as appropriate internal controls, and corporate governance.

Statutory Liability

Corporate statutes impose two principal duties on directors: a fiduciary duty and a duty of care. Directors cannot contract out of these responsibilities and may be personally liable for any breach of them. There is also a broad array of statutes, such as labor laws, which either charge corporate directors with additional responsibilities or make them directly liable for the actions of the corporation.

Types of Authorized and Issued Share Capital

Every corporation must have share capital.

Authorized share capital is the maximum number or value of shares that a corporation may issue as prescribed in its charter. A corporation is not obliged to issue all of its share capital. The portion it issues is called *issued capital* (same as *paid-up capital*).

A *share* is the shareholder's proportionate interest in the capital of a corporation, while a *common share* represents equity or ownership in a corporation.

Preferred shares have some characteristics of common shares, but carry preferential rights with regard to the receipt of dividends or redemption upon dissolution of the corporation.

Qualified Small Business Corporation Shares Criteria

Shares of CCPC where all or substantially all of the fair market value (FMV) of the assets are used to carry on active business, primarily in Canada.

With some exceptions, shares are owned for at least 24 months prior to disposition and more than 50% of the FMV of the corporation's assets were used to carry on active business, primarily in Canada.

Holding Companies

There are two kinds of holding companies:

- **Opco.** The company actively carrying on business.
- **Holdco.** This company's primary purpose is to hold assets or investments.

Benefits of Holding Companies

Credit Protection

If Opco produces revenue greater than shareholder needs, money can be transferred to Holdco as tax free inter-corporate dividends.

Investment Opportunity

Earnings in excess of need for a closely-held corporation can be left within the corporation so more assets are available for investment.

Differing Shareholder Compensation Needs

Establishing holding companies owned by each shareholder of a closely-held, private corporation increases flexibility since each holding company can distribute income to a shareholder based on the shareholder's circumstances needs. Operating companies can pay dividends to each holding company without immediate taxation.

Estate Planning

Holdcos are valuable to accumulate and diversify investments. When a shareholder dies, only shares of Holdco must be dealt with instead of each individual investment. The assets in Holdco continue, reducing the need to liquidate or transfer investment holdings. Upon the death of the taxpayer, Holdco shares can pass through the estate in accordance with the will, or through intestate succession laws if there is no will.

Estate Freeze

An estate freeze allows the owner of Opco to freeze growth in the interest of Opco to avoid further capital gain on his shares triggered at his death. The shareholder transfers Opco shares to Holdco, in exchange for fixed value preferred shares (often dividend bearing, carrying voting rights to control Holdco). The shareholder's family can subscribe to common shares of Holdco at nominal cost to benefit from the growth of the corporation. Estate freezes are common where the shareholder has accumulated long-term wealth.

For shareholder agreements, see section 114, "Tax Consequences of Death", in Module 21.

Unit 4
Contract Law and Trusts

507. CONTRACT LAW

- **Public Law.** Public law deals with an individual or society as a whole, and the relationship between an individual and the state. Examples include criminal and constitutional laws.

- **Private Law.** Private law deals with the relationship between individuals and the settlement of disputes. Examples include contract law, tort law, and trust law.

Contracts

A *contract* is a formal agreement between two parties entered in to voluntarily. Contract law involves legal, binding promises. This unit considers written, enforceable, and legal contracts.

Formation of a Contract

The criteria set forth by common law to make a contract legal and enforceable are:

- A valid offer and acceptance;

- Consideration;

- The intention to create a legal contract (some circumstances that could result in a contract being considered void or unenforceable include a mistake about the terms or assumptions, undue influence, duress, or misrepresentation);

- The capacity to contract; and

- Legal intent.

Discharging a Contract

A contract may be discharged by performance, agreement, frustration, operation of law, or breach of contract.

Law of Torts

The term *law of torts* falls within common law, and is used when a wrongful act is committed against another person or that person's property because the offending party failed to meet a legal duty of proper care.

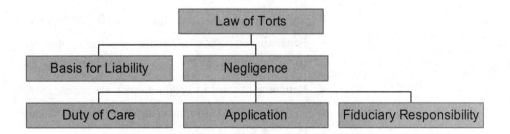

Basis for Liability

With *basis for liability*, fault or blame is assessed under the law as conduct or an action which is intentional or careless and which results in harm to others.

Negligence

Negligence is failure to exercise reasonable care that results in injury to another individual.

A litigant who sues for negligence must prove:

- The defending party owed the litigant a duty of care;
- The defending party breached the duty of care; and
- The defending party's actions caused the injury to the litigant.

Fiduciary Responsibility

Fiduciary responsibility is a duty where there is a special relationship of trust, confidence or responsibility and is generally viewed as part of most professional-client relationships.

Agency Relationship

An agency relationship is formed between one party acting as an agent on behalf of another party, referred to as the principal, in an effort to create a contractual arrangement between the principal and a third party. The agent generally operates under a contract between him and the principal, and is remunerated for the role. Insurance brokers would be an example. They work on behalf of the insurance company to sell insurance.

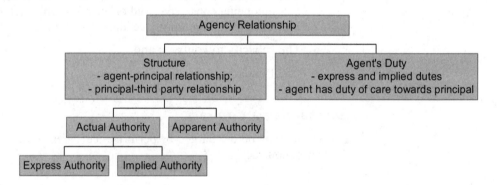

508. TRUST LAW

Uses of a Trust

There are many uses of a trust. These can include:

- Providing for the maintenance of children in a variety of circumstances.
- Benefiting of a spouse/partner or an ex-spouse/ex-partner.
- Providing for the maintenance of an elderly family.
- Retaining control of business interests during or after the settlor's lifetime.
- Maintaining and administering the cottage or vacation property for future generations.
- Enhancing the creditor protection of assets.

The only reporting requirement for an *inter vivos* trust is with the CRA; the trust, therefore, offers privacy in moving assets and can provide income tax planning opportunities, such as income and capital gains splitting.

Characteristics of a Trust

The characteristics of a trust are based on the "three certainties".

- **Certainty of Intention.** The settlor intended that the property be held in trust for the benefit of the beneficiary.

- **Certainty of Subject Matter.** The property must be clearly described and pass absolutely to the trust.

- **Certainty of Objects.** Beneficiaries must be clearly identifiable based on criteria.

Creating a Trust

- **Settlor.** The individual who transfers ownership and control of his property into a trust.

- **Trustee.** The person taking responsibility for the property who holds legal title to the property to administer it for the beneficiary.

There is a fiduciary relationship between the trustee and the beneficiaries. The trustee is legally obliged to act in the best interest of the beneficiaries, act impartially between different beneficiaries, and act with reasonable and prudent judgment.

The statutory powers, duties, and obligations of a trustee are dictated by each province. The settlor will often expand on the limited provincial provisions in the trust deed.

Provincial legislation limits the types of investment permitted. Expansion of authority in trust document ensures the trustee is empowered to invest according to the objectives of the settlor.

With *legal capacity*, the settlor must be of the age of majority, sound mind, and solvent at the trust's creation. The beneficiary can be any legal entity. With *legal purpose*, the trust's purpose must be legal, not unreasonable, or contrary to public policy.

A trust is established by the transfer of property to a trust. Residency of the trust is based on the residency of the trustee or the controlling individual, or the majority thereof.

Beneficiaries of a Trust

The *beneficiary* of a trust receives the benefit of the funds or property.

The trust is viewed as an individual for tax purposes, but is not a separate legal entity; it does not have rights separate from those of the parties involved.

Income Interest

The absolute or contingent right to receive all or part of the income of the trust.

Capital Interest

The right to receive the capital of the trust after a certain period of time or event.

Important Distinctions

A beneficiary can be named as an income beneficiary, capital beneficiary, or both. Common law dictates that trust income retained after the end of the fiscal year becomes capital property of the trust.

Life and Remainder Interest

The beneficiary has the right to use the property for his lifetime, after which the property passes to the capital beneficiary. A beneficiary with life interest is referred to as a *life tenant*, while a beneficiary entitled to property after the life tenant is referred to as a *remainderman*. The capital interest is referred to as the *remainder interest*.

Fixed and Discretionary Interest

The settlor of a trust can grant fixed interest or discretionary interest to the trust. *Discretionary interest* is when the trustee is given authority to determine if, when, and the amount of proceeds the beneficiary receives.

Vested and Contingent Interest

- **Vested Interest.** The beneficiary has possession or is entitled to possession of property upon the completion of specified conditions, even if the interest would terminate for failure to meet conditions.
- **Vested Absolutely.** This is when all conditions have been met, or there are no conditions, but he has not yet received possession of the property.
- **Vested Subject to Divestment.** The term for if there is a condition that could terminate a beneficiary's interest after the interest is created.

509. INTER VIVOS TRUSTS

Types of Inter Vivos Trusts

Personal Trust

A *personal trust* is either a testamentary or *inter vivos* trust; no beneficial interest is acquired for consideration payable either to the trust or the trust contributor. The trust creator may acquire all interest without losing personal trust status.

Revocable versus Irrevocable Trust

With a *revocable trust*, all or part of property of the trust may revert back to the settlor or the settlor retains the right to approve distributions. With an *irrevocable trust*, transfer of the property to the trust is automatic, unless a document specifies that the trust is revocable.

A testamentary trust is always irrevocable as the settlor is deceased and unable to revoke.

Commercial Trust

A *commercial trust* is one that does not meet the definition of a personal trust, such as a mutual fund trust.

Spousal or Common-Law Partner Trust

A *spousal or common-law partner trust* can be *inter vivos* or testamentary.

The living beneficiary is entitled to all income arising in his lifetime. No one other than the spouse can obtain any income or capital of the trust during the spouse's lifetime.

Family Trust

Family trust is a generic term covering a variety of trusts created by persons for the benefit of their family members. It includes *inter vivos* and testamentary trusts. A typical trust may hold property in trust for a parent or spouse during their lifetimes, with the remainder of the trust capital going to the children.

Alter Ego Trust

An *alter ego trust* is an *inter vivos* trust that is created after 1999, and is created by a settlor who is at least 65 years of age at the time of creation. The settlor is entitled to all income during his lifetime, and is the only person with trust access.

The settlor can elect out of the *alter ego* designation by filing an election with the first trust tax return.

Joint Spousal or Common-Law Partner Trust

A *joint spousal or common-law partner trust* is an *inter vivos* trust that was created after 1999, was created by a settlor at least 65 years of age at the time of the trust's creation, and where the settlor or spouse is entitled to all income from trust before the latter's death.

Charitable Trust

A *charitable trust* is a trust that was set up for charitable purposes.

Bare Trust

In a *bare trust*, the beneficiary has sole absolute interest in the trust property, and may demand possession at any time. The trustee is simply holding the property to transfer upon demand to the beneficiary. This kind of trust is commonly used to maintain confidentiality.

TAXATION OF TRUSTS

Property Transfers

Testamentary Trust

Property has been transferred from the deceased's estate to the trusts since the property has already been subject to the deemed disposition rules, the ACB of the estate is equal to the FMV of the property (except for spousal rollovers where ACB equals the ACB of the deceased individual's property).

Future gains and losses are based on the difference between the proceeds of disposition at the time of the property's sale and the property's ACB. Property transferred from the testamentary trust to the beneficiary is transferred at the trust's ACB and rolls tax-free to the beneficiary.

Inter Vivos Trust

There is a deemed disposition by the settlor at the time the property was transferred into the trust. The settlor will realize an accrued capital gain with possible income tax liability (with some exceptions).

Preservation of Character of Income

The income allocated by a trust to its beneficiaries retains its character. If a trust receives dividend income and allocates it to a beneficiary, the beneficiary is deemed to have received dividend income.

The beneficiary would gross-up the dividend by 25% (or 45%) and be entitled to the dividend credit.

Taxation Year

Once taxation year is established, the trust's year end cannot be changed without prior approval from the CRA.

- **Inter Vivos Trust.** December 31 year end, except mutual fund trust that may elect a December 15 year end.
- **Testamentary Trust.** Begins the day after the testator dies. The trustee may select the first year end, but it cannot be more than 12 months after the trust was established.

Taxation of Trust Income

A testamentary trust is taxed at the same rates as personal income tax, while an *inter vivos* trust has a flat tax equal to the top marginal tax rate (federal and provincial combined).

21-Year Deemed Disposition Rule

The Act includes deemed disposition of trust property rules and requires tax be paid on accrued but unrealized capital gains every 21 years.

Deemed disposition of capital property generally occurs for:

- Spousal trust, on the day the beneficiary spouse dies
- *Alter ego* trust, on the day in which the settlor dies
- Joint partner trust, on the day that the settlor or spouse dies, whichever is later
- All other trusts, 21 years after the trust was created

Revocable Trust

Revocable if all or part of property may revert back to the settlor or if the settlor retains right to approve distributions. All income and gains taxed to the settlor; tax-free rollover is denied to the beneficiary.

Irrevocable Trust

If the settlor is one of discretionary capital beneficiaries of irrevocable trust, the trust is viewed as revocable for tax purposes.

Income Attribution

The Act disallows certain tax provisions for revocable trusts that are available to irrevocable trusts.

With a revocable trust, all income and capital gains is taxed to the settlor, and the tax-free rollout to beneficiaries is denied.

Multiple Trusts

When multiple trusts exist where a single person contributed substantially all of the property to the trusts and income accrues for the benefit of the same beneficiary or class of beneficiary, the CRA may group trusts and treat them as a single trust.

Trusts must be made as distinct as possible to avoid this grouping.

Preferred Beneficiary Election

For preferred beneficiaries, the option to allocate income but not distribute cash can be beneficial if the beneficiary does not need the full amount of income, but where tax minimization planning dictates income allocation.

A preferred beneficiary is:

- An individual resident in Canada;

- Beneficiary of the trust;

- Eligible to claim non-refundable tax credit for mental or physical impairment; and

- Related to the settlor as follows:

  — The settlor;

  — Spouse or former spouse of the settlor; or

  — A child of the settlor.

510. TESTAMENTARY TRUSTS

Integration

A *testamentary trust* is a trust created on the day a person dies. The terms of a testamentary trust are established by the deceased person's will or by law if there is no will, or by a court order under provincial legislation.

Testamentary trusts may be used as part of a will for a variety of purposes, including:

- Hold assets for minor children

- Provide ongoing income for minor children

- Provide for a disabled child or relative

- Provide for a spouse or common-law partner

- Provide for a wide variety of special needs

Types of Trusts

Spousal Trust

This type of trust is created at the time of the testator's death in which the surviving beneficiary spouse or common-law partner is entitled to receive all income that may arise during his lifetime and is the only person who can receive or access use of any income or capital of the trust during his lifetime.

Non-Spousal Trust

If a trust does not meet the definition of a qualified spousal trust, it falls into the category of a non-spousal testamentary trust for income tax purposes. These may be established for the benefit of minor children, a disabled child or perhaps even an elderly parent.

Taxation

Testamentary trusts are taxed at the same marginal tax rates as those for personal income tax. All income received by the trust is initially reported by the trust, but income tax is only paid at the trust level on income retained by the trust. Beneficiaries are taxed at their marginal tax rates. Trusts must file a tax return within 90 days after the year end of the trust (in contrast to December 31 as for *inter vivos* trusts).

Property Transfers

Property is transferred by the deceased's estate into the testamentary trust. Since the transfer is from the estate, the property has already been subject to the deemed disposition rules upon death.

Multiple Trusts

Where more than one trust exists, but where a single person contributed substantially all of the property into the trusts. The CRA may group these separate trusts and treat them as a single trust.

Unit 5
Self-Test Questions

QUESTIONS

Question 1

Tom's will provided for the establishment of a separate trust for each of his six children with the net assets of his estate being divided equally into the trusts. With regard to the taxation of the trusts, which one of the following statements is **true**?

a. Each trust is treated as a separate taxable entity.

b. Income earned by the trust is taxable in the hands of the beneficiary, with no other option available.

c. Income earned by the trust is taxable in the hands of the trust, with no other option available.

d. The trust pays tax at the top tax rate, so it is always advantageous to have the income taxed in the hands of the beneficiary.

Question 2

After the death of David's first wife, Trudy, he had a new will prepared that left everything to his parents. David moved on with his life and three years later married his childhood sweetheart, Rita. Neither David nor Rita felt an urgent need to update their wills. If David were to die under the current circumstances, how will his estate be distributed?

a. Rita will automatically split David's estate with his parents.

b. David's parents will be the beneficiaries of his estate.

c. David will be considered to have died intestate and Rita will receive a share of his estate based on the rules of provincial intestate succession.

d. Upon David's marriage to Rita, David's will is automatically updated and Rita becomes the sole beneficiary of his estate.

Question 3

Mary-Anne was the only surviving child of Hannah and Frederik, who both died in a common disaster. Neither of Mary-Anne's parents left a valid will, so Mary-Anne has applied to the courts for appointment as estate administrator. Prior to receiving the court's approval, what financial transactions can Mary-Anne legally undertake on behalf of the estate?

a. Negotiate an extension of the mortgage on her parent's home.

b. None.

c. Sell the family home registered jointly to her parents.

d. Use funds in her parent's bank accounts to make loan payments that are due or to pay off existing loans.

Question 4

If Donald, an employee of XYZ Inc., died on March 15, 2009, what is the latest date by which his final income tax return must be filed?

    a. April 30, 2009

    b. April 30, 2009

    c. December 31, 2009

    d. September 15, 2009

Question 5

Angelo, who lives in ABC Province, is reviewing his estate plan. He has the following assets registered in his own name:

- RRSP assets valued at $100,000 (spouse Anita named as beneficiary)

- RRIF assets valued at $100,000 (estate named as beneficiary)

- universal life insurance policy with a face value of $1,000,000 (estate is named as beneficiary)

- pension assets valued at $43,000 (son named as beneficiary)

- cottage valued at $225,000

- bond portfolio (non-registered) valued at $60,000

- stock portfolio (non-registered) valued at $90,000

- segregated funds valued at $30,000 (spouse Anita named as beneficiary)

In addition, he and Anita have the following assets registered in joint title with the right of survivorship:

- personal residence valued at $280,000

- segregated funds (non-registered) valued at $100,000

Calculate the probate fees on Angelo's estate, as of today. Probate fees are $5 per $1,000 on the first $50,000, and $15 per $1,000 over $50,000.

    a. $21,625

    b. $22,270

    c. $23,575

    d. $6,625

Question 6

Nadine is the executor for her father's estate. Her father has recently passed away and has left his entire estate to Jennifer, his spouse of ten years. With regard to tax issues, which of the following statements is true?

a. The spousal rollover provision is not automatic, but rather must be elected through the filing of specific forms.

b. If Nadine elects to opt out of a spousal rollover provision, she must do so with respect to all property.

c. If the spousal rollover provision is utilized, any applicable assets will roll to Jennifer with an ACB equal to the FMV.

d. If an election is made to opt out of the spousal rollover provision with respect to a specific piece of property, Jennifer's ACB for the property will be set at the FMV.

Question 7

When Tim died this year, he had an allowable capital loss of $47,000 but no taxable capital gains. That same year, he had earned income of $140,000. With regard to this scenario, which one of the following statements is true?

a. A maximum of 75% of the $47,000 in allowable capital losses can be claimed against Tim's current year income.

b. Tax rules allow for one-half of any outstanding allowable capital loss, $23,500 in this case, to be claimed in the year of death.

c. The full $47,000 can be deducted against Tim's earned income.

d. There is no opportunity to claim the $47,000 in allowable capital losses against Tim's income.

Question 8

When 23-year-old Kaitlyn became incapacitated because of a recent car accident, her parents Nadine and Rick were immediately ready to assume responsibility for managing her affairs. After all, Kaitlyn has never been married and is very close to her parents. With regard to the role that Nadine and Rick will assume, which of the following statements is true?

a. Nadine and Rick do not have automatic legal authority to act on Kaitlyn's behalf.

b. Nadine and Rick have automatic authority over Kaitlyn's financial affairs but not health-related issues.

c. Nadine and Rick have automatic authority over Kaitlyn's health-related affair but not her financial affairs.

d. Nadine and Rick will automatically assume the role of power of attorney, responsible for Kaitlyn's affairs.

Question 9

When Denny died, his son found a handwritten document that provided clear directions as to how Denny wanted his estate to be distributed. The document, dated August 29, 1973, was in Denny's handwriting and was signed by him although there was no witness to Denny's signature. After an extensive search, Denny's son was unable to locate any other formal or informal document that provided similar direction as to Denny's testamentary wishes. It is likely that the handwritten document will be treated as:

a. a notorial will

b. a modified English form will

c. a holograph will

d. an invalid will because Denny's signature was not witnessed

Question 10

Thirty-three-year-old Ralph was surprised to learn that all of his assets do not pass automatically to his wife, Janice, when he dies. His financial planner explained that the purpose of the will is to communicate Ralph's testamentary wishes. From the following list, which items can Ralph achieve through the completion of a will?

1. Indicate how he wants his distributable assets divided upon his death.

2. Indicate his preference regarding guardianship of his minor children, in the event that Janice does not survive him.

3. Make an irrevocable beneficiary designation.

4. Indicate how he wants Janice's distributable assets divided upon her death.

5. Create an *inter vivos* trust to take care of his six nephews.

a. 1 and 2 only

b. 1 and 4 only

c. 2, 3, 4 and 5 only

d. 3 and 5 only

Question 11

When Harry created his will in 1985, he left his antique car collection, valued at $250,000, to his eldest son, Rod. At the same time, Harry's will provided for his registered retirement savings plan (RRSP), also valued at $250,000, to pass to his youngest son, Andrew. The residual balance of the estate was to be divided evenly between Rod and Andrew. When Harry fell ill in 1998, he disposed of the antique car collection. Harry died this past year. At the time of Harry's death, his RRSP assets were valued at $347,000, with the remainder of his net estate valued at $650,000. The will created in 1985 was accepted as his last will and testament, with no changes having occurred since it was originally signed. Based on this scenario, which of the following statements is true?

    a. Andrew will receive the full value of the RRSP assets but will automatically become responsible for any income taxes arising from the disposition.

    b. Because the antique car collection no longer exists within the estate; it is removed as a bequest.

    c. Rod and Andrew will share equally in the estate including an equal split of the RRSP assets.

    d. Since the antique car collection was disposed of prior to Harry's death, Rod will automatically receive $250,000 from the estate as a substitute item.

Question 12

Gord's will provided for the distribution of his net estate to his five children in equal shares. At the time of Gord's death, his youngest son, age 23, was beginning medical school and needed immediate access to $50,000. The two eldest children, Ted and Todd, were executors and decided that in order to be fair they would immediately distribute $50,000 to each of the five children. After making this $250,000 distribution, Ted and Todd realized that the estate was short $30,000 in order to pay taxes owing. Given this shortfall, which of the following statements is true?

    a. The CRA will typically forego the shortfall.

    b. The CRA will typically divide the shortfall equally across the estate beneficiaries and add it to their personal tax bill for the subsequent year.

    c. Ted and Todd can be held personally liable for this shortfall.

    d. Ted and Todd can claim an administrative error and apply to have the estate treated as insolvent.

Question 13

Last year, when Raymond's brother and sister-in-law died, Raymond accepted the role of trustee on a Henson trust established for the benefit of his nephew, Alex. Which of the following statements describe Raymond's responsibilities under the trust?

1. Raymond likely has complete and absolute discretion as to how the money within the trust is used for Alex's benefit.

2. Raymond must act in Alex's best interest.

3. Raymond must act with reasonable and prudent judgment.

4. Raymond does not have a fiduciary relationship to Alex, but is expected to consistently demonstrate good judgment.

    a. 1 only

    b. 1, 2 and 3 only

    c. 2, 3 and 4 only

    d. 4 only

Question 14

Which of the following types of trust arrangements may be established as either a testamentary trust or as an *inter vivos* trust?

1. Personal trust

2. Spousal or common-law partner trust

3. Joint spousal or common-law partner trust

4. *Alter ego* trust

    a. 1 and 2 only

    b. 2, 3 and 4 only

    c. 3 and 4 only

    d. 3 only

Question 15

Where a beneficiary is entitled to take possession of trust property upon the completion of specified conditions, the beneficiary is viewed as having:

    a. A discretionary interest

    b. A non-obligatory interest

    c. A short-term interest

    d. A vested interest

Question 16

Angie is the settlor of an *inter vivos* trust under which her two adult daughters are the sole beneficiaries. The trust was established on July 1, 2007. On what date does the trust's first taxation year end?

    a. April 30, 2008

    b. December 31, 2007

    c. June 30, 2008

    d. September 28, 2007

Question 17

Rick is the sole beneficiary of an irrevocable *inter vivos* trust settled by his Aunt Edith. With regard to the transfer of assets into and out of the trust, which of the following statements is/are true?

1. Property transferred into the trust will trigger a deemed disposition that may result in a possible income tax liability for Edith.

2. If the trust disposes of capital property, the trustee may retain the gain/loss within the trust or may allocate it to the beneficiary.

3. Property may be transferred from the trust to Rick at the trust's ACB.

4. There will always be double taxation when assets transfer between the trust and Rick, but Rick can reclaim the excess tax when he disposes of the capital property.

    a. 1 and 3 only

    b. 1, 2 and 3 only

    c. 2 only

    d. 2, 3 and 4 only

QUESTIONS & SOLUTIONS

Question 1

Tom's will provided for the establishment of a separate trust for each of his six children with the net assets of his estate being divided equally into the trusts. With regard to the taxation of the trusts, which one of the following statements is **true**?

    a. Each trust is treated as a separate taxable entity.

    b. Income earned by the trust is taxable in the hands of the beneficiary, with no other option available.

    c. Income earned by the trust is taxable in the hands of the trust, with no other option available.

    d. The trust pays tax at the top tax rate, so it is always advantageous to have the income taxed in the hands of the beneficiary.

Answer: a

    ⇨   A testamentary trust is established on the day that the settlor dies. This type of trust is taxed at the same marginal tax rates as those for personal income tax. All income received by the trust is initially reported by the trust, but income tax is only paid at the trust level on the income retained in the trust.

Question 2

After the death of David's first wife, Trudy, he had a new will prepared that left everything to his parents. David moved on with his life and three years later married his childhood sweetheart, Rita. Neither David nor Rita felt an urgent need to update their wills. If David were to die under the current circumstances, how will his estate be distributed?

    a. Rita will automatically split David's estate with his parents.

    b. David's parents will be the beneficiaries of his estate.

    c. David will be considered to have died intestate and Rita will receive a share of his estate based on the rules of provincial intestate succession.

    d. Upon David's marriage to Rita, David's will is automatically updated and Rita becomes the sole beneficiary of his estate.

Answer: c

    ⇨   David's marriage to Rita nullifies his existing will. He will be considered to have died intestate.

Question 3

Mary-Anne was the only surviving child of Hannah and Frederik, who both died in a common disaster. Neither of Mary-Anne's parents left a valid will, so Mary-Anne has applied to the courts for appointment as estate administrator. Prior to receiving the court's approval, what financial transactions can Mary-Anne legally undertake on behalf of the estate?

     a. Negotiate an extension of the mortgage on her parent's home.

     b. None.

     c. Sell the family home registered jointly to her parents.

     d. Use funds in her parent's bank accounts to make loan payments that are due or to pay off existing loans.

Answer: b

    ⇨   When an individual dies without a valid will, an application must be made to the courts for the appointment of an estate administrator. Until an administrator is appointed, no one, including the spouse, has the immediate authority to represent the estate or deal with the deceased's assets.

Question 4

If Donald, an employee of XYZ Inc., died on March 15, 2009, what is the latest date by which his final income tax return must be filed?

     a. April 30, 2009

     b. April 30, 2010

     c. December 31, 2009

     d. September 15, 2009

Answer: b

    ⇨   Normally, the final income tax return for a deceased taxpayer is due the later of: six months after the date of the taxpayer's death or April 30th of the year following death.

Question 5

Angelo, who lives in ABC Province, is reviewing his estate plan. He has the following assets registered in his own name:

- RRSP assets valued at $100,000 (spouse Anita named as beneficiary)

- RRIF assets valued at $100,000 (estate named as beneficiary)

- universal life insurance policy with a face value of $1,000,000 (estate is named as beneficiary)

- pension assets valued at $43,000 (son named as beneficiary)

- cottage valued at $225,000

- bond portfolio (non-registered) valued at $60,000

- stock portfolio (non-registered) valued at $90,000

- segregated funds valued at $30,000 (spouse Anita named as beneficiary)

In addition, he and Anita have the following assets registered in joint title with the right of survivorship:

- personal residence valued at $280,000

- segregated funds (non-registered) valued at $100,000

Calculate the probate fees on Angelo's estate, as of today. Probate fees are $5 per $1,000 on the first $50,000 and $15 per $1,000 over $50,000.

a. $21,625

b. $22,270

c. $23,575

d. $6,625

Answer: a

⇨ Probatable assets may be determined by the structure under which the asset is owned. Assets that were wholly owned by the deceased or that were owned as tenants in common are typically subject to the probate process. Therefore, the RRSP with a named beneficiary, pension assets with the named beneficiary and the segregated funds will not be included for the probate calculation.

Question 6

Nadine is the executor for her father's estate. Her father has recently passed away and has left his entire estate to Jennifer, his spouse of ten years. With regard to tax issues, which of the following statements is true?

    a. The spousal rollover provision is not automatic, but rather must be elected through the filing of specific forms.

    b. If Nadine elects to opt out of a spousal rollover provision, she must do so with respect to all property.

    c. If the spousal rollover provision is utilized, any applicable assets will roll to Jennifer with an ACB equal to the FMV.

    d. If an election is made to opt out of the spousal rollover provision with respect to a specific piece of property, Jennifer's ACB for the property will be set at the FMV.

Answer: d

    ⇨   The legal representative for the deceased can elect to opt out of a spousal rollover. If they opt out, the property is deemed disposed at the FMV and Jennifer's ACB will be set at the FMV.

Question 7

When Tim died this year, he had an allowable capital loss of $47,000 but no taxable capital gains. That same year, he had earned income of $140,000. With regard to this scenario, which one of the following statements is true?

    a. A maximum of 75% of the $47,000 in allowable capital losses can be claimed against Tim's current year income.

    b. Tax rules allow for one-half of any outstanding allowable capital loss, $23,500 in this case, to be claimed in the year of death.

    c. The full $47,000 can be deducted against Tim's earned income.

    d. There is no opportunity to claim the $47,000 in allowable capital losses against Tim's income.

Answer: c

    ⇨   In the year of the taxpayer's death, the allowable capital loss may be used against any type of income realized in that year. This is an exception as generally an allowable capital loss can only be used against a taxable capital gain in a given year.

Question 8

When 23-year-old Kaitlyn became incapacitated because of a recent car accident, her parents Nadine and Rick were immediately ready to assume responsibility for managing her affairs. After all, Kaitlyn has never been married and is very close to her parents. With regard to the role that Nadine and Rick will assume, which of the following statements is true?

a. Nadine and Rick do not have automatic legal authority to act on Kaitlyn's behalf.

b. Nadine and Rick have automatic authority over Kaitlyn's financial affairs but not health-related issues.

c. Nadine and Rick have automatic authority over Kaitlyn's health-related affair but not her financial affairs.

d. Nadine and Rick will automatically assume the role of power of attorney, responsible for Kaitlyn's affairs.

Answer: a

⇨ Kaitlyn would needed to have established a valid or enduring power of attorney naming her parents for them to be able to act on her behalf. In the absence of a power of attorney, provincial authorities through the public guardian and trustee office typically assume responsibility for an incapacitated adults' affairs.

Question 9

When Denny died, his son found a handwritten document that provided clear directions as to how Denny wanted his estate to be distributed. The document, dated August 29, 1973, was in Denny's handwriting and was signed by him although there was no witness to Denny's signature. After an extensive search, Denny's son was unable to locate any other formal or informal document that provided similar direction as to Denny's testamentary wishes. It is likely that the handwritten document will be treated as:

a. a notorial will

b. a modified English form will

c. a holograph will

d. an invalid will because Denny's signature was not witnessed

Answer: c

⇨ A holograph will is one written completely in the handwriting of the deceased whose signature it bears. This form of will is recognized in all provinces although each may have slightly different criteria for acceptance including that it be signed and dated.

Question 10

Thirty-three-year-old Ralph was surprised to learn that all of his assets do not pass automatically to his wife, Janice, when he dies. His financial planner explained that the purpose of the will is to communicate Ralph's testamentary wishes. From the following list, which items can Ralph achieve through the completion of a will?

1. Indicate how he wants his distributable assets divided upon his death.

2. Indicate his preference regarding guardianship of his minor children, in the event that Janice does not survive him.

3. Make an irrevocable beneficiary designation.

4. Indicate how he wants Janice's distributable assets divided upon her death.

5. Create an *inter vivos* trust to take care of his six nephews.

    a. 1 and 2 only

    b. 1 and 4 only

    c. 2, 3, 4 and 5 only

    d. 3 and 5 only

Answer: a

    ⇨ A will typically communicates directions according to the division of assets, appointing an executor, guardianship of minor children, and conveying specific powers and duties of the executor.

Question 11

When Harry created his will in 1985, he left his antique car collection, valued at $250,000, to his eldest son, Rod. At the same time, Harry's will provided for his registered retirement savings plan (RRSP), also valued at $250,000, to pass to his youngest son, Andrew. The residual balance of the estate was to be divided evenly between Rod and Andrew. When Harry fell ill in 1998, he disposed of the antique car collection. Harry died this past year. At the time of Harry's death, his RRSP assets were valued at $347,000, with the remainder of his net estate valued at $650,000. The will created in 1985 was accepted as his last will and testament, with no changes having occurred since it was originally signed. Based on this scenario, which of the following statements is true?

    a. Andrew will receive the full value of the RRSP assets but will automatically become responsible for any income taxes arising from the disposition.

    b. Because the antique car collection no longer exists within the estate; it is removed as a bequest.

    c. Rod and Andrew will share equally in the estate including an equal split of the RRSP assets.

    d. Since the antique car collection was disposed of prior to Harry's death, Rod will automatically receive $250,000 from the estate as a substitute item.

Answer: b

    ⇨ Ademption refers to the removal of a bequest within the will because the asset no longer exists in the estate at the time of death. Unfortunately for Rod, there are no subsequent actions to make up for the missed bequest and so he is left without the $250,000 bequest noted in the will.

Question 12

Gord's will provided for the distribution of his net estate to his five children in equal shares. At the time of Gord's death, his youngest son, age 23, was beginning medical school and needed immediate access to $50,000. The two eldest children, Ted and Todd, were executors and decided that in order to be fair they would immediately distribute $50,000 to each of the five children. After making this $250,000 distribution, Ted and Todd realized that the estate was short $30,000 in order to pay taxes owing. Given this shortfall, which of the following statements is true?

   a. The CRA will typically forego the shortfall.

   b. The CRA will typically divide the shortfall equally across the estate beneficiaries and add it to their personal tax bill for the subsequent year.

   c. Ted and Todd can be held personally liable for this shortfall.

   d. Ted and Todd can claim an administrative error and apply to have the estate treated as insolvent.

Answer: c

   ⇨   The CRA will not typically forego any income taxes owning. In priority order, income taxes fall second only to final expenses in provincial jurisdictional order. The role of the executor is to be accountable for the accounting of the estate assets and payment of outstanding debts, which would include any income taxes triggered by death.

Question 13

Last year, when Raymond's brother and sister-in-law died, Raymond accepted the role of trustee on a Henson trust established for the benefit of his nephew, Alex. Which of the following statements describe Raymond's responsibilities under the trust?

1. Raymond likely has complete and absolute discretion as to how the money within the trust is used for Alex's benefit.

2. Raymond must act in Alex's best interest.

3. Raymond must act with reasonable and prudent judgment.

4. Raymond does not have a fiduciary relationship to Alex, but is expected to consistently demonstrate good judgment.

   a. 1 only

   b. 1, 2 and 3 only

   c. 2, 3 and 4 only

   d. 4 only

Answer: b

   ⇨   A Henson Trust is a discretionary testamentary trust intended to provide financially for a disabled child without impacting any provincial benefits that they be eligible for. For the Henson trust to meet it's objectives it must ensure that the trust is fully discretionary so that the trustee retains all discretion related to the property rights. As with any trustee, they are obligated to act in the best interest of the beneficiary, act impartially between multiple beneficiaries and exercise reasonable and prudent judgment in their role. Undertaking a trustee role establishes a fiduciary relationship with the beneficiary, so the fourth point above is false.

Question 14

Which of the following types of trust arrangements may be established as either a testamentary trust or as an *inter vivos* trust?

1. Personal trust

2. Spousal or common-law partner trust

3. Joint spousal or common-law partner trust

4. *Alter ego* trust

      a. 1 and 2 only

      b. 2, 3 and 4 only

      c. 3 and 4 only

      d. 3 only

Answer: a

    ⇨ A joint spousal trust is created as an *inter vivos* trust by a settlor who is at least 65 years of age and the income is accessible only to the settlor or the settlor's spouse before the latter death. The *alter ego* trust also requires the settlor be at least 65 years of age with the settlor being the only individual eligible to receive the income or capital of the trust during the settlor's lifetime.

Question 15

Where a beneficiary is entitled to take possession of trust property upon the completion of specified conditions, the beneficiary is viewed as having:

      a. A discretionary interest

      b. A non-obligatory interest

      c. A short-term interest

      d. A vested interest

Answer: d

Question 16

Angie is the settlor of an *inter vivos* trust under which her two adult daughters are the sole beneficiaries. The trust was established on July 1, 2009. On what date does the trust's first taxation year end?

      a. April 30, 2010

      b. December 31, 2009

      c. June 30, 2010

      d. September 28, 2009

Answer: b

    ⇨ The taxation year for an *inter vivos* trust is December 31, except in the case of a mutual fund trust. A mutual fund trust may elect December 15th as their year end.

Question 17

Rick is the sole beneficiary of an irrevocable *inter vivos* trust settled by his Aunt Edith. With regard to the transfer of assets into and out of the trust, which of the following statements is/are true?

1. Property transferred into the trust will trigger a deemed disposition that may result in a possible income tax liability for Edith.

2. If the trust disposes of capital property, the trustee may retain the gain/loss within the trust or may allocate it to the beneficiary.

3. Property may be transferred from the trust to Rick at the trust's ACB.

4. There will always be double taxation when assets transfer between the trust and Rick, but Rick can reclaim the excess tax when he disposes of the capital property.

    a. 1 and 3 only

    b. 1, 2 and 3 only

    c. 2 only

    d. 2, 3 and 4 only

Answer: b

> ⇨ Unfortunately for Rick, when the capital property is disposed of by the trust, the trust will incur the capital gain or loss. The trustee can allocate the capital gain to a beneficiary or retain the gain/loss in the trust and reflect it on the trust's tax return.

THE CFP
EDUCATION PROGRAM

CCH/ADVOCIS FPSC-APPROVED CAPSTONE COURSE

MODULE 26
FINANCIAL MANAGEMENT

Module 26
FINANCIAL MANAGEMENT

Appendices

Module 26
Financial Management

Unit 1
Financial Calculations and Ratios

601. ANALYSIS OF FINANCIAL INFORMATION

This section provides a foundation for determining investment performance covering interest calculations, the time value of money (present value, future value, annuities), and investment returns. The following section assumes that the Hewlett Packard HP10BII calculator is being used. If a different calculator is being used, refer to the owner's manual for how to do the calculations.

First Function (white print)	
N	Number of payments or compounding periods
I/YR	Annual nominal interest rate
PV	The present value
PMT	The amount of the periodic payment
FV	Future value

Second Function (orange print)	
XP/YR	Optional shortcut for storing N. The number entered in the display is multiplied by the value in P/YR and stored the result in N
NOM%	Nominal interest percent
EFF%	Effective interest percent
P/YR	Stores the number of periods per year

- Use the SHIFT Key to shift between first function and second function keys.

- BEG and END Mode — If first payment occurs at "beginning of the period", press [SHIFT] BEG/END key to get the word BEGIN to appear on the screen.

- Use the [+/-] key to change sign of a number; i.e., -100. Cash outflows are negative, cash inflows are positive numbers.

- Calculator keeps entries in memory, so before doing a new calculation, press [SHIFT] C ALL to clear the memory.

Interest Calculations

Understanding time value of money concepts including simple interest and compound interest allows the financial planner to identify issues and counsel a client on appropriate financial planning strategies within retirement planning and portfolio analysis of fixed income and equity investments. Time value of money is based on the concept that there is an opportunity cost to using money today versus saving it and investing it for the future.

See Appendix One for the financial formulae sheet that is provided at the actual CFP Examination. In general, the formulae sheet is not beneficial since most candidates use financial calculators during the examination.

Interest is the rate of return earned (or paid) for the use of money for a period of time.

Simple interest does not include the re-investment of any interest that is earned in a previous period in the calculation of principal and interest in subsequent periods.

The formula for calculating simple interest is: Interest = Amount invested (Principal) × Interest rate per period × Time period.

With *compound interest*, the interest earned during a preceding period is added to the principal amount for calculating interest in a subsequent period.

The formula for calculating compound interest is: Interest = (Amount invested + Accumulated interest) × Interest rate per period × Time period.

MARVIN

Marvin invested $1,000 for two years at 10%. Using simple interest, interest earned would be $1,000 × 10% × 1 year = $100, compared to compound interest of ($1,000 + ($1,000 × 10%)) × 10% × 1 year = $110 in year two.

The *nominal yield* (or *rate*) is the basic interest rate that is charged or earned for any compounding period. The *effective yield* (or *rate*) is the actual interest rate earned or paid based on the number of compounding periods.

$$\text{Effective Yield} = \frac{\text{Total Future Value - Original Value}}{\text{Original Value}} \times 100$$

MATTHEW

Matthew invests $100 in a bond that pays 6% compounded twice per year. The nominal interest rate is 6% (the stated interest rate).

Interest earned 1st six months = 100 × 6% ÷ 2 = $3.00
Interest earned 2nd six months = (100 + 3) × 6% ÷ 2 = $3.09
                                                 $6.09

$$\text{Effective Interest Rate} = \frac{(106.09 - 100)}{100} \times 100 = \quad 6.9\%$$

Interest Rate Conversion

Knowing the annual nominal rate allows for conversion to the corresponding effective interest rate or vice versa.

CHARLENE

Charlene has an investment that pays 6.5% annual interest, compounded daily. What is the annual effective rate of interest?

Keystrokes
- [SHIFT] C ALL
- 6.7 [SHIFT] NOM%
- 365 [SHIFT] P/YR
- [SHIFT] EFF%
- Display shows 6.9289

The effective rate of interest is 6.9289%.

TIME VALUE OF MONEY

Present Value. What a sum of money received in the future is equivalent to in current dollars today.

Future Value. Defines the final or terminal value of an investment if the investment compounds at a given rate for a period of time.

Two Types of Cash Flows

A *single amount* has only one payment versus an *annuity*, where they are a series of periodic payments.

Present Value of a Single Amount

What is the present value of $10,000 received in four years? Assume a 10% interest rate compounded annually? (Disregard taxes.)

Keystrokes
- [SHIFT] C ALL
- 1 [SHIFT] P/YR
- 4 [SHIFT] XP/YR
- 10 I/YR
- 0 PMT
- 10,000 FV
- PV
- Display shows -6,830.1346

The investment is worth $6,830.13 today.

Today	4 years
PV = ??	$10,000

Future Value of a Single Amount

What is the future value of $1,000 to be received in 15 years? Assume a 3% interest rate compounded annually. (Disregard taxes.)

Keystrokes
- [SHIFT] C ALL
- 1 [SHIFT] P/YR
- 15 [SHIFT] XP/YR
- 3 I/YR
- 0 PMT
- 1,000 [+/-] PV
- FV
- Display shows 1,557.9674

The investment will be worth $1,557 in 15 years.

Today	15 years
$1,000	FV =??

Present Value of a Periodic Payment Stream (Annuity)

What is the present value of $2,500 received at the end of each year for four years? Assume a 10% interest rate compounded annually. (Disregard taxes.)

Keystrokes
- [SHIFT] C ALL
- 1 [SHIFT] P/YR
- 4 [SHIFT] XP/YR
- 10 I/YR
- 2,500 PMT
- 0 FV
- [SHIFT] END
- PV
- Display shows -7,924.6636

The PV of $2,500 received over four years is $7,925.

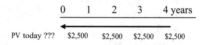

Future Value of Periodic Payment Stream (Annuity)

What is the future value of $6,000 invested at the end of each year for three years? Assume a 4.4% interest rate compounded annually. (Disregard taxes.)

Keystrokes
- [SHIFT] C ALL
- 1 [SHIFT] P/YR
- 3[SHIFT] XP/YR
- 4.4 I/YR
- 6,000 [+/-] PMT
- 0 PV
- [SHIFT] END
- FV
- Display shows $18,803.6160

The investment will be worth $18,803.62.

Solving for an Unknown Variable

Any unknown value can be solved if the values of all other variables are known.

In this example, TVM will be used to determine the interest rate.

What is the nominal interest rate of the following loan assuming monthly compounding? The loan amount is $25,000, with $525 monthly payments at the beginning of the month for five years.

Keystrokes

- [SHIFT] C ALL
- 12 [SHIFT] P/YR
- 5 [SHIFT] XP/YR
- 25,000 PV
- 525 [+/-] PMT
- 0 FV
- [SHIFT] BEG
- I/YR
- Display shows 9.8480

The nominal interest rate is 9.85%.

Calculation for Perpetuity

To solve for perpetuities that do not have a fixed maturity date, set the term very long. (XP/YR = 999)

JILL

Jill wants to invest in an investment that never matures, but pays $1,000 at the end of each month in perpetuity. The prevailing market interest rate is 8%. What should the market price of the security be?

Keystrokes

- [SHIFT] C ALL
- 12 [SHIFT] P/YR
- 999 [SHIFT] XP/YR
- 8 I/YR
- 1,000 PMT
- 0 FV
- [SHIFT] END
- PV
- Display shows -150,0000 or $150,000

Internal Rate of Return/Net Present Value

To solve problems where cash flows occur over regular intervals but are of different amounts, use the cash flow application (CFA) on the calculator instead of the TVM calculations. Use the "CFj" key on the calculator (middle key in the third row on the calculator).

Net Present Value

For an investment to make financial sense, the PV (future cash flows) must be > Amount invested.

An investor would not invest $10,000 in a project if it only produced $6,000 in cash flow. The NPV finds the present value of a stream of cash flows.

- IF NPV ≥0 → Do the project.
- IF NPV <0 → Do *not* do the project.

CARMAN

Carman is considering investing $12,000 in Project ABC that will generate cash flows of:

> End of yr 1   ($20,000)
>   yr 2   ($1,000)
>   yr 3 $15,000
>   yr 4 $27,000
>   yr 5 $32,000

Using a discount factor of 13%, what is the present value of this investment?

Keystrokes
- [SHIFT] C ALL
- 1 [SHIFT] P/YR (sets all periods per year to one)
- 12,000 [+/-] CFj (enters cash flow of initial investment cf0)
- 20,000 [+/-] CFj (enters cash flow for year 1 cf1)
- 1,000 [+/-] CFj (enters cash flow for year 2 cf2)
- 15,000 CFj (enters cash flow for year 3 cf3)
- 27,000 CFj (enters cash flow for year 4 cf4)
- 32,000 CFj (enters cash flow for year 5 cf5)
- 13 I/YR
- [SHIFT] NPV
- Display shows 13,841.4143

Since NPV > 0, Carman would *do* the project.

Internal Rate of Return

Similar to NPV, except with the internal rate of return (IRR), the answer is a percentage compared to a dollar amount under NPV.

IRR calculates the annual nominal interest rate that is required in the project to give a NPV = 0.

- If IRR > Cost of Capital, do the project.
- If IRR < Cost of Capital, do *not* do the project.

Use the same keys on the calculator as NPV, except press IRR/YR instead of NPV at the end, using the same Carman example.

Keystrokes
- [SHIFT] C ALL
- 1 [SHIFT] P/YR (sets all periods per year to one)
- 12,000 [+/-] CFj (enters cash flow of initial investment cf0)
- 20,000 [+/-] CFj (enters cash flow for year 1 cf1)
- 1,000 [+/-] CFj (enters cash flow for year 2 cf2)
- 15,000 CFj (enters cash flow for year 3 cf3)
- 27,000 CFj (enters cash flow for year 4 cf4)
- 32,000 CFj (enters cash flow for year 5 cf5)
- 13 I/YR
- [SHIFT] IRR/YR
- Display shows 25.7259 (or 25.7%)

Since IRR > 13% (the cost of the capital), *do* the project.

Rates of Return Calculations

There are eight types of rates of return that you must know for the CFP® Examination. The student should be able to calculate:

- Holding period return (HPR)
- Yield to maturity (YTM)
- Time-weighted return
- Dollar-weighted return
- Real return
- After-tax return
- Real after-tax return
- Dividend yield

Holding Period Return

= (Closing value - Opening value) ÷ (Opening value) × 100

LUCY

Lucy purchased a stock for $40.00 and eventually sells it for $55.00. What is the HPR?

HPR = ($55 - 40) ÷ $40

= 0.375 or 37.5%

Yield to Maturity

Yield to maturity (YTM) measures the total return of a security (usually a bond) over its lifetime. It is the bond's internal rate of return. The YTM of a bond purchased at face value and held to maturity is equal to the bond's coupon rate.

A bond is purchased for $17,000. The bond was originally issued for $15,000 at a coupon rate of 12% and has ten years remaining. What is the yield to maturity?

- P/YR = 2 (bonds have two interest payments per year)
- XP/YR = 10
- PMT = 900
- FV = 15,000
- PV = -17,000
- MODE = END

SOLVE FOR I/YR, which equals 9.8718

Time-Weighted Rate of Return

Time-weighted rate of return (TWR) measures that part of the return due to the performance of a single investment at the beginning of a period and measuring the growth or loss of market value to the end of that period only. It ignores any new cash inflows or withdrawals.

SIMON

Simon invests $100,000 at the start of year one. The money earns $5,000 (5%) by the end of the year. At the beginning of year two, Simon invests another $95,000 (total now $200,000). By the end of year two, $20,000 is earned (10% return in the year).

The TWR = $((1.05 \times 1.10)^{1/2} - 1) \times 100$

= $(1.0747 - 1) \times 100$

= 7.47%

For the *dollar-weighted return*, see the *internal rate of return*.

Real Rate of Return

If the nominal interest rate is less than expected rate of inflation, there is no real rate of return.

$$\text{Real Rate of Return} = \frac{(\text{nominal interest rate - inflation rate})}{(1 + \text{inflation rate})}$$

Assume the investment has a nominal return of 4% while the expected inflation rate is 2%.

$$\text{Real Rate of Return} = \frac{(\text{nominal interest rate - inflation})}{(1 + \text{inflation})}$$
$$= (0.04 - 0.02) \div (1 + 0.02)$$
$$= 0.0196$$

The investment has a real rate of return of 1.96%.

Real After-Tax Rate of Return

Takes into account inflation and taxation on the real rate of return.

$$\text{Real After-Tax Rate of Return} = \frac{(\text{nominal interest rate } (1 - \text{MTR}) - \text{inflation rate})}{(1 + \text{inflation rate})}$$

Assume an investment has a nominal return of 4% while the expected inflation rate is 2% and the marginal tax rate (MTR) = 30%.

$$\text{Real Rate of Return} = (\text{nominal interest rate } (1 - 0.30) - \text{inflation}) \div (1 + \text{inflation})$$
$$= (0.04(0.7) - 0.02) \div (1 + 0.02)$$
$$= 0.0078$$

The investment has a real rate of return of 0.78%.

AL

At retirement Al hopes to have an income of $60,000 after-tax, for 25 years, indexed for inflation of 2%. Assume Al can earn an annual return of 7% compounded annually before tax, he has a 35% MTR, and his retirement funds will be paid annually at the beginning of each year. How much does Al need to have at retirement?

Keystrokes

- [SHIFT] C ALL
- 1 [SHIFT] P/YR
- 25 [SHIFT] XP/YR
- $(0.07 \times (1 - 0.35) - 0.02)) \div (1 + 0.02) \times 100$ I/YR*
- 60,000 [+/-] PMT
- 0 FV
- [SHIFT] BEG
- SOLVE FOR PV
- Display shows $1,133,099.1500

Al will need savings of $1,133,099 to fund his retirement.

* Do all calculations on the calculator without writing down intermediate answers since the calculator calculates up to 15 significant digits.

Dividend Yield

Dividend yield = ((Annual dividend payment) ÷ (Current market price)) × 100

JOHN

John purchased $100 par value preferred shares offering a dividend rate of 6.95% at the current market price of $90. What is the dividend yield?

Dividend Yield = ((Annual dividend payment) ÷ (current market price)) × 100
$$= ((\$100 \times 6.95\%) \div \$90) \times 100$$
$$= 7.72\%$$

---

602. PERSONAL FINANCIAL RATIOS

Debt is the amount of money an individual owes. It may include mortgages, bank loans, car loans, and personal loans.

Assets are things an individual owns of monetary value. Examples include money in bank accounts, cars, paintings, homes, and computers.

Equity is the difference between assets and debt.

Debt-to-Equity Ratio = Total Debt ÷ Total Equity.

Debt-to-Total Assets Ratio = Total Debt ÷ Total Assets.

Total Debt Service

$$= \frac{((\text{Monthly housing costs})) + (\text{all other monthly debt payments})}{\text{Gross Monthly income}} \times 100$$

- Debts include housing costs such as mortgage payments, property taxes, heating, and other liabilities such as credit cards, car loans, and other personal loans.
- The ratio should be less than 40%.
- It is used in credit assessment to ensure individuals are not over-extended and become high-risk candidates for default on debt payments.

Gross Debt Service

$$= \frac{((\text{Monthly mortgage payment}) + (\text{Property taxes}) + (\text{Heat}) + (\text{Condo fees}))}{\text{Gross Monthly income}} \times 100$$

- Used by mortgage lenders to evaluate a person's ability to pay her mortgage debt.
- Acceptable range is 25% to 35%.

TOM

Tom applied for a $250,000 mortgage on a $350,000 home that will require monthly payments of $900. Property taxes are expected to be $200 and heating costs are $25 per month. He pays $80 for credit cards bills and $75 monthly on his $5,000 car loan. The market value of the car is $8,000. Tom's gross annual salary is $48,000. Calculate the total debt service (TDS), gross debt service (GDS), debt-to-assets, and debt-to-equity ratios. Should Tom receive the mortgage?

TDS = (900 + 200 + 25 + 80 + 75) ÷ (48,000 ÷ 12)
= 1,280 ÷ 4,000
= 32%. The ratio is within a reasonable range of less that 40%.

GDS = (900 + 200 + 25) ÷ (48,000 ÷ 12)
= 1,125 ÷ 4,000
= 28.1%. The ratio is within a reasonable range of 25% to 35%.

Debt-to-Assets ratio = (250,000 + 5,000) ÷ (350,000 + 8,000)
= 71.2%

This is very high. It means that Tom owes 71 cents for every dollar of assets he owns.

Debt-to-Equity Ratio = (250,000 + 5,000) ÷ (350,000 - 250,000 + 8,000 - 5,000)
= 255,000 ÷ 103,000
= 2.476 times

This is very high. It can be interpreted to mean that Tom owes $2.47 for every dollar of equity. Overall, Tom would qualify for a mortgage under the TDS and GDS ratios.

---

603. BUDGETING

Cash Flow Analysis

Personal money management involves the management of cash inflows and cash outflows within a budget in an effort to achieve the desired financial goals.

Cash inflows or income are summarized in a budget, usually on a monthly basis, to determine the total amount of money available to cover expenditures. The two main sources of cash are regular inflows such as monthly salary and infrequent lump-sum amounts like dividend income. The timing of expenses is also estimated on a monthly basis as regular and lump-sum amounts. It is important to ensure the all income and expenses are included in the budget. See Appendix Three for an example of a cash flow.

If income > expenses, there is a surplus of cash. If income < expenses, there is a deficit and additional cash is required from available savings or by increasing debt to fund the deficit.

Emergency Fund

An emergency fund is a source of readily accessible liquid funds (i.e., savings account, Canada Savings Bonds, or cashable GIC) to cover an unexpected need for cash. Historically, the rule of thumb has been 10% of gross income should be set aside in a liquid asset to finance emergency needs. A family may be able to have a smaller emergency fund than 10% if they have access to other easily accessible resources like a line of credit.

604. PERSONAL FINANCIAL STATEMENTS

Net Worth Statement

Net Worth = Assets - Liabilities

An individual's net worth can be compared to her personal goals and objectives to develop financial plans. Net worth statements are usually presented at current or fair market values and they do not usually include the tax liability of selling the assets, if applicable.

Asset Allocation

Asset allocation refers to the diversification of an investment portfolio towards an appropriate mix of investments (fixed income and equity) based on the individual's specific investment objectives that maximize the portfolio's performance while managing investment risk at an appropriate level. The goal is to generate more consistent returns, lower volatility on the portfolio, and increase the chance of achieving the financial objectives.

Cash Flow Statement

The cash flow statement denotes the cash inflows and outflows over a period of time. It is important to differentiate discretionary expenses like travel, meals and entertainment from essential expenses such as groceries, rent, and utilities to identify areas where better cash management would benefit the individual. The cash flow statement also helps identify periods of surplus cash where additional savings could be used for investments.

SHARON AND MAX WEST

Sharon and Max West, a married couple aged 42 and 45, live in XYZ province. They know saving for retirement is important but are unsure if they have the resources to save any money. The couple have provided a statement of net worth and monthly cash flow statements in Appendices Two and Three. Review the West's Statement of Net Worth and Projected Monthly Cash Flow Statement and comment on the net worth statement and cash flow statements.

Suggested recommendations include:

Net Worth Statement

- The debt to equity ratio of 75.9% (244,400 ÷ 322,200) is quite high due to the mortgage. Debt to total assets is also high at 43% (244,400 ÷ 566,600). The TDS is reasonable at 30.8% (($28,000 + $4,000 + $1,000) ÷ $107,200).

- The non-registered assets are more weighted to equities than conservative investments like GICs. Given their age, they will need to significantly increase their retirement savings to be able to enjoy retirement.

- The Wests should try to pay down their credit card/consumer debt since it is most likely at high interest rates.

Cash Flow Statement

- Income each month varies significantly. April has the lowest income at $7,088, and December has the highest at $14,927.

- There is variability in the monthly expenses. Expenses are the highest in July ($9,450), and the lowest in October ($4,533).

- The Wests will need to identify how they are going to fund the months of January and July where they have negative cash flow.

- At a high level, it appears the Wests should have the resources to save for retirement. According to the cash flow statement, they will have $30,400 available for savings and investing for retirement.

701. ECONOMIC ENVIRONMENT

Economic Indicators

The analysis of business cycles and "economic indicators" enables economists to forecast economic trends by examining the repetitive sequences that occur and to use indicators to provide predictions. Economic indicators are measurable economic phenomena that move in concert with changes in the business cycle

- **Leading Indicators.** A measurable economic factor that changes before the economic output starts to move in a way that indicates a trend. Some examples of common leading indicators include changes in business and consumer credit, new orders for equipment and durable goods, housing starts, new businesses formed, material prices, and stock prices.

- **Coincident Indicators.** A measurable economic factor that moves in concert, both directly and simultaneously, with economic output, indicating a trend. Examples include non-agricultural payrolls, personal income, industrial production, manufacturing, and trade sales.

- **Lagging Indicators.** A measurable economic factor that begins to change after the economy has changed to a new pattern or trend. Examples include the duration of unemployment, outstanding loans, average prime interest rate charged by banks, change in labour cost per unit of output, ratio of manufacturing, and trade inventories to sales.

Inflation and Deflation

Inflation is the percentage change in the purchasing power of a unit of currency over a specific period of time. The *Consumer Price Index* (CPI) is an indicator of changes to the general level of consumer prices.

The CPI is used in four unique ways:

- As a benchmark to escalate the given value of a dollar over time;
- As a tool to deflate current dollar estimates;
- As an integral part in the establishment of Canadian economic policy; and
- In economic research and analysis relative to the causes and effects of inflation along with regional disparities in price changes.

Causes

Inflation results when money is produced at a more rapid pace than the supply of goods and services. This causes a shortage of goods and services relative to the supply of money.

Inflation Control

The Bank of Canada and Canadian government agreed upon a target inflation rate in the range of 1% to 3% for the period between 2006 and 2011.

Effects of Inflation

High inflation erodes purchasing power. Investments tend to be more speculative as individuals attempt to leverage the effects of inflation.

With low inflation, wage and price demands tend to be less onerous when an economy is not experiencing significant price changes.

$$\text{Unexpected inflation} = (\text{Actual inflation}) - (\text{Expected inflation})$$

Deflation is a sustained decrease in prices, represented by negative changes to the CPI year over year. Deflation should not be confused with "disinflation", which is a decline in the rates of average increases in the rate of the CPI. Deflation can cause harmful effects on a country's economy, such as causing spending habits to contract, resulting in lower prices as economic uncertainty intensifies.

Employment and Unemployment Measures

To be classified as unemployed, a person must not have worked in the week; must have actively sought work in the previous four weeks; and, must be currently available to take a job. Persons who have not looked for work because they are on temporary layoff or because they have a new job scheduled to start within four weeks are also counted as unemployed. The official unemployment rate shows the unemployed as a percentage of the total labour force.

Monetary Policy

Monetary policy is the efforts to manage and control the supply of money in the Canadian economy by the Bank of Canada, which is ultimately accountable to the federal government.

The total demand for money is comprised of two elements:

- Transaction demands; and
- Asset demands.

There are three basic ways that the Bank of Canada can affect the money supply:

- Conducting open market operations;
- Transferring government deposits to/from private banks; and

- Changing the bank rate, which affects the target for the overnight rate.

Open Market

Open market operations involve the sale and purchase of Canadian government bonds and other government securities.

Transfers of Government Deposits

The transferring of government deposits to private banks provides the private banking system with excess reserves that can be used to increase the money supply through the demand–deposit multiplier or money multiplier.

Changing the Bank Rate

The bank rate is the interest rate charged by the Bank of Canada when private banks have loans with the Bank of Canada.

When interest rates increase, it causes private banks to incur greater costs, if forced to borrow.

Expansionary versus Contractionary Monetary Policy

Expansionary monetary policy increases the money supply while contractionary monetary policy decreases the money supply, and is achieved through buying government securities, transferring government deposits to private banks, and lowering the bank rate.

Contractionary monetary policy is achieved through selling government securities, transferring government deposits from private banks, and increasing the bank rate.

Monetary Policy and the Interest Rate

When the Bank of Canada is pursuing an *expansionary monetary policy*, the interest rate falls. When a *contractionary monetary policy* is in place, and money is relatively scarce, interest rates increase.

Fiscal Policy

Fiscal policy are the actions taken by the Canadian government to influence the economy through government behaviour regarding spending decisions and tax policy. Fiscal policy can generally be divided into three categories:

- Government purchases of goods and services;
- Taxes; and
- Transfer payments to households (i.e., Old Age Security, Unemployment Insurance).

Expansionary fiscal policy, which involves increased government spending, low taxes, and increased transfer payments, results in consumers having more disposable income and increased economic output.

Contractionary fiscal policy leads to decreases in economic output. Increased taxes lowers income and reduced government spending and transfers decrease consumers' disposable income.

Business Cycles

Business cycles are significant swings or fluctuations in economic activity. The boom years are periods of economic expansion; the periods of economic decline are labeled as recessions or depressions.

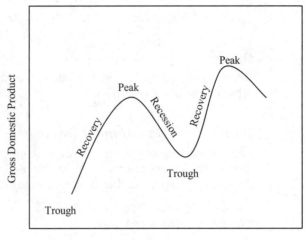

There are four main business cycles:

- **Trough.** This cycle follows a recession, and less frequently, a depression, during which output and employment reach their lowest point.

- **Recovery/Expansion.** Also referred to as a period of "expansion" and output and employment expand with movement toward full employment and full capacity output.

- **Peak.** During this period, production output is increasing or steady as the economy reaches full production capacity.

- **Recession.** Characterized by a period of at least two consecutive quarters (six months) where there is obvious and continued decline in output, employment and income.

Business Cycle Economic Impact

	Trough (1)	Recovery/Expansion (2)	Peak (3)	Recession (4)
Savings	High	Begins to decrease	Decreasing	Increasing
Spending	Low	Begins to increase	Increasing	Decreasing
Output/Production	Reaches lowest point	Increasing and moving toward full capacity	Increasing or steady as economy reaches full production capacity	Decreasing
Employment	Unemployment reaches highest point.	Increasing and moving toward full employment	Steady or increasing as economy reaches full employment during this phase	Decreasing
Notes		Further into the recovery and before reaching full employment and full capacity production, price levels tend to rise	Price levels tend to increase Note: Statistics Canada normally defines a recession as two consecutive quarters of negative economic growth.	

Note: Statistics Canada normally defines a recession as two consecutive quarters of negative economic growth.

Foreign Exchange Rates

Canada has a floating exchange rate where there is no pre-determined value of the Canadian dollar relative to the currency of other countries. In addition to the influences of interest rates and inflation, exchange rates are also affected by Canada's balance of trade and investors' expectations relative to Canada's economic outlook.

Gross Domestic Product

The Gross Domestic Product (GDP) is a formal measure of the total productive output of the final goods and services produced within Canada during a single year. The GDP takes into account all labour and capital within the geographical boundaries of Canada, ignoring the residency of the labour and ownership of the capital. The GDP can be calculated in two ways: the expenditure approach or the income approach. The *expenditure approach* measures the amount spent on all final goods. The *income approach* measures all the income received by all factors of production integral to producing the final goods.

Gross National Product

The Gross National Product (GNP) measures the output generated by residents of Canada, regardless of where the output is produced. The GNP includes such direct items as wages and salaries, company profits and rents.

- The GDP emphasizes production within the boundaries of Canada.

- The GNP emphasizes Canadian income that is generated by Canadian residents, regardless of the geographical origin.

Financial Markets

Money markets are financial markets for short-term borrowing and lending of Treasury bills, commercial paper and banker's acceptances.

Bond markets are financial markets where debt securities, usually bonds, are bought and sold.

Equity markets are financial markets where common and preferred shares are bought and sold. The primary market is that part of the capital markets that deal with initial offering of stocks and bonds. After a financial security has been sold in the primary market, it gets traded in the secondary market between individual investors.

Foreign exchange markets are financial markets where one currency is traded for another currency.

Commodity markets are financial markets where raw or primary products are bought and sold in standardized contracts.

Term Structure of Interest Rates and Yield Curves

The interest rate yield curve is a graphical representation that depicts the relationship between rates of return on fixed-income securities and the maturity dates of those securities.

Types of Curves

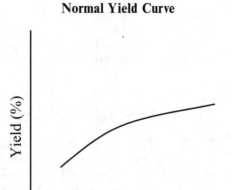

Normal Yield Curve

With a *normal yield curve*, long-term rates are higher than short-term rates, resulting in the upward slope to the right.

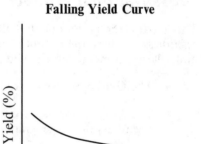

Falling Yield Curve

With a *falling yield curve*, the yield curve is downward sloping, or inverted, which means yields fall as maturity increases.

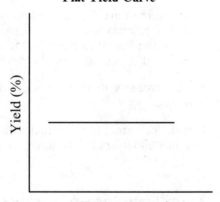

Flat Yield Curve

With a *flat yield curve*, the yield curve is flat, which means yields are identical across all maturities.

There are three significant theories or schools of thought that are generally used to explain the term structure of interest rates:

Expectation Theory

The yield curve represents what people expect rates to be in the future.

Liquidity Preference Theory

Investors will accept lower yields on short-term investments when it allows them to maintain liquidity. They demand a higher yield on long term investment due to the non-liquid nature of long term investments.

Market Segmentation Theory

The yield curve is segmented into short-term (banks), medium term (mutual funds, casualty insurance carriers) and long-term investors (pension funds, life insurance companies). The yield curve is a composite of the three segments' requirements.

Forecasting Economic Trends

The predictive power of yield curves comes from their ability to predict significant interest-rate movements. Yield curves are better relative predictors of economic output than other macroeconomic and financial variables, but also need to be utilized with caution — they did not successfully predict the 1990 recession, for example.

The Effect of Government Borrowing

When the government increases spending, it often must also issue debt to fund the increases; this can shift the slope of the yield curve.

Supply and Demand

It is the forces of supply and demand that coordinate and set the price in the production and sale of goods and services.

Demand

The demand curve is the amount of a commodity or service that a consumer desires to own, combined with the capacity to purchase it at a given price. The lower the price, the more quantity will be demanded. The demand curve slopes down and to the right.

The basic determinants of demand include:

- Price of the good or service

- Changes to price of related goods (substitute or complementary goods)

- Changes to consumers' income or wealth

- Changes to consumers' expectations (i.e., regarding income, price, and/or product availability)

- Changes to consumers' tastes or preferences

Movements along the demand curve are caused by changes in price. Shifts in the demand curve are caused by changes in the four other factors (price of related goods, consumers' wealth, consumers' expectations, and tastes/preferences).

Movements Along the Demand Curve

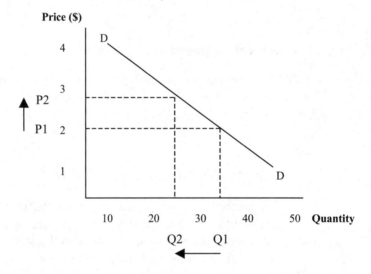

An increase in price results in decreased quantity demanded (movement along the demand curve).

Shifts in the Demand Curve

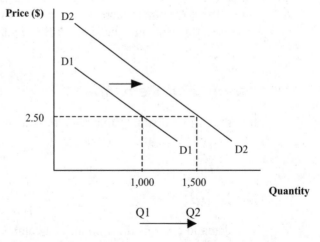

An increase in one factor other than price shifts the demand curve to the right (changes in consumers' wealth, tastes, expectations, or the price of other goods).

Supply

Supply is the quantity supplied or the amount of a good or service a producer is willing and able to sell at a given price during a given period of time. The curve slopes upwards. As price increases, the quantity supplied increases. Conversely, as price decreases, the quantity supplied decreases.

The basic determinants of supply include:

- Price of the good or service;
- Cost of producing the good or service (i.e., available technologies, price of inputs such as labour or capital);
- Price of related goods or services; and
- Expectations regarding the future price of the good or service.

Movements Along the Supply Curve

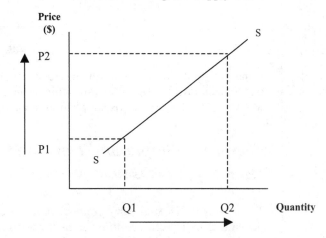

Movements along the supply curve result from changes in prices.

Shifts in the Supply Curve

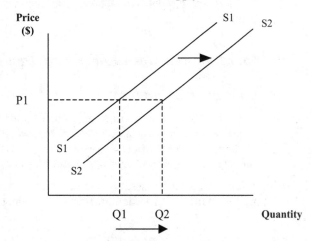

Shifts in the supply curve result from changes in other factors (cost of producing a good, price of related goods, and future price expectations).

Market Equilibrium

Market equilibrium occurs when the quantity of goods or services supplied equals the quantity demanded.

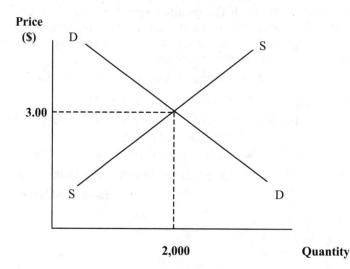

Market Equilibrium

A market shortage occurs when the quantity demanded at a given price exceeds the quantity that producers are willing and able to supply at that price. A market surplus occurs when the quantity of goods supplied exceeds the quantity that is demanded.

Aggregate Supply and Demand

Aggregate supply and demand is when all the individual markets in a domestic economy are combined.

The *aggregate demand curve* represents the overall quantity of goods and services that is demanded in a given economy at each possible price level (real GDP). It takes into account the purchases made by consumers, businesses, government, and foreign markets for Canada's entire domestic economy.

The *aggregate supply curve* takes into account the total production of the domestic economy.

Four Determinates of Aggregate Demand

Consumer Spending

Consumer spending is a function of disposable income and wealth. Real wealth includes financial and physical assets. When real wealth declines, consumers are inclined to buy less at each price level in order to save more, causing aggregate demand to decrease. As a result the aggregate demand curve will **shift left**.

When real wealth rises, consumers tend to buy more at each price level, increasing aggregate demand and the demand curve will **shift right**.

Investment Spending

Investment spending is the purchase of capital goods. When investment spending declines, consumers in turn buy less equipment, machinery, and buildings. The result is a decrease in aggregate demand; the curve will **shift left**.

A decline in real interest rates (caused by factors other than price changes) leads to higher investment spending, causing an increase in aggregate demand; the demand curve will **shift right**.

Government Spending

Government spending includes all expenditures made by the government, but excludes transfer payments to the provinces. When government spending increases, the demand curve will **shift left**.

Net Exports Spending

Net exports spending is the difference between total exports and total imports. The real GDP in other countries affects Canadian aggregate demand because real GDP in foreign countries determines their consumption, both domestic and foreign. When net exports increase, the demand curve will **shift left**.

Three Determinants of Aggregate Supply

Resource Prices

As resource costs increase, production costs increase and aggregate supply decreases, the supply curve will **shift left**.

As lower resource costs reduce production costs and aggregate supply increases, the curve will **shift right**.

Productivity

This is a measure of average real output per unit of input.

Taxes and Regulations

Increasing business taxes drives up production costs and decreases the aggregate supply; the curve will **shift left**.

The lowering of business taxes could lower production costs and increase aggregate supply; the curve will **shift right**.

702. REGULATORY ENVIRONMENT

Regulatory Agencies for Financial Institutions

Federal Jurisdiction

The Department of Finance oversees operations of financial institutions. Their power comes from: The *Bank Act, Insurance Companies Act, Trust and Loan Companies Act, Co-operative Credit Associations Act,* and the *Pension Benefits Standards Act*.

Three federal agencies supervise the operations of institutions:
- Superintendent of Financial Institutions (OSFI)
- Financial Consumer Agency of Canada (FCAC)
- Canada Deposit Insurance Corporation (CDIC)

Provincial Jurisdiction

There are four general components for provincial insurance regulation: regulation and supervision of provincial incorporated and registered insurance companies, licensing of insurance companies, statutory requirements for contracts of insurance, and the licensing of agents and brokers.

Provincial regulators formed four organizations to work towards uniformity of regulations:
- Canadian Council of Insurance Regulators (CCIR)
- Canadian Association of Pension Supervisory Authorities (CAPSA)
- Joint Forum of Financial Market Regulators (Joint Forum)
- Canadian Securities Administrators (CSA)

Consumer Protection

Canada Deposit Insurance Corporation

The Canada Deposit Insurance Corporation (CDIC) is a Federal Crown corporation created to insure deposits in banks, trust companies and loan companies against loss in case of member failure. It is financed through member premiums.

- A maximum of $100,000 per member institution;
- Joint accounts, trust deposits, RRSP, and RRIF deposits are all insured separately to a maximum of $100,000;
- Eligible deposits include savings and chequing accounts, money orders, certified drafts and cheques, traveller's cheques, debentures issued by loan companies, and term deposits with a term of five years or less. Eligible deposits are automatically protected; and
- Products not covered include foreign-currency deposits, term deposits with terms greater than five years, bonds and debentures issued by governments or corporations, treasury bills, and investments in stocks, mutual funds and mortgages.

RACHEL

Rachel has the following deposits held at Corner Bank and at West Munroe Bank. Both banks are members of the CDIC.

Corner Bank — Cherry Street branch

Savings account*	$ 8,000
Chequing account*	$14,500
One-year, non-registered term deposit*	$26,000
Total	$48,500

Corner Bank — Walnut Grove branch

An RRSP that holds the following investments:

Three-year term deposit*	$18,000
Mutual funds*	$23,000
Total RRSP	$41,000

West Munroe Bank — Ford Road branch

Four-year term deposit*	$120,000
U.S. dollar savings account	$ 26,000

* Canadian dollars.

How does the CDIC insurance apply to Rachel's situation? (Assume all amounts include principal and interest.)

The deposits at West Munroe Bank are viewed independent of the deposits held at Corner Bank. However, deposits at the Cherry Street and Walnut Grove branches of Corner Bank are combined as deposits in a single institution.

The three deposits at Corner Bank (Cherry Street branch) total $48,500 and are all eligible deposits that fall within the $100,000 maximum. The full $48,500 is insured.

The RRSP held at the Corner Bank (Walnut Grove branch) includes $23,000 in mutual funds that are excluded from the CDIC coverage. The $18,000 term deposit within the RRSP is an eligible deposit and would be insured separate from the $48,500 discussed in the paragraph above. Note that deposits at the two branches of Corner Bank must be considered together; however, the RRSP is eligible for a $100,000 maximum, separate from the other non-registered deposits.

Only $100,000 of Rachel's $120,000 term deposit at West Munroe Bank is covered through CDIC, because of the insurance plan maximum. The $26,000 in the U.S.-dollar savings account is not a deposit eligible for CDIC insurance.

Credit Union Deposit Protection Organizations

These are provincially regulated. The organizations exist to protect the deposits of credit union members in the event of failure, and are funded by premiums of assessments levied on individual participating credit unions. Coverage ranges from $100,000 to 100% guarantee of the amount on deposit.

Assuris

Assuris is a private, not-for-profit corporation which provides life insurance policyholders with protection against loss of benefits due to the financial failure of a member life insurance company. Policyholders are protected automatically.

Benefits are covered up to:

Monthly income	$ 2,000
Health Expense	$ 60,000
Death Benefit	$ 200,000
Cash Value	$ 60,000
Accumulated Value	$ 100,000

If a policyholder's benefits exceed these amounts, except for the accumulated value, Assuris covers 85% of the promised benefits, but not less than these amounts.

Benefits that exceed Assuris coverage will be adjusted to the greater of:

- The amount continued by the liquidator of the failed insurer;
- Assuris maximum coverage; and
- 85% of the promised benefits.

The benefits cover individual and group benefit programs (life, critical illness, disability, heath insurance) and registered individual and group benefit programs (RPP, RRSPs, LIFs, and related annuities). Each program is treated separately for Assuris protection purposes.

TOM

Tom's life is insured under a term life policy for $300,000. The liquidator supported only 70% of the policy benefits. Tom would receive $255,000, since it is the greater of:
- (a) liquidation amount — $210,000 ($300,000 × 70%);
- (b) maximum coverage — $200,000; or
- (c) 85% of the promised benefits — $255,000 (85% × $300,000).

Canadian Investor Protection Fund

The Canadian Investor Protection Fund (CIPF) is a private trust fund established to protect customers in case of insolvency of a member of the following SROs: Toronto Stock Exchange; Canadian Venture Exchange; Montreal Exchange; and the Investment Industry Regulatory Organization of Canada (IIROC). Generally, individual customer and joint accounts are covered for $1 million for losses related to securities and cash balances. RRSPs and RESPs are covered separately for up to $1 million.

Consumer Protection Policy

Consumer Protection Policy is legislation to protect consumers from unsafe products, improper business practices and the use of personal information collected.

Stock Exchanges

A *stock exchange*, *share market*, or *bourse* is a corporation or mutual organization that provides facilities for its members' stock brokers to trade company stocks and other securities. Stock exchanges also provide facilities for the issue and redemption of securities as well as other financial instruments and other capital transactions. In the past, stock exchanges have been physical locations. Due to the increased use of electronic networks, many exchanges today are done electronically.

The main benefits of stock exchanges include: it is a formal meeting place for buyers and sellers of securities, it provides companies with the facility to raise capital to fund the business and growth, and the movement of share prices and stock indexes can be an indicator of the trends in the economy.

The main Canadian exchanges are the Toronto Stock Exchange (TSX), which trades equities, the Montreal Exchange which focuses on derivative securities, and the TSX Venture Exchange (TSX V) which deals with equity and debt of junior and emerging companies. NASDAQ, Chicago and the New York Stock exchanges are the main American exchanges. London and Tokyo are the largest international stock exchanges.

Self-Regulatory Organizations

Self-regulatory organizations (SROs) are responsible for ensuring their members adhere to provincial standards and established business and/or market or trading practices.

Mutual Fund Dealers Association

The Mutual Fund Dealers Association is the mutual fund dealers' SRO and it regulates the business practices of the distribution side of the mutual fund industry for the purpose of investor protection. Its rules cover business structures, individual qualifications for membership, financial and operational requirements, and business conduct.

Investment Industry Regulatory Organization of Canada

In June 2008, the Investment Industry Regulatory Organization of Canada (IIROC) was created through the consolidation of the Investment Dealers Association (IDA) and Market Regulation Services Inc. (RS). IIROC is now the self-regulatory organization overseeing all investment dealers and trading activity on equity and debt market places in Canada. It regulates the business activities and licensing of investment dealers who sell all investment products, including mutual funds, in order to maximize investor protection.

IIROC's mandate is to foster investor confidence in the Canadian securities market and to safeguard investor protection through the administration, interpretation and enforcement of a common set of trading rules consistently in all markets in Canada called the Universal Market Integrity Rules (UMIR). IIROC regulates securities trading practices covering manipulative trading methods, short selling, front-running, execution of client orders, compliance, and assessing penalties for non-compliance to the rules.

Financial Planners Standards Council

Financial Planners Standards Council (FPSC) benefits the public by leading the evolution of the financial planning profession in Canada through the development, enforcement and promotion of financial planning competency and ethical standards for Certified Financial Planners (CFPs).

Securities Regulation

There is no signal national securities regulator in Canada. The current system of 13 provincial/territorial securities regulatory authorities (SRAs) is inefficient because of the multiple provincial securities rules. The SRAs work as members of the Canadian Securities Administrators, a virtual national securities commission, to coordinate and harmonize provincial security regulations.

The objectives of security regulation are to protect investors from unfair, improper or fraudulent practices, foster fair, efficient access to markets, and the reduction of systemic risk by reducing the risk of failure of market intermediaries.

Provincial Securities Legislation

The 13 SRAs administer and enforce provincial/territorial securities legislation and regulations involving individual securities, such as stocks, bonds, futures, and mutual funds.

Public Company Disclosure and Investor Rights

Fair treatment of investors requires full disclosure of information that is material to investment decisions. Disclosure is made available to the public through SEDAR (system for Electronic Document Analysis and Retrieval (www.sedar.com)), company Web sites, securities regulators, and investment dealers.

Insurance Regulation

Insurance is regulated at the provincial/territorial level in Canada. The Canadian Council of Insurance Regulators (CCIR), whose members come from the provincial/territorial regulators, works to harmonize insurance policy and regulations across Canada.

Provincial insurance legislation usually covers: regulation, supervision and licensing of insurance companies, statutory requirements for insurance contracts, and the licensing of agents and brokers.

900. DEBT

Understanding personal credit, debt and money management is integral to the process of financial planning. While retirement and investment planning are important to the outcome of a family's personal financial goals, these types of planning initiatives are most successful when integrated into the family's debt and budget management process.

Debt management covers optimizing the structure of an individual's serviceable debt to allow for the most effective use of available funds. This process involves an analysis of the situation taking into account assets, cash flow and personal requirements. Some strategies include using the interest-free period on credit card purchases as a source of short-term money, optimizing deductible interest where possible, and reducing mortgage debt.

901. CREDIT

Usually, any time an individual attempts to borrow money, the lending institution will automatically undertake a credit assessment. This assessment looks into such things as: current income, payment history on previous or current loans, assets, outstanding liabilities, and the ability to meet the required payment schedule.

Two key ratios used in the course of credit evaluation are:

The *total debt service ratio* (TDSR) is a mathematical equation used to estimate how much of an individual's income can be allocated to a monthly loan payment.

$$TDSR = \frac{(\text{Monthly housing costs}) + (\text{All other monthly debt payments})) \times 100}{(\text{Gross monthly income})}$$

The *gross debt service ratio* (GDSR) is used by mortgage lenders to evaluate an applicant's ability to service her mortgage debt

$$\text{GDSR} = \frac{((\text{Monthly mortgage payment}) + (\text{Property taxes}) + (\text{Heat})) \times 100}{(\text{Gross monthly income})}$$

Line of Credit

A credit facility where the borrower has access to a specific amount of credit from which she can borrow and repay as needs arise, without seeking credit approval each time that she uses the credit facility.

Credit Cards

Approval of the application is one aspect of the credit application, while the decision as to the amount of credit is a second aspect. Normally, purchases can be made on a credit card and no interest applies until the cardholder is billed for the purchase and the bill becomes due. The majority of credit cards allow a cardholder to carry an outstanding balance. Less expensive credit options to help eliminate an outstanding credit card balance include: using available liquid assets, using funds from a line of credit or getting a personal loan.

Single Purpose Personal Loans

This is a loan sought for a single purpose, such as borrowing funds to purchase a car. The terms established for a personal loan could include a fixed or variable rate of interest and a fixed monthly payment schedule.

Investment Loan

For interest on the investment loan to be tax deductible, the money borrowed must be used for the purpose of earning income from a business or property and directly traceable to the investment. The interest must be paid or payable in respect of the year it is being deducted and a legal obligation to pay the interest must exist.

Money borrowed for an investment where the sole purpose is to realize a capital gain may not be tax non-deductible.

Insurance Loan

If an individual holds an insurance policy such as a whole life policy with a cash value, they may borrow from the cash value of the policy. Interest rates are usually established on a floating basis. The benefits include easy, immediate access to cash. There is no repayment schedule, although interest charges apply as long as the loan is outstanding.

Company Loan

A company may issue loans to employees to assist them in purchasing a home or relocation loans to a new place of work. The tax impact of each loan is as follows:

Home Loan to Purchase a Home

Taxable interest benefit uses the lesser of the prescribed interest rate at the time of the loan and prescribed rate for each quarter.

If the term of the loan exceeds 5 years, the home loan's prescribed interest rate is reset every five years.

$$\textit{Interest benefit} = \text{Prescribed interest rate} \times \text{Loan amount} \times \text{Time period}$$

Home Relocation Loan

A *home relocation loan* is a loan to an employee that moves at least 40 kilometres closer to work. The employee reports total interest benefit, but can claim a deduction equal to the taxable benefit charged on the first $25,000 for five years.

902. REFINANCING AND DEBT CONSOLIDATION

Refinancing is an activity where an individual uses a new source of debt to pay off an existing source of debt. For example, a homeowner who has an open mortgage may be able to negotiate a new mortgage at a lower interest rate. They will use the new mortgage to pay off the higher interest rate mortgage.

Debt consolidation involves negotiating a new source of debt and then paying off the various other sources of debt one has. For example, an individual has $1,000 in credit card debt at 28% and a $5,000 car loan at 10%. They would be better off negotiating a line of credit of $6,000 at 6% and then paying off the credit card and car loan debt. As a result, they will be paying a lower rate of interest of 6% instead of 28% and 10%.

903. MORTGAGES

A mortgage is money lent by a financial institution to a borrower who is purchasing real estate and requires additional financial resources to complete the purchase of the property.

A *fixed rate mortgage* is one where the rate of interest applied over the term of the mortgage is locked in and will not change.

A *variable rate mortgage* is one where the interest rate applied during the term of the mortgage will vary based on changes to the Bank of Canada or similar rates.

With an *open mortgage*, the debtor has the complete freedom to pay off the entire outstanding balance or any portion, at any time, without penalty. With a *closed mortgage* the borrower cannot pay off the balance without paying penalties.

Amortization

Amortization is the period over which the payments associated with the repayment of a debt, including interest and principal, is based. The length of the amortization period is an important element in the calculation of the monthly payments. It is usually 20 or 25 years.

Longer amortization period = Lower payment amount and a higher total amount of interest paid

Shorter amortization period = Higher payment amount and a lower total amount of interest paid

Payment Schedule

Most lending institutions offer a variety of schedules including weekly, bi-weekly, semi-monthly, and monthly payments.

Term

The mortgage term is the period during which the lender extends funds to the debtor. The term is important because it is the period for which the interest rate conditions are established.

Conventional versus High Ratio Mortgages

When an individual takes out a mortgage, the size of the debt is assessed relative to the value of the property against which the debt will apply.

Conventional Mortgage

A *conventional mortgage* is when the debt represents an amount that is less than 80% of the property's appraised value or purchase price, whichever is less.

High Ratio Mortgage

A *high ratio mortgage* is when a mortgage exceeds 80% of the value of the home, and where the value is defined as the lower of the appraised value or the purchase price. These mortgages are considered higher risk mortgages. Lenders will require the mortgagor to obtain mortgage payment insurance from the Canadian Housing and Mortgage Corporation or a private insurer. If the mortgagor cannot pay the insurance premiums, which is usually the case, the amount of the premium is added to the mortgage principal and adds 1.5% to 2% of the principal to the mortgage.

Prepayment Options and Penalties

Many mortgages allow the individual to pay down or prepay up to 10%–15% of the mortgage each year without any penalties. If the mortgage is a closed mortgage, the individual may have to pay up to three months interest penalty or an interest rate differential (IRD) penalty for early payment of the full mortgage. The IRD is the difference between the borrower's stated interest rate and the rate at which the lender could currently loan money for an equivalent term.

IRD formula = (((Mortgage interest rate - Current interest rate) × Outstanding balance) × (Remaining months) ÷ 12)

BETH

Beth has 6 months left on her 5-year, 6% mortgage. The principle is $50,000 and the current interest rate on 6-month mortgages is 4%. The penalty would be:

IRD = [((6% - 4%) × 50,000) × (6 ÷ 12)
   = 2% × 50,000 × 0.5
   = $500

Reverse Mortgages

For many Canadians, a significant portion of their savings is tied up in the value of the home in which they live. A reverse mortgage allows an individual to access the equity in her home while still living in it. The individual must be at least 62 years old and can access between 10% and 40% of the home's appraised value.

Nature of a Reverse Mortgage

With a traditional mortgage, an individual takes out a mortgage to buy a home and makes regular payments to the financial institution against the debt obligation represented by the mortgage. With a reverse mortgage, the individual uses the equity portion of her property for collateral on a loan that only becomes due when she dies, or sooner if she sells her home. As with a regular mortgage, the individual who takes out a reverse mortgage continues to own her home but there becomes a debt obligation on which interest accumulates, although no payments are required until the debt obligation becomes due at death or when the house is sold.

Types of Reverse Mortgages

Reverse mortgages are relatively new in Canada and have not caught on as a significant trend; generally, there is very low public awareness. The three main types are: reverse annuity mortgage, line of credit reverse mortgage, and a fixed term reverse mortgage.

With a reverse annuity mortgage, a lump-sum amount is borrowed and invested in an annuity with monthly income payments for the rest of the homeowner's life. The mortgage is repaid upon death of the homeowner or sooner if the home is sold.

A line of credit mortgage allows the homeowner to borrow funds as needed from a line of credit secured by the value of the home. Interest only accumulates when the funds are withdrawn.

A fixed term reverse mortgage provides funds to a homeowner for a fixed period of time, often five to ten years. The repayment of the borrowed funds and accumulated interest occurs at end of the fixed term.

Taxation

According to the CRA, simple reverse mortgage payments and lines of credit are not taxable since they are equivalent to loan advances from a traditional mortgage. The income generated by a reverse mortgage annuity is not taxable.

When reversed mortgages are used for investment purposes, the accruing mortgage interest is tax-deductible against any investment returns generated by the mortgage proceeds, providing individuals with a stream of tax-sheltered income.

904. LEASES

Leasing is similar to renting an item for a period of time. Examples of items leased include automobiles, furniture and equipment. The main benefit of leasing is that an individual gets to use the item without incurring a large upfront cost. They pay for the items through periodic payments over the term of the lease.

The term of the lease varies based on the life of the item being leased and may be a fixed term. The interest rate, initial payment and residual value of the item are used in the calculation of the monthly lease payment.

905. INSOLVENCY AND BANKRUPTCY

Consumer Proposal

A consumer proposal is a legal agreement prepared by a debtor to her creditors to reduce the level of debts. Proposals to creditors were created to provide people who had the ability to repay some of the debt with an alternative to filing for personal bankruptcy. Once you file a proposal, none of your unsecured creditors can garnish your wages or take you to court until the proposal has been dealt with and all of your unsecured debts are frozen and no more interest accumulates against them.

Bankruptcy

An individual is financially insolvent if her liabilities are greater than her assets.

Bankruptcy is the legal process that allows the individual to be released from most of her unsecured debts to creditors. The process is performed under the federal *Bankruptcy and Insolvency Act* and it involves the assignment of all assets, except those exempt by law, to a trustee in bankruptcy who arranges for an orderly distribution of the proceeds from the assets as compensation to creditors. The notation of bankruptcy on an individual's credit rating will directly impact future applications for credit. Once the bankruptcy process is complete, the individual will receive a discharge. During the taxation year in which a bankruptcy is filed, two tax returns are filed: one for the period from January 1 to the date of bankruptcy and the post-bankruptcy period during the remainder of the year.

The following debts are not released through bankruptcy: debts which included a co-signer or guarantee of another individual, student loans if the bankruptcy occurs while the debtor is still a student, student loans if the bankruptcy occurs within 10 years after having ceased to be a student, claims for alimony, spousal or child support payments, debts related to any involvement with fraud, court fines, and damages owed to another individual due to an assault.

Unit 2
Government Benefit Plans

1001. CANADA PENSION PLAN/QUEBEC PENSION PLAN

The Canada Pension Plan (CPP) is a mandatory defined benefit pension program that is intended to supplement retirement savings plans of Canadians. It is administered federally through the Human Resource Development Corporation and the Canada Revenue Agency (the "CRA"). The CPP/Quebec Pension Plan (QPP) provides retirement, survivor, disability and death benefits.

Eligibility for Benefits

An individual is eligible to receive retirement benefits if the individual has made one contribution and:

- is at least 65; or
- is between 60 and 64 and ceased employment, or has low earnings.

It is important to recognize that an individual cannot contribute to the CPP/QPP and receive benefits at the same time. To facilitate this, if an individual returns to work once they have begun to receive benefits, they no longer contribute to the pension but will continue to receive CPP/QPP benefits.

Amount of Benefits

Retirement benefits are a function of the contributions, contributory period, and the age when benefits are chosen to commence relative to the normal retirement age of 65 where full benefits are received by the pensioner. The calculation recognizes that individuals may incur work interruptions through their careers and allows for some parts of an individual's contributory period to be dropped from the calculation for benefits in these instances. Examples of these recognized low income periods include:

- Time spent raising children under the age of seven;
- Time spent working after age 65; and
- 15% of the individual's lowest earning years.

The benefits will represent approximately 25% of the earnings on which the CPP/QPP contributions were made adjusted for inflation. To calculate the basic retirement benefit for a client, apply the formula below:

CALCULATIONS

Simplified CPP Basic Retirement Calculation

= 25% of the average YMPE for the current and four previous years × the average earnings ratio

The Average Earnings Ratio Calculation

= YMPE ÷ the unadjusted pensionable earnings

The maximum CPP retirement benefit for 2009 is $908.75 per month.

Benefits will be reduced by 0.5% per month that the individual retires prior to the normal retirement age to a maximum reduction of 30% at the earliest allowable retirement benefit age of 60.

Benefits will be increased by 0.5% per month that the individual delays their retirement beyond the normal retirement age up to age 70.

Disability Benefits are available for disabled contributors and their dependants to replace income when they are not able to work. Eligibility for the benefit requires that a contributor meet the following criteria:

- Contribute to CPP for four of the past six years and must have at least 10% of YMPE;
- Considered to be disabled under the CCP definition of severe and prolonged disability; and
- Be under the age of 65.

Benefits under the Disability Coverage are comprised of a flat amount and a variable component adjusted each year to reflect the cost of living. These two components cannot exceed the amount of the maximum monthly benefit. For 2009, the maximum disability benefit is $1,105.99.

Disability Benefits cannot be combined with retirement benefits but can be combined with Survivor's Benefits. The Benefits will terminate when the contributor is no longer disabled, or when normal retirement benefits begin or upon death.

An additional flat amount of benefit is available for the Dependent Children of Disabled Contributors. A child is eligible to receive up to two full benefits from the program after a 4-month qualifying period. For 2009, this amount is $213.99 per month.

Benefits for survivors are intended to provide benefits to surviving family members of a deceased contributor. These benefits fall into three general categories.

- **Death Benefit.** A one-time lump-sum payment calculated as the lesser of six times the contributor's age 65 monthly pension, 10% of contributor's MPE, or $2,500.
- **Survivor's Pension.** Payable, upon application, to the legal spouse at the time of death. The maximum benefit available for 2009 is $545.25 for survivors age 65+ and $506.38 for survivors under the age of 65.
- **Children's Benefit.** An additional flat amount of benefit is available for the dependent children of deceased contributors. A dependent child must be under age 18; or between 18 and 24, and in school full-time. A child who becomes married while receiving the benefits does not lose their benefits. A child is eligible to receive up to two full benefits from the program after a four-month qualifying period. For 2009, this benefit amount is $213.99 per month.

Contribution Levels

The CPP is a contributory plan. A *contributory plan* is one where contributions are made by the employee. In the case of CPP, both the employee and the employer contribute funds to the pension. Contributions toward CPP begin from the date an individual reaches age 18.

Most employment is considered to be pensionable employment and the earnings are subject to CPP contributions. The following employment situations are exempt from CPP contributions:

- Workers earning less than $3,500;
- Casual workers (i.e., babysitters);
- Migratory workers (working less than 25 days a year or less than $250 per employer); and
- Religious workers whose income is turned over to the order.

The amount required for contributions in a year is based on an individual's earnings between a minimum level and a maximum amount of income. The minimal level before which no CPP contributions are required is known as the Year's Basic Exemption (YBE) which for 2009 was $3,500. The maximum amount for which contributions are payable is known as the *year's maximum pensionable earnings* (YMPE) which was $46,300 for 2009. Any earnings in excess of the YMPE do not require CPP contributions to be deducted. The amount of earnings a person has between the YBE and the YMPE, is the pensionable earnings for which CPP contributions are made. The contribution rate is 4.95% for both the employee and employer to a maximum of $2,118.60 each. The maximum for self-employed individuals is $4,237.20 (9.9%).

Contributions will continue until the earlier of when an individual begins to receive CPP benefits, reaches age 70, or dies.

Tax Treatment of Contributions and Receipts

Employer contributions to the CPP are a deductible business expense for the employer, and not a taxable benefit to the employee.

Employee contributions to the pension are not tax-deductible but can be claimed under the non-refundable tax credit system. Benefits are included as income for recipients. The CPP retirement benefits do not qualify for the $1,000 pension income non-refundable tax credit when received.

Application Requirements and Deadlines

Retirement pension requires the completion of an application in order to start receiving CPP pension benefits.

1002. OLD AGE SECURITY

The Old Age Security (OAS) program provides benefits that include the regular OAS retirement pension, the Guaranteed Income Supplement (GIS) designed to assist low-income seniors and an Allowance benefit.

Eligibility for Benefits

An individual will be eligible for benefits if she is a Canadian citizen at least 65 years old. She will receive a full pension with 40 years residency after July 1, 1977. If an individual has not resided in Canada for periods of time totalling 40 years, she may still qualify if, on July 1, 1977, she was 25 years of age or over, and lived in Canada on July 1, 1977; or had lived in Canada before July 1, 1977, after reaching age 18; or held an immigration visa on July 1, 1977.

Amount of Benefits

Old Age Security benefits are a flat monthly benefit designed to help support the lower to middle income individuals over the age of 65. The maximum OAS benefit for 2009 is $516.96. The benefits are adjusted quarterly and are tied to the CPI. Benefits must be applied for by the recipient.

Clawback of Benefits

Repayment is made by reducing the monthly income at source by $1/12$ of the anticipated payback. Repayment is at 15% of the amount that the individual's net income (including OAS) exceeds the minimum (for 2009 the minimum threshold is $66,335 for individuals). OAS is completely clawed back at $107,692 for 2009.

Tax Treatment of Receipts

Benefits received under the OAS pension are fully taxable by the recipient as income.

GUARANTEED INCOME SUPPLEMENT

The GIS is a pension income source for OAS recipients with little or no other sources of income. The benefit is a flat amount subject to an income means test. The means test reduces the GIS proportionately to the amount the individual's income increases until reaching a maximum income amount where the GIS is discontinued. The maximum benefit for 2009 is $652.51 monthly and must be applied for annually by the pensioner.

The GIS is subject to clawback, which is calculated by taking 50% of pensioner's previous years income and subtracting this amount from the maximum income. For a single person, the base level at which the entire GIS is clawed back is $15,672. For married or common-law couples, the entire GIS is clawed back at $37,584. When determining a pensioner's base income, the OAS benefits are not included.

Special considerations for the GIS relate to travel and termination of benefits. When a pensioner travels out of country, the benefit will continue to be payable for six months, then will terminate. It can be restarted with an application when the pensioner returns to Canada. In addition to out of country travel, an individual GIS will terminate when no income tax return or other application has been submitted by April 30.

Survivor Benefits

OAS provides an allowance for the survivor of low-income individuals between ages of 60–64, who were married to or the common-law partner of an OAS pension recipient who died.

The Survivor Benefits pay a flat monthly benefits amount tied to the amount of an individual's previous year's income. The maximum allowance is $1,050.68 per month for 2009.

Similar to GIS, the benefits are subject to clawback based on the recipient's base income. The GIS clawback is calculated as $3 per month for $4 of the survivor's base income (up to 133% of the OAS maximum pension), and $1 for every $2 of base income thereafter. Benefits will terminate when income exceeds the allowable maximum. In addition, the benefits will terminate when traveling out of country for more than 6 months, if no application for benefits was submitted by April 30, or if the recipient remarries or dies.

Application Requirements and Deadlines

Application for benefits must be received by April 30th with benefits commencing one month following eligibility.

1003. CHILD TAX BENEFIT

The Canada Child Tax Benefit (CCTB) is a tax-free monthly payment made to eligible families to help them with the cost of raising children under the age of 18. The benefit may include both the Basic Benefit and be supplemented by the National Child Benefit Supplement (NCBS) if needed.

Eligibility for Benefits

An individual may be eligible for benefits if they are the primary caregiver of a child under the age of 18 and are a Canadian resident.

Amount of Benefits

The CCTB provides a basic benefit plus additional benefits to provide support to low income families for their children. Benefit year is July 2009–June 2010. Benefits are recalculated at the beginning of each benefit year.

Basic Benefit

The basic benefit is a monthly benefit for each child under the age of 18 with a top up per child when there are three or more children. For the benefit year, the benefit amount is $111.66 per month per child under 18, and an additional $7.75 per month for the individual's third and each additional child.

The benefit is reduced when the family net income exceeds a maximum dollar amount. For the current benefit year, this maximum is $40,726 (as of July 2009) and will be reduced by 2% of the excess amount of the family income over the maximum for the first child. When there are two or more children, the benefit is reduced by 4%.

National Child Benefit Supplement

The NCBS is an enhancement to the basic benefit by an additional monthly benefit to help lower income families. The flat monthly benefit for the current benefit year is $173.00 per month for a family with one child. For a family with two children, the monthly benefit for the second child is reduced to $153.08 per month.

Additionally, the NCBS is reduced on a quickly reclining calculation as follows:

- *One child* — 12.2% of excess family net income over $23,710;
- *Two children* — 23% of excess family net income over $23,710; and
- *Three or more* — 33.3% of excess family net income over $23,710.

Child Disability Benefit

Families caring for a child diagnosed with severe and prolonged mental or physical impairments under the age of 18 with a net family income amount equal to or less than a set annual threshold ($40,726 for 2009) will receive a monthly benefit. For 2008, the monthly benefit amount is $204.58.

1004. EMPLOYMENT INSURANCE

Employment Insurance (EI) is funded through the contributions by both the employer and the employee. The benefits payable include benefits for unemployed individuals; on maternity/parental leave; or those who are not working due to disability.

Eligibility for Benefits

In Canada, participation in the EI program is mandatory for employees. Some individuals are not eligible to participate. These include self-employed individuals, individuals owning more than 40% of a corporation's voting shares, and employed individuals not at arm's-length.

Most people will need between 420 and 700 insurable hours of work in their qualifying period to qualify, depending on the unemployment rate in their region.

Amount and Calculation of Benefits

The basic benefit rate is 55% of an individual's average insured earnings up to a yearly maximum insurable amount of $42,300. For 2009, this results in a maximum payment of $447 per week, and there is a two-week waiting period. Benefits are reduced dollar for dollar if the claimant works during the period they were on claim. When the benefit is payable for disability, EI stands as the second payer following the CPP/QPP programs.

Contribution Levels

Individuals contribute premiums based on their earnings up to the annual maximum salary. For 2009, the maximum salary is set at $42,300. The EI premium rate is set to $1.73 for every $100 of salary until the maximum has been reached. Based on this contribution rate, the maximum contribution amount will be $711.03 for 2009.

Tax Treatment of Contributions and Receipts

All EI benefit payments are treated as taxable income.

Types of Benefits

For individuals, benefits are payable as regular unemployment benefits, maternity/parental benefits and disability benefits.

1005. UNIVERSAL CHILD CARE BENEFIT

The Universal Childcare Benefit (UCCB) provides childcare support for children under the age of 6. This benefit provides level $100 per month benefit per eligible child. This benefit is taxable to the recipient but no annual tax return filing is required to be eligible to receive the benefit.

Income Qualification

Based on the family net income minus any amount the taxpayer or the taxpayer's common-law spouse reported for the UCCB (line 117 of the tax return). Net income is the amount on line 236 of the tax return.

Tax Treatment of Benefits

The benefits from the Child Benefits program are taxable.

1006. WORKERS' COMPENSATION PROGRAMS

Provincial and territorial based programs compensate workers for income lost due to a job-related accident or illness. The program requires that the accident or injury occurs while on the job and results in a severe and prolonged injury.

For Worker's Compensation programs, premiums paid by employers are based on the relative risk of the business activities and are a tax-deductible expense for employers. Premiums are a percentage of the total payroll for covered employees.

The benefit is not taxable for employees when received and represents between 75% of net earnings and 90% of gross earnings depending on the province. These benefits are usually paid monthly but may be paid as a lump-sum benefit to the recipient. The benefit commences the day following an injury and will continue for the lifetime of the employee. While needing to be included in the income of the employee, the benefits are eligible for an offsetting deduction.

1007. INCOME ASSISTANCE PROGRAMS

Income assistance programs include government pension programs (CPP, OAS, GIS), Employment Insurance, and child tax benefit programs, covered in Unit 2.

1101. BEHAVIOURAL FINANCE

Behavioural finance studies the relationship between psychology and money, examining how one's perceptions, desires, and fears affect the financial decision making process. If advisors can learn to recognize and understand what drives people to make irrational investment decisions, they may be able to prevent both themselves and their clients from making these mistakes. Those interested in reading more on the subject should consider "Beyond Greed and Fear", written by Hersh Shefrin, and published by the Oxford University Press in 2002.

1102. HUMAN BEHAVIOUR

Heuristics

Heuristics are rules of thumb, mental shortcuts, guidelines, or strategies which people use to solve problems and make decisions. Behavioural finance is interested in how relying on heuristics may lead to biases and/or errors in judgment. The three key elements are: availability, representativeness, and anchoring.

Availability

When asked to assess the probable frequency of an event, people tend to base their answer on recently acquired information. This heuristic helps to explain why new information can have a short-term, disproportionate effect on the price of a company's shares. If a company announces particularly good first quarter results, for example, it will be widely reported and the share price may surge temporarily, but unless these results are indicative of a fundamental change in the company, the share price is likely to revert to its previous level.

Representativeness

If someone is asked to predict the likelihood that A belongs to category B, they will often think something similar — a comparable known thing or experience — and base their response on that. For example, one may be inclined to think that simply because a firm shares some of the traits of, and is in the same industry as, under performing companies that it is also a poor investment.

Anchoring and Adjustment

This describes a person's tendency to focus heavily on, or anchor to, one specific piece of information or reference point, and adjust expectations from there. An investor may not react appropriately to a positive earnings announcement from a company that, in the past, did not perform very well. If she ignores fundamentals and dismisses the improvement as temporary, she may miss out on an opportunity to buy because she has mentally anchored the stock price at a low level.

Prospect Theory

The "Prospect Theory" attempts to explain how people make choices when they are confronted with risk, or when an outcome is unknown. Basically, people prefer sure things, but they also found that the pain people experience as a result of a loss is stronger than the pleasure they derive from an equal gain. It may feel good to find a $100 bill, but it hurts more to lose one. This phenomenon is called *loss aversion*. Another example occurs when an investor holds on to investments that have lost a significant amount of value in hopes that the stock will increase in the future and she will break even.

Endowment Effect or Divestiture Aversion

If people already own something, they attribute a higher value to it. As a result, they will demand more to give up an object they already possess than they would be prepared to pay to acquire it. For example, a home owner may expect to sell her home for a higher price than comparable homes because she thinks it is worth more.

Status Quo Bias

Given the choice people prefer to stick with the *status quo* even though it is no more attractive than the other options available to them. For instance, if the employer's contributions to a defined contribution pension plan are automatically deposited into one fund, members may be more likely to remain in that fund even though it is unsuitable given their financial circumstances. *Status quo* bias is also tied to the concept of loss aversion, since people may fear the loss of the *status quo* more than they value the potential gain that could result from making change.

Overconfidence

When people are overly confident in their ability to make a rational decision, or an accurate prediction about the direction the stock market is heading, they may be prepared to accept more risk than the situation really warrants. Overconfidence can also cause investors to under-react to new information, fixed in a belief that their initial investment choice was a good one. One way to deal with overconfidence is to eliminate part of decision making process. Rather than try to select individual securities, the investor can purchase the entire market through an index fund, for example.

Demographics

A person's age, culture, social and educational background may also affect the ability to make decisions. A study found that highly-educated males who are nearing retirement, who have received investment advice, and who have experience investing for themselves, tend to have a higher certainty level and are therefore more prone to overconfidence.

Escalation Bias

Once someone has made a decision they may remain emotionally attached to it, becoming more even committed despite being presented with new information that proves their initial choice was a poor one. It explains why, instead of selling, investors will ride losing investments into oblivion, pouring new money into a losing and doomed investment while telling themselves that they are "averaging down" and buying the stock a bargain price. Investors can counteract escalation bias by consistently re-evaluating their portfolio using pre-determined, fixed criteria, e.g., the investor decides she will only hold shares that have P/E Ratio less than X, or by asking an independent person for an opinion.

Mental Accounting

Many people do not see their finances as a whole, but instead divide their funds into several separate accounts, assigning a specific purpose to each one. The rules of mental accounting are not neutral — the source of the funds affects how they are spent. For example, if someone were to receive a $1,000 tax refund, she may have no qualms spending it on an expensive holiday. She would be reluctant, however, to withdraw the very same $1,000 from her retirement savings.

Herd Mentality

The human tendency to follow the actions of the larger group is sometimes called the herd mentality, herding, or crowding. The most recent Canadian example of herding is the widespread enthusiasm for Bre-X, a mining company which in the early and mid-1990s claimed to have found a massive gold deposit in Busang, Indonesia, which increased the stock price widely. Eventually, the gold find was discovered to be untrue and the company went bankrupt.

Like mental accounting, herding contradicts traditional economic theory, which suggests that fundamentals and the law of supply and demand regulate prices, and that agents act independently of others.

Unit 3
Self-Test Questions

QUESTIONS

Question 1

Lisa has $100,000 to invest. She anticipates earning an annual return of 7%, compounded annually, for each of the next 10 years. How much will Lisa's investment be worth at the end of 10 years? (Disregard taxes.)

    a. $107,225

    b. $196,715

    c. $200,966

    d. $206,103

Question 2

Walter invested $100 in mutual funds at the end of each month for five years. At the end of the five years, his investment had accumulated to $9,000. Assuming monthly compounding, what is the effective annual rate of return? (Disregard taxes.)

    a. 15.13%

    b. 15.58%

    c. 16.22%

    d. 16.75%

Question 3

John purchased preferred shares of Alpha, which have a $100 par value and a dividend rate of 5.75%. The current market price of the shares is $92. What is the current yield of the Alpha preferred share?

    a. 4.00 %

    b. 5.75 %

    c. 6.25 %

    d. 8.00 %

Question 4

Susan hopes to draw an annual income of $40,000 after taxes, indexed for inflation at 1.5%, at the beginning of each year for 20 years during retirement. During retirement, she can earn 6%, compounded annually and she will be in the 29% marginal tax bracket. How much does Susan need at the beginning of retirement to fund her retirement plan?

    a. $433,701

    b. $610,846

    c. $627,456

    d. $796,432

Question 5

James put $20,000 in a non-registered interest-bearing investment that pays an annual nominal interest rate of 7.5% compounded annually. James's marginal tax rate is 40%. The annual inflation rate is 2%. What is James's real after-tax rate of return?

    a. 2.45%

    b. 3.75%

    c. 4.50%

    d. 5.39%

Question 6

Martha signed a lease for a brand new car. The monthly payments are $520 for seven years. The first payment is due today. Using an interest rate of 10.8% compounded monthly, what is the value of the lease?

    a. 30,406

    b. 30,557

    c. 30,832

    d. 34,858

Question 7

Belinda, a media relations consultant, has applied for a car loan. Her monthly obligations include:

- $600 to reduce an outstanding credit card balance;
- $200 student loan payment; and
- housing costs of $1,200.

The monthly payment on the car loan will be $700. Belinda's gross monthly income is $7,000. What would Belinda's total debt service ratio be?

    a. 28.6%

    b. 25.7%

    c. 38.6%

    d. 10.0%

Question 8

A Gross Debt Service Ratio:

1. is commonly used by lenders when considering a loan application for purchase of an automobile.

2. is calculated in order to evaluate an applicant's ability to service her mortgage debt.

3. is almost always higher than an individual's total debt service ratio.

4. that is between 25% and 35% is deemed acceptable by lenders.

    a. 1 and 3 only

    b. 2 and 4 only

    c. 3 and 4 only

    d. 1 and 2 only

Question 9

A bankrupt individual is not released from which of the following debts through the process of bankruptcy?

1. Court fines

2. Claims for alimony

3. Child support payments

4. Credit card debt

     a. 1, 2 and 3 only

     b. 2, 3 and 4 only

     c. 1, 3 and 4 only

     d. 1, 2, 3, and 4

Question 10

With regard to the Employment Insurance (EI) program, which of the following statements are true?

1. Sickness benefits are calculated based on 75% of the claimant's average weekly earnings.

2. EI sick benefits are reduced by any money an EI claimant receives from Workers' Compensation or group insurance plans.

3. EI sick benefits are not reduced if the EI claimant receives money from an individual disability insurance policy.

4. Sickness benefits are subject to a four-week waiting period.

     a. 1 and 3 only

     b. 1 and 4 only

     c. 2 and 3 only

     d. 2 and 4 only

Question 11

With regard to premiums for Workers' Compensation programs, which of the following statements are correct?

1. Premiums assessed against an employer take into consideration the relative level of risk pertaining to the employer's business activities.

2. Premiums are based on a percentage of an employer's payroll for covered employees working within a particular province or territory.

3. Employees who opt to participate in the Workers' Compensation program pay premiums based on a percentage of their salary.

4. Employer premiums are paid to the Canadian Workplace Safety Board, a federal government agency.

     a. 1 and 2 only

     b. 1, 2 and 3 only

     c. 2, 3 and 4 only

     d. 3 and 4 only

Question 12

With regard to CPP benefits, which of the following statements is/are correct?

1. Children of a deceased contributor are entitled to a lifetime pension.

2. In some circumstances, spouses may elect to share their retirement pension.

3. Only those credits earned during a relationship are subject to credit splitting.

4. A surviving spouse of a deceased contributor may be entitled to survivor's benefits.

    a. 1 and 2 only

    b. 1, 2 and 3 only

    c. 2, 3 and 4 only

    d. 3 and 4 only

Question 13

Which of the following individuals are currently eligible for retirement benefits under the CPP? (Assume each individual meets the contribution requirements.)

1. Fifty-five-year-old Amanda, who ceased employment last month when her sixty-five year old spouse began to receive CPP retirement benefits.

2. Sixty-three-year-old Peter, who retired three months ago, and has no plans for alternative employment.

3. Sixty-five-year-old Albert, who continues to work as a sales manager for his long-term employer.

4. Sixty-year-old Samantha, who retired two months ago, and has accepted another job to begin six months from now.

    a. 1 and 2 only

    b. 1, 2 and 3 only

    c. 2, 3 and 4 only

    d. 3 and 4 only

Question 14

The basic determinants of demand include which of the following?

1. Price of good or service

2. Changes in price of substitute goods

3. Changes in price of complementary goods

4. Changes in producers' tastes

    a. 1 only

    b. 2 and 4 only

    c. 3 and 4 only

    d. 1, 2 and 3 only

Question 15

The following profile indicates an economy in which stage of a business cycle?

- Profits: *declining*
- Savings: *increasing*
- Spending: *decreasing*
- Employment: *decreasing*
- Output: *decreasing*

a. Recession

b. Trough

c. Peak

d. Recovery

QUESTIONS & SOLUTIONS

Question 1

Lisa's has $100,000 to invest. If she anticipates earning an annual return of 7%, compounded annually for each of the next 10 years. How much will Lisa's investment be worth at the end of 10 years? (Disregard taxes.)

    a. $107,225

    b. $196,715

    c. $200,966

    d. $206,103

Answer: b.

Given:

    ⇨ P/YR = 1

    ⇨ XP/YR = 10

    ⇨ I/YR = 7

    ⇨ PMT = 0

    ⇨ PV = -100,000

    ⇨ FV = $196,715.14

Question 2

Walter invested $100 in mutual funds at the end of each month for five years. At the end of the five years, his investment had accumulated to $9,000. Assuming monthly compounding, what is the effective annual rate of return? (Disregard taxes.)

    a. 15.13%

    b. 15.58%

    c. 16.22%

    d. 16.75%

Answer: d

    ⇨ Given

    ⇨ P/YR = 12

    ⇨ XP/YR = 5

    ⇨ PMT = -100

    ⇨ PV = 0

    ⇨ FV = 9,000

    ⇨ MODE = END

SOLVE FOR I/YR, which equals 15.5833 (nominal interest rate). The effective interest is 16.746%. Press [SHIFT] EFF% to get 16.746%

Question 3

John purchased preferred shares of Alpha, which have a $100 par value and a dividend rate of 5.75%. The current market price of the shares is $92. What is the current yield of the Alpha preferred share?

     a. 4.00%

     b. 5.75%

     c. 6.25%

     d. 8.00%

Answer: c

     ⇨   Yield = (annual dividend payment) ÷ (current market price) × 100

     ⇨   Yield = ($100 × 0.0575) ÷ 92 × 100

     ⇨   Yield = 6.25%

Question 4

Susan hopes to draw an annual income of $40,000 after taxes, indexed for inflation at 1.5%, at the beginning of each year for 20 years during retirement. During retirement, she can earn 6%, compounded annually and she will be in the 29% marginal tax bracket. How much does Susan need at the beginning of retirement to fund her retirement plan?

     a. $433,701

     b. $610,846

     c. $627,456

     d. $796,432

Answer: c

     ⇨   Given:

     ⇨   P/YR = 1

     ⇨   XP/YR = 20

     ⇨   I/YR = [(0.06 × (1 - 0.29) - 0.015) ÷ (1 + 0.015)] × 100

     ⇨   PMT = -40,000.00

     ⇨   FV = 0

     ⇨   MODE = BEG

SOLVE FOR PV, which equals $627,456.49

Question 5

James put $20,000 in a non-registered interest-bearing investment that pays an annual nominal interest rate of 7.5% compounded annually. James's marginal tax rate is 40%. The annual inflation rate is 2%. What is James's real after-tax rate of return?

     a. 2.45%

     b. 3.75%

     c. 4.50%

     d. 5.39%

Answer: a

     ⇨   Real after-tax rate of return = (Nominal rate of return × (1 - MTR)) - inflation)) ÷ (1 + inflation)

     ⇨   = [(0.075 × (1 - 0.40)) - 0.02))] ÷ (1 + 0.02)

     ⇨   = 0.02451 (or 2.45%)

Question 6

Martha signed a lease for a brand new car. The monthly payments are $520 for seven years. The first payment is due today. Using an interest rate of 10.8% compounded monthly, what is the value of the lease?

    a. 30,406

    b. 30,557

    c. 30,832

    d. 34,858

Answer: c

    ⇨ Given:

    ⇨ P/YR = 12

    ⇨ XP/YR = 7

    ⇨ I/YR = 10.8

    ⇨ PMT = -520.00

    ⇨ FV = 0

    ⇨ MODE = BEGIN

SOLVE FOR PV, which equals $ 30,831.87

Question 7

Belinda, a media relations consultant, has applied for a car loan. Her monthly obligations include:

- $600 to reduce an outstanding credit card balance;
- $200 student loan payment; and
- housing costs of $1,200.

The monthly payment on the car loan will be $700. Belinda's gross monthly income is $7,000. What would Belinda's total debt service ratio be?

    a. 28.6%

    b. 25.7%

    c. 38.6%

    d. 10.0%

Answer: c

    ⇨ (600 + 200 + 1,200 + 700) ÷ 7,000 = 38.57%

Question 8

A Gross Debt Service Ratio:

1. is commonly used by lenders when considering a loan application for purchase of an automobile.

2. is calculated in order to evaluate an applicant's ability to service her mortgage debt.

3. is almost always higher than an individual's total debt service ratio.

4. between 25% and 35% is deemed acceptable by lenders.

    a. 1 and 3 only

    b. 2 and 4 only

    c. 3 and 4 only

    d. 1 and 2 only

Answer: b

Question 9

A bankrupt individual is not released from which of the following debts through the process of bankruptcy?

1. Court fines

2. Claims for alimony

3. Child support payments

4. Credit card debt

     a. 1, 2 and 3 only

     b. 2, 3 and 4 only

     c. 1, 3 and 4 only

     d. 1, 2, 3, and 4

Answer: a

     ⇨   All of the statements are correct except for 4. A bankrupt individual is released from her credit card debt.

Question 10

With regard to the Employment Insurance (EI) program, which of the following statements are true?

1. Sickness benefits are calculated based on 75% of the claimant's average weekly earnings.

2. EI sick benefits are reduced by any money an EI claimant receives from Workers' Compensation or group insurance plans.

3. EI sick benefits are not reduced if the EI claimant receives money from an individual disability insurance policy.

4. Sickness benefits are subject to a four-week waiting period.

     a. 1 and 3 only

     b. 1 and 4 only

     c. 2 and 3 only

     d. 2 and 4 only

Answer: c

     ⇨   Statement 1 is incorrect since there is a maximum limit to the benefits. Statement 4 is incorrect since the waiting period is two weeks, not four weeks.

Question 11

With regard to premiums for Workers' Compensation programs, which of the following statements are correct?

1. Premiums assessed against an employer take into consideration the relative level of risk pertaining to the employer's business activities.

2. Premiums are based on a percentage of an employer's payroll for covered employees working within a particular province or territory.

3. Employees who opt to participate in the Workers' Compensation program pay premiums based on a percentage of their salary.

4. Employer premiums are paid to the Canadian Workplace Safety Board, a federal government agency.

    a. 1 and 2 only

    b. 1, 2 and 3 only

    c. 2, 3 and 4 only

    d. 3 and 4 only

Answer: a

    ⇨   Statements 3 and 4 are incorrect because employers pay workers' compensation premiums, calculated as a percentage of the payroll of covered employees, based on the risk pertaining to their business activities.

Question 12

With regard to CPP benefits, which of the following statements is/are correct?

1. Children of a deceased contributor are entitled to a lifetime pension.

2. In some circumstances, spouses may elect to share their retirement pension.

3. Only those credits earned during a relationship are subject to credit splitting.

4. A surviving spouse of a deceased contributor may be entitled to survivor's benefits.

    a. 1 and 2 only

    b. 1, 2 and 3 only

    c. 2, 3 and 4 only

    d. 3 and 4 only

Answer: c

    ⇨   Children of deceased contributors are entitled to a pension up to age 18 or, if in school full-time, age 18 to 24.

Question 13

Which of the following individuals are currently eligible for retirement benefits under the CPP? (Assume each individual meets the contribution requirements.)

1. Fifty-five-year-old Amanda, who ceased employment last month when her sixty-five year old spouse began to receive CPP retirement benefits.

2. Sixty-three-year-old Peter, who retired three months ago, and has no plans for alternative employment.

3. Sixty-five-year-old Albert, who continues to work as a sales manager for his long-term employer.

4. Sixty-year-old Samantha, who retired two months ago, and has accepted another job to begin six months from now.

    a. 1 and 2 only

    b. 1, 2 and 3 only

    c. 2, 3 and 4 only

    d. 3 and 4 only

Answer: c

    ⇨ Amanda needs to be at least 60 years old to receive the CPP. All of the other individuals qualify to receive the CPP.

Question 14

The basic determinants of demand include which of the following?

1. Price of good or service

2. Changes in price of substitute goods

3. Changes in price of complementary goods

4. Changes in producers' tastes

    a. 1 only

    b. 2 and 4 only

    c. 3 and 4 only

    d. 1, 2 and 3 only

Answer: d

    ⇨ The determinates of demand are the price of the good or service, changes in the price of substitute or complementary goods, changes to consumer's income or wealth, changes to consumers' expectations regarding income, price, and/or product availability, and changes to consumer's tastes or preferences, not producer's tastes.

Question 15

The following profile indicates an economy in which stage of a business cycle?

- Profits: *declining*
- Savings: *increasing*
- Spending: *decreasing*
- Employment: *decreasing*
- Output: *decreasing*

a. Recession

b. Trough

c. Peak

d. Recovery

Answer: a

Appendix One

CFP Examination — Financial Formulae Reprint

CFP Examination – Financial Formulae Reprint

The following formulae page will be reprinted on the CFP Examination. The list of formula is not all-inclusive and others may be necessary to answer questions on the CFP Examination. Candidates writing the CFP Examination should bring a financial calculator to their examination sitting. No calculators will be supplied at the writing centre.

Legend

FV	= future value	e	= effective, annual rate of return
PV	= present value	k	= periodic rate of return (i/m)
i	= nominal, annual rate of return	r	= real, annual rate of return
n	= number of years	y	= yield to maturity, or IRR
m	= number of compounding periods per year	infl	= annual rate of inflation
I_t	= amount returned or paid in year t		

The effect of non-annual compounding:

$$FV_n = PV(1 + i/m)^{n \times m}$$

Simple interest (return) calculation:

$$I_t = PV \times i$$

Effective, annual rate:

$$e = (1 + k)^m - 1$$

Future value of a single payment:

$$FV_n = PV(1 + i)^n$$

Present value of a single payment:

$$PV = \frac{FV_n}{(1 + i)^n}$$

Future value of a stream of payments:

$$FV = \frac{\left((1 + k)^n - 1\right)}{k}$$

Present value of a stream of payments:

$$PV = \frac{1 - \left(\frac{1}{(1 + k)^n}\right)}{k}$$

Real rate of return:

$$r = \frac{i - infl}{1 + infl}$$

Appendix Two
Ms. Sharon West and Mr. Max West
Statement of Net Worth
As of December 31, 2009

	Sharon ($)	Max ($)	TOTAL ($)
ASSETS			
Non-Registered Assets			
Cash and Equivalents	8,500	4,000	12,500
GICs		12,000	12,000
Bonds			
Equities	15,500	8,000	23,500
Mutual Funds	2,000		2,000
Stock Options (vested)			
Real Estate			
Life Insurance CVS			
Total Non-Registered Assets	**26,000**	**24,000**	**50,000**
Registered Assets			
RESP	3,300		3,300
RPP		44,000	44,000
RRSP	28,000	12,000	40,000
Total Registered Assets	31,300	56,000	87,300
Other Assets			
Business Equity			
CVS of Life Insurance		8,000	8,000
Total Other Assets		8,000	8,000
Personal Assets			
Home/Residence		265,000	265,000
Personal Effects	5,500	7,800	13,300
Cottage/Recreational Property	125,000		125,000
Vehicles	6,000	10,000	16,000
Other	1,000	1,000	2,000
Total Personal Assets	137,500	283,800	421,300
TOTAL ASSETS	**194,800**	**371,800**	**566,600**
LIABILITIES			
Credit Cards/Consumer Debt	2,300	7,100	9,400
Loan — Vehicles		9,000	9,000
Business Loan			
Investment Loan	2,000	4,000	6,000
Mortgage		220,000	220,000
TOTAL LIABILITIES	**4,300**	**240,100**	**244,400**
NET WORTH	**190,500**	**131,700**	**322,200**

Note: Assets at market value could have income tax consequences that have not been accounted for in this Statement of Net Worth.

Appendix Three
Ms. Sharon West and Mr. Max West
Projected Cash Flow Statement
For 12 Months Ending December 31, 2009

	Sharon	Max	Total	Jan	Feb	Mar	Apr	May	June	July	Aug	Sept	Oct	Nov	Dec
INCOME															
Salary	54,200	98,500	152,700	12,725	12,725	12,725	12,725	12,725	12,725	12,725	12,725	12,725	12,725	12,725	12,725
Self-employment earnings	12,000		12,000			3,000			3,000						6,000
Dividend income		1,200	1,200	125	200	225	30	300	60	150	50	25			35
Interest income		500	500												500
Alimony/Child Support															
Other/Miscellaneous	800		800					400					400		
Less source deductions: income tax	17,000	35,000	52,000	4,333	4,333	4,333	4,333	4,333	4,333	4,333	4,333	4,333	4,333	4,333	4,333
Less source deductions: CPP/QPP	1,500	2,800	4,300	717	717	717	717	717	717						
Less source deductions: E.I.	1,200	2,500	3,700	617	617	617	617	617	617						
Total Net Income	**47,300**	**59,900**	**107,200**	**7,183**	**7,258**	**10,283**	**7,088**	**7,758**	**10,118**	**8,542**	**8,442**	**8,417**	**8,792**	**8,392**	**14,927**
EXPENSES															
Mortgage		28,000	28,000	2,333	2,333	2,333	2,333	2,333	2,333	2,333	2,333	2,333	2,333	2,333	2,333
Property Taxes		4,000	4,000	667	667	667				667	667	667			
Utilities	1,000		1,000	83	83	83	83	83	83	83	83	83	83	83	83
Food	4,000		4,000	333	333	333	333	333	333	333	333	333	333	333	333
Day Care	1,200		1,200		250			250						700	
Education															
Vehicle - Loan/Lease		4,800	4,800	400	400	400	400	400	400	400	400	400	400	400	400
Vehicle - Gasoline & Repair	1,500	3,000	4,500	375	375	375	375	375	375	375	375	375	375	375	375
Insurance - Life	1,200	1,500	2,700	1,500		1,200									
Insurance - General	800	1,500	2,300	800					1,500						
Insurance - Vehicle	1,400	2,200	3,600	1,800		1,200				600					
Personal	2,500	3,000	5,500	389	389	389	389	255	389	800	300	300	300	300	1,300
Entertainment	900	1,000	1,900	150	150	150	150	250	250	250	100	100	100	100	150
Vacations		4,000	4,000		1,000					3,000					
Consumer Debt	2,500	2,500	5,000	417	417	417	417	417	417	417	417	417	417	417	417
Donations	500	500	1,000		250		100		50						600
Recreational property expenses		2,300	2,300	192	192	192	192	192	192	192	192	192	192	192	192
Other/Miscellaneous	500	500	1,000			250			250			250			250
Total Expenses	**18,000**	**58,800**	**76,800**	**9,439**	**6,839**	**7,989**	**4,772**	**4,888**	**6,572**	**9,450**	**5,200**	**5,450**	**4,533**	**5,233**	**6,433**
NET INCOME AVAILABLE FOR SAVINGS	**29,300**	**1,100**	**30,400**	**-2,256**	**419**	**2,294**	**2,316**	**2,870**	**3,546**	**-908**	**3,242**	**2,967**	**4,258**	**3,158**	**8,493**
Non-registered savings	2,000	4,000	6,000												
RRSP contributions	7,000	12,000	19,000												
RESP contributions															
Total Savings & Reinvestment	**9,000**	**16,000**	**25,000**												
UNALLOCATED CASH FLOW	**20,300**	**-14,900**	**5,400**												

THE CFP
EDUCATION PROGRAM

CCH/ADVOCIS FPSC-APPROVED CAPSTONE COURSE

MODULE 27

PATH TO THE CFP CERTIFICATION AND EXAMINATION REVIEW

Module 27
PATH TO THE CFP CERTIFICATION AND EXAMINATION REVIEW

Module 27
Path to the CFP Certification and Examination Review

Unit 1
CFP® Certification Requirements

OVERVIEW

The Financial Planners Standards Council (FPSC) introduced new certification requirements effective July 1, 2010. The new requirements will affect all candidates who have not passed the CFP examination by June 2010. Currently, accredited education candidates (AE) who have completed an FPSC-approved core curriculum education program, such as the CCH/Advocis CFP education program, or are holders of an approved prior credential (APC) (CGA, CMA, CA, CFA, CLU, FCIA, LL.B., or Ph.D. in Business, Finance, or Economics) are required to pass one six-hour multiple-choice examination and complete a minimum of two years of work experience prior to obtaining their CFP certification. Candidates are also required to agree to adhere to the Code of Ethics and FPSC's Practice Standards once they are granted the CFP certification.

The June 2010 CFP examination is comprised of two, three-hour sessions. Each session consists of stand alone multiple-choice questions and two cases with related multiple-choice questions. There are approximately 150 questions in each exam. Each question on the examination is based on one or more of the competencies listed in the CFP Professional Competency Profile. The June 2010 examination is the last time the current exam format will be offered. The FPE1 examination study skills discussed in Unit 2, which focuses on writing multiple-choice exams, are also applicable to the June 2010 CFP examination.

The new CFP certification requirements, which come into effect July 2010, were introduced to help candidates better develop the competencies and professional skills required of a financial planner and integrate their knowledge of the large amount of information CFPs are expected to know. CFP certification is based on 4Es: education (core curriculum and Capstone Course or prior professional credentials), examinations (FPE1 and FPE2), experience (three years), and ethics (adhering to the FPSC Codes of Ethics and Professional Standards).

The new CFP certification path will include two separate financial planning examinations (FPE1 and FPE2), completion of an FPSC-approved Capstone Course, including a comprehensive financial plan, and three years of qualifying financial planning work experience instead of the current two years. FPE1 will be comprised of competency-based multiple-choice questions. To remain eligible for CFP certification, all candidates must maintain continuous registration with FPSC from approval to write the FPE1 until CFP certification. FPE2 will cover a variety of competency-based questions types like short answer and written case responses. Candidates can attempt each exam a maximum of four times. In addition, new time limits for completing the certification process have been introduced. Candidates must attempt FPE1 within four years of completing an FPSC-approved core curriculum program and attempt FPE2 within four years of completing an FPSC-approved Capstone Course. AE candidates have a maximum of twelve years and APC candidates have eight years to complete the whole CFP certification process. For further information, see http://www.fpsccanada.org/public/new_cfp_certification_guidelines.

Path to CFP Certification

- Complete an FPSC-approved Core Curriculum education program (or hold a professional designation under the Approved Prior Credential policy);

- Upon registration for the Financial Planning Examination (FPE1), candidates must register and remain in good standing with FPSC;

- Pass the FPE1 examination;

- Complete a FPSC-approved Capstone Course and at least one year of financial planning related work experience;

- Pass the FPE2 examination;

- Complete the remaining two years of financial planning related work experience; and

- Apply to FPSC for CFP certification.

Work Experience Requirement

All candidates need to provide evidence of three years of qualifying work experience when applying for CFP certification. At least one year must be completed prior to writing the FPE2. Qualifying work experience is based on a 35-hour work week, full-time personal financial planning (or part-time equivalent) related employment. Experience may be gained within the performance of financial planning, financial management, asset management, risk management, tax planning, retirement planning, estate planning, portfolio management or teaching at a post-secondary level (two years maximum). FPSC will consider other relevant experience. Experience earned within the last eight years prior to obtaining the CFP certification may be used to satisfy the work experience requirement.

Unit 2
CFP Professional Competence Examinations

OVERVIEW

The CFP Financial Planning Examinations (FPE1 and FPE2) are quite different than other exams that student candidates may have written in the past. The exams are competency-based and require the candidates not only to know the technical knowledge, but also to apply and integrate the knowledge when answering the exam questions. In contrast to academic exams, which usually involve direct testing of knowledge of a single subject or course material, the CFP examinations consists of multi-subject type questions that require a higher level of professional judgment and demonstration of competencies. Furthermore, since FPSC does not release old exams, and it is moving towards a new format for the FPE1 and FPE2 exams in 2010/2011, it is difficult to determine the exact nature of the questions.

The FPE1 and FPE2 examinations will be held twice yearly in June and November and are available in both official languages. The first FPE1 sitting will be November 2010 and the first sitting of FPE2 will be June 2011. Registration for each examination closes one month prior to each exam date. Academic Education candidates (AE) must write the FPE1 exam within four years of completing a FPSC-accredited education program. Holders of an Approved Prior Credential (APC) are not required to complete core curriculum courses prior to applying for the FPE1. All candidates must maintain continuous registration with FPSC and abide by the CFP Code of Ethics from the time they register to write the FPE1 until the time they attain the CFP certification. Prior to applying for the FPE2, all candidates must have completed a FPSC-approved Capstone Course and have at least one year of financial services work experience completed. The Capstone course may be completed prior to writing the FPE1. The entire CFP certification program must be completed within 12 years for AE candidates and eight years for APC candidates. Additional information on the examinations is available at www.fpsccanada.org/earn.

FPSC has a student associate section within their Web site that provides additional information on the examinations, located at www.fpsccanada.org/candidates. By registering as a student associate, candidates get access to sample questions and solutions, financial planning tips of the day, and a job site. They can also connect with other candidates through discussion forums and FPSC events. It is highly recommended that candidates join as student associates to gain access to the available information.

THE CFP PROFESSIONAL COMPETENCY PROFILE

The FPE1 and FPE2 are based on the CFP Professional Competency Profile. In December 2006, FPSC issued the "CFP® Professional Competency Profile: FPSC's Standards of Competence for CFP® Professionals" (Competency Profile), which outlines a set of financial planning competencies required of a CFP professional. It distinguishes financial planning from other financial services, and it distinguishes the role and value proposition of the CFP professional from those of other advisors. It will help everyone better understand both the profession's purpose and value. The Profile is based on financial planning being defined as "the process of creating strategies to help clients manage their financial affairs to meet life goals".

The Competency Profile is structured around activities, financial planning components, professional skills, and technical knowledge. There are three levels of activities: collection (gathering, calculating and determining facts), analysis (identifying potential opportunities and strategies), and synthesis (development and the evaluation of recommendations and strategies). Five core competencies were identified and then further defined in terms of every possible aspect of performance that may be required to demonstrate each competency. Within each financial planning activity, there are six financial planning components: financial management, asset management, risk management, tax planning, retirement planning and estate planning; four sets of professional skills: ethical judgment, professional practice, written and oral communication and cognitive abilities and eleven areas of technical knowledge: taxation, insurance, investment, retirement/savings/income programs, law, financial analysis, economics/regulatory environment, ethics/standards, debt, government benefit programs, and behavioural finance. For further details, see http://www.cfp-ca.org/licensees/licensees_competencyprofile.asp.

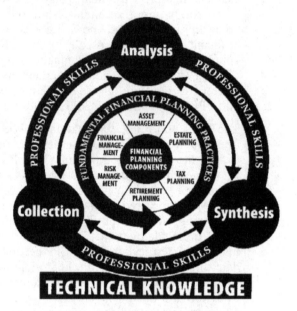

In summary, there are three basic functions or activities (collection, analysis, and synthesis), six financial planning components (financial management, asset management, risk management, tax planning, retirement planning, and estate planning), and four sets of professional skills (ethics, practice, communication, and cognitive). The eleven areas of technical knowledge provide the foundation for the above activities.

EXAMINATION WRITING TIPS

Exam Preparation Tips

- **Stay healthy!** Get the optimum amount of sleep each night; eat regular, well-balanced meals and exercise. Take breaks when studying. Maintain a positive attitude.

- **Begin studying early.** Confidence comes from good planning and following a systematic study plan. Multiple-choice exams tend to focus on details, and you cannot retain all of the details effectively in your short-term memory. Starting early will also allow you time to repeat and synthesize the information. The CFP exam is moving away from single subject questions to competency-based questions that require a better level of comprehension. Set up a study schedule and stick to it!

- **Gain as much information about the format and structure of the exam as possible.** This can be done by reviewing the FPSC Examination Web site. Candidates should ensure they use the CFP Professional Competency Profile, Professional Competency Matrix and CFP Examination Blueprints. The FPSC also has a "Guide to the CFP Examination", available on the FPSC Web site. FPSC usually gives candidates a sample of past exam questions. Practice the sample FPSC questions. Generally, FPSC exam questions do not have extraneous information in the questions. Candidates should also join as a

FPSC student associate to get access to additional questions. Note the subjects that keep recurring frequently and analyze the answer solutions.

- **Understand the material, not just memorize it.** The wording of the question may be different from the way you originally learned the material. Pay particular attention to fundamental terms and concepts that tie related ideas together.

- **Make lists, tables and topic summaries from your course materials.** Concentrate on understanding and summarizing the main concepts and look for similarities and differences that might be used to distinguish correct choices from distractors on an exam. Include examples to help you remember the concepts.

- **Brainstorm possible questions.** This can be done with several other students who are also taking the exam. Try to predict test questions. Ask other students what they think will be tested.

Exam Day Strategies

- Bring the correct materials to the exam, including the admission letter, photo identification, a noiseless, non-programmable calculator, #2 HB pencils, and erasers. See the FPSC Guide to CFP examination, available from the FPSC Web site, for further details.

- Before the candidate begins taking the exam, RELAX!

- Enter all pieces of required information on your answer sheet such as your name, student number, etc. If you forget to enter your name and ID number, your results may never be scored.

- Preview the exam. Survey the test completely and read directions carefully. As you browse through the exam, take note of those questions which seem easier.

- Calculate the amount of time you can spend on each section or question according to the number of marks it's worth. For example, the 50 stand-alone questions on the current CFP exam are worth ½ mark each and the 25 case questions are worth one mark each on each exam. Do the easy questions or sections first — this will increase your confidence, and help you relax and recall information better.

- Read the questions carefully. Careless mistakes are often made when students rush through the "stem", or first part of the question, and miss important information. Avoid jumping to conclusions about what you think the question asks.

- Read the case study related questions before reading the whole case study. Reviewing the questions will help you focus on the necessary areas when you read the case study.

- Budget your time well. The current CFP exam is a challenge to complete within the allotted time period.

EXAMINATION WRITING TECHNIQUES

In order for a candidate to be successful in passing the CFP exams, he must not only know the content of the CFP syllabus, but also be able to demonstrate that knowledge on the examination. Establishing an effective approach to studying for the CFP exam will play a significant role in successful completion of the exam. This section covers exam writing techniques for multiple-choice format exams (June 2010 and FPE1 exams) and candidate written response essay and short answer exams like FPE2.

FPSC had not finalized the format of the FPE1 and FPE2 exams as of September 2009. The published FPE1 and FPE2 Exam Blueprints provide the most current information on the structure of the exams. FPE1 will be a competency-based multiple-choice exam which will focus on the collection and analysis activities of the CFP Competency Profile. It may be very close in format to the existing CFP examination by including single-subject and multiple-topic questions. FPE2, which will focus more on analysis and synthesis activities, is expected to require written responses to the questions and case studies. The first sitting of the FPE1 exam will occur November 2010 and FPE2 in June 2011. FPSC plans to release further details on the FPE1 and FPE2 thorough its Web site in 2010.

The following section and Module 28 provide the student with practice on answering case study and multiple-choice exam questions.

Multiple-Choice Examinations (June 2010 and FPE1)

Studying for a multiple-choice exam requires a special method of preparation. Multiple-choice exams ask a student to recognize a correct answer among a set of options that include several wrong answers (called "distractors"), rather than asking the student to produce a correct answer directly. Some students consider multiple-choice exams easier than essay exams because the correct answer is guaranteed to be among the possible responses, and due to the large number of questions, each question has a lower point value. Despite these factors, however, multiple-choice exams can actually be very difficult. Since multiple-choice exams contain many questions, they force students to be familiar with a much broader range of material and have a greater familiarity with details such as specific terms and concepts than essay exams.

There are many strategies for maximizing success on multiple-choice exams. The best way to improve the candidate's chances of being successful is to study carefully before the exam. There is no substitute for knowing the right answer. Even a well-prepared student can make silly mistakes on a multiple-choice exam or select distractors that look like the correct answer. One of the most frequent reasons, other than a lack of preparedness, why students do poorly on exam questions is that they do not read the questions properly or they fail to understand them. They often miss a key word or phrase and misinterpret the entire question. Consequently, they do not answer the question asked.

Basic-Type Question

All questions on the CFP exam are either *basic-type* or *combination-type* multiple-choice questions. For the CFP exam, there is only one correct answer for each question and marks are not deducted for incorrect answers.

The *basic-type question* has a lead-in sentence, called a "stem", followed by four or five possible answers.

BASIC-TYPE QUESTION EXAMPLE

The term GAAP refers to:

    a. generally accepted accounting principles.

    b. generally accepted auditing practices.

    c. good accounting and auditing practices.

    d. guaranteed audited accounting presentations.

Answer: a

FPSC SAMPLE QUESTION — BASIC-TYPE QUESTION

Jared plans to leave his life insurance and his home to his second wife, Kathy, and his RRSPs to his married adult children from his first marriage. When Jared dies, which of the following statements is true?

    a. The RRSP proceeds will be included as income on Jared's final income tax return.

    b. The RRSP proceeds can be declared as income of the estate.

    c. Jared's children must declare the RRSPs as income on their tax returns.

    d. Jared's children can roll the RRSPs into their own RRSPs.

Answer: a

The RRSP proceeds are not passing to a surviving spouse or to minor or dependent children, so the proceeds must be declared on Jared's final income tax return.

Question Relationship to CFP Professional Competency Profile

Element of Competency Assessed	Description
Core Competency 1.1	Collects the quantitative information required to develop a financial plan.
Financial Planning Component	Tax Planning.
Element of Competency 1.111	Identifies the taxable nature of assets and liabilities.

Relevant Linked Technical Knowledge

Category	Description
I. Taxation	114. Tax Consequences of Death
IV. Retirement, Savings and Income Plans	404. Registered Retirement Savings Plans

Combination-Type Question

The *combination-type question* lists four or more alternative statements where one, some, or all of the statements are true. The candidate then selects the correct combination of statements.

COMBINATION-TYPE QUESTION EXAMPLE

With regard to GAAP, which of the following statements are true?

1. GAAP contains the guidelines that accountants use to measure, process and communicate financial information.

2. GAAP is inapplicable in the area of personal financial reports.

3. GAAP is developed under the guidance of the Canadian Management Institute of Accountants.

4. It is mandatory for public companies to adhere to GAAP.

    a. 1 and 2 only

    b. 1, 2 and 4 only

    c. 1, 3 and 4 only

    d. 2, 3 and 4 only

Answer: b

FPSC SAMPLE QUESTION — COMBINATION-TYPE QUESTION

Lorraine, age 70, would like to invest $250,000. Her objectives are a regular income flow and preservation of her capital so that she can leave $250,000 to her adult children. She is in very good health. Which of the following are suitable investments for her?

1. A portfolio of GICs.

2. An insured annuity.

3. An index-linked GIC.

4. An investment in a bond fund.

    a. 1 and 2 only

    b. 1 and 3 only

    c. 2 and 4 only

    d. 3 and 4 only

Answer: a

Option 1 is correct. A portfolio of GICs would provide Lorraine with a regular income flow while preserving capital for her estate. Option 2 is correct. The annuity will provide her with regulare income and the insurance policy will provide a death benefit for her children.

Question Relationship to CFP Professional Competency Profile

Element of Competency Assessed	Description
Core Competency 2.1	Identifies potential opportunities and constraints.
Financial Planning Component	Asset Management.
Element of Competency 2.108	Identifies potential investment vehicles.

Relevant Linked Technical Knowledge

Category	Description
III. Investment	301. Investment Vehicles 302. Investment Structures
IV. Retirement, Savings and Income Programs	411. Annuities

How to Answer a Question Strategically

After reading a question, the candidate must interpret it. What does it ask? Does it have more than one part? If so, break it into smaller parts and deal with each one separately. By doing this, you are less likely to forget to deal with some important aspect of the question. Also, be on the lookout for questions which may answer other questions.

If you cannot answer a question or are unsure of an answer within a minute or two, skip it and come back to it later. If you run out of time, it's better to answer the easier questions than to have missed some questions because you spent too much time on the more difficult questions.

Try this *10-step approach* to make sure you read each question thoroughly.

1. Cover up the alternatives before you read the stem (the first part of the question).

2. Read the stem carefully. You should process the stem: underline key words; translate the question into your own words, and watch for small but important qualifying words, such as "not", "always", "never", and "usually". You should try to rephrasing the question in your own words.

3. Predict an answer.

4. Uncover the alternatives and read all of them carefully, even if the first choice seems correct. Sometimes alternatives only differ by one or two words or terms. Treat each

alternative as a true/false question, and eliminate alternatives you know to be incorrect by striking out the words. Put a question mark beside alternatives you are uncertain about.

5. Responses that use absolute words, such as "always" or "never" are less likely to be correct than ones that use conditional words like "usually" or "probably". "All of the above" is often a correct response. If you think more than one of the responses is correct, then choose "all of the above". "None of the above" is seldom a correct response.

6. Look for grammatical rules and verbal associations. If a stem ends with an "an", then the correct response probably begins with a vowel. Watch for agreement between subjects and verbs.

7. The alternative which differs most in length from the others tends to be the correct one because it contains qualifying phases or adjectives.

8. Pay attention to an alternative that contains negative words such as "not" or "none". Try to rephrase stems with two negatives in positive terms. If the question asks "which of the following are NOT applicable?", be sure modify your thinking accordingly.

9. For combination-type questions, if you can eliminate one or more of the alternative responses, you may be able to eliminate one or more of the possible answers.

10. Identify the best response. Guess if you still don't know the answer since there is no penalty on the CFP exam for wrong answers.

In multiple-choice questions, your first inclination is usually correct, so consider carefully before changing your answer after you have made your initial selection. In general, when reviewing answers, you should only change an answer if you have a specific reason for doing so (for example, you remembered a new piece of information). Even if you're not entirely sure that your answer is correct, it's usually better to keep it than to switch to another answer at the last minute.

Once you have marked all the questions on your exam, transfer all the responses to the answer sheet at the same time. Saving the relatively mindless job of filling in bubbles until the last step reduces the probability of making silly errors. Always check that you have answered all the questions and that you have transferred all your answers to the answer sheet properly. Be sure that you have filled the appropriate bubbles carefully. Erase any accidental marks completely. Take the time to check your work before you hand in the answer sheet.

JUNE 2010 EXAMINATION

The June 2010 Examination is a six-hour multiple-choice examination divided into two three-hour sessions, a morning and afternoon session. Each session consists of stand-alone multiple-choice questions and two cases with related multiple-choice questions. There are approximately 150 questions. The June 2010 examination is the last time the current exam format will be offered. All questions are either "basic-type" or "combination-type" multiple-choice questions. There is only one correct answer for each question, and marks are not deducted for incorrect answers. CFP Examination candidates should use the CFP Professional Competency Profile, Competency Profile Matrix, and the CFP Examination Blueprint as reference material when preparing for the exam to ensure they cover all of the required knowledge components of the exam. For further details see, www.fpsccanada.org/students/cfp_exam_preparing.

FPSC issued a CFP Examination Blueprint document which provided a summary of the focus of the exam. Content of the CFP exam is allocated within a matrix of Financial Planning Functions: *Collection* (36%–40%), *Analysis* (36%–40%), and *Synthesis* (22–26%)); by *Fundamental Financial Planning Practices* (10%–14%) and *Financial Planning Components* (90%–86%). The Financial Planning Components exam coverage is further segmented by each of the six components. See the following table.

The CFP® Examination Blueprint

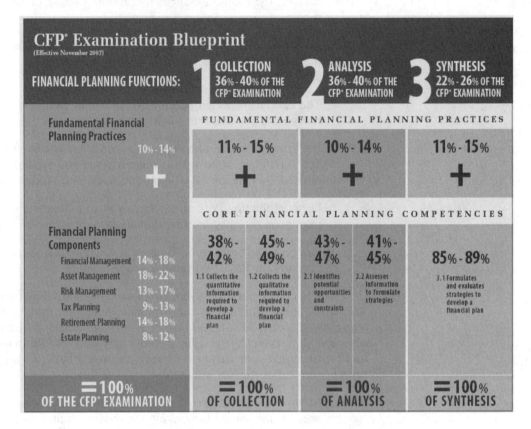

Source: http://www.cfp-ca.org/pdf/CFP_Exam_Blueprint_Charts_FINAL.pdf

FINANCIAL PLANNING EXAMINATION LEVEL 1 (FPE1)

The new CFP certification process will apply to any one who has not passed the CFP examination by July 1, 2010. To be eligible to write the FPE1, a candidate must apply to the FPSC with documentation demonstrating completion of an FPSC-approved Core Curriculum program, or for APC candidates, a current letter from the conferring institution/organization showing that his designation is in good standing.

It is anticipated that 60% to 70% of the exam will be made up of independent multiple-choice questions and 30% to 40% of the exam will be based on case studies with multiple-choice questions. FPSC issued a FPE1 Blueprint which provides a summary of the focus of the exam. Content of the CFP exam will be allocated within a matrix of Financial Planning Functions, with *Collection* being the biggest area (50%–54%), followed by *Analysis* (36%–40%), and *Synthesis* (8%–12%). *Fundamental Financial Planning Practices* will represent 8%–12% of the exam. The main Financial Planning Components will be *Asset Management*, *Financial Management*, and *Retirement Planning*. The Financial Planning Components coverage is segmented by each of the six components. See the following table.

FPE1 Blueprint

Source: http://www.fpsccanada.org/files/FPE1%20Blueprint.pdf.

FINANCIAL PLANNING EXAMINATION LEVEL 2 (FPE2)

To qualify to write the FPE2 exam, a candidate must have:

- passed FPE1;

- completed an approved Capstone Course with the last four years of applying to write the FPE2;

- completed at least one year of financial planning related work experience; and

- continue to maintain his Registered Candidate status in good standing with FPSC.

There is no limitation on time between passing the FPE1 and attempting the FPE2, except that the entire CFP certification program must be complete within 12 years for candidates under the approved Core Curriculum program path. (The number of years to obtain CFP certification can be no more than eight years from first attempt at FPE1 to CFP certification for candidates under the Approved Credential Policy.) Applications for FPE2 will be available in January 2011.

The structure of FPE2 will include written responses and fewer multiple-choice type questions. Based on the FPE2 Blueprint, the focus of the examination will also shift from the lower-level Collection functions to higher-level Analysis and Synthesis functions. There will be a slightly higher emphasis on Financial Planning Practices and the proportional weighting of the financial planning components will remain comparable to the FPE1 breakdown. See the following table.

FPE2 Blueprint

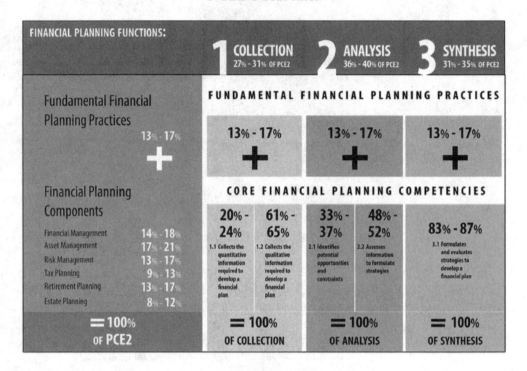

Source: http://www.fpsccanada.org/files/FPE2%20Blueprint.pdf.

KATHLEEN (FPE2 SAMPLE QUESTION)

Kathleen wishes to leave a sum of money to each of her minor grandchildren upon her death. She wants the investment income to be used to support them until they finish their education, and she wants the investment income from the funds to be taxed at as low a rate as possible. She does not want them to have access to the capital until the age of 25. Provide recommendations to Kathleen.

There are several ways Kathleen could leave the money to her minor grandchildren. For example, she could gift the money directly in her will to the grandchildren, or establish a discretionary testamentary trust for each of her grandchildren as beneficiaries. Establishing a discretionary testamentary trust for each child would be the best alternative to meet her objectives. It would allow income splitting between the trusts and the child to minimize income taxes. The trustee would have discretion to disburse the funds as needed for education purposes. In addition, a condition of the trusts could also be that the grandchild only get access to the capital at age 25. Gifting the money would not be the best option because the child would have access to the capital prior to age 25, so the money may not be available to fund the children's education. An *inter vivos* trust is not applicable due to her wish to leave the money to the grandchildren upon her death.

Question Relationship to CFP Professional Competency Profile

Element of Competency Assessed	Description
Core Competency 2.1	Identifies potential opportunities and constraints.
Financial Planning Component	Estate Planning.
Element of Competency 2.118	Identifies potential estate planning vehicles.

Relevant Linked Technical Knowledge

Category	Description
V. Law	502. Wills 509. *Inter Vivos* Trusts 510. Testamentary Trusts

Unit 3
Self-Test Questions

QUESTIONS

Question 1

Which of the following people is exempt from making Canada Pension Plan (CPP) contributions?

    a. Jeannine, who has an adult paper route, which pays her about $80 per week.

    b. George, a migratory worker who only works about 60 days per year.

    c. Jacqueline, who earns $7,000 per year as a result of her part-time job in the mall.

    d. Francine, who babysits two days each week.

Question 2

Lilly is a personal financial planner. Her client, Megan, has been separated from her husband for some time. She now resides in one province while her estranged husband resides in another. When her divorce is granted in a few months time, she plans to travel to a third province to marry again. Megan is confused about how the divorce and subsequent marriage will affect her financial plans. She asks Lilly which level of government governs which aspects of family law. Which of the following statements is true?

    a. In the event of divorce, corollary relief such as custody, access and support are governed by provincial legislation.

    b. In the event of divorce, the division of property and civil rights are governed by federal legislation.

    c. There is a federal *Divorce Act* that has uniform application across Canada.

    d. Each province has its own *Divorce Act* that applies to those who are resident in the province at the time of the divorce.

Question 3

Which of the following is a correct comment on the subject of electing out of the spousal rollover upon the death of a taxpayer?

    a. Electing out of the spousal rollover will always result in more tax being paid by the deceased taxpayer's estate.

    b. Electing out of the spousal rollover will always result in more tax being paid by the deceased taxpayer's spouse.

    c. The best solution in a rollover situation is to elect a partial rollover.

    d. Electing to opt out of the spousal rollover might make sense if the deceased has a net capital loss carried forward from previous years, or other deductions which could offset the gain.

Question 4

Henrietta is 64 years of age and has withdrawn $1,000 per month from her registered retirement savings plans (RRSP) holdings that she intends to use to qualify for the "pension income amount" on line 314 of her tax return. Which of the following statements is correct?

    a. The pension income amount is only available to those who have attained age 65.

    b. Withdrawals from Henrietta's RRSP will not qualify her to claim a pension income amount.

    c. Henrietta will be limited to a pension income amount of $2,000.

    d. As Henrietta is not 65, her pension income amount, as described above, may be claimed by her spouse, if he is age 65.

Question 5

Mr. Chan has capital property with an ACB of $10,000 and a current market value of $20,000. He is considering giving the property either to his wife or to his brother, who is currently financially distressed. Which of the following statements is correct?

    a. If he gives the property to his wife, he will incur a capital gain.

    b. If he gives the property to his wife, and she opts out of the spousal rollover treatment, he will incur a capital gain.

    c. If he gives the property to his brother, he will be deemed to have disposed of the property at fair market value (FMV), and a capital gain will be incurred.

    d. Mr. Chan may eliminate his taxable capital gain if he sells the property to his brother for $10,000.

Question 6

Nelson owned a cottage from 1987 that he sold in 2009. He had designated it as his principal residence when he purchased it; however he changed that election to his house in town from 1999 to 2007, at which time he sold the house. He purchased the cottage for $15,000, and sold it for $75,000, paying a 5% sales commission. What is his principal residence exemption?

    a. $14,674

    b. $35,795

    c. $41,576

    d. $41,739

Question 7

In an effort to reduce taxes, Mr. Warner proposes the following:

1. He transfers, as a rollover, stock shares to his wife, Wilma, who sells them one month later for $5,000 more than their adjusted cost base (ACB).

2. He gives a $50,000 GIC to each of his three minor children (one of whom, Buck, will turn 18 before year-end).

3. Mr. Warner also lends Wilma $100,000 interest-free in order that she can purchase stocks in her own name. A written repayment agreement is signed, but no interest rate is specified, and no interest is paid.

Which of the above tactics will be successful in reducing Mr. Warner's taxes?

    a. 2 and 3

    b. 3 only

    c. 2, in part

    d. None will achieve any tax reduction

Question 8

Which of the following statements regarding *inter vivos* trusts is correct?

    a. Paul transfers property to an *inter vivos* trust in favour of his brother. There is a deemed disposition of the property by Paul at this time, with possible income tax liability.

    b. Paul transfers property to an *inter vivos* trust in favour of his common-law partner. There is a deemed disposition of the property by Paul at this time, with possible income tax liability.

    c. Paul transfers property to an *alter ego* trust. There is a deemed disposition of the property by Paul at this time, with possible income tax liability.

    d. Paul transfers property to a joint partner trust. There is a deemed disposition of the property by Paul at this time, with possible income tax liability.

Question 9

A CFP licensee makes a radio commercial, identifying his organization as "John Brown, CFP, and Associates" when, in fact, he is not professionally associated with anyone else. He also promises in the commercial to save tax dollars for anyone engaging his services. Which Principle is being violated?

    a. Integrity.

    b. Competence.

    c. Professionalism.

    d. Objectivity.

Question 10

Financial advisor A.J. is starting to work through the risk management process with client Adam. Adam has identified a number of risk management objectives. Which of the following objectives best defines the scope of the task at hand and provides the best direction in achieving the objective?

    a. To have adequate retirement income to ensure the independence of Adam and his spouse.

    b. To ensure $2,000 a month of income to his widow from the time of Adam's death until their young daughter is age 22.

    c. To regularly save money and avoid going into debt.

    d. To have enough money after retirement to allow for large bequests for the daughter and any future children.

Question 11

With regard to individual disability insurance, which of the following statements are correct?

1. The incidence of mortality is generally higher than the incidence of morbidity.

2. When assessing the occupational risk, an applicant with varied duties will likely be assessed based on the most hazardous duties, even if they only represent 5% of total job duties.

3. An individual's high net worth might cause him/her to be declined for individual disability insurance.

4. The policy owner of an individual disability insurance contract must be the individual himself — i.e., third-party disability insurance is not available.

    a. 1 and 2 only

    b. 1 and 3 only

    c. 2 and 3 only

    d. 2 and 4, only

Question 12

Advisors and their clients sometimes must decide between an IPP and an RRSP. Which of the following statements in this regard is correct?

    a. If there is uncertainty as to whether the company can meet its long-term contribution requirements, an IPP may be the more advantageous retirement savings vehicle.

    b. Indexing assumptions can be incorporated into the income projections for an RRSP.

    c. An RRSP has greater flexibility than an IPP in accessing funds for emergency purposes.

    d. An IPP provides an income-splitting arrangement that is not available with an RRSP.

Question 13

With regard to the Home Buyers' Plan (HBP), which of the following statements is correct?

    a. A locked-in RRSP may be used as a source of funds for an HBP.

    b. An RRSP owner can participate in an HBP, even when funds have been withdrawn from RRSPs under the Lifelong Learning Plan and have not been fully repaid.

    c. An owner of more than one RRSP wishing to use the HBP may only select one RRSP to be used for this purpose.

    d. For homes purchased jointly, each purchaser may withdraw up to $25,000 from their respective RRSPs, but the joint owner must be a spouse or common-law partner.

Question 14

Bertie has decided to invest $5,000 each year, after tax, in his RRSP. He is in a 40% marginal tax bracket and asks how much he must deposit to achieve his goal this year.

    a. $8,333.33

    b. $7,142.86

    c. $7,000.00

    d. $6,500.00

Question 15

The basic determinants of demand include which of the following?

1. Price of good or service.

2. Changes in price of substitute goods.

3. Changes in price of complementary goods.

4. Changes in producers' tastes.

    a. 1 only

    b. 2 and 4 only

    c. 3 and 4 only

    d. 1, 2 and 3 only

Question 16

Which one of the following statements regarding economic indicators is true?

    a. Leading indicators include stock prices, housing starts and new orders for durable goods.

    b. Leading indicators include housing starts and the duration of unemployment.

    c. Coincident indicators include personal income, stock prices, and industrial production.

    d. Coincident indicators include outstanding loans and personal income.

Question 17

Gerry purchased a 180-day Canadian T-bill for $97,000 with a maturity value of $100,000. What is the quoted yield on Gerry's T-bill?

    a. 6.00%

    b. 6.17%

    c. 6.27%

    d. 10.14%

Question 18

Belinda, a media relations consultant, has applied for a car loan. Her monthly obligations include:

- $600 to reduce outstanding her credit card balance
- $200 student loan payment
- Housing cost of $1,200

The monthly payment on the car loan will be $700. Belinda's gross monthly income is $7,000. What would Belinda's total debt service ratio (TDSR) be?

    a. 28.6%

    b. 25.7%

    c. 38.6%

    d. 10.0%

Question 19

A bankrupt individual is not released from which of the following debts through the process of bankruptcy?

1. Court fines

2. Claims for alimony

3. Child support payments

4. Credit card debt

    a. 1, 2 and 3 only

    b. 2, 3 and 4 only

    c. 1, 3 and 4 only

    d. 1, 2, 3 and 4

Question 20

With reference to a deceased taxpayer, which of the following is/are reported on a "rights or things" return?

1. Employment salary owed to the deceased but not paid at the time of death.

2. Uncashed matured bonds.

3. Income from a registered retirement income fund (RRIF).

4. Old Age Security (OAS) benefits due and payable prior to the taxpayer's death.

    a. 1 only

    b. 2 and 3 only

    c. 1, 2 and 4 only

    d. 1, 2, 3 and 4

Question 21

With reference to property owned as joint tenants, which of the following statements are correct?

1. The death of one of the joint tenants causes the deceased tenant's share to pass to the surviving tenant.

2. The deceased tenant is deemed to have disposed of his interest in the property at 50% of FMV immediately preceding death.

3. The surviving tenant is deemed to have acquired his interest in the property at FMV.

4. The death of one of the joint tenants causes the deceased tenant's share to be acquired by the executor appointed by the deceased tenant.

    a. 1 and 4 only

    b. 2 and 3 only

    c. 2 and 4 only

    d. 1 and 3 only

Question 22

Larry has been offered a retirement package that includes a $75,000 settlement that is to be paid today. If Larry accepts the package, he will immediately invest the $75,000 for the next three years, after which he will use the savings to purchase an annuity. If Larry receives an annual interest rate of 5.8% compounded annually, for each of the next three years, how much money will Larry have available to purchase the annuity? (Disregard taxes.)

    a. $76,092.76

    b. $88,821.53

    c. $99,423.63

    d. $89,216.76

Question 23

Charlie anticipates that he can accumulate sufficient non-registered savings to allow him an annual income of $40,000 after-tax, for 25 years, indexed for annual inflation of 2%. He feels he can earn an annual nominal return of 10% before tax (compounded annually) and he anticipates a 35% marginal tax rate. Assuming Charlie's retirement income is paid annually at the beginning of each year, how much money does he require at the beginning of retirement to support this stream of payments?

    a. $520,494.70

    b. $525,184.97

    c. $598,552.44

    d. $624,959.17

Question 24

Derek has accumulated $100,000 of savings and would like to retire in 10 years. By that time, he hopes to have accumulated $250,000 in total savings. Assuming Derek can earn an annual nominal return of 5% compounded monthly, how much will Derek need to invest at the end of each month for the next 10 years to meet his $250,000 objective? (Disregard taxes.)

    a. $1,603.29

    b. $1,609.97

    c. $547.04

    d. $549.32

Question 25

Using the following balance sheet, calculate the debt-to-equity ratio.

Current Assets

Cash	$ 10,000
Marketable securities (near-cash)	$ 23,500
Accounts receivable	$ 86,545
Inventory	$ 223,685
Total Current Assets	$ 343,730

Capital Assets

Land	$ 190,000
Building	$ 95,000
Accumulated depreciation	$ 15,000
Total Capital Assets	$ 270,000

TOTAL ASSETS	$ 613,730

Current Liabilities

Note payable	$ 6,000
Income taxes payable	$ 12,250
Total Current Liabilities	$ 18,250

Long-Term Liabilities

Mortgage payable	$ 37,000
Total Liabilities	$ 55,250

Shareholder's Equity

Common shares (100,000)	$ 12,000
Retained earnings	$ 546,480
Total Shareholders' Equity	$ 558,480
TOTAL LIABILITIES AND SHAREHOLDERS' EQUITY	$ 613,730

Calculate the debt-to-equity ratio.

     a. 0.033

     b. 0.099

     c. 0.990

     d. 4.604

Question 26

Under which of the following circumstances might a contract be considered void or unenforceable?

1. Undue influence.

2. Inadequate consideration.

3. Misrepresentation.

4. Duress.

     a. 1 and 3 only

     b. 1, 2, 3 and 4

     c. 1, 3 and 4 only

     d. 2, 3 and 4 only

Question 27

Together, Helen and her sister, Barbara, own a piece of land. Upon Helen's death, the land passes automatically to Barbara rather than to Helen's heirs. In turn, upon Barbara's death, the land passes automatically to Helen rather than to Barbara's heirs. What is the type of property ownership?

     a. Co-owner with transfer rights

     b. Joint tenants with right of survivorship

     c. Survivorship tenancy

     d. Tenants in common

Question 28

If brother and sister Roberta and Mahood own a family cottage as joint tenants, which of the following statements are true?

1. Mahood and Roberta share equally in the right to use the family cottage.

2. If Mahood should die, his share of the family cottage becomes part of his estate.

3. During Mahood's lifetime, he can transfer his interest in the family cottage to someone else without obtaining Roberta's prior consent.

4. During Roberta's lifetime, she can transfer her interest in the family cottage to someone else but first must obtain Mahood's prior consent.

    a. 1 and 2 only

    b. 1 and 3 only

    c. 2 and 3 only

    d. 2 and 4 only

Question 29

With regard to credit splitting of Canada Pension Plan (CPP) benefits, which of the following statements are true?

1. Credit splitting is triggered only upon the dissolution of a relationship.

2. Upon credit splitting, both spouses become immediately eligible to receive the benefits associated with the credits that have been split.

3. If both spouses have qualifying credits, the couple may elect to share both sets of credits or only the credits that apply to one spouse.

4. Credit splitting affects only the credits accumulated during the period when the couple lived together.

    a. 1 and 2 only

    b. 1 and 4 only

    c. 2 and 3 only

    d. 3 and 4 only

Question 30

To be eligible to receive the guaranteed income supplement (GIS), an individual must meet specific criteria. Which of the following statements together make up the eligibility criteria?

1. The recipient must be receiving Canada Pension Plan benefits.

2. The recipient must be age 65 or older.

3. The recipient must meet certain income requirements.

4. The recipient must be resident in Canada.

5. The recipient must be in receipt of the OAS pension.

    a. 1 and 5 only

    b. 1, 2, 3, 4 and 5

    c. 2, 3 and 4 only

    d. 2, 3, 4 and 5 only

Question 31

Keith, a self-employed carpenter, has lived common-law with Amanda for seven years. Amanda is employed at New Brook Corporation, where she has worked for two years. By what date must Amanda file her 2009 income tax return?

    a. April 30, 2009

    b. December 31, 2009

    c. June 15, 2009

    d. June 30, 2009

Question 32

Fiona, an employee of Statler Industries, died on December 17, 2009. Her spouse, Stewart, is a self-employed electrician. By what date is Fiona's 2009 income tax return due?

    a. April 30, 2010

    b. December 31, 2010

    c. June 15, 2010

    d. June 17, 2010

Question 33

Bold Corporation makes an automobile available for the exclusive use of Raji, who has been employed at the firm for three years. The automobile cost $33,000 (including PST and GST) and was available to Raji throughout the year. The vehicle is required for business purposes. Maintenance costs on the vehicle were $4,600 while the total kilometres travelled that same year were 35,000. Raji's records showed that he used the automobile for business purposes at least 90% of the kilometres travelled, with total personal kilometres of 1,800. Given these circumstances, calculate the minimum standby charge applicable to Raji.

    a. $713

    b. $3,960

    c. $660

    d. $7,920

Question 34

In 2007, Gina's employer granted her 2,000 options to buy common shares of the firm. The options had an exercise price of $5 each and were issued at a time when the shares were worth $5 each. In 2008, Gina exercises her right to buy 2,000 shares by paying $10,000 to her employer while the shares have an actual market value of $15 each. In 2009, Gina sells her shares on the open market for $50 each. What income tax consequence, if any, will Gina incur relative to the 2009 taxation year? Assume Gina operates at arm's length from her employer, she does not file any elections, and the calculation is made under the basic rules.

    a. Gina will have a taxable benefit of $10,000, plus a $5,000 offsetting deduction.

    b. Gina will have a taxable benefit of $20,000, plus an offsetting deduction of $10,000.

    c. Gina will have taxable benefit of $30,000, plus an offsetting deduction of $15,000.

    d. No income tax consequences.

Question 35

Dan and Miriana Scott have two children who turned ages six and nine this year. The children attended overnight camp for five weeks during the summer, at a cost of $500 per week for each child. The children's absence allowed Miriana to completely focus on her work. The family incurred no other child care expenses this year. Miriana's income is $40,000 while Dan's is $100,000. How much can the Scotts claim as child care expenses?

    a. $1,375

    b. $5,000

    c. $500

    d. $0

Question 36

When Liz bought property in 2003, the land was valued at $300,000 and the building at $700,000. She took $100,000 of CCA during her ownership (leaving $600,000 in undepreciated capital cost (UCC) for the building). Liz sold the property in 2009 for $1.5 million, with the land portion valued at $600,000. What will be the total income addition in her 2009 tax return from this transaction?

    a. $250,000

    b. $300,000

    c. $350,000

    d. $600,000

Question 37

Which of the following statements support the concept that the capital gains system is a tax-advantaged system?

1. The system allows for only a portion of a gain on capital property to be included in income, rather than the full gain.

2. Appreciation of all capital property is accounted for annually.

3. The system allows for some exceptions where a gain on capital property can be excluded from income.

4. The system allows some deductions that offset the income inclusion of a capital gain.

    a. 1 and 2 only

    b. 1, 2 and 3 only

    c. 1, 3 and 4 only

    d. 3 and 4 only

Question 38

Which of the following statements are generally considered advantages relative to the sole proprietorship form of business structure?

1. Business continuity in the event of the owner's death.

2. Owner's ability to retain control of the business.

3. Ease of formation.

4. Start-up costs.

5. Limited liability for the owner.

    a. 1 and 5 only

    b. 1, 2 and 5 only

    c. 2, 3 and 4 only

    d. 3 and 4 only

Question 39

Which of the following statements regarding corporations is correct?

    a. In the event of a business failure, a creditor can claim against the personal assets of the shareholder.

    b. A Canadian-controlled private corporation (CCPC) may not be controlled directly or indirectly by a Crown corporation or a public corporation.

    c. A corporation continues in perpetual existence, except in the case of the death of an owner/manager.

    d. A corporation's authorized share capital must be issued and paid for within the firm's first year of existence.

Question 40

Rachel owns the following investments at PQR Bank:

- Savings account — $22,000

- Savings account (U.S. dollars) — $15,000

- Term deposit #1 (non-registered) — $97,000

- Term deposit #2 (non-registered) — $83,000

- Mutual funds (RRIF) — $45,000

- Term deposit #3 (RRSP) — $200,000

All amounts are in Canadian dollars, unless otherwise noted.

Assuming PQR Bank is a member of the Canada Deposit Insurance Corporation (CDIC), which of the following statements is/are true with regard to CDIC insurance coverage on Rachel's investments?

1. $60,000 of Rachel's investments do not qualify for coverage under the CDIC program.

2. Half of the value of Rachel's RRSP is protected by insurance while the other half exceeds the maximum limit.

3. All of Rachel's investments qualify for coverage under the CDIC program.

4. Rachel's term deposits #1 and #2 are combined with her savings account for CDIC coverage, up to the maximum limit.

5. Rachel's RRIF qualifies for $45,000 of CDIC insurance coverage, separate from all other limits.

    a. 1 only

    b. 1, 2 and 4 only

    c. 2, 3 and 5 only

    d. 3 and 5 only

Question 41

Terry is insured for $125,000 under a group life insurance policy at XYZ Insurance Company. As well, she is insured for a $1,500 monthly disability benefit under her employer's group benefit program, also through XYZ Insurance Company. With regard to Assuris insurance coverage, which one of the following statements is true?

    a. Coverage on these two policies is combined and is capped at a maximum payout of $200,000.

    b. Each of these two policies is covered through different categories, but they are subject to an overall maximum payout of $200,000.

    c. Each of these two policies is fully covered through two different categories.

    d. The full amount of the group life insurance policy is covered, but there is no coverage for the monthly disability benefit.

Question 42

John, a CFP professional, was thrilled when his brother introduced him to George Brown, a world-famous humourist. John and George enjoyed each other's company and, within a short time, George became one of John's clients. At a meeting last week, John met another individual who is also in the entertainment business. John was tempted to mention his association with George, but he realized that he had not yet sought George's permission to use his name in this regard. As such, John did not mention his association or work with George. Which one of the following Principles, under the FPSC code of ethics, did John likely consider in this decision?

a. Confidentiality

b. Diligence

c. Objectivity

d. Professionalism

Question 43

Anna, a CFP professional, worked on the development of a financial plan for her client, Anita. They are now in the monitoring step of the process. During a recent call to Anna, Anita explained that she has become engaged and plans to elope shortly. As well, Anita has assumed responsibility for her six-year-old nephew whose parents died prematurely. At this point in time, what should be suggested to Anita as the most appropriate next step?

a. Anita should determine if her fiancé has a financial plan; and if so, his plan should be merged with Anita's.

b. Develop a second plan for Anita that takes into account her responsibility for her nephew.

c. Given the magnitude of the changes, suggest a complete revisiting of the six-step planning process.

d. Meet with Anita and make revisions to her current financial plan.

Question 44

Mo is very committed to professional development and acquired a total of 55 continuing education (CE) credits in 2009. All courses were completed in 2009. Mo's 55 CE credits are comprised of 30 non-verifiable credits and 25 verifiable credits. How many CE credits can Mo carry forward into 2010?

a. Fifteen non-verifiable credits and 10 verifiable credits.

b. Twenty non-verifiable credits and 5 verifiable credits.

c. Any combination of 25 credits.

d. Five non-verifiable credits.

Question 45

Joan hired a university student as a part-time gardener to care for her lawns and gardens throughout the summer. While trimming the shrubs, the gardener tripped on the hose that was filling the pool and broke his ankle. Joan runs her graphic design business out her home, with three employees working out of Joan's basement office. The same day that the gardener tripped, Joan's office secretary also fell and broke her wrist. And, to make things even worse, later that week Joan fell on the pool deck and broke her kneecap. Which of these accidents would normally be covered under the liability portion of Joan's home insurance policy?

1. Gardener's accident.

2. Secretary's accident.

3. Joan's accident.

    a. 1 and 2 only

    b. 1 only

    c. 2 only

    d. 3 only

Question 46

Ervin owns a life insurance policy with a cash surrender value of $27,500 and an ACB of $12,600. To address an immediate cash need, Ervin borrows $20,000 from the life insurance policy to use as working capital within his accounting practice. With regard to interest on this policy loan, which of the following statements is/are true?

1. The interest expense is tax deductible.

2. The interest expense is not tax deductible.

3. When interest is paid on a policy loan, it is treated as a premium and decreases the ACB.

4. If interest paid on the policy loan has been deducted as a business expense, it will not affect the policy's ACB when paid.

    a. 1 and 4 only

    b. 1 only

    c. 2 and 3 only

    d. 2 only

Question 47

Ralph and Stan are equal shareholders of Opco and have a share redemption buy-sell arrangement that is funded with life insurance. Under this arrangement, which of the following statements are typically true?

1. Ralph and Stan will each incur an annual taxable benefit associated with the life insurance.

2. Opco is the life insurance policy owner and beneficiary.

3. If either Ralph or Stan dies, the corporation will redeem his respective shares from his estate.

4. If either Ralph or Stan dies, the surviving shareholder will have a new ACB.

    a. 1 and 2 only

    b. 1 and 4 only

    c. 2 and 3 only

    d. 2 and 4 only

Question 48

At the end of 2009, Bill retired after 30 years of participation in his employer's pension plan. The pension plan provides a benefit based on 1.8% of the average of his best four consecutive year's earnings. Bill's career has progressed steadily, with his promotion six years ago having caused a substantial jump in his earnings. Given the following earnings history, calculate Bill's annual pension.

Year	Amount
2004	$60,000
2005	$65,000
2006	$70,000
2007	$75,000
2008	$71,000
2098	$60,000

   a. $32,400.

   b. $37,260.

   c. $37,935.

   d. $42,150.

Question 49

Gina joined her employer's defined contribution pension plan when it was first established fifteen years ago. Gina is eight years from retirement, and she is working with her financial planner to assess her retirement savings. With regard to Gina's participation in the company pension plan, which of the following statements is/are true?

1. The investment performance of the assets held in Gina's pension plan will directly affect the amount of Gina's pension.

2. Gina's pension provides a specific benefit amount at retirement, regardless of investment performance.

3. Gina's pension plan likely allows her to select investments for her pension assets that suit her risk preferences.

4. While Gina has participated in the company pension plan for fifteen years, there is no guarantee as to her level of pension income at retirement.

   a. 1 and 3 only

   b. 1, 3 and 4 only

   c. 2 only

   d. 4 only

Question 50

Ruth, a widow, joined her employer's defined contribution pension plan 28 years ago, and is now reaching age 65. Ruth would like to use her pension assets of $167,432 to purchase a life annuity with monthly payments beginning at the end of her first month of retirement. Assuming an annual nominal return of 5%, compounded monthly, and a life expectancy of 25 years, what monthly income will Ruth receive from her current pension assets?

    a. $923.01

    b. $926.86

    c. $974.73

    d. $978.79

Question 51

Vickie and Victor are discussing the differences between an individual pension plan (IPP) and an RRSP. Together they have made the following conclusions:

1. If an emergency arises, participants in either type of plan may withdraw funds as needed.

2. Once established, an employer is obligated to make annual contributions in order to maintain the solvency of both plans.

3. An RRSP allows income splitting, whereas an IPP does not.

4. The plan member assumes responsibility for investment risk associated with an RRSP but this is not the case with an IPP.

5. An IPP allows the member to count on a guaranteed level of income, whereas the RRSP provides no guarantee.

From the above list, which of the statements are true?

    a. 1 and 4 only

    b. 1, 2 and 3 only

    c. 2 and 5 only

    d. 3, 4 and 5 only

Question 52

In 2001, Stanley made HBP withdrawals that totalled $18,000. During the 2009 taxation year, Stanley failed to make his regular minimum repayment. He had never previously over-paid on any minimum required repayment. What is the consequence of missing the payment?

    a. $1,200 is treated as taxable income to Stanley.

    b. $1,800 is treated as taxable income to Stanley.

    c. $15,600 is treated as taxable income.

    d. Stanley may file an election to extend his repayment schedule by one year.

Question 53

Rhonda is a LLP participant who withdrew $6,000 from her RRSP in 2007, during her first year of university, and $6,000 during her second year. At the end of 2008, Rhonda had an outstanding LLP balance of $12,000. In 2009, Rhonda will begin her third year of a four-year, full-time program at university. During 2009, Rhonda's husband plans to access funds for the first time from his RRSP under the LLP rules, where he will be the LLP participant and Rhonda will be the LLP student. If Rhonda withdraws the maximum amount permitted under the LLP rules where she is the LLP participant and student, how much can her husband withdraw in 2009?

    a. $0

    b. $10,000

    c. $6,000

    d. $8,000

Question 54

With regard to a pension adjustment (PA), which of the following statements is/are true?

1. A PA is intended to ensure equity with regard to tax-assisted savings.

2. Through the use of a PA, individuals with comparable income will have access to comparable tax-assisted savings.

3. A PA represents the value of benefits earned or accrued to a taxpayer because of her participation in a registered pension plan or deferred profit sharing plan (DPSP).

4. Every taxpayer will have a PA, although the amount will differ by individual with the minimum being $600.

    a. 1 and 4 only

    b. 1, 2 and 3 only

    c. 2 only

    d. 3 only

Question 55

Florence has participated in her employer's defined contribution pension plan for the past ten years, and has assembled the following information:

For 2008

- Earned income — $50,000
- Employer pension contributions — $2,500
- Employee pension contributions — $2,500

For 2009

- Earned income — $55,000
- Employer pension contributions — $2,750
- Employee pension contributions — $2,750

If Florence has $12,500 of carry-forward contribution room from years prior to 2008, what is the total amount that she can contribute to an RRSP with respect to 2009?

    a. $16,500

    b. $16,900

    c. $19,000

    d. $21,000

Question 56

Jane purchased a registered annuity in April 2009, and began to receive a monthly payment of $900 starting in May 2009. With regard to the taxation of the $900 monthly payment, which one of the following statements is true?

    a. Jane can elect on her tax return to have tax on the monthly payment deferred for up to three years.

    b. Jane has the option to utilize prescribed tax treatment for the monthly payments, which could substantially reduce her 2009 taxable income.

    c. Jane will pay tax on the $7,200 received in 2009.

    d. Jane's monthly payment is not taxable because the money originates from a registered plan.

Question 57

With regard to a RRIF, which of the following statements are true?

1. An annuitant can accumulate additional capital by making new regular, tax-deductible contributions.

2. An annuitant can accumulate additional capital through investment earnings.

3. In a low-return environment, withdrawals from a RRIF could erode the capital base of a RRIF.

4. RRIFs typically provide the annuitant with a guaranteed level of income throughout his lifetime.

    a. 1 and 2 only

    b. 1 and 4 only

    c. 2 and 3 only

    d. 3 and 4 only

Question 58

Bonnie purchased a non-registered annuity with $175,000 of capital. She established it as a life annuity with no guarantee period and will receive a monthly income of $1,200, beginning immediately. Bonnie's life expectancy was 22.6 years. If Bonnie opts for prescribed tax treatment on the annuity, what total amount of the monthly payment is non-taxable?

    a. $0

    b. $1,200.00

    c. $554.76

    d. $645.24

Question 59

Audrey and Stuart, who have been living as common-law spouses for the past five years, plan to marry in the spring of 2010. During the fall of 2009, Stuart converted his RRSP to a RRIF when the assets had a market value of $250,000. On January 1, 2010, the plan is expected to have a market value of $240,000. Stuart was born in July 1940, while Audrey was born in September 1942. If Stuart structured his RRIF to allow for the lowest possible minimum withdrawal, how much must he withdraw in 2010?

    a. $10,434.78

    b. $10,909.09

    c. $11,428.57

    d. $12,000.00

Question 60

Martin and his spouse, Annette, have recently become quite serious about their retirement planning. Currently, they have accumulated $850,000 in non-registered assets, and are wondering how much pre-tax income can be generated on an annual basis, based on the following assumptions:

- Retirement begins in exactly five years.

- Payout period should align with the standard rule of thumb: the period of retirement begins when the first individual retires and extends to the point in time when the youngest spouse reaches age 90.

- Annual nominal return of 5%, compounded annually, during accumulation phase.

- Annual nominal return of 7%, compounded annually, during payout phase.

- No additional contributions will be made, other than the investment earnings.

- Income during retirement will be received annually at the beginning of each year.

- Martin turns age 55 today, while Annette turns age 53 today.

Calculate the total amount of annual pre-tax income that the asset base will provide throughout retirement, based on the assumptions outlined above.

    a. $67,209.86

    b. $70,570.35

    c. $80,169.54

    d. $85,781.41

Question 61

Joyce has non-registered savings that she would like to use in the provision of an annual income during retirement. She hopes to have an after-tax income of $30,000, indexed for annual inflation of 1.75%, and paid at the beginning of each year. She is using a 30-year planning horizon. If Joyce can earn a pre-tax annual nominal investment return of 6.5%, compounded annually, and if she anticipates a 35% marginal tax rate, calculate the total amount of savings she requires when retirement begins in order to support her income objective.

    a. $474,613

    b. $497,157

    c. $633,603

    d. $649,015

Question 62

Erin and Ted, a married couple, plan to retire on January 1, 2010. Ted is retiring from ABC Inc., with an annual pension of $20,000 from his defined benefit pension plan. Ted joined ABC Inc. on January 1, 1970, and joined the company's pension plan on January 1, 1992, when he first became eligible. ABC Inc. plans to pay Ted a $100,000 retiring allowance. Ted owns an RRSP with a market value of $175,000 and a book value of $78,000. Erin will retire from XYZ Ltd., where she has worked for the past ten years, although there is no pension plan. Erin has made regular contributions into a self-directed RRSP where she is the annuitant. On January 1, 2010, Erin's RRSP is expected to have a current market value of $216,000, and a book value of $112,000. Erin was born on March 1, 1946, while Ted was born December 2, 1944. Ted plans to work part-time, as a consultant, during his retirement.

How much of the retirement allowance can Ted roll into his RRSP?

    a. $31,500

    b. $77,000

    c. $80,500

    d. $84,000

Question 63

With regard to business risk, which of the following statements is/are true?

1. It is a company-specific risk.

2. It is a form of systematic risk.

3. It can be reduced through diversification of portfolio holdings.

    a. 1 and 2 only

    b. 1 and 3 only

    c. 2 only

    d. 3 only

Question 64

Which of the following activities will shift the aggregate demand curve?

1. Increases in consumer spending.

2. Decreases in investment spending.

3. Increases in government spending.

4. Increases to productivity.

5. Decreases in the cost of resources.

    a. 1, 2 and 3 only

    b. 1, 3 and 4 only

    c. 2, 4 and 5 only

    d. 5 only

Question 65

Which of the following measurements are considered to be leading economic indicators?

1. Personal income.

2. Duration of unemployment.

3. Stock prices.

4. Housing starts.

5. Industrial production.

6. Average prime rate charged by banks.

    a. 1 and 2 only

    b. 1, 3 and 6 only

    c. 3 and 4 only

    d. 5 and 6 only

Question 66

Which of the following factors will normally influence the coupon rate that is initially established on a bond offering?

1. General interest rates in the market.

2. The type of asset pledged as security by the bond issuer, if any.

3. The market volatility of the bond issuer's common stock.

4. The credit rating of the bond issuer.

5. The beta of the bond issuer's stock.

    a. 1, 2 and 4 only

    b. 1, 3 and 5 only

    c. 2 and 4 only

    d. 3 and 5 only

Question 67

With regard to a stock option, which of the following statements are true?

1. The call option holder hopes that the price of the security will increase before the option expires.

2. The put option holder hopes that the price of the security will increase before the option expires.

3. The call option holder hopes that the price of the security will decrease before the option expires.

4. The put option holder hopes that the price of the security will decrease before the option expires.

    a. 1 and 2 only

    b. 1 and 4 only

    c. 2 and 3 only

    d. 2 and 4 only

Question 68

Jason holds a position in both a put option and a call option on Reply Inc. shares, each with the same strike price and each for the same three-month period. With regard to Jason's strategy, which of the following statements is/are true?

1. Jason has undertaken an investment strategy typically referred to as a sprawl.

2. To calculate the break-even price at which Jason would make a profit, he would need to factor in the cost of both the put and call options.

3. If the market price of Reply Inc. shares rises above the strike price, the call option becomes attractive.

4. If the market price of Reply Inc. shares falls below the strike price, the put option becomes attractive.

    a. 2, 3 and 4 only

    b. 1 and 2 only

    c. 1 only

    d. 3 and 4 only

Question 69

Ken has decided to purchase a Save Inc. bond with a face value of $15,000 and eight years remaining until maturity. The coupon rate is 6.15%, while the current market rate is 3.85%. What price should Ken pay for the Save Inc. bond? (Disregard taxes.)

    a. $14,212.45

    b. $17,337.25

    c. $17,356.13

    d. $17,477.41

Question 70

With regard to the concept of fundamental analysis, which of the following statements is/are true?

1. It involves the underlying premise that there is a relationship between the price of a stock and the health of the company.

2. It involves the identification of mispriced securities.

3. The intrinsic value of a stock is an important aspect of this analysis.

4. Ratio analysis is an important component of the evaluation.

    a. 1 and 2 only

    b. 3 only

    c. 4 only

    d. 1, 2, 3 and 4

Question 71

Which of the following types of investments would typically be acceptable within a portfolio where income is the primary investment objective?

1. Mortgage-backed securities

2. Common stocks

3. Preferred shares

4. Guaranteed investment certificates

5. Equity-based segregated funds

    a. 1 and 5 only

    b. 1, 3 and 4 only

    c. 2 and 5 only

    d. 3 and 4 only

Question 72

As part of her divorce settlement this year, Dawn became the new subscriber of the family RESP under which her former husband, Andrew, was the original subscriber. With regard to Dawn's new role as subscriber of the RESP, which of the following statements is/are true?

1. Dawn will be considered to have made all contributions into the plan.

2. Andrew will be considered the contributor for all past and future contributions into the plan.

3. Dawn will be responsible for any future tax consequences arising from contributions made after 1997 and prior to the divorce.

4. Andrew will be responsible for any future tax consequences arising from contributions made after 1997 and prior to the divorce.

5. Dawn and Andrew will share equally in any future tax consequences rising from contributions made after 1997.

    a. 1 and 3 only

    b. 2 and 4 only

    c. 2 only

    d. 5 only

Question 73

Under which of the following scenarios would repayment of a grant under the CESG program typically be required?

1. Dan, who is the subscriber of a RESP, has qualified to receive an AIP from the plan.

2. Twenty-year-old Alena, who has decided not to attend post-secondary school, is being replaced as beneficiary of a non-family RESP by her 22-year-old cousin who attends a Canadian university on a full-time basis.

3. Donna, a joint subscriber of a RESP, has qualified to receive an AIP from the plan.

4. A total of $10,000 in CESG money was received by a family RESP but only one of the two beneficiaries under the plan will pursue any post-secondary education.

    a. 1 and 3 only

    b. 1, 2, 3 and 4

    c. 2 and 4 only

    d. 4 only

Question 74

Maxine is buying a new car and plans to apply for a car loan from Fast Forward Bank, to help fund the purchase. Maxine's current monthly payments toward debt obligations include:

- Housing costs of $2,200

- Student loan of $150

- Personal loan of $600

Maxine's gross annual income is $78,000, while her net income after taxes is $56,000. Calculate Maxine's current TDSR.

    a. 37%

    b. 45%

    c. 55%

    d. 63%

Question 75

With regard to the concept of budgeting within a family unit, which of the following statements is/are true?

1. The primary purpose of this process is to assist families who have debt management issues.

2. The concept involves prioritizing cash flows in and out of a family unit.

3. It can be a valuable process to ensure that financial goals can be optimized.

4. The financial planner is in the best position to prepare a budget based on what he believes are reasonable expenditures in key areas.

    a. 1 and 2 only

    b. 1 only

    c. 2 and 3 only

    d. 3 and 4 only

Question 76

Hew made a $50,000 donation to the local hospital. During the same year, his net income was $28,000, which was $10,000 lower than the prior year. Hew is now filing his income tax return. Which of the following is a valid option for Hew?

    a. Hew can claim $21,000 as a charitable donation and can carry forward the remaining $29,000 to the next year.

    b. Hew can claim $28,000 as a charitable donation and carry forward $22,000 to the next year.

    c. Hew can claim $28,000 as a charitable donation and carry back $22,000 to the prior year.

    d. Hew can claim $50,000 as a charitable donation on his income tax return.

Question 77

Nelly is thinking through the design of her estate plan. She plans to leave all of her assets to her twenty-year-old daughter Amanda, but is concerned about Amanda's ability to handle a large sum of money without strong guidance from a financially astute person. Nelly feels that if she explains to Amanda that she must accept guidance from Harold and Derek, the family's lawyer and accountant respectively, she will simply disregard the advice. Nelly does not want to create any formal structure to address this issue prior to her death. With regard to this scenario, which of the following approaches would be most appropriate to address Nelly's concerns?

a. Establish an *inter vivos* trust today with Amanda as beneficiary and Nelly as trustee.

b. Leave the money directly to Amanda but include a letter of direction that puts Nelly's wishes in writing to Amanda.

c. Nelly could establish a testamentary trust in her will with Amanda as beneficiary and Harold and Derek as joint trustees.

d. Nelly could establish a testamentary trust in her will with Amanda as beneficiary and trustee.

Question 78

Ellen, who lived in ABC Province, died without a will and left an estate with a net value of $180,000. If Ellen's next of kin includes her 55-year-old husband, Hank, and her three adult sons, how will her estate be distributed? ABC Province's intestate distribution laws provide for the estate to be distributed ⅓ to the spouse and ⅔ to the children of the intestate in equal shares *per stirpes*.

a. Hank will receive $120,000, and each of Ellen's three sons will receive $20,000.

b. Hank will receive $45,000, and so will each of the three sons.

c. Hank will receive $60,000, and each of Ellen's three sons will receive $40,000.

d. Hank will receive the entire $180,000.

Question 79

Six years ago, Donny executed a general power of attorney for property in XYZ Province, and named his spouse, Ellen, as the attorney. With regard to this scenario, which of the following statements are true?

1. Ellen would typically have the authority to renew an investment in XYZ Province on Donny's behalf.

2. Donny's power of attorney may or may not be valid in OPQ Province.

3. If Ellen were to die, the power of attorney would terminate automatically.

4. If Donny were to die, the power of attorney would terminate automatically.

5. Ellen has the authority to create and execute Donny's personal will.

a. 1 and 4 only

b. 1, 2, 3 and 4 only

c. 2 and 5 only

d. 3 and 5 only

Question 80

Which of the following are deemed to be estate-planning techniques that can serve as a substitute to a will?

1. Named-beneficiary designation
2. Ownership as joint tenants
3. Tenancy in common law
4. Multiple named executors

     a. 3 and 4 only

     b. 2 and 3 only

     c. 1 and 2 only

     d. 1 and 4 only

QUESTIONS & SOLUTIONS

Question 1

Which of the following people is exempt from making CPP contributions?

    a. Jeannine, who has an adult paper route, which pays her about $80 per week.

    b. George, a migratory worker who only works about 60 days per year.

    c. Jacqueline, who earns $7,000 per year as a result of her part-time job in the mall.

    d. Francine, who babysits two days each week.

Answer: d

⇨   Persons falling into the following categories are not considered to be engaging in pensionable employment, and, as such, are exempt from contributing to the CPP:

- Workers who do not earn more than the exempt amount of $3,500;

- Casual workers (i.e., babysitters), like Francine;

- Migratory workers who work less than 25 days a year or earn less than $250 from any one employer; and

- Members of religious orders, whose income is turned over to the order.

Jeannine and Jacqueline earn more than $3,500, and George works more than 25 days a year.

Question 2

Lilly is a personal financial planner. Her client, Megan, has been separated from her husband for some time. She now resides in one province while her estranged husband resides in another. When her divorce is granted in a few months time, she plans to travel to a third province to marry again. Megan is confused about how the divorce and subsequent marriage will affect her financial plans. She asks Lilly which level of government governs which aspects of family law. Which of the following statements is true?

    a. In the event of divorce, corollary relief such as custody, access and support are governed by provincial legislation.

    b. In the event of divorce, the division of property and civil rights are governed by federal legislation.

    c. There is a federal *Divorce Act* that has uniform application across Canada.

    d. Each province has its own *Divorce Act* that applies to those who are resident in the province at the time of the divorce.

Answer: c

⇨   Family law is an area of shared constitutional responsibility between the federal government and the provinces/territories. Federal laws govern divorce through the federal *Divorce Act*. The federal government is responsible for divorce legislation and issues involving support and children in the context of divorce. The provinces/territories are responsible for custody and access as well as the administration of justice that includes the courts and community services.

Question 3

Which of the following is a correct comment on the subject of electing out of the spousal rollover upon the death of a taxpayer?

    a. Electing out of the spousal rollover will always result in more tax being paid by the deceased taxpayer's estate.

    b. Electing out of the spousal rollover will always result in more tax being paid by the deceased taxpayer's spouse.

    c. The best solution in a rollover situation is to elect a partial rollover.

    d. Electing to opt out of the spousal rollover might make sense if the deceased has a net capital loss carried forward from previous years, or other deductions which could offset the gain.

Answer: d

    ⇨   An election to opt out of the rollover provision, partially or fully, or not at all, would be made based on which decision would be most beneficial in each case.

Question 4

Henrietta is 64 years of age and has withdrawn $1,000 per month from her registered retirement savings plans (RRSP) holdings that she intends to use to qualify for the "pension income amount" on line 314 of her tax return. Which of the following statements is correct?

    a. The pension income amount is only available to those who have attained age 65.

    b. Withdrawals from Henrietta's RRSP will not qualify her to claim a pension income amount.

    c. Henrietta will be limited to a pension income amount of $2,000.

    d. As Henrietta is not 65, her pension income amount, as described above, may be claimed by her spouse, if he is age 65.

Answer: b

    ⇨   Those not yet 65 by the end of the tax year may only claim the pension income amount of the lesser of $2,000 and the individual's qualified pension income, which does not include RRSP withdrawals. Even at age 65, the eligible pension income would only include life annuity payments out of an RRSP, not lump-sum withdrawals.

Question 5

Mr. Chan has capital property with an ACB of $10,000 and a current market value of $20,000. He is considering giving the property either to his wife or to his brother, who is currently financially distressed. Which of the following statements is correct?

    a. If he gives the property to his wife, he will incur a capital gain.

    b. If he gives the property to his wife, and she opts out of the spousal rollover treatment, he will incur a capital gain.

    c. If he gives the property to his brother, he will be deemed to have disposed of the property at fair market value (FMV), and a capital gain will be incurred.

    d. Mr. Chan may eliminate his taxable capital gain if he sells the property to his brother for $10,000.

Answer: c

    ⇨   For statement a, under the automatic spousal rollover rule, the asset will be transferred at Mr. Chan's ACB, not FMV. Statement b is incorrect, as it is the transferring spouse who makes the election, not the receiving spouse. Statement d is incorrect because the parties are deemed to be transacting at FMV.

Question 6

Nelson owned a cottage from 1987 that he sold in 2009. He had designated it as his principal residence when he purchased it; however he changed that election to his house in town from 1998 to 2007, at which time he sold the house. He purchased the cottage for $15,000, and sold it for $75,000, paying a 5% sales commission. What is his principal residence exemption?

    a. $14,674

    b. $35,795

    c. $41,576

    d. $41,739

Answer: c

    ⇨ Principal residence is 1987 to 1999 (13 years) and 2007 to 2009 (3 years) = 16. Total years owned 1987 to 2009 = 23 years.

    ⇨ Capital gain is $60,000, less 5% of $75,000 ($3,750), or $56,250.

    ⇨ Principal residence exemption is $56,250 ((1 + 16) ÷ 23) = $41,576.

Question 7

In an effort to reduce taxes, Mr. Warner proposes the following:

1. He transfers, as a rollover, stock shares to his wife, Wilma, who sells them one month later for $5,000 more than their adjusted cost base (ACB).

2. He gives a $50,000 GIC to each of his three minor children (one of whom, Buck, will turn 18 before year-end).

3. Mr. Warner also lends Wilma $100,000 interest-free in order that she can purchase stocks in her own name. A written repayment agreement is signed, but no interest rate is specified, and no interest is paid.

Which of the above tactics will be successful in reducing Mr. Warner's taxes?

    a. 2 and 3

    b. 3 only

    c. 2, in part

    d. None will achieve any tax reduction

Answer: c

    ⇨ Statement 1 will not work, as the taxable capital gain will be attributed back to Mr. Warner. Similarly, in statement 3, all income earned and all future income is attributed back to the spouse. Statement 2 works in part, because Buck will turn 18 before year-end, but income from the GICs of the other children will be attributed back to Mr. Warner.

Question 8

Which of the following statements regarding *inter vivos* trusts is correct?

    a. Paul transfers property to an *inter vivos* trust in favour of his brother. There is a deemed disposition of the property by Paul at this time, with possible income tax liability.

    b. Paul transfers property to an *inter vivos* trust in favour of his common-law partner. There is a deemed disposition of the property by Paul at this time, with possible income tax liability.

    c. Paul transfers property to an *alter ego* trust. There is a deemed disposition of the property by Paul at this time, with possible income tax liability.

    d. Paul transfers property to a joint partner trust. There is a deemed disposition of the property by Paul at this time, with possible income tax liability.

Answer: a

    ⇨ Transfers as in statements b, c, or d are deemed to have occurred at the settlor's ACB, although the settlor of any of these trusts may elect out of the rollover.

Question 9

A CFP licensee makes a radio commercial, identifying his organization as "John Brown, CFP, and Associates" when, in fact, he is not professionally associated with anyone else. He also promises in the commercial to save tax dollars for anyone engaging his services. Which Principle is being violated?

    a. Integrity.

    b. Competence.

    c. Professionalism.

    d. Objectivity.

Answer: a

    ⇨ Pretending to have a larger organization is dishonest, and raising expectations of tax savings is misleading, both of which contravene Integrity Rule 103.

Question 10

Financial advisor A.J. is starting to work through the risk management process with client Adam. Adam has identified a number of risk management objectives. Which of the following objectives best defines the scope of the task at hand and provides the best direction in achieving the objective?

    a. To have adequate retirement income to ensure the independence of Adam and his spouse.

    b. To ensure $2,000 a month of income to his widow from the time of Adam's death until their young daughter is age 22.

    c. To regularly save money and avoid going into debt.

    d. To have enough money after retirement to allow for large bequests for the daughter and any future children.

Answer: b

    ⇨ Only b is specific enough to be useful. The other objectives, if quantified and made more specific, would become more useful in the risk management process.

Question 11

With regard to individual disability insurance, which of the following statements are correct?

1. The incidence of mortality is generally higher than the incidence of morbidity.

2. When assessing the occupational risk, an applicant with varied duties will likely be assessed based on the most hazardous duties, even if they only represent 5% of total job duties.

3. An individual's high net worth might cause him/her to be declined for individual disability insurance.

4. The policy owner of an individual disability insurance contract must be the individual himself or herself — i.e., third-party disability insurance is not available.

  a. 1 and 2 only

  b. 1 and 3 only

  c. 2 and 3 only

  d. 2 and 4 only

Answer: c

  ⇨ For statement 1, the opposite is true. Regarding statement 4, third party insurance, such as key employee coverage, is available.

Question 12

Advisors and their clients sometimes must decide between an IPP and an RRSP. Which of the following statements in this regard is correct?

  a. If there is uncertainty as to whether the company can meet its long-term contribution requirements, an IPP may be the more advantageous retirement savings vehicle.

  b. Indexing assumptions can be incorporated into the income projections for an RRSP.

  c. An RRSP has greater flexibility than an IPP in accessing funds for emergency purposes.

  d. An IPP provides an income-splitting arrangement that is not available with an RRSP.

Answer: c

  ⇨ All answers are reversed, except c.

Question 13

With regard to the Home Buyers' Plan (HBP), which of the following statements is correct?

  a. A locked-in RRSP may be used as a source of funds for an HBP.

  b. An RRSP owner can participate in an HBP, even when funds have been withdrawn from RRSPs under the Lifelong Learning Plan and have not been fully repaid.

  c. An owner of more than one RRSP wishing to use the HBP may only select one RRSP to be used for this purpose.

  d. For homes purchased jointly, each purchaser may withdraw up to $25,000 from their respective RRSPs, but the joint owner must be a spouse or common-law partner.

Answer: b

  ⇨ Statement a is incorrect since a locked-in RRSP can not be used. One can use one or several RRSPs, so statement c is incorrect. For statement d, the joint owner need not be the spouse, etc., but the home must be the principal residence of both parties.

Question 14

Bertie has decided to invest $5,000 each year, after tax, in his RRSP. He is in a 40% marginal tax bracket and asks how much he must deposit to achieve his goal this year.

    a. $8,333.33

    b. $7,142.86

    c. $7,000.00

    d. $6,500.00

Answer: a

    ⇨ RRSP gross-up factor = $5,000 ÷ (100% - MTR). At a 40% marginal tax rate, RRSP gross-up factor is $8,333.33 ($5,000 ÷ (100% - 0.40)).

Question 15

The basic determinants of demand include which of the following?

1. Price of good or service.

2. Changes in price of substitute goods.

3. Changes in price of complementary goods.

4. Changes in producers' tastes.

    a. 1 only

    b. 2 and 4 only

    c. 3 and 4 only

    d. 1, 2 and 3 only

Answer: d

    ⇨ The basic determinants of demand include: price of the good or service, changes to the price of related goods (substitute or complementary goods), changes to consumers' income or wealth, changes to consumers' expectations (i.e., regarding income, price, and/or product availability), and changes to consumers' tastes or preferences). Movements along the demand curve are caused by changes in price. Shifts in the demand curve are caused by changes in the four other factors (price of related goods, consumers' wealth, consumers' expectations, and tastes/preferences).

Question 16

Which one of the following statements regarding economic indicators is true?

    a. Leading indicators include stock prices, housing starts and new orders for durable goods.

    b. Leading indicators include housing starts and the duration of unemployment.

    c. Coincident indicators include personal income, stock prices, and industrial production.

    d. Coincident indicators include outstanding loans and personal income.

Answer: a

    ⇨ Leading indicators include stock prices, housing starts and new orders for durable goods.

Question 17

Gerry purchased a 180-day Canadian T-bill for $97,000 with a maturity value of $100,000. What is the quoted yield on Gerry's T-bill?

   a. 6.00%

   b. 6.17%

   c. 6.27%

   d. 10.14%

Answer: c

   ⇨ Yield = (((Face value) - (Purchase price)) ÷ (Purchase price)) × 365 ÷ Days to maturity) × 100

   ⇨ Yield = (((100,000) - (97,000)) ÷ (97,000)) × 365 ÷ 180) × 100

   ⇨ Yield = 6.27%

Question 18

Belinda, a media relations consultant, has applied for a car loan. Her monthly obligations include:

   • $600 to reduce her outstanding credit card balance

   • $200 student loan payment

   • Housing cost of $1,200

The monthly payment on the car loan will be $700. Belinda's gross monthly income is $7,000. What would Belinda's total debt service ratio (TDSR) be?

   a. 28.6%

   b. 25.7%

   c. 38.6%

   d. 10.0%

Answer: c

   ⇨ (600 + 200 + 1,200 + 700) ÷ 7,000 = 38.6%

Question 19

A bankrupt individual is not released from which of the following debts through the process of bankruptcy?

1. Court fines

2. Claims for alimony

3. Child support payments

4. Credit card debt

   a. 1, 2 and 3 only

   b. 2, 3 and 4 only

   c. 1, 3 and 4 only

   d. 1, 2, 3 and 4

Answer: a

Question 20

With reference to a deceased taxpayer, which of the following is/are reported on a "rights or things" return?

1. Employment salary owed to the deceased but not paid at the time of death.

2. Uncashed matured bonds.

3. Income from a registered retirement income fund (RRIF).

4. Old Age Security (OAS) benefits due and payable prior to the taxpayer's death.

    a. 1 only

    b. 2 and 3 only

    c. 1, 2 and 4 only

    d. 1, 2, 3 and 4

Answer: c

Question 21

With reference to property owned as joint tenants, which of the following statements are correct?

1. The death of one of the joint tenants causes the deceased tenant's share to pass to the surviving tenant.

2. The deceased tenant is deemed to have disposed of his interest in the property at 50% of FMV immediately preceding death.

3. The surviving tenant is deemed to have acquired his interest in the property at FMV.

4. The death of one of the joint tenants causes the deceased tenant's share to be acquired by the executor appointed by the deceased tenant.

    a. 1 and 4 only

    b. 2 and 3 only

    c. 2 and 4 only

    d. 1 and 3 only

Answer: d

Question 22

Larry has been offered a retirement package that includes a $75,000 settlement that is to be paid today. If Larry accepts the package, he will immediately invest the $75,000 for the next three years, after which he will use the savings to purchase an annuity. If Larry receives an annual interest rate of 5.8% compounded annually, for each of the next three years, how much money will Larry have available to purchase the annuity? (Disregard taxes.)

    a. $76,092.76

    b. $88,821.53

    c. $99,423.63

    d. $89,216.76

Answer: b

    ⇨ PV = 75,000

    ⇨ I/YR = 5.8

    ⇨ P/YR = 1

    ⇨ XP/YR = 3

    ⇨ PMT = 0

SOLVE FOR FV, which equals $88,821.53

Question 23

Charlie anticipates that he can accumulate sufficient non-registered savings to allow him an annual income of $40,000 after-tax, for 25 years, indexed for annual inflation of 2%. He feels he can earn an annual nominal return of 10% before tax (compounded annually) and he anticipates a 35% marginal tax rate. Assuming Charlie's retirement income is paid annually at the beginning of each year, how much money does he require at the beginning of retirement to support this stream of payments?

    a. $520,494.70

    b. $525,184.97

    c. $598,552.44

    d. $624,959.17

Answer: d

      ⇨   P/YR = 1

      ⇨   Mode = BEG

      ⇨   PMT = 40,000

      ⇨   XP/YR = 25

      ⇨   I/YR = [((i 1 - MTR) - inflation) ÷ (1 + inflation)] × 100

      ⇨   I/YR = [(0.10 (1 - 0.35) - 0.02) ÷ (1 + 0.02)] × 100

SOLVE FOR PV, which equals $624.959.17

Question 24

Derek has accumulated $100,000 of savings and would like to retire in 10 years. By that time, he hopes to have accumulated $250,000 in total savings. Assuming Derek can earn an annual nominal return of 5% compounded monthly, how much will Derek need to invest at the end of each month for the next 10 years to meet his $250,000 objective? (Disregard taxes.)

    a. $1,603.29

    b. $1,609.97

    c. $547.04

    d. $549.32

Answer: d

      ⇨   Mode = End

      ⇨   P/YR = 12

      ⇨   XP/YR = 10

      ⇨   I/YR = 5

      ⇨   PV = 100,000

      ⇨   FV = -250,000

SOLVE FOR PMT, which equals $549.32

Question 25

Using the following balance sheet, calculate the debt-to-equity ratio.

Current Assets

Cash .... $ 10,000

Marketable securities (near-cash) $ 23,500

Accounts receivable .... $ 86,545

Inventory .... $ 223,685

Total Current Assets .... $ 343,730

Capital Assets

Land .... $ 190,000

Building.......................... $ 95,000

Accumulated depreciation .... $ 15,000

Total Capital Assets .... $ 270,000

TOTAL ASSETS .... $ 613,730

Current Liabilities

Note payable .... $ 6,000

Income taxes payable .... $ 12,250

Total Current Liabilities .... $ 18,250

Long-Term Liabilities

Mortgage payable .... $ 37,000

Total Liabilities .... $ 55,250

Shareholder's Equity

Common shares (100,000)........ $ 12,000

Retained earnings................ $ 546,480

Total Shareholders' Equity......... $ 558,480

TOTAL LIABILITIES AND
  SHAREHOLDERS' EQUITY...... $ 613,730

Calculate the debt-to-equity ratio.

    a. 0.033

    b. 0.099

    c. 0.990

    d. 4.604

Answer: b

    ⇨   Debt is $55,250, Equity is $558,480.

    ⇨   Debt-to-equity is $55,250 ÷ $558,480 = 0.099.

Question 26

Under which of the following circumstances might a contract be considered void or unenforceable?

1. Undue influence.

2. Inadequate consideration.

3. Misrepresentation.

4. Duress.

    a. 1 and 3 only

    b. 1, 2, 3 and 4

    c. 1, 3 and 4 only

    d. 2, 3 and 4 only

Answer: c

    ⇨   Inadequate consideration is not grounds for voiding a contract.

Question 27

Together, Helen and her sister, Barbara, own a piece of land. Upon Helen's death, the land passes automatically to Barbara rather than to Helen's heirs. In turn, upon Barbara's death, the land passes automatically to Helen rather than to Barbara's heirs. What is the type of property ownership?

    a. Co-owner with transfer rights

    b. Joint tenants with right of survivorship

    c. Survivorship tenancy

    d. Tenants in common

Answer: b

Question 28

If brother and sister Roberta and Mahood own a family cottage as joint tenants, which of the following statements are true?

1. Mahood and Roberta share equally in the right to use the family cottage.

2. If Mahood should die, his share of the family cottage becomes part of his estate.

3. During Mahood's lifetime, he can transfer his interest in the family cottage to someone else without obtaining Roberta's prior consent.

4. During Roberta's lifetime, she can transfer her interest in the family cottage to someone else but first must obtain Mahood's prior consent.

    a. 1 and 2 only

    b. 1 and 3 only

    c. 2 and 3 only

    d. 2 and 4 only

Answer: b

    ⇨   Ownership as joint tenants is unique because of the right of survivorship. The death of one of the joint tenants causes the deceased tenant's share to pass immediately upon death to the surviving tenant. As such, a joint tenant cannot sever his share of a piece of property through his will because property held as joint tenants passes automatically to the surviving joint tenant(s). When property is owned as joint tenants, it is subject to the creditors of any of the joint tenants. A surviving tenant has full control of the property and is under no obligation to provide for the heirs of the deceased tenant.

Question 29

With regard to credit splitting of Canada Pension Plan (CPP) benefits, which of the following statements are true?

1. Credit splitting is triggered only upon the dissolution of a relationship.

2. Upon credit splitting, both spouses become immediately eligible to receive the benefits associated with the credits that have been split.

3. If both spouses have qualifying credits, the couple may elect to share both sets of credits or only the credits that apply to one spouse.

4. Credit splitting affects only the credits accumulated during the period when the couple lived together.

    a. 1 and 2 only

    b. 1 and 4 only

    c. 2 and 3 only

    d. 3 and 4 only

Answer: b

Question 30

To be eligible to receive the guaranteed income supplement (GIS), an individual must meet specific criteria. Which of the following statements together make up the eligibility criteria?

1. The recipient must be receiving Canada Pension Plan benefits.

2. The recipient must be age 65 or older.

3. The recipient must meet certain income requirements.

4. The recipient must be resident in Canada.

5. The recipient must be in receipt of the OAS pension.

    a. 1 and 5 only

    b. 1, 2, 3, 4 and 5

    c. 2, 3 and 4 only

    d. 2, 3, 4 and 5 only

Answer: d

Question 31

Keith, a self-employed carpenter, has lived common-law with Amanda for seven years. Amanda is employed at New Brook Corporation, where she has worked for two years. By what date must Amanda file her 2009 income tax return?

    a. April 30, 2010

    b. December 31, 2010

    c. June 15, 2010

    d. June 30, 2010

Answer: c

    ⇨   Self-employed individuals and their spouses have to file their tax returns by June 30, of the year following the taxation year. Any amounts due are required to be paid by April 30.

Question 32

Fiona, an employee of Statler Industries, died on December 17, 2009. Her spouse, Stewart, is a self-employed electrician. By what date is Fiona's 2009 income tax return due?

    a. April 30, 2010

    b. December 31, 2010

    c. June 15, 2010

    d. June 17, 2010

Answer: d

> ⇨ The final/terminal tax return for deceased individuals must be filed the later of six months after death and April 30.

Question 33

Bold Corporation makes an automobile available for the exclusive use of Raji, who has been employed at the firm for three years. The automobile cost $33,000 (including PST and GST) and was available to Raji throughout the year. The vehicle is required for business purposes. Maintenance costs on the vehicle were $4,600 while the total kilometres travelled that same year were 35,000. Raji's records showed that he used the automobile for business purposes at least 90% of the kilometres travelled, with total personal kilometres of 1,800. Given these circumstances, calculate the minimum standby charge applicable to Raji.

    a. $713

    b. $3,960

    c. $660

    d. $7,920

Answer: a

> ⇨ (2% × 12 months × $33,000) × 1,800 personal kilometres ÷ 20,004 km = $713

Question 34

In 2007, Gina's employer granted her 2,000 options to buy common shares of the firm. The options had an exercise price of $5 each and were issued at a time when the shares were worth $5 each. In 2008, Gina exercises her right to buy 2,000 shares by paying $10,000 to her employer while the shares have an actual market value of $15 each. In 2009, Gina sells her shares on the open market for $50 each. What income tax consequence, if any, will Gina incur relative to the 2009 taxation year? Assume Gina operates at arm's length from her employer, she does not file any elections, and the calculation is made under the basic rules.

    a. Gina will have a taxable benefit of $10,000, plus a $5,000 offsetting deduction.

    b. Gina will have a taxable benefit of $20,000, plus an offsetting deduction of $10,000.

    c. Gina will have taxable benefit of $30,000, plus an offsetting deduction of $15,000.

    d. No income tax consequences.

Answer: b

> ⇨ The employment taxable benefit occurs when the shares are purchased, not at the date the options were granted. Taxable benefit = (value of shares acquired) - (cost to acquire the shares). There is an offsetting deduction available if the FMV of shares when the options were granted was equal to or greater than the exercise price of the shares plus any costs associated with acquiring the options. The employee can claim a deduction equal to 50% of the taxable benefit.

Question 35

Dan and Miriana Scott have two children who turned ages six and nine this year. The children attended overnight camp for five weeks during the summer, at a cost of $500 per week for each child. The children's absence allowed Miriana to completely focus on her work. The family incurred no other child care expenses this year. Miriana's income is $40,000 while Dan's is $100,000. How much can the Scotts claim as child care expenses?

    a. $1,375

    b. $5,000

    c. $500

    d. $0

Answer: a

    ⇨ $175/week × 5 weeks + $100/week × 5 weeks = $1,375

Question 36

When Liz bought property in 2003, the land was valued at $300,000 and the building at $700,000. She took $100,000 of CCA during her ownership (leaving $600,000 in undepreciated capital cost (UCC) for the building). Liz sold the property in 2009 for $1.5 million, with the land portion valued at $600,000. What will be the total income addition in her 2009 tax return from this transaction?

    a. $250,000

    b. $300,000

    c. $350,000

    d. $600,000

Answer: c

    ⇨   "Profit" of $300,000 on the land, $300,000 on the building (the difference between UCC and the building sale price) = $600,000, which is capital gains of $300,000 on the land and $200,000 on the building, **plus** recapture of capital cost allowance (CCA) of $100,000. $500,000 of capital gains is included at 50% = $250,000 taxable capital gain. Recapture of CCA is taxable at 100% = $100,000, for a total of $350,000 in income.

Question 37

Which of the following statements support the concept that the capital gains system is a tax-advantaged system?

1. The system allows for only a portion of a gain on capital property to be included in income, rather than the full gain.

2. Appreciation of all capital property is accounted for annually.

3. The system allows for some exceptions where a gain on capital property can be excluded from income.

4. The system allows some deductions that offset the income inclusion of a capital gain.

    a. 1 and 2 only

    b. 1, 2 and 3 only

    c. 1, 3 and 4 only

    d. 3 and 4 only

Answer: c

    ⇨   All of the statements are correct except for 2. The appreciation of capital property is accounted for when the item is sold, not annually.

Question 38

Which of the following statements are generally considered advantages relative to the sole proprietorship form of business structure?

1. Business continuity in the event of the owner's death.

2. Owner's ability to retain control of the business.

3. Ease of formation.

4. Start-up costs.

5. Limited liability for the owner.

    a. 1 and 5 only

    b. 1, 2 and 5 only

    c. 2, 3 and 4 only

    d. 3 and 4 only

Answer: c

    ⇨ All of the statements are correct except for 1 and 5. In a sole proprietorship, the business stops upon the death of the owner, and there is unlimited liability.

Question 39

Which of the following statements regarding corporations is correct?

    a. In the event of a business failure, a creditor can claim against the personal assets of the shareholder.

    b. A Canadian-controlled private corporation (CCPC) may not be controlled directly or indirectly by a Crown corporation or a public corporation.

    c. A corporation continues in perpetual existence, except in the case of the death of an owner/manager.

    d. A corporation's authorized share capital must be issued and paid for within the firm's first year of existence.

Answer: b

Question 40

Rachel owns the following investments at PQR Bank:

- Savings account — $22,000
- Savings account (U.S. dollars) — $15,000
- Term deposit #1 (non-registered) — $97,000
- Term deposit #2 (non-registered) — $83,000
- Mutual funds (RRIF) — $45,000
- Term deposit #3 (RRSP) — $200,000

All amounts are in Canadian dollars, unless otherwise noted.

Assuming PQR Bank is a member of the Canada Deposit Insurance Corporation (CDIC), which of the following statements is/are true with regard to CDIC insurance coverage on Rachel's investments?

1. $60,000 of Rachel's investments do not qualify for coverage under the CDIC program.

2. Half of the value of Rachel's RRSP is protected by insurance while the other half exceeds the maximum limit.

3. All of Rachel's investments qualify for coverage under the CDIC program.

4. Rachel's term deposits #1 and #2 are combined with her savings account for CDIC coverage, up to the maximum limit.

5. Rachel's RRIF qualifies for $45,000 of CDIC insurance coverage, separate from all other limits.

    a. 1 only

    b. 1, 2 and 4 only

    c. 2, 3 and 5 only

    d. 3 and 5 only

Answer: b

    ⇨ Statements 3 and 5 are incorrect because the U.S. dollar account, the mutual fund account, and RRIFs are not covered by CDIC.

Question 41

Terry is insured for $125,000 under a group life insurance policy at XYZ Insurance Company. As well, she is insured for a $1,500 monthly disability benefit under her employer's group benefit program, also through XYZ Insurance Company. With regard to Assuris insurance coverage, which one of the following statements is true?

    a. Coverage on these two policies is combined and is capped at a maximum payout of $200,000.

    b. Each of these two policies is covered through different categories, but they are subject to an overall maximum payout of $200,000.

    c. Each of these two policies is fully covered through two different categories.

    d. The full amount of the group life insurance policy is covered, but there is no coverage for the monthly disability benefit.

Answer: c

Question 42

John, a CFP professional, was thrilled when his brother introduced him to George Brown, a world-famous humourist. John and George enjoyed each other's company and, within a short time, George became one of John's clients. At a meeting last week, John met another individual who is also in the entertainment business. John was tempted to mention his association with George, but he realized that he had not yet sought George's permission to use his name in this regard. As such, John did not mention his association or work with George. Which one of the following Principles, under the FPSC Code of Ethics, did John likely consider in this decision?

    a. Confidentiality

    b. Diligence

    c. Objectivity

    d. Professionalism

Answer: a

    ⇨ John was considering Rule 501 under Confidentiality.

Question 43

Anna, a CFP professional, worked on the development of a financial plan for her client, Anita. They are now in the monitoring step of the process. During a recent call to Anna, Anita explained that she has become engaged and plans to elope shortly. As well, Anita has assumed responsibility for her six-year-old nephew whose parents died prematurely. At this point in time, what should be suggested to Anita as the most appropriate next step?

    a. Anita should determine if her fiancé has a financial plan; and if so, his plan should be merged with Anita's.

    b. Develop a second plan for Anita that takes into account her responsibility for her nephew.

    c. Given the magnitude of the changes, suggest a complete revisiting of the six-step planning process.

    d. Meet with Anita and make revisions to her current financial plan.

Answer: c

    ⇨ Given the significant changes in Anita's life, Anna should revisit all steps in the financial planning process.

Question 44

Mo is very committed to professional development and acquired a total of 55 continuing education (CE) credits in 2009. All courses were completed in 2009. Mo's 55 CE credits are comprised of 30 non-verifiable credits and 25 verifiable credits. How many CE credits can Mo carry forward into 2010?

    a. Fifteen non-verifiable credits and 10 verifiable credits.

    b. Twenty non-verifiable credits and 5 verifiable credits.

    c. Any combination of 25 credits.

    d. Five verifiable credits.

Answer: d

    ⇨ Only verifiable credits can be carried forward. Of the 25 verifiable credits he acquired, he needs 20 for 2009.

Question 45

Joan hired a university student as a part-time gardener to care for her lawns and gardens throughout the summer. While trimming the shrubs, the gardener tripped on the hose that was filling the pool and broke his ankle. Joan runs her graphic design business out her home, with three employees working out of Joan's basement office. The same day that the gardener tripped, Joan's office secretary also fell and broke her wrist. And, to make things even worse, later that week Joan fell on the pool deck and broke her kneecap. Which of these accidents would normally be covered under the liability portion of Joan's home insurance policy?

1. Gardener's accident.

2. Secretary's accident.

3. Joan's accident.

    a. 1 and 2 only

    b. 1 only

    c. 2 only

    d. 3 only

Answer: b

    ⇨   Since Joan runs a business out of her home, the secretary's accident would not be covered by her home insurance. Joan's accident on her own property would not be covered either.

Question 46

Ervin owns a life insurance policy with a cash surrender value of $27,500 and an ACB of $12,600. To address an immediate cash need, Ervin borrows $20,000 from the life insurance policy to use as working capital within his accounting practice. With regard to interest on this policy loan, which of the following statements is/are true?

1. The interest expense is tax deductible.

2. The interest expense is not tax deductible.

3. When interest is paid on a policy loan, it is treated as a premium and decreases the ACB.

4. If interest paid on the policy loan has been deducted as a business expense, it will not affect the policy's ACB when paid.

    a. 1 and 4 only

    b. 1 only

    c. 2 and 3 only

    d. 2 only

Answer: a

    ⇨   Interest on a policy loan may be deductible for income tax purposes if the money is borrowed to earn income from a business or property. Normally when interest is paid on a policy loan, the interest payment is treated as a premium and added to the ACB of the policy. If the interest expense has been deducted for income purposes, as in this case, the ACB increase is not allowed.

Question 47

Ralph and Stan are equal shareholders of Opco and have a share redemption buy-sell arrangement that is funded with life insurance. Under this arrangement, which of the following statements are typically true?

1. Ralph and Stan will each incur an annual taxable benefit associated with the life insurance.

2. Opco is the life insurance policy owner and beneficiary.

3. If either Ralph or Stan dies, the corporation will redeem his respective shares from his estate.

4. If either Ralph or Stan dies, the surviving shareholder will have a new ACB.

    a. 1 and 2 only

    b. 1 and 4 only

    c. 2 and 3 only

    d. 2 and 4 only

Answer: c

    ⇨   Under a share redemption arrangement, corporate life insurance is placed on the life of each shareholder with the corporation named as the beneficiary. Upon the death of a shareholder, the insurance proceeds above the ACB are placed in the capital dividend account. The proceeds from the capital dividend account are used to redeem the shares held by the deceased shareholder's estate.

Question 48

At the end of 2009, Bill retired after 30 years of participation in his employer's pension plan. The pension plan provides a benefit based on 1.8% of the average of his best four consecutive year's earnings. Bill's career has progressed steadily, with his promotion six years ago having caused a substantial jump in his earnings. Given the following earnings history, calculate Bill's annual pension.

Year	Amount
2004	$60,000
2005	$65,000
2006	$70,000
2007	$75,000
2008	$71,000
2098	$60,000

    a. $32,400.

    b. $37,260.

    c. $37,935.

    d. $42,150.

Answer: c

    ⇨   The best four years of earnings cover 2005 to 2008.

    ⇨   ($65,000 + $70,000 + $75,000 + $71,000) ÷ 4 years × 1.8% × 30 years = $37,935

Question 49

Gina joined her employer's defined contribution pension plan when it was first established fifteen years ago. Gina is eight years from retirement, and she is working with her financial planner to assess her retirement savings. With regard to Gina's participation in the company pension plan, which of the following statements is/are true?

1. The investment performance of the assets held in Gina's pension plan will directly affect the amount of Gina's pension.

2. Gina's pension provides a specific benefit amount at retirement, regardless of investment performance.

3. Gina's pension plan likely allows her to select investments for her pension assets that suit her risk preferences.

4. While Gina has participated in the company pension plan for fifteen years, there is no guarantee as to her level of pension income at retirement.

    a. 1 and 3 only

    b. 1, 3 and 4 only

    c. 2 only

    d. 4 only

Answer: b

    ⇨   Since the plan is a defined contribution plan, the amount of pension income Gina will receive is not guaranteed and will be based on the investment performance of the assets she selected.

Question 50

Ruth, a widow, joined her employer's defined contribution pension plan 28 years ago, and is now reaching age 65. Ruth would like to use her pension assets of $167,432 to purchase a life annuity with monthly payments beginning at the end of her first month of retirement. Assuming an annual nominal return of 5%, compounded monthly, and a life expectancy of 25 years, what monthly income will Ruth receive from her current pension assets?

    a. $923.01

    b. $926.86

    c. $974.73

    d. $978.79

Answer: d

    ⇨   MODE = END

    ⇨   P/YR = 12

    ⇨   XP/YR = 25

    ⇨   I/YR = 5%

    ⇨   PV = 167,432

    ⇨   FV = 0

SOLVE FOR PMT, which equals $978.79

Question 51

Vickie and Victor are discussing the differences between an individual pension plan (IPP) and an RRSP. Together they have made the following conclusions:

1. If an emergency arises, participants in either type of plan may withdraw funds as needed.

2. Once established, an employer is obligated to make annual contributions in order to maintain the solvency of both plans.

3. An RRSP allows income splitting, whereas an IPP does not.

4. The plan member assumes responsibility for investment risk associated with an RRSP but this is not the case with an IPP.

5. An IPP allows the member to count on a guaranteed level of income, whereas the RRSP provides no guarantee.

From the above list, which of the statements are true?

    a. 1 and 4 only

    b. 1, 2 and 3 only

    c. 2 and 5 only

    d. 3, 4 and 5 only

Answer: d

    ⇨   In contrast to RRSP funds, which can be accessed easily, funds within an IPP can not be accessed if an emergency arises. An employer does not normally make contributions to an individual's RRSP, and if they do they are not obligated to make annual contributions. The remaining statements are correct.

Question 52

In 2001, Stanley made HBP withdrawals that totalled $18,000. During the 2009 taxation year, Stanley failed to make his regular minimum repayment. He had never previously overpaid on any minimum required repayment. What is the consequence of missing the payment?

    a. $1,200 is treated as taxable income to Stanley.

    b. $1,800 is treated as taxable income to Stanley.

    c. $15,600 is treated as taxable income.

    d. Stanley may file an election to extend his repayment schedule by one year.

Answer: a

    ⇨   A taxpayer who participates in the HBP has a 15-year period to repay the RRSP amount withdrawn from the plan. The repayment period begins the second calendar year following the year in which the taxpayer made the withdrawals. Stanley's minimum repayment amount is $1,200 ($18,000 ÷ 15 years). Any payments not made during the year or within the first 60 days of the following year are included in the taxpayer's income for the year that the payment was due.

Question 53

Rhonda is a LLP participant who withdrew $6,000 from her RRSP in 2007, during her first year of university, and $6,000 during her second year. At the end of 2008, Rhonda had an outstanding LLP balance of $12,000. In 2009, Rhonda will begin her third year of a four-year, full-time program at university. During 2009, Rhonda's husband plans to access funds for the first time from his RRSP under the LLP rules, where he will be the LLP participant and Rhonda will be the LLP student. If Rhonda withdraws the maximum amount permitted under the LLP rules where she is the LLP participant and student, how much can her husband withdraw in 2009?

    a. $0

    b. $10,000

    c. $6,000

    d. $8,000

Answer: b

⇨   Rhonda's husband, as the LLP participant, can withdraw up to $10,000 from his RRSP to fund Rhonda's education.

Question 54

With regard to a pension adjustment (PA), which of the following statements is/are true?

1. A PA is intended to ensure equity with regard to tax-assisted savings.

2. Through the use of a PA, individuals with comparable income will have access to comparable tax-assisted savings.

3. A PA represents the value of benefits earned or accrued to a taxpayer because of his participation in a registered pension plan or deferred profit sharing plan (DPSP).

4. Every taxpayer will have a PA, although the amount will differ by individual with the minimum being $600.

    a. 1 and 4 only

    b. 1, 2 and 3 only

    c. 2 only

    d. 3 only

Answer: b

⇨   All of the statements are correct except for statement 4. Only taxpayers who are members of a registered pension plan or DPSP have pension adjustments. The $600 is the exemption used in calculating the PA.

Question 55

Florence has participated in her employer's defined contribution pension plan for the past ten years, and has assembled the following information:

For 2008

- Earned income — $50,000
- Employer pension contributions — $2,500
- Employee pension contributions — $2,500

For 2009

- Earned income — $55,000
- Employer pension contributions — $2,750
- Employee pension contributions — $2,750

If Florence has $12,500 of carry-forward contribution room from years prior to 2008, what is the total amount that she can contribute to an RRSP with respect to 2009?

    a. $16,500

    b. $16,900

    c. $19,000

    d. $21,000

Answer: a

⇨ For Florence, her current year RRSP contribution room is calculated as 18% of earned income from 2008, less RRSP contributions and pension adjustments, plus any carry-forward RRSP room (up to a maximum yearly amount of $21,000 for 2009).

⇨ $50,000 × 18% - ($2,500 + $2,500) + $12,500 = $16,500

Question 56

Jane purchased a registered annuity in April 2009, and began to receive a monthly payment of $900 starting in May 2009. With regard to the taxation of the $900 monthly payment, which one of the following statements is true?

    a. Jane can elect on her tax return to have tax on the monthly payment deferred for up to three years.

    b. Jane has the option to utilize prescribed tax treatment for the monthly payments, which could substantially reduce her 2009 taxable income.

    c. Jane will pay tax on the $7,200 received in 2009.

    d. Jane's monthly payment is not taxable because the money originates from a registered plan.

Answer: c

⇨ All of the statements are incorrect except c. Jane does not have an option to use the prescribed tax treatment for the monthly payments because the annuity is a registered annuity.

Question 57

With regard to a RRIF, which of the following statements are true?

1. An annuitant can accumulate additional capital by making new regular, tax-deductible contributions.

2. An annuitant can accumulate additional capital through investment earnings.

3. In a low-return environment, withdrawals from a RRIF could erode the capital base of a RRIF.

4. RRIFs typically provide the annuitant with a guaranteed level of income throughout his lifetime.

    a. 1 and 2 only

    b. 1 and 4 only

    c. 2 and 3 only

    d. 3 and 4 only

Answer: c

⇨ Only statements 2 and 3 are correct. The annuitant can not contribute additional capital, and RRIFs require that a minimum withdrawal be done annually beginning the year after it is established, which may erode the capital base of the RRIF.

Question 58

Bonnie purchased a non-registered annuity with $175,000 of capital. She established it as a life annuity with no guarantee period and will receive a monthly income of $1,200, beginning immediately. Bonnie's life expectancy was 22.6 years. If Bonnie opts for prescribed tax treatment on the annuity, what total amount of the monthly payment is non-taxable?

    a. $0

    b. $1,200.00

    c. $554.76

    d. $645.24

Answer: d

⇨ The capital is $175,000 and the number of payments is 22.6 years × 12 = 271.2 months.

⇨ The proportion of capital in each payment is $175,000 ÷ (271.2 × $1,200) = 53.77%. The non-taxable portion of each monthly payment is $645.24 (53.77% × 1,200).

Question 59

Audrey and Stuart, who have been living as common-law spouses for the past five years, plan to marry in the spring of 2010. During the fall of 2009, Stuart converted his RRSP to a RRIF when the assets had a market value of $250,000. On January 1, 2010, the plan is expected to have a market value of $240,000. Stuart was born in July 1940, while Audrey was born in September 1942. If Stuart structured his RRIF to allow for the lowest possible minimum withdrawal, how much must he withdraw in 2010?

    a. $10,434.78

    b. $10,909.09

    c. $11,428.57

    d. $12,000.00

Answer: a

⇨ To minimize the withdrawals, it is advantageous to use Audrey's age at January 1 since she is younger than Stuart, the annuitant. For a non-qualifying RRIF, where the annuitant is under age 71 as of January 1 (Stuart is 69 at January 1, 2009), the minimum payment is equal to the market value of the plan at January 1 divided by (90 - age at January 1). Age refers to the age of the annuitant as of January, or the age of the annuitant's spouse or common-law partner if the election is made.

⇨ $240,000 ÷ (90 - 67) = $10,434.78

Question 60

Martin and his spouse, Annette, have recently become quite serious about their retirement planning. Currently, they have accumulated $850,000 in non-registered assets, and are wondering how much pre-tax income can be generated on an annual basis, based on the following assumptions:

- Retirement begins in exactly five years.

- Payout period should align with the standard rule of thumb: the period of retirement begins when the first individual retires and extends to the point in time when the youngest spouse reaches age 90.

- Annual nominal return of 5%, compounded annually, during accumulation phase.

- Annual nominal return of 7%, compounded annually, during payout phase.

- No additional contributions will be made, other than the investment earnings.

- Income during retirement will be received annually at the beginning of each year.

- Martin turns age 55 today, while Annette turns age 53 today.

Calculate the total amount of annual pre-tax income that the asset base will provide throughout retirement, based on the assumptions outlined above.

    a. $67,209.86

    b. $70,570.35

    c. $80,169.54

    d. $85,781.41

Answer: c

First, calculate the accumulation of assets up to retirement.

    ⇨   P/YR =1

    ⇨   XP/YR = 5

    ⇨   I/YR = 5

    ⇨   PV = 850,000

    ⇨   PMT = 0

SOLVE FOR FV, which equals $1,084,839.33

Then, calculate the retirement income based on the asset value at retirement.

    ⇨   MODE = BEG

    ⇨   P/YR = 1

    ⇨   XP/YR = (90 - 58 years (Annette's age in 5 years))

    ⇨   PV = 1,084,839.33

    ⇨   I/YR = 7%

    ⇨   FV = 0

SOLVE FOR PMT, which equals $80,169

Question 61

Joyce has non-registered savings that she would like to use in the provision of an annual income during retirement. She hopes to have an after-tax income of $30,000, indexed for annual inflation of 1.75%, and paid at the beginning of each year. She is using a 30-year planning horizon. If Joyce can earn a pre-tax annual nominal investment return of 6.5%, compounded annually, and if she anticipates a 35% marginal tax rate, calculate the total amount of savings she requires when retirement begins in order to support her income objective.

    a. $474,613

    b. $497,157

    c. $633,603

    d. $649,015

Answer: d

    ⇨ MODE = BEG

    ⇨ P/YR = 1

    ⇨ XP/YR = 30

    ⇨ PMT = 30,000

    ⇨ FV = 0

    ⇨ I/YR = (0.065 (1 - 0.35) - 0.0175) ÷ (1 + 0.0175) × 100

SOLVE FOR PV, which equals $649,015

Note: To get the most accurate interest rate, do not round off any of the interest calculations during the calculation.

Question 62

Erin and Ted, a married couple, plan to retire on January 1, 2010. Ted is retiring from ABC Inc., with an annual pension of $20,000 from his defined benefit pension plan. Ted joined ABC Inc. on January 1, 1970, and joined the company's pension plan on January 1, 1992, when he first became eligible. ABC Inc. plans to pay Ted a $100,000 retiring allowance. Ted owns an RRSP with a market value of $175,000 and a book value of $78,000. Erin will retire from XYZ Ltd., where she has worked for the past ten years, although there is no pension plan. Erin has made regular contributions into a self-directed RRSP where she is the annuitant. On January 1, 2010, Erin's RRSP is expected to have a current market value of $216,000, and a book value of $112,000. Erin was born on March 1, 1946, while Ted was born December 2, 1944. Ted plans to work part-time, as a consultant, during his retirement.

How much of the retirement allowance can Ted roll into his RRSP?

    a. $31,500

    b. $77,000

    c. $80,500

    d. $84,000

Answer: c

    ⇨ $2,000 × Number of years employed before 1996, 26 years (1995 - 1970 + 1)

    ⇨ *plus*

    ⇨ $1,500 × Number of years before 1989 where Ted was not a member of a pension plan or DPSP (1988 - 1970 + 1) = 19 years

    ⇨ $2,000 × 26 = $52,000 + $1,500 × 19 = 28,500 = $80,500

Question 63

With regard to business risk, which of the following statements is/are true?

1. It is a company-specific risk.

2. It is a form of systematic risk.

3. It can be reduced through diversification of portfolio holdings.

    a. 1 and 2 only

    b. 1 and 3 only

    c. 2 only

    d. 3 only

Answer: b

    ⇨   All of the statements are correct except 2. Business risk is classified as non-systematic risk.

Question 64

Which of the following activities will shift the aggregate demand curve?

1. Increases in consumer spending.

2. Decreases in investment spending.

3. Increases in government spending.

4. Increases to productivity.

5. Decreases in the cost of resources.

    a. 1, 2 and 3 only

    b. 1, 3 and 4 only

    c. 2, 4 and 5 only

    d. 5 only

Answer: a

    ⇨   The four determinants of aggregate demand are consumer spending, investment spending, government spending, and net export spending.

Question 65

Which of the following measurements are considered to be leading economic indicators?

1. Personal income.

2. Duration of unemployment.

3. Stock prices.

4. Housing starts.

5. Industrial production.

6. Average prime rate charged by banks.

     a. 1 and 2 only

     b. 1, 3 and 6 only

     c. 3 and 4 only

     d. 5 and 6 only

Answer: c

     ⇨ Leading economic indicators are measurable economic factors that change before the economic output starts to move in a way that indicates a trend. Some examples of common leading indicators include: changes in business and consumer credit, new orders for equipment and durable goods, housing starts, new businesses formed, material prices, and stock prices.

Question 66

Which of the following factors will normally influence the coupon rate that is initially established on a bond offering?

1. General interest rates in the market.

2. The type of asset pledged as security by the bond issuer, if any.

3. The market volatility of the bond issuer's common stock.

4. The credit rating of the bond issuer.

5. The beta of the bond issuer's stock.

     a. 1, 2 and 4 only

     b. 1, 3 and 5 only

     c. 2 and 4 only

     d. 3 and 5 only

Answer: a

     ⇨ All of the factors affect the coupon rate except the volatility and beta of the common stock.

Question 67

With regard to a stock option, which of the following statements are true?

1. The call option holder hopes that the price of the security will increase before the option expires.

2. The put option holder hopes that the price of the security will increase before the option expires.

3. The call option holder hopes that the price of the security will decrease before the option expires.

4. The put option holder hopes that the price of the security will decrease before the option expires.

    a. 1 and 2 only

    b. 1 and 4 only

    c. 2 and 3 only

    d. 2 and 4 only

Answer: b

    ⇨   The value of a call option increases if the price of the security increases, and a put option increases in value if the security decreases in value.

Question 68

Jason holds a position in both a put option and a call option on Reply Inc. shares, each with the same strike price and each for the same three-month period. With regard to Jason's strategy, which of the following statements is/are true?

1. Jason has undertaken an investment strategy typically referred to as a sprawl.

2. To calculate the break-even price at which Jason would make a profit, he would need to factor in the cost of both the put and call options.

3. If the market price of Reply Inc. shares rises above the strike price, the call option becomes attractive.

4. If the market price of Reply Inc. shares falls below the strike price, the put option becomes attractive.

    a. 2, 3 and 4 only

    b. 1 and 2 only

    c. 1 only

    d. 3 and 4 only

Answer: a

    ⇨   All of the statements are correct except 1, which describes a straddle strategy.

Question 69

Ken has decided to purchase a Save Inc. bond with a face value of $15,000 and eight years remaining until maturity. The coupon rate is 6.15%, while the current market rate is 3.85%. What price should Ken pay for the Save Inc. bond? (Disregard taxes.)

    a. $14,212.45

    b. $17,337.25

    c. $17,356.13

    d. $17,477.41

Answer: c

    ⇨   Mode = END

    ⇨   P/YR = 2

    ⇨   XP/YR = 8

    ⇨   I/YR = 3.85% (current market rate)

    ⇨   FV = 15,000

    ⇨   PMT = $461.25 ($15,000 × 6.15% × ½)

SOLVE FOR PV, which equals $17,356.13

Question 70

With regard to the concept of fundamental analysis, which of the following statements is/are true?

1. It involves the underlying premise that there is a relationship between the price of a stock and the health of the company.

2. It involves the identification of mispriced securities.

3. The intrinsic value of a stock is an important aspect of this analysis.

4. Ratio analysis is an important component of the evaluation.

    a. 1 and 2 only

    b. 3 only

    c. 4 only

    d. 1, 2, 3 and 4

Answer: d

    ⇨   All of the statements are correct in regard to fundamental analysis.

Question 71

Which of the following types of investments would typically be acceptable within a portfolio where income is the primary investment objective?

1. Mortgage-backed securities

2. Common stocks

3. Preferred shares

4. Guaranteed investment certificates

5. Equity-based segregated funds

     a. 1 and 5 only

     b. 1, 3 and 4 only

     c. 2 and 5 only

     d. 3 and 4 only

Answer: b

    ⇨ Only the investment types in statements 1, 3, and 4 produce regular income.

Question 72

As part of her divorce settlement this year, Dawn became the new subscriber of the family RESP under which her former husband, Andrew, was the original subscriber. With regard to Dawn's new role as subscriber of the RESP, which of the following statements is/are true?

1. Dawn will be considered to have made all contributions into the plan.

2. Andrew will be considered the contributor for all past and future contributions into the plan.

3. Dawn will be responsible for any future tax consequences arising from contributions made after 1997 and prior to the divorce.

4. Andrew will be responsible for any future tax consequences arising from contributions made after 1997 and prior to the divorce.

5. Dawn and Andrew will share equally in any future tax consequences rising from contributions made after 1997.

     a. 1 and 3 only

     b. 2 and 4 only

     c. 2 only

     d. 5 only

Answer: a

    ⇨ Dawn, as the new subscriber, will be considered to have made all of the contributions to the RESP plan and she is also responsible for any future tax consequences.

Question 73

Under which of the following scenarios would repayment of a grant under the CESG program typically be required?

1. Dan, who is the subscriber of a RESP, has qualified to receive an AIP from the plan.

2. Twenty-year-old Alena, who has decided not to attend post-secondary school, is being replaced as beneficiary of a non-family RESP by her 22-year-old cousin who attends a Canadian university on a full-time basis.

3. Donna, a joint subscriber of a RESP, has qualified to receive an AIP from the plan.

4. A total of $10,000 in CESG money was received by a family RESP but only one of the two beneficiaries under the plan will pursue any post-secondary education.

    a. 1 and 3 only

    b. 1, 2, 3 and 4

    c. 2 and 4 only

    d. 4 only

Answer: b

    ⇨   All of the scenarios would require repayment of the CESG.

Question 74

Maxine is buying a new car and plans to apply for a car loan from Fast Forward Bank, to help fund the purchase. Maxine's current monthly payments toward debt obligations include:

- Housing costs of $2,200

- Student loan of $150

- Personal loan of $600

Maxine's gross annual income is $78,000, while her net income after taxes is $56,000. Calculate Maxine's current TDSR.

    a. 37%

    b. 45%

    c. 55%

    d. 63%

Answer: b

Total debt service ratio

$$= \frac{(\text{Monthly housing costs} + \text{All other monthly debt payments})}{\text{Gross monthly income}} \times 100$$

$$= (2,200 + 150 + 600) \div (78,000 \div 12 \text{ months}) \times 100$$

$$= 45.4\%$$

    ⇨   Debts include housing costs, such as mortgage payments, property taxes, heating, and other liabilities, such as credit cards, car loans, and other personal loans. The ratio should be less than 40%.

Question 75

With regard to the concept of budgeting within a family unit, which of the following statements is/are true?

1. The primary purpose of this process is to assist families who have debt management issues.

2. The concept involves prioritizing cash flows in and out of a family unit.

3. It can be a valuable process to ensure that financial goals can be optimized.

4. The financial planner is in the best position to prepare a budget based on what he believes are reasonable expenditures in key areas.

     a. 1 and 2 only

     b. 1 only

     c. 2 and 3 only

     d. 3 and 4 only

Answer: c

     ⇨   A budget is useful for everyone to prepare, not just those with debt management problems. The client, and not the financial planner, should prepare the budget since he is most knowledgeable about his expenses and cash flow.

Question 76

Hew made a $50,000 donation to the local hospital. During the same year, his net income was $28,000, which was $10,000 lower than the prior year. Hew is now filing his income tax return. Which of the following is a valid option for Hew?

     a. Hew can claim $21,000 as a charitable donation and can carry forward the remaining $29,000 to the next year.

     b. Hew can claim $28,000 as a charitable donation and carry forward $22,000 to the next year.

     c. Hew can claim $28,000 as a charitable donation and carry back $22,000 to the prior year.

     d. Hew can claim $50,000 as a charitable donation on his income tax return.

Answer: a

     ⇨   Charitable donations can be claimed up to a maximum of 75% of the yearly income, which is $21,000 ($28,000 × 75%). The remaining amount can be carried forward for up to five years. One hundred per cent of donations can be claimed only in the year of death.

Question 77

Nelly is thinking through the design of her estate plan. She plans to leave all of her assets to her twenty-year-old daughter Amanda, but is concerned about Amanda's ability to handle a large sum of money without strong guidance from a financially astute person. Nelly feels that if she explains to Amanda that she must accept guidance from Harold and Derek, the family's lawyer and accountant respectively, she will simply disregard the advice. Nelly does not want to create any formal structure to address this issue prior to her death. With regard to this scenario, which of the following approaches would be most appropriate to address Nelly's concerns?

    a. Establish an *inter vivos* trust today with Amanda as beneficiary and Nelly as trustee.

    b. Leave the money directly to Amanda but include a letter of direction that puts Nelly's wishes in writing to Amanda.

    c. Nelly could establish a testamentary trust in her will with Amanda as beneficiary and Harold and Derek as joint trustees.

    d. Nelly could establish a testamentary trust in her will with Amanda as beneficiary and trustee.

Answer: c

    ⇨   Only c meets all of Nelly's requirements.

Question 78

Ellen, who lived in ABC Province, died without a will and left an estate with a net value of $180,000. If Ellen's next of kin includes her 55-year-old husband, Hank, and her three adult sons, how will her estate be distributed? ABC Province's intestate distribution laws provide for the estate to be distributed ⅓ to the spouse and ⅔ to the children of the intestate in equal shares *per stirpes*.

    a. Hank will receive $120,000, and each of Ellen's three sons will receive $20,000.

    b. Hank will receive $45,000, and so will each of the three sons.

    c. Hank will receive $60,000, and each of Ellen's three sons will receive $40,000.

    d. Hank will receive the entire $180,000.

Answer: c

    ⇨   The $180,000 will be split ⅓ to Hank ($60,000), and ⅔ to the children ($120,000 or $40,000 each).

Question 79

Six years ago, Donny executed a general power of attorney for property in XYZ Province, and named his spouse, Ellen, as the attorney. With regard to this scenario, which of the following statements are true?

1. Ellen would typically have the authority to renew an investment in XYZ Province on Donny's behalf.

2. Donny's power of attorney may or may not be valid in OPQ Province.

3. If Ellen were to die, the power of attorney would terminate automatically.

4. If Donny were to die, the power of attorney would terminate automatically.

5. Ellen has the authority to create and execute Donny's personal will.

      a. 1 and 4 only

      b. 1, 2, 3 and 4 only

      c. 2 and 5 only

      d. 3 and 5 only

Answer: b

     ⇨   The general power of attorney grants Ellen all of the powers except statement 5 to create a personal will for Donny.

Question 80

Which of the following are deemed to be estate-planning techniques that can serve as a substitute to a will?

1. Named-beneficiary designation

2. Ownership as joint tenants

3. Tenancy in common law

4. Multiple named executors

      a. 3 and 4 only

      b. 2 and 3 only

      c. 1 and 2 only

      d. 1 and 4 only

Answer: c

THE CFP
EDUCATION PROGRAM

CCH/ADVOCIS FPSC-APPROVED CAPSTONE COURSE

MODULE 28
FPSC FINANCIAL PLAN AND CASE STUDIES

Module 28
FPSC FINANCIAL PLAN AND CASE STUDIES

Module 28
FPSC Financial Plan and Case Studies

LEARNING OBJECTIVES

Upon completion of the financial plan requirement and case studies, the student will be able to:[1]

- Address issues across a wide range of financial planning components.

- Integrate the financial planning components and clearly prioritize the components that may be most relevant given the client's position in her life cycle.

- Demonstrate the fundamental financial planning competencies.

- Make recommendations, supported by appropriate analysis and synthesis.

- Demonstrate appropriate professionals skills when creating and presenting financial plans.

- Communicate a completed comprehensive financial plan clearly and professionally.

Completion of a financial plan is a key requirement of the Financial Planners Standards Council (FPSC) Capstone Course. The FPSC has developed case studies based on several financial planning scenarios. The cases are designed to provide the student with real-life client situations and an opportunity to demonstrate their competence in financial planning. In this course, you will be required to complete a comprehensive financial plan to address the specific issues facing the client(s) in one case study.

FPSC has established several expectations for the comprehensive financial plan. Each student must prepare their own financial plan. The student is expected to complete qualitative and quantitative analysis to formulate strategies and support their recommendations. They are expected to be able to prioritize client issues and defend their approach, assumptions and financial planning component recommendations. The written financial plan should be well presented and geared to the level of sophistication of the client. Finally, the student should apply the CFP Standards of Practice and CFP Code of Ethics throughout the financial planning process.

This section begins with six case studies which address several different client scenarios. The cases are written in a similar style to the FPSC-approved cases and include information that addresses the financial planning components. The information presented may seem incomplete in some respects, but this reflects the reality faced by CFP professionals every day as part of their financial planning practice. Each case is followed by case-specific questions.

The following Sheldon and Victoria sample case will provide an example of the components that should be included in a financial plan. The case uses CCH's Financial Planning Solutions software which is included in your textbook.

---

[1] FPSC Capstone Course Guidelines, August 2009.

SAMPLE CASE STUDY — SHELDON AND VICTORIA HUI[2]

Background

Sheldon and Victoria Hui retired in 2002 with the intention of enjoying a more leisurely lifestyle. While they have worked hard to accumulate savings, they have never discussed their retirement plans with a financial planner. Victoria's cautious instinct led the couple to you, a financial planner who has provided retirement planning advice to Victoria's sister for the past seven years. The couple has asked you to review their retirement income. The date of the meeting was early 2003.

Fact-Finding

Dates of birth:

Sheldon: April 12, 1942

Victoria: July 13, 1942

Sheldon and Victoria require sufficient financial resources to support only the two of them, as they have no other financially dependent family or relatives. Married for 22 years, the Huis have two grown children who are both married and live in another town a short distance away. The couple lives in a rented condominium. Discussions with Victoria and Sheldon indicate that they are both in very good health, with generally good longevity in each of their families. After significant discussion, the Huis felt that they would like to work with a 30-year planning horizon and, if feasible, the couple would like annual after-tax income of $55,000.

Victoria previously participated in her employer's defined benefit pension plan where she accumulated 25 years of eligible pension service. The pension plan provided a 2% unit benefit for each year of eligible pension service while using career average earnings in the pension formula calculation. A report of Victoria's earnings history over the 25 years of pensionable service shows total pensionable earnings of $1,250,000. Victoria selected a joint and last survivor option with 66⅔% continuation.

Sheldon previously participated in a defined contribution pension plan. When he terminated employment, he transferred his eligible pension assets to a locked-in RRSP. The book value of the assets in Sheldon's locked-in RRSP is $46,750, whereas the market value is $91,500. Throughout his working years, whenever possible, Sheldon has consciously contributed to an RRSP where he has accumulated assets with a book value of $87,000 and a market value of $143,000.

The couple each has $63,000 of non-registered assets, because the Huis have consciously allocated all purchases equally between the two of them. All asset values are as of January 1, 2003. The family is debt free.

Victoria and Sheldon have both taken early Canada Pension Plan retirement benefits, beginning at age 60.

Preparing the Retirement Plan

While the CFP courses utilize a financial calculator as a tool to support the calculation of time value of money applications, the calculator on its own has limitations, particularly when undertaking integrated financial planning solutions. Financial planners often utilize software packages as a valuable tool when working with integrated planning situations, such as a comprehensive retirement plan. Good quality software allows the planner to enter a series of variables that reflect facts and assumptions relative to the client's specific situation, and then readily produces a variety of output that can be used to analyze case-specific issues.

CCH's *Financial Planning Solutions* (FPS), offers extensive software support for completing comprehensive and single need planning. Using fully integrated workbooks with the

---

[2] *Note:* The case does not take into account any changes to RRSP rules that took effect in 2007.

spreadsheet format of Microsoft Excel, the software allows a planner to enter data, make assumptions and update assumptions in order to analyze the client-specific situation. The software produces output that is client-friendly.

The planner will need to carefully review the client's knowledge level and depth of understanding when deciding how best to present the information. While software will help in the analysis and in the production of client output, the planner should be selective in preparing the client package presenting only those pages that address the issues at hand.

To demonstrate the concept of integrated retirement planning, we have taken the information gathered through discussions with Sheldon and Victoria and entered it into CCH's Financial Planning Solutions. The Personal Financial Plan presented as the end of this case contains some of the output produced with the software, which can be used to analyze the Hui's situation and will support the compilation of a retirement planning report for the Huis. Keep in mind that the information acquired through client discussions needs to be converted into the variables needed for entry into the software.

Using the information contained in the sample report entitled *Personal Financial Plan prepared for Sheldon and Victoria Hui*, the following observations can be made. Note that in Table 5 the number in the column entitled *Section* refers to a corresponding number on Sheldon and Victoria's pension report, presented in Appendix One.

Review of the Personal Financial Plan for Sheldon and Victoria Hui

Section	Notes and Comments
1	The title page of the report should clearly set out the name of the client. This is important because in some situations only one spouse may be the client of the financial planner.
2	The financial planner's name should be clearly set out on the report in order to demonstrate who prepared the report and who will take responsibility for its content.
3	A disclaimer gives the financial planner an opportunity to reinforce the issues in respect of financial projections (i.e., values projected within the report should not be construed as a prediction or guarantee of future performance) and relative to the importance of periodic revisions.
4	The *Personal Details* page sets out some facts of the situation. This is important because the analysis is based on certain facts and, by placing the facts in the report, they can be reviewed for accuracy or referred to when explaining the recommendations. It should be noted that Sheldon and Victoria are born in the same year and are both currently retired at their respective age 60. The report is dated January 1, 2003 and both Sheldon and Victoria retired in 2002.
5	The *Financial Situation* page sets out more facts of the situation. As noted above, it is important to re-establish the facts that the planner used in creating the report.
6	The top one-third of the page summarizes, in graphical and numerical form, the current financial information relative to the Huis. The Huis have $547,651 of investments comprised of: — non-registered assets of $126,000 derived as ($63,000 × 2); and — registered assets of $421,651, derived as $91,500 plus $143,000, both of which are given facts in the case plus an assumed present value of $187,151 for Victoria's pension.
7	The middle one-third of the page summarizes the Hui's current income information. Sheldon has $9,676 of income from pensions and government benefits. Victoria's income from pension and government benefits totals $31,626, which includes her $25,000 pension benefit and her CPP retirement benefit. The equal split of non-registered assets results in projected annual investment income of $2,496.

Section	Notes and Comments
8	The row entitled *Taxes & Government programs* shows income taxes of $722 for Sheldon and $5,767 for Victoria, based on their total income. The income tax calculations in this software are based on actual tax calculations.
	After allowing for income taxes, the couple has combined after-tax income of $39,804. An important observation relates to the total combined after-tax income, which is projected at $39,804, whereas the family's goal is $55,000 (in today's dollars), leaving a projected shortfall of $15,196.
	The bottom one-third of the page summarizes the Hui's retirement income objectives. Based on the client's objectives, the report assumes an inflation-adjusted annual income of $55,000 throughout the couples' joint lifetimes, with the $55,000 continuing for the surviving spouse, after the first death. Using the client's 30-year planning horizon, the income is needed until age 90.
	The report notes that CPP and OAS benefits are incorporated into the income stream, when applicable.
9	The *Assumptions* page sets out the assumptions that were made in order to complete projections within the report.
10	Certain assumptions had to be made in respect of taxation. This report assumed that the current income tax rules and rates stayed in effect for the term of the projection. In addition, it was assumed that the investment earnings were taxed at 30% to reflect the fact that investment earnings would be a mix of interest, dividends and capital gains (an assumption for simplicity).
10.5	Inflation is assumed to be 2% for the projection.
11	This report uses a diverse portfolio of investments where each type of investment has its own assumptions with respect to rates of return, types of income reported, and mix of income reported. Later in the report, other analysis will show the results of changing the mix of investments.
12	Assumptions in respect of investment portfolio turnover are important in order to better project the cash flow needs of paying taxes on realized capital gains caused by portfolio turnover.
13	The last set of assumptions on this page set out the timing of cash flows into and out of the client's investments (registered and non-registered).
14	This *Projected Cash Flow* page summarizes how Sheldon and Victoria will generate their retirement income. To the extent that their income is less than their needs, the deficiency will be funded from savings.
	In the first year, their deficiency is $15,196. This is presented in three fashions on this page (as described in numbers 15, 16 and 17).
15	On the top one-third of the page is a summary that presents the financials for the couple's first year of retirement. In order to meet their goal of $55,000 for lifestyle needs, they will need to draw $15,196 from savings.
16	On the middle one-third of the page, the bar graph presents the deficiency as the financial gap between income and lifestyle needs. In the first year, the couple's income is less than their lifestyle goal.
	The deficiency between income and lifestyle goal is funded from savings. This graph shows that under the current financial arrangements, draws from savings will be required for ages 61 to 69. From ages 70 to 82, Sheldon and Victoria's total income is sufficient to meet their lifestyle needs. However, from age 83 onward, Sheldon and Victoria will not have sufficient resources to meet their goals.
17	On the bottom one-third of the page, the deficiency is presented in its own graph. This is meant to highlight the issue specific to their situation. A deficiency will exist for the first nine years of their retirement and reappears when they are 83 years old.

Section	Notes and Comments
18	The *Projected Cash Flow* page sets out the numerical summary that was used to create the second and third graphs, shown on the prior page.
19	The *Total Income* column represents the total retirement income that will be received by Sheldon and Victoria from various sources.
20	The *Total Tax Payable* column represents the income tax provision on the Hui's retirement income. As noted on the top of the page entitled *Assumptions,* the income tax provision reflects the current income tax rates and provisions.
21	The *Lifestyle Needs* column represents the Hui's retirement income goal. As noted on the page entitled *Financial Situation,* they would like to have $55,000 of total after-tax income, adjusted for 2% inflation, to support their lifestyle. Inflation of 2% as noted on the page entitled *Assumptions* (point 10.5), is used to adjust their income annually.
22	The *Retirement Capital Needs* page uses three sample asset allocation models, with varying degrees of risk, to provide a comparison that shows the amount of capital required to meet the couple's income goal. This is an opportunity to incorporate different interest assumptions into the discussion regarding the projections of retirement income.
23	The purpose of this page is to start the process for finding solutions to the Hui's situation, where there is an obvious income deficiency throughout a number of retirement years.
	The information and chart on the top one-third of the page sets out the capital required at January 1, 2003 to meet the Hui's income goal, based on three different rates of return.
	The Huis currently have $360,500 in assets (incorporates current assets of $541,651 less $187,151 as the value of Victoria's pension), which if invested at 7% will not be sufficient to accomplish their retirement income objective.
	A conservative investment assumption of 6% would require a net investment portfolio of $493,179 to provide the desired retirement goal.
	A moderate investment assumption of 7.4% would require a net investment portfolio of $415,216 to provide the desired retirement goal.
	An aggressive investment assumption of 8.4% would require a net investment portfolio of $370,539 to provide the desired retirement goal.
24	The chart in the middle one-third of the page presents the decline of the Hui's current investment assets as their retirement progresses. The assets can never fully dissipate during the couple's lifetime because the value will exist until the second estate (i.e., joint and last survivor pension). The graph also presents the erosion of the various asset pools, each with their own investment assumptions, which support the Hui's retirement income goal.

Next Steps

From the information provided through the software analysis, the planner recognizes that Victoria and Sheldon's base of assets is insufficient to provide their desired goal of an annual after-tax retirement income of $55,000, adjusted for a 2% inflation factor. Given the original set of assumptions, the couple will experience a shortfall of income from now through to age 69 and again beginning at age 83 onward. During the shortfall periods, the couple will need to access savings to meet the desired income goal.

During the original discussion with the couple, they positioned their desired income goal with the words, "if feasible". Using the reports developed through the software analysis, the planner will prepare the appropriate pages to package into a retirement report for discussion with the couple. If you decide to access the CCH software to review the analysis and run alternatives, you will notice that while the software provides extensive output, we have selected only key pages to include with this material and assist in the explanation of the issues at hand.

The planner's discussion with the couple will focus on the areas noted in the chart above. First, it should begin with a review of the key information used in the analysis, assumptions made and then move to a discussion about the feasibility of the retirement income goal. The discussion will address the current issues, followed by a discussion relative to the implications and options available to the couple.

If the couple decides to realign elements of their goals or assumptions, the changes can be incorporated and a revised analysis may be in order to determine if the problem has been fully addressed.

The planner should fully document the discussions and decisions throughout the process. Once the retirement plan is implemented, a follow-up appointment should occur, at least annually, to monitor the couple's retirement plan.

SHELDON AND VICTORIA HUI
"INCOME REVIEW"

Personal Financial Plan

(1) Prepared for:

Sheldon & Victoria Hui

(2) Prepared by:

Advisor Name

(3) **Disclaimer**

This document has been prepared to assist in the analysis of your current financial position, thereby helping to identify potential problem areas. Although great care has been taken to ensure the accuracy of all aspects of the document, it should be kept in mind that the various projections are based on numerous assumptions, and as such it is unlikely that the future will unfold exactly as illustrated. The investment and/or life insurance values projected within this plan should not be construed as a prediction or guarantee of future performance. This document is designed to help you to chart the appropriate courses of action, and should be reviewed and revised regularly to ensure its timeliness and relevance to your changing financial position.

Personal Details   (4)

Date of Financial Analysis	Jan 1, 2003
Start of Financial Analysis	Jan 1, 2003
Plan Notes	

Title	Mr.	Mrs.
First Name	Sheldon	Victoria
Middle Name		
Last Name	Hui	Hui
SIN		
Date of Birth	Apr 12, 1942	Jul 13, 1942
Retirement Age	60	60
Date of Retirement	May 1, 2002	Aug 1, 2002
Occupation		
Employer / Company		
Address		
City		
	Ontario	Postal Code
Home phone #		
Business phone #		
Business fax #		
Mobile phone #		
E-mail		
Web Page		

Dependants	Date of Birth	Relationship

Financial Situation   (5)

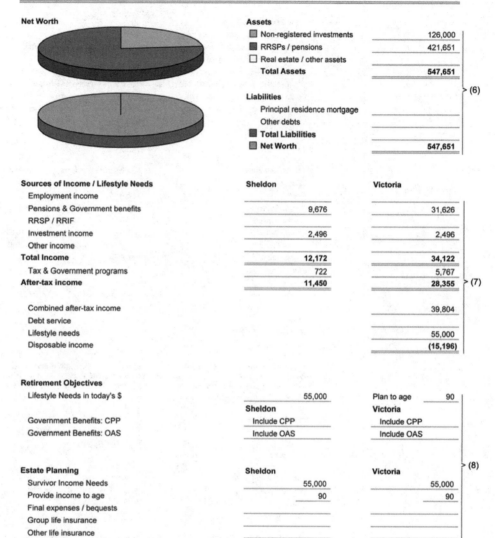

Net Worth

Assets

▨ Non-registered investments	126,000
▨ RRSPs / pensions	421,651
☐ Real estate / other assets	
Total Assets	**547,651**

> (6)

Liabilities

Principal residence mortgage	
Other debts	
▨ **Total Liabilities**	
▨ **Net Worth**	**547,651**

Sources of Income / Lifestyle Needs	Sheldon	Victoria
Employment income		
Pensions & Government benefits	9,676	31,626
RRSP / RRIF		
Investment income	2,496	2,496
Other income		
Total Income	**12,172**	**34,122**
Tax & Government programs	722	5,767
After-tax income	**11,450**	**28,355**

> (7)

Combined after-tax income		39,804
Debt service		
Lifestyle needs		55,000
Disposable income		(15,196)

Retirement Objectives

Lifestyle Needs in today's $	55,000	Plan to age	90
	Sheldon	**Victoria**	
Government Benefits: CPP	Include CPP	Include CPP	
Government Benefits: OAS	Include OAS	Include OAS	

> (8)

Estate Planning

	Sheldon		Victoria	
Survivor Income Needs		55,000		55,000
Provide income to age		90		90
Final expenses / bequests				
Group life insurance				
Other life insurance				

Assumptions (9)

Income Tax Assumptions

The first-year tax calculations are based on the current CCRA T1 schedule.

The tax calculations beyond the first year of the projections are based on the current CCRA T1

schedule with the following assumptions: } (10)

    - Tax brackets and other income thresholds are indexed at inflation minus 0.00%

    - CPP & OAS benefits are indexed at inflation minus 2.00% (when included)

Estate tax is calculated at second death (with no tax triggered on first death), at the top marginal rate of 46.41%

The growth in non-sheltered investments is compounded after-tax at the following assumed marginal tax rates:

Sheldon	30.00%
Victoria	30.00%
Joint-owned	

Index Assumptions (10.5)

	Rate	Interest	Dividends	Capital Gain	Realized Gains	
Inflation	2.00%					
Cash	5.00%					
Bonds: Canadian	7.00%	85.00%		15.00%	20.00%	
Bonds: Foreign	7.00%	80.00%		20.00%	20.00%	(11)
Equity: Canadian	8.00%		10.00%	90.00%	10.00%	
Equity: Foreign	9.00%		5.00%	95.00%	10.00%	
U.S. Equity	10.00%			100.00%	5.00%	
Small Cap	10.00%			100.00%	5.00%	

Portfolio Turnover

	Non-registered	RRSP / RRIF Can.	For.	LRSP / MPP Can.	For.	
Sheldon		25.00%	25.00%	25.00%	25.00%	(12)
Victoria						
Joint-owned						

The projected returns for the various investment portfolios are calculated based on each year's asset allocation and the assumed return for each asset class. All index rates shown, including the rates of portfolio turnover, are the rates used in the first year of the projections. The assumed rates used beyond the first year may be different. Refer to the Return Assumptions documents for complete details.

Investment savings

	Non-registered	RRSP / RRIF	LRSP / MPP	
Sheldon	Monthly, Last Day	Monthly, Last Day	Monthly, Last Day	
Victoria	Monthly, Last Day			
Joint-owned				(13)

Investment withdrawals

	Non-registered	RRSP / RRIF	LRSP / MPP	
Sheldon	Monthly, First Day	Monthly, First Day	Monthly, First Day	
Victoria	Monthly, Last Day			
Joint-owned				

Note: The assumed frequency and timing of all investment activity is material to projected results.

Projected Cash Flow   (14)

Your future projected after-tax income compared to income needs

Prepared for: **Sheldon & Victoria Hui**
Prepared by: **Advisor Name**

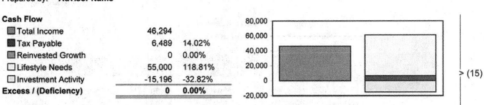

Cash Flow		
▦ Total Income	46,294	
■ Tax Payable	6,489	14.02%
▦ Reinvested Growth	0	0.00%
☐ Lifestyle Needs	55,000	118.81%
☐ Investment Activity	-15,196	-32.82%
Excess / (Deficiency)	**0**	**0.00%**

(15)

The chart above compares your current total income from all sources to your needs including income taxes, investment activity and your lifestyle. The chart below compares your future projected lifestyle needs and investment activity to your after tax income from all sources.

Excess income in the earning years must be invested to ensure that there is sufficient capital to provide for a secure retirement. To correct a projected shortfall in the retirement years, you must invest more during the earning years, invest more efficiently, plan on working longer, or reduce your expectations for retirement income.

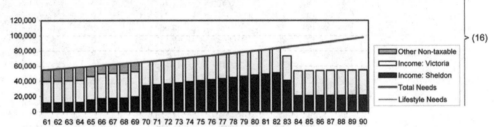

(16)

The chart below illustrates any excess income after taxes and lifestyle needs, but before investment activity. Normally referred to as disposable income, this is the amount annually that you have to invest for the future.

Also presented are income deficiencies, after-tax amounts that are needed in addition to your after-tax income to meet your lifestyle needs. In a successful financial plan, there will be a minimum amount of income deficiencies that will be offset by non-taxable principal withdrawals from non-registered investments.

(17)

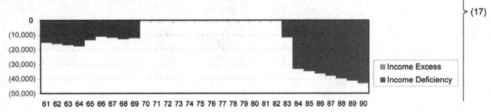

Projected Cash Flow   (18)

Your future projected after-tax income compared to income needs

Prepared for: **Sheldon & Victoria Hui**
Prepared by: **Advisor Name**

Year	Age	Total Income	Total Tax Payable	Re-invested Growth	Lifestyle Needs	Disposable Income	Investment Activity	Excess (Deficiency)
1	61	46,294	6,489	0	55,000	(15,196)	(15,196)	0
2	62	46,522	6,354	0	56,100	(15,931)	(15,931)	0
3	63	46,734	6,209	0	57,222	(16,697)	(16,697)	0
4	64	46,927	6,068	0	58,366	(17,507)	(17,507)	0
5	65	52,348	6,148	0	59,534	(13,333)	(13,333)	0
6	66	57,053	7,349	0	60,724	(11,020)	(11,020)	0
7	67	57,336	7,181	0	61,939	(11,784)	(11,784)	0
8	68	57,611	7,005	0	63,178	(12,571)	(12,571)	0
9	69	59,737	7,257	0	64,441	(11,960)	(11,960)	0
10	70	77,445	11,715	0	65,730	(0)	0	0
11	71	79,109	12,064	0	67,045	(0)	0	0
12	72	80,806	12,420	0	68,386	(0)	0	0
13	73	82,536	12,783	0	69,753	(0)	0	0
14	74	84,301	13,153	0	71,148	(0)	0	0
15	75	86,102	13,531	0	72,571	(0)	0	0
16	76	87,953	13,930	0	74,023	(0)	0	0
17	77	89,853	14,350	0	75,503	(0)	0	0
18	78	91,791	14,778	0	77,013	(0)	0	0
19	79	93,768	15,215	0	78,554	(0)	0	0
20	80	95,785	15,660	0	80,125	(0)	0	0
21	81	97,841	16,114	0	81,727	(0)	0	0
22	82	99,939	16,578	0	83,362	(0)	0	0
23	83	84,670	11,334	0	85,029	(11,693)	0	(11,693)
24	84	58,857	5,387	0	86,729	(33,259)	0	(33,259)
25	85	58,920	5,257	0	88,464	(34,802)	0	(34,802)
26	86	58,981	5,125	0	90,233	(36,377)	0	(36,377)
27	87	59,042	4,990	0	92,038	(37,986)	0	(37,986)
28	88	59,105	4,852	0	93,879	(39,625)	0	(39,625)
29	89	59,164	4,710	0	95,756	(41,303)	0	(41,303)
30	90	59,220	4,565	0	97,671	(43,016)	0	(43,016)
		(19)	(20)		(21)			

Retirement Capital Needs   (22)

Capital required at retirement compared to your available capital

Prepared for: **Sheldon & Victoria Hui**
Prepared by: **Advisor Name**

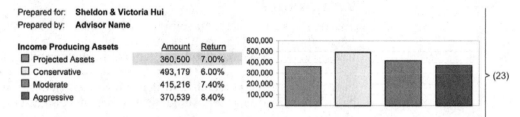

Income Producing Assets	Amount	Return
Projected Assets	360,500	7.00%
Conservative	493,179	6.00%
Moderate	415,216	7.40%
Aggressive	370,539	8.40%

(23)

The chart above is based on your savings and retirement lifestyle goals. It compares your projected income producing assets at retirement, with a required amount of income producing assets assuming three sample asset allocations with varying degrees of risk.

The chart below compares accumulations projected to be available with accumulations that would be required for each of the three investment strategies. Each crossover point, which is where a line representing the three sample allocations meets the projected assets, indicates a point in time where accumulations should be sufficient to meet your goals assuming the investment strategy indicated by the line graph is employed. The more conservative the approach, the larger the pool of capital that will be required at retirement. Your investment strategy between now and retirement will dictate the annual savings level required to meet your goals.

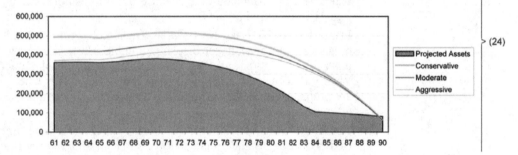

(24)

With any retirement planning analysis, if there is an indication that you may not be able to meet your goals, there are generally only three courses of action you can take.

First, you can choose to do nothing, this will ultimately force you to reduce your need for income in the future by working longer or spending less resulting in a lowering of planned lifestyle.

Second, you can save more now, this will have an impact on your current standard of living, forcing you to reduce what you are now spending on such things as entertainment, vacations and other discretionary items.

Third, you can better manage your resources, this requires developing strategies for investment and taxes to maximize the future growth of your assets so you will have the capital necessary at your planned retirement date to provide you with the lifestyle you want.

CASE STUDY 1 — TOM AND VIV ELIOT

Background

Tom and Viv Eliot met with you on April 1, 2009 in order to get a second opinion on their financial situation. They say that they are unhappy with their current advisor, who they feel has sometimes pressured them into purchasing investment and insurance products they did not completely understand. They are particularly concerned about the taxes they pay on their non-registered portfolio, and they are also worried they may not be able to leave enough money to their son Alfred, who is mentally disabled.

They tell you that they've never really had anyone prepare a complete financial plan for them in the past, but Viv has prepared net worth and cash flow statements to give you a better idea of their situation (see Tables).

Personal Information

Tom Eliot (age 70) and Viv Eliot (age 58) live in a small town outside of Ottawa, Ontario. They have been married for 33 years. Both live a very healthy lifestyle. They exercise regularly, eat a balanced diet, and are both non-smokers. They have two children — Ernest (age 31) and Alfred (age 17).

Ernest has just finished his Ph.D. in English literature and is working as an associate professor at a university in British Columbia. He is married to Mary (age 30), who is also a university professor, and they have a three-month-old daughter named Hannah. Tom and Viv say that they were happy to help Ernest financially when he went to school, and they are prepared to do the same for his daughter. They would like to set aside $3,600 every year for her education.

The Eliots' other son, Alfred, was born with Down's Syndrome. He is able to attend specialized classes at the local high school, but Tom and Viv say that he relies on them completely. They have retained the services of a part-time support worker to help them look after Alfred, and they worry about whether he will be able to manage financially after their deaths.

Employment Information

Details of Tom's Business

Tom is the sole proprietor of a small media company, Eliot Publishing, which he runs from an office in his home. He has no employees, but he does contract the services of several freelance editors to help him edit manuscripts and co-ordinate the printing of the books he publishes. Tom has few expenses besides production costs, such as a cell phone and a separate business phone line and fax line, and usually takes home about $120,000 before taxes. He is considering incorporating the business.

Tom says he has no plans to retire, and hopes to keep working for at least another 10 years. One of the freelance editors has expressed an interest in investing in the company and becoming a partner, but Tom says that he isn't prepared to give up control just yet.

Details of Viv's Employment

Viv works as an in-house translator at Big Time Translations, an independent agency in Ottawa. She earns $66,000 a year and has worked at Big Time since 1993. Big Time has lost several important contracts over the last few years, and her boss has just offered her a $35,000 severance package. She will be leaving the company at Christmas.

Viv says that she plans to start her own business and will work as a part-time freelance translator next year. She says she won't miss commuting, and her employer did not provide health, dental, or retirement benefits anyway. She is wondering if it would be worthwhile renovating an extra bedroom that she could use as her own office at home, or whether she should just share the room Tom already uses as his office.

Financial Position

Real Estate

Tom and Viv purchased their home 31 years ago for $40,000 and paid off the mortgage quite a few years ago. It is an old Victorian farmhouse, and they own it jointly. After all the improvements the Eliots have made, its value has grown significantly. It has 10 bedrooms and was recently appraised at $550,000.

They are also own a 1,600 square foot townhouse in a fashionable part of Toronto, which they purchased in 1997 for $180,000. They own it jointly as well. A friend of theirs who is a real estate agent recently told them that the property is now worth $600,000. They currently rent out the bottom floor and keep the small apartment (about 700 square feet) at the top of the house for personal use. The Eliots spend at least one weekend a month there, as well as a good part of their summer holidays.

Viv also owns half of a cottage in the Muskokas with her sister, Susan. They are tenants in common. When they inherited it from her mother 10 years ago, the cottage was valued at $50,000. It is now worth $250,000. Neither Susan nor Viv spend much time there, especially now that Susan lives in Newfoundland. However, Susan's daughter, Samantha, spends most of the summer there and often has Alfred up to stay for several weeks to give Tom and Viv a bit of time to themselves — Susan does not pay any rent for the cottage, but Viv says she is happy to have someone so reliable looking after the place for them. She says it means a great deal to Alfred to be able to spend time there with Susan.

Tom's Investments, Registered

Tom's RRSP portfolio consists of the following investments:

- $28,000 GrowGreat Canadian Precious Metals Fund
- $27,000 GrowGreat American Small Cap Fund
- $48,000 GrowGreat Canadian Aggressive Growth Fund
- $20,000 GrowGreat S&P/TSX 60 Index Fund
- $18,000 GrowGreat Telecommunications Fund
- $15,000 GrowGreat Labour-Sponsored Fund

On the advice of their current advisor, Tom has put $5,000 into the GrowGreat Labour-Sponsored Fund every year, for a total investment of $30,000. The market value of the investment has declined to $15,000. Tom says he is very unhappy with the way most of the funds have performed, especially the Labour-Sponsored Fund.

Tom also has $89,000 in a locked-in retirement account. The money is in a money-market fund and the account is held by the same company that managed his former employer's pension plan. Tom wants to know what, if anything, he can do with these funds.

Tom's Investments, Non-Registered

Tom says that, in an attempt to make up for all the money he was losing in his RRSPs, he opened up an account at a discount brokerage. Based on information he read in the newspaper, he decided to invest a total of $60,000 in the ABC Bond Fund. The market value of the fund is now $80,000. Tom says he's happy to earn the extra money, currently about 7% a year, but hates having to pay tax on this interest income. He says he has already maximized his RRSP, or he would transfer the money there.

Viv's Investments, Registered

Like Tom, Viv has invested most of her registered funds in very aggressive GrowGreat Funds:

- $8,000 GrowGreat Canadian Precious Metals Fund
- $12,000 GrowGreat Japan Small Cap Fund
- $37,000 GrowGreat Canadian Aggressive Growth Fund
- $18,000 GrowGreat Canadian Telecommunications Fund

- $15,000 GrowGreat Labour-Sponsored Fund

She is as displeased as Tom with the performance of her investments, and says that she has lost sleep worrying about her investments. She also invested $30,000 in the Labour-Sponsored Fund, and her other investments have a book value of $100,000. She says she would prefer a more conservative portfolio.

Viv's Investments, Non-Registered

Viv has always purchased Canada Savings Bonds (CSBs), and currently holds $27,000 in various series, with earnings averaging 4% annually. While she likes the regular interest income the CSBs generate, she would like to find a way to reduce the taxes she pays. She wishes she could transfer them to her RRSP but she has no more contribution room available.

Liabilities

Tom and Viv pay their entire credit card bill each month, and do not have any outstanding personal loans except for a small car loan of $15,000 at 4%. They still have a $150,000 mortgage at 6.9% on their Toronto property, and the rate is locked in for the next two years. They are paying $1,250 every month in principal and interest.

Viv says that she will have to either purchase or lease a computer when she starts working from home. The computer she is looking at retails for $3,500.

Insurance Information

Tom has a T-100 life insurance policy with a face value of $300,000, and Viv has a $280,000 five-year term life insurance coverage through her university alumni plan. Tom was unable to find his last statement from the insurance company, but the policy is more than 10 years old and he thinks it may have a cash surrender value. Viv is worried about what will happen when she reaches age 65, and her term insurance policy expires. They have named each other as beneficiaries on their policies. Neither Tom nor Viv have disability insurance.

Children

They want to make sure that Alfred is provided with a decent and reliable level of income for the rest of his life. They love their son Ernest very much, but they say that he is not at all good with money. They say that he is a terrible spendthrift, and they are worried he would spend any money they give to him. They would like whatever money that is left after Alfred dies to go to their granddaughter, Hannah.

Risk Profile

Both Tom and Viv describe themselves as extremely conservative investors who cannot tolerate short-term volatility. They say that they would rather earn a lower rate of return than face the ups and downs of the stock market. They say that they told their advisor this, but that he later telephoned and pushed them into buying growth investment funds anyway.

They have shown you copies of their original investment applications, and they have pointed to where they checked off boxes indicating they had "little or no" tolerance for risk. They say their advisor often makes "adjustments" to their investment mix, and only informs them of changes after the fact. They do not remember ever signing a form to authorize him to do this, and wonder if it is a common practice.

Goals and Objectives

Tom and Viv say that their number one priority is to make sure that Alfred is able to live comfortably after their deaths. They have heard that if they leave money in a trust for Alfred, he might not be able to receive his disability benefits. They want to know if there is any way to deal with this problem.

Tom says he doesn't want to retire. He enjoys his job and wants to keep working as long as he is physically able. He's deferred CPP income as long as possible, and he hasn't converted his RRSP to a RRIF yet, but now that he's approaching 71 he knows he'll have to act soon. He wants to receive as little income as possible, and wants to minimize his income taxes.

Viv says she'd like to stop working at age 60 and spend more time with Alfred, and perhaps help Tom with his business. She says that her needs are quite modest; she'd like to have a retirement income of about $30,000 before taxes.

Wills and Powers of Attorney

Tom and Viv last updated their wills in 1987, shortly after Alfred was born. They have named each other as beneficiaries and executors, and in the event of both their deaths Tom's younger brother Jack (current age 65, widower) would act as executor, guardian and trustee. The will allows Ernest to inherit half of the estate, since he has now reached 21 years of age. The remainder is to be held in trust for Alfred, with Jack as trustee. Tom and Viv say that Jack spends most of the winter in Florida now, and they are considering naming someone else.

Neither Tom nor Viv have powers of attorney, although they know they probably should. They have also heard about something called a living will, and want to know if that's the same thing.

Tom and Viv Eliot
Statement of Net Worth at December 31, 2008

ASSETS	Tom	Viv	Total
Liquid Assets			
Joint Chequing Account	$ 1,200	$ 1,200	$ 2,400
Business Chequing Account	4,600		4,600
Cash Surrender Value	?		
Total Liquid Assets	**$ 5,800**	**$ 1,200**	**$ 7,000**
Investment Assets			
Non-Registered Assets	80,000	27,000	107,000
Registered Assets	260,000	120,000	380,000
Total Investment Assets	**$ 340,000**	**$ 147,000**	**$ 487,000**
Personal-Use Assets			
Residence (farmhouse)	275,000	275,000	550,000
Residence (Toronto)	300,000	300,000	600,000
Cottage (Muskokas)		125,000	125,000
Automobile	25,000		25,000
Personal Effects (owned jointly)	10,000	10,000	20,000
Total Personal-Use Assets	**$ 610,000**	**$ 710,000**	**$ 1,320,000**
TOTAL ASSETS	**$ 955,800**	**$ 858,200**	**$ 1,814,000**
LIABILITIES			
Short-Term Liabilities			
Car Loan	15,000		15,000
Long-Term Liabilities			
Mortgage (Toronto)	75,000	75,000	150,000
TOTAL LIABILITIES	**$ 90,000**	**$ 75,000**	**$ 165,000**
NET WORTH	**$ 865,800**	**$ 783,200**	**$ 1,649,000**

Tom and Viv Eliot
Monthly and Annual Cash Flow as of December 31, 2008

	Monthly	Annually
INCOME		
Tom's Business Income	$ 10,000	$ 120,000
Viv's Employment Income	5,500	66,000
Investment Interest Income	490	5,880
Rental Income	1,000	12,000
Total Income	**$ 16,990**	**$ 203,880**
EXPENSES		
Tax Instalments — Tom	3,555	42,660
Withholdings at Source — Viv		
Taxes, CPP and EI	1,532	18,384
Professional Dues	28	336
Mortgage Payment (Toronto)	1,250	15,000
Maintenance, Repairs		
Townhouse	250	3,000
Farmhouse	100	1,200
Home Insurance		
Townhouse	200	2,400
Farmhouse	75	900
Heating, Water and Electricity		
Townhouse	240	2,880
Farmhouse	400	4,800
Property Taxes		
Townhouse	675	8,100
Farmhouse	290	3,480
Cottage	75	900
Automobile Insurance	95	1,140
Operating Expenses	165	1,980
Repairs and Maintenance	62	744
Loan Payments		
Life Insurance Premiums		
Tom	419	5,028
Viv	162	1,944
Telephone (personal)	100	1,200
Food	600	7,200
Clothing	525	6,300
Personal Care	75	900
Entertainment	100	1,200
Support Worker for Alfred	3,000	36,000
RRSP Contribution — Tom	1,291	15,492
RRSP Contribution — Viv	990	11,880
Savings for Hannah	300	3,600
Miscellaneous Cash	100	1,200
TOTAL EXPENSES	**$ 16,654**	**$ 199,848**
SURPLUS	**$ 336**	**$ 4,032**

QUESTIONS

Question 1

What portion of Tom's GrowGreat RRSP portfolio could be said to have a beta of one?

- a. $18,000
- b. $20,000
- c. $48,000
- d. $72,000

Question 2

If Viv were to die tomorrow, how much would her estate have to include as a taxable capital gain on her terminal income tax return?

- a. $152,000
- b. $125,000
- c. $50,000
- d. $0

Question 3

If Viv were to die tomorrow, ownership of her half of the cottage would be transferred to:

- a. Tom
- b. Susan
- c. Tom and Susan equally
- d. Samantha

Question 4

How much will Viv have to contribute to the Canada Pension Plan in 2009 if she were to earn the same net taxable income as she did in 2008? (The 2009 YMPE is $46,300, contribution rates for employees and employers are 4.95% each.)

- a. $2,118.60
- b. $2,291.85
- c. $4,237.20
- d. $4,398.50

Question 5

If Tom were to redeem all of his units in the GrowGreat Labour-Sponsored Funds tomorrow, how much of the federal and provincial tax credits would he have to repay?

- a. $2,250
- b. $4,500
- c. $5,000
- d. $9,000

Question 6

Which of the following is the *most likely* cash surrender value for Tom's life insurance policy?

- a. Nil
- b. $20,000
- c. $50,000
- d. $300,000

Question 7

If Tom and Viv were to deposit $3,600 into a registered education savings plan (RESP) at the beginning of each year for Hannah, what will the account balance be after 10 years, including grants and assuming a 4% rate of return, compounded annually?

- a. $43,222
- b. $44,951
- c. $51,194
- d. $51,866

Question 8

If Tom continues to work, he will:

1. Not be able to contribute to his own RRSP next year

2. Be able to contribute to a spousal RRSP

3. Have to decide if he wants to convert his RRSP to a RRIF and/or purchase an annuity before the end of this year

4. Be able to defer his CPP pension for another two years, increasing the pension he will receive by 30%.

Which of the above statements is/are true?

- a. 1 and 2 only
- b. 2 only
- c. 3 only
- d. 2 and 4 only

Question 9

How much of his farm housing costs should Tom be deducting as home office expenses?

- a. $828
- b. $918
- c. $1,038
- d. $1,557

Question 10

Which of the following best describes the purpose of a living will?

- a. It divides assets among beneficiaries while you are still alive, and is sometimes referred to as an *inter vivos* trust.
- b. It divides assets among beneficiaries after your death, and is sometimes referred to as a testamentary trust.
- c. It allows someone to make decisions about your finances and property should you become unable to do so.
- d. It states your wishes about end-of-life medical treatment, and may include a request dealing with life support and resuscitation.

Question 11

If Tom and Viv were to establish a Henson Trust with Alfred named as beneficiary:

1. The trustee would have absolute discretion over both the amount of money paid from the trust, and when it would be paid.

2. Alfred would stop receiving his disability support payments from the government.

3. The capital held in trust could not exceed $100,000.

4. It would not be possible to leave the remaining funds to Hannah after Alfred's death.

    a. 1 only

    b. 2 and 3 only

    c. 1 and 3 only

    d. 4 only

Question 12

How much of Viv's severance package is she eligible to transfer to her RRSP as a retiring allowance under the terms of the *Income Tax Act*?

    a. $0

    b. $6,000

    c. $14,500

    d. $35,000

Question 13

If Viv were to sell all of her current RRSP investments today except her labour-sponsored investment fund, how much could she then reinvest in funds that qualify as "foreign content"?

    a. $52,500

    b. $37,500

    c. $31,500

    d. $75,000

Question 14

Viv has mentioned that she is interested in starting her own business and will work as a freelance translator next year to earn some income. She wondered if it would be worthwhile to renovate an extra bedroom to use as her home office or just share Tom's office. As her financial planner, you would advise the following:

    a. Viv should renovate the extra bedroom and claim $1/10$ of the household expenses as business expenses to deduct from her income as business expense.

    b. Viv should move into Tom's office to take advantage of the $1/10$ of the household expenses that he claims as business expenses to deduct from her income as business expense.

    c. Viv should renovate the extra bedroom to have her own office but cannot claim it as a business expense as there is already one home office being claimed in the household.

    d. Viv should not renovate the extra bedroom because there is no allowable business expense deduction for renovations.

Question 15

Tom and Viv have expressed a concern about their current advisor who has his CFP designation. They feel he has pressured them into purchasing investment and insurance products that they did not fully understand and did not match their objectives for investing. This has contributed to their unhappiness with the results of their Labour-Sponsored Venture Fund Investments — which, in hindsight, they may not have invested in if they had understood them better. Which of the Principles of the Financial Planners Code of Ethics did their current advisor not follow?

  a. Diligence
  b. Integrity
  c. Professionalism
  d. Fairness

DISCUSSION QUESTIONS

Question 16

In preparation for meeting the Eliots in April, identify the elements of establishing the client–planner engagement phase of financial planning that you should address during the meeting.

Question 17

What are the Eliot's responsibilities in regards to the financial planning engagement?

Question 18

Summarize and prioritize what you see as the Eliot's priorities, personal and financial goals, and needs.

Question 19

Discuss the major problems areas or opportunities that you have identified.

Question 20

What are your professional responsibilities in regards to the conduct of their prior financial advisor?

Question 21

Viv and Tom would like to know how much an annuity would cost to look after Alfred's annual expenses of $36,000, if the annual expenses are paid at the beginning of each month. Assume Alfred lives to be 60 and the annuity offers 3% interest a year.

Question 22

The Eliots set up a savings account in trust for Hannah's future education at their local bank. Assume the bank's interest rate will be 2.5% every year. Tom and Viv plan to contribute $3,600 at the end of each year towards Hannah's education.

  a. How much money will be in the bank account when Hannah starts school in 11 years?
  b. If post secondary school is expected to cost $10,000 at the beginning of each year when Hannah begins, will she have enough money in the bank account to pay for four years of school? (Show your calculations.)
  c. Do you have any alternative recommendations for financing Hannah's education?

Question 23

Viv prepared a Statement of Net Worth and a Cash Flow Statement for you. Comment on the Eliot's financial position regarding the following items:

a. Based on the December statement, do the Eliot's have sufficient assets to cover their monthly needs in case Tom becomes ill and cannot work for three months?

b. The Eliot's rental income comes from renting the Toronto townhouse. Prepare an annual rental property income statement in good form. Are the Eliot's making a profit? How much more (or less) monthly rent would you suggest they charge to fully cover the expenses?

c. Comment on the Eliot's overall financial position based on the net worth statement and cash flow statement.

Question 24

The Eliots are interested in talking to you about their retirement options including the Canada Pension Plan (CPP) and Employment Insurance (EI), the main government sponsored benefit programs.

a. Will Viv qualify for any of the CPP, OAS, and GIS after she retires in December?

b. Calculate how much Tom would receive as a CPP pension if he decided to retire with Viv. Assume he would have earned a CPP of $840 if he had retired at age 65.

c. If Tom were to retire with Viv is he allowed to assign or share his retirement pension with Viv? What are the conditions under which CPP pensions can be assigned? Calculate the amount of pension that Tom and Viv will each have if they assign their CPP retirement income. For purposes of this section only, assume Tom earned a monthly retirement benefit of $980 and Viv earned a monthly benefit of $550.

Question 25

If Viv were to pass away, she would like see Samantha get the Muskoka cottage in return for all the time she has spent with Alfred each summer. She would like to see the Toronto townhouse go to both of her sons, Ernest and Alfred. Comment on Viv's plan.

QUESTIONS & SOLUTIONS

Question 1

What portion of Tom's GrowGreat RRSP portfolio could be said to have a beta of one?

- a. $18,000
- b. $20,000
- c. $48,000
- d. $72,000

Answer: b

⇨ Beta measures an investment's volatility in relation to the market. A fund with a volatility of one will match the movements of the market, while a fund with a beta of greater than one will be more volatile than the benchmark — the highs will be higher, and the lows will be lower.

⇨ Tom holds $20,000 in an index fund, which is structured to follow the movements of the underlying S&P/TSX 60. All his other funds are aggressive growth or specialty funds and would have a beta of more than one.

Question 2

If Viv were to die tomorrow, how much would her estate have to include as a taxable capital gain on her terminal income tax return?

- a. $152,000
- b. $125,000
- c. $50,000
- d. $0

Answer: c

⇨ Although Viv holds most assets jointly with her husband, allowing for a tax-free rollover, she owns half of the cottage with her sister as tenants in common.

⇨ The cottage was worth $50,000 when they acquired it, and it is now valued at $250,000. Viv's death would trigger a deemed disposition of her half, a $100,000 gain, 50% of which would be taxable as income to her estate. The Canada Savings Bonds (CSBs) she holds would not generate a taxable gain since they only pay interest. Since her average rate of return on the CSBs equals the current market rate of 4%, they would be disposed of at a value equal to their book value and a capital gain would not result.

Question 3

If Viv were to die tomorrow, ownership of her half of the cottage would be transferred to:

- a. Tom
- b. Susan
- c. Tom and Susan equally
- d. Samantha

Answer: a

⇨ The case study indicates that Susan and Viv are "tenants in common". They are not joint tenants with right of survivorship. This means that Viv's interest in the cottage would not revert to Susan, but would pass to her heir — namely Tom. In the event of Viv's death, Tom would become part owner of the cottage along with Susan.

Question 4

How much will Viv have to contribute to the Canada Pension Plan in 2009 if she were to earn the same net taxable income as she did in 2008? (The 2009 MPE is $46,300, contribution rates for employees and employers are 4.95% each.)

   a. $2,118.60

   b. $2,291.85

   c. $4,237.20

   d. $4,398.50

Answer: c

   ⇨ The maximum pensionable earnings under the Canada Pension Plan (CPP) for 2009 have been raised to $46,300. The actual CPP contribution rates for 2009 remain unchanged at 4.95% for employees and 9.9% for the self-employed. The maximum employee contribution to the plan for 2009 is $2,118.60, and the maximum self-employed contribution is $4,237.20. Since Viv will be in business for herself next year, she will have to pay the latter.

Question 5

If Tom were to redeem all of his units in the GrowGreat Labour-Sponsored Funds tomorrow, how much of the federal and provincial tax credits would he have to repay?

   a. $2,250

   b. $4,500

   c. $5,000

   d. $9,000

Answer: d

   ⇨ If an investor withdraws his or her money from a labour-sponsored fund before eight years have elapsed, he or she must repay all of the tax credits originally received. The calculation is based on the value of the fund at the time of purchase, and not the current market value.

   ⇨ Tom invested $5,000 each year for six years for a total of $30,000. He would have received 15% in tax credits from the federal government and another 15% in tax credits from the provincial government each year, for a total of $1,500 in credits each year, or $9,000 in total.

Question 6

Which of the following is the *most likely* cash surrender value for Tom's life insurance policy?

   a. Nil

   b. $20,000

   c. $50,000

   d. $300,000

Answer: a

   ⇨ Unlike a whole life insurance policy, which can grow in value over time, term to 100 life insurance policies offer little or no cash surrender value (CSV).

Question 7

If Tom and Viv were to deposit $3,600 into a registered education savings plan (RESP) at the beginning of each year for Hannah, what will the account balance be after 10 years, including grants and assuming a 4% rate of return, compounded annually?

    a. $43,222

    b. $44,951

    c. $51,194

    d. $51,866

Answer: c

    ⇨ The Canada Education Savings Grant will add 20% on the first $2,500 of contributions, or $500, to the $3,600 annual contribution that Tom and Viv intend to make, for a total of $4,100.

    ⇨ The Eliot's income exceeds the income threshold to get $600 in CESGs.

    ⇨ The steps on a business calculator are as follows:

    ⇨ Set mode to BEGIN

    ⇨ P/YR = 1

    ⇨ xP/YR = 10

    ⇨ I/YR = 4

    ⇨ PV = 0

    ⇨ PMT = (4,100)

SOLVE FOR FV, which equals $51,194

Question 8

If Tom continues to work, he will:

1. Not be able to contribute to his own RRSP next year

2. Be able to contribute to a spousal RRSP

3. Have to decide if he wants to convert his RRSP to a RRIF and/or purchase an annuity before the end of this year

4. Be able to defer his CPP pension for another two years, increasing the pension he will receive by 30%.

Which of the above statements is/are true?

    a. 1 and 2 only

    b. 2 only

    c. 3 only

    d. 2 and 4 only

Answer: b

    ⇨ Re 1: Tom is 70, and will be turning 71 next year. He can contribute to his own RRSP up to and including the year in which he reaches age 71.

    ⇨ Re 2: Because Viv is younger, Tom could make contributions to a spousal RRSP until she reaches age 71, so long as he is still working and has earned income.

    ⇨ Re 3: Tom will have to decide what to do with his RRSP by the end of next year, when he turns 71.

    ⇨ Re 4: Those who delay receiving their CPP can increase their pensions by 0.5% per month, up to a maximum of 30% at age 70.

Question 9

How much of his farm housing costs should Tom be deducting as home office expenses?

    a. $828

    b. $918

    c. $1,038

    d. $1,557

Answer: c

    ⇨ The case does not indicate the precise square footage of Tom's office, but it does say that he uses one of the ten rooms in their farmhouse, meaning that the calculation can be based on 1/10th of his total allowable costs. The $100 in personal telephone costs is not included, since the case says Tom already has a separate business phone line.

- $1,200 maintenance

- $900 home insurance

- $4,800 heating, water and electricity

- $3,480 property taxes

- $10,380 total, times 10% equals $1,038

Question 10

Which of the following best describes the purpose of a living will?

    a. It divides assets among beneficiaries while you are still alive, and is sometimes referred to as an *inter vivos* trust.

    b. It divides assets among beneficiaries after your death, and is sometimes referred to as a testamentary trust.

    c. It allows someone to make decisions about your finances and property should you become unable to do so.

    d. It states your wishes about end-of-life medical treatment, and may include a request dealing with life support and resuscitation.

Answer: d

    ⇨ A living will, or advance health care directive, does not distribute assets or confer power over assets to another person, but rather allows an individual to place limits on the treatment they wish to receive should they become incapacitated.

Question 11

If Tom and Viv were to establish a Henson Trust with Alfred named as beneficiary:

1. The trustee would have absolute discretion over both the amount of money paid from the trust, and when it would be paid.

2. Alfred would stop receiving his disability support payments from the government.

3. The capital held in trust could not exceed $100,000.

4. It would not be possible to leave the remaining funds to Hannah after Alfred's death.

    a. 1 only

    b. 2 and 3 only

    c. 1 and 3 only

    d. 4 only

Answer: a

    ⇨ A Henson Trust allows families to provide funds to disabled family members without being limited by the $100,000 limit set by the 1997 *Ontario Disability Support Program Act*, and without preventing them from receiving their support payments. A condition is that the trustee must have "absolute discretion" over both how much and how often funds are paid to the beneficiary. After the death of the Henson Trust beneficiary, assets can be distributed to other people named by the settlor.

Question 12

How much of Viv's severance package is she eligible to transfer to her RRSP as a retiring allowance under the terms of the *Income Tax Act* (the "Act")?

    a. $0

    b. $6,000

    c. $14,500

    d. $35,000

Answer: b

    ⇨ The amount that is eligible for transfer under section 60(j.1) of the Act is limited to:

      • $2,000 for each year or part of a year before 1996 that the retiree worked for the company; plus

      • $1,500 for each year or part of a year before 1989 of that employment in which the employee was not a member of or had any vested contributions to RPP or DPSP when the retiring allowance was paid. The number can be a fraction.

    ⇨ For every year of service prior to 1996, an employee is allowed to roll $2,000 into his or her RRSP as a retiring allowance. Viv has worked for Big Time Translations since 1993, which means she can transfer $2,000 for each of the years between 1993 and 1995, for a total of $6,000. Big Time did not have RPP or DPSP.

Question 13

If Viv were to sell all of her current RRSP investments today except her labour-sponsored investment fund, how much could she then reinvest in funds that qualify as "foreign content"?

    a. $52,500

    b. $37,500

    c. $31,500

    d. $75,000

Answer: d

    ⇨ The 2005 federal Budget eliminated the limitation on foreign property that RRSPs are permitted to hold.

Question 14

Viv has mentioned that she is interested in starting her own business and will work as a freelance translator next year to earn some income. She wondered if it would be worthwhile to renovate an extra bedroom to use as her home office or just share Tom's office. As her financial planner, you would advise the following:

    a. Viv should renovate the extra bedroom and claim $1/10$ of the household expenses as business expenses to deduct from her income as business expense.

    b. Viv should move into Tom's office to take advantage of the $1/10$ of the household expenses that he claims as business expenses to deduct from her income as business expense.

    c. Viv should renovate the extra bedroom to have her own office but cannot claim it as a business expense as there is already one home office being claimed in the household.

    d. Viv should not renovate the extra bedroom because there is no allowable business expense deduction for renovations.

Answer: a

    ⇨ Self employment income is reported on line 162 (gross income) and line 135 (net income) of the T1 General. The difference between the amounts on these two lines is the allowable business expense. Included in these expenses can be a claim for a percentage of household expenses incurred relative to the number of rooms or square footage. It is important for the business to keep accurate records and receipts for all expenses claimed by the business.

Question 15

Tom and Viv have expressed a concern about their current advisor who has his CFP designation. They feel he has pressured them into purchasing investment and insurance products that they did not fully understand and did not match their objectives for investing. This has contributed to their unhappiness with the results of their Labour-Sponsored Venture Fund Investments — which, in hindsight, they may not have invested in if they had understood them better. Which of the Principles of the Financial Planners Code of Ethics did their current advisor not follow?

    a. Diligence

    b. Integrity

    c. Professionalism

    d. Fairness

Answer: a

    ⇨ According to the Financial Planner Code of Ethics, Tom and Viv's current financial advisor did not invest the Eliot's money in investments that they understood or met their needs. This is in conflict with the Principle of Diligence. Specifically, Rule 703, which states that: A CFP professional shall make and/or implement only those recommendations that are suitable for the client.

CASE STUDY 2 — SHAKIR AND WATJARNA NAGI

Background

You met Shakir and Watjarna through a mutual friend. They are a young couple and they have never worked with a financial advisor before. As a result, they have never had a written financial plan prepared for them. It is March 2, 2009 today.

During 2008, Shakir and Watjarna had their first child, Shabnam. Now that they are parents, they tell you they think that the time has come for them to get their finances in order. The friend who referred them to you said that Shakir and Watjarna have quite a few questions about home ownership, education savings plans and life insurance.

Up until this point, they have relied on informal financial advice from friends and family members despite none of them having a financial education or designation. They tell you they have also read a couple of personal finance books. Because they have relatively little in the way of assets at the moment, they tell you they believed that no advisor would be prepared to see them. Their first questions to you were about how you are paid and the sort of fees you charge as a Certified Financial Planner. You explain to them that you charge a flat fee for a financial plan that includes all the steps of the financial planning process as defined by the Financial Planning Standards Council and you only sell no-load mutual funds. You also tell them that you are licensed to sell life insurance products to help support their risk management needs.

Personal Information

Shakir (age 31) and Watjarna (age 30) are both elementary teachers at a small private school in Edmonton, Alberta. Watjarna just finished her graduate degree in English and they both just started their jobs this September. Watjarna teaches history and Shakir is the school music teacher. They have been married for two years, and are both in excellent health and enjoy a healthy lifestyle. Shabnam was born last year.

At the moment, they are living in a house located on campus and owned by the school. They say they only have to pay $250 a month in rent, including all utilities. They are very happy with the arrangement since a comparable apartment in the city would cost them at least $500 more a month. They are able to eat their meals in the dining hall for free.

Both Shakir and Watjarna come from relatively large families; he has three brothers and one sister, while she has two brothers and two sisters. Because of this, they have been (and still are) extremely reluctant to ask their parents for financial assistance.

Employment Information

Details of Shakir and Watjarna's Employment

Shakir earns $45,000 a year. Watjarna has a graduate degree, and is therefore higher on the provincial pay grid, earning $54,000 a year. Last year, Shakir also started to supplement his income by teaching piano to local children and young adults three nights a week during the school year. He earns $1,000 a month from this extra work through all 12 months of the year.

Both Shakir and Watjarna are members of the Alberta private school teacher's defined benefit pension plan, and have health, dental and disability benefits through their employer. They tell you that their pension plan is currently in a surplus position, and they expect to be on "contribution holiday" for the next two years. This will provide each of them with an extra $200 a month and they would like to set aside these funds for either their RRSP or for a down payment on their first house.

Financial Position

Real Estate

Shakir and Watjarna would like to buy a home in the new development across from their school. The model they like is priced at $350,000. They know this is a bit much for a first home, but they have fallen in love with the design. They are not sure if they will be able to qualify for the mortgage, and would like your advice on the matter.

They would also like to know more about the Home Buyers Plan, and how they might be able to withdraw funds from their RRSPs to purchase this home. They say they have some cash on hand, about $3,000, and did not know whether they should put it in their RRSP or use it as part of their down payment.

Education Savings

As soon as Shabnam was born, Shakir and Watjarna opened a high interest savings account with an online bank and have been depositing small amounts from time to time — mostly money given to Shabnam as gifts from aunts and uncles. The balance has grown to $4,000, and they would now like to invest the funds in the stock market — in something that would yield higher returns over the long run. They have heard about registered education savings plans (RESPs), and tell you they picked up a brochure at the doctor's office for a pooled scholarship trust fund. They would like to know more about the different education savings plans available.

Shakir's Investments, Registered

Shakir opened an RRSP Daily Interest Savings account at Massive Bank two years ago. He says that, because he was uncertain of what kind of investment to make, he has simply left the funds in a high interest savings account, where he is earning 2.5% interest. He tells you that he just added $1,000 to the account last week that has a current value of $4,000.

Shakir's Investments, Non-Registered

Shakir has non-registered money invested in Canada Savings Bonds, which he purchased in 2001. He is earning 4.8% rate of interest.

- $1,000 Series 9 Canada Savings Bond, Compound Interest

Watjarna's Investments, Registered

Watjarna banks at the local Community Credit Union, and has purchased GICs with her RRSP contributions.

- $2,000 GIC, 3% rate of interest, matures this month
- $2,500 GIC, 2.5% rate of interest, matures this month

Watjarna's Investments, Non-Registered

Watjarna has an interest in fine art, and two years ago she purchased a painting at an auction when she was visiting friends in the country. The painting is by a well-known Canadian artist from the 1930s. She bought the painting for $500, but believes it is probably worth nearly $10,000.

While she is very attached to the work, she is thinking about selling it to a friend of hers who is an art dealer.

Liabilities

Shakir has a student loan with an outstanding balance of $5,000 with Massive Bank and is paying 8.5% in interest. He is also carrying a $1,000 balance on his Massive Bank Visa card, and is paying 22% interest on the card.

Shakir and Watjarna have a car lease for their small four-door sedan that costs them $300 a month. They say that, living on campus, they don't use the car as much as other people probably do. As a result the current mileage on the vehicle is quite low; averaging only 15,000 kilometers per year. They figure that 30% of the car's actual use is from Shakir driving to his students' houses to give lessons.

Watjarna has no outstanding debts, and pays off her credit card every month.

Insurance Information

Both Shakir and Watjarna have group life insurance through their employer for two times their annual salaries. They also have disability, health and dental insurance coverage. Both of them say they are concerned they do not have adequate life insurance coverage, and are worried about what would happen to Shabnam if either of them where to die prematurely. If one spouse were to die, they believe that the survivor would require additional income equal to at least 45% of their current combined gross income for the next 35 years. They would prefer that the mortgage on their home should be completely paid off should one of them die.

When they were researching mortgages and home buying, they spoke with an advisor at Massive Bank who told them they could obtain mortgage life insurance through the Bank. They want to know if they are required to purchase mortgage life insurance through the lender, and if it is a good idea to do so.

Shakir and Watjarna have also heard about mortgage insurance offered by the Canada Mortgage and Housing Corporation (CMHC), and want to know if that is the same thing as mortgage life insurance.

Risk Profile

Shakir and Watjarna agree that they are both fairly conservative investors. They are prepared to accept some risk in return for potentially higher returns, but since stock market investing is new to them they say they want to start slowly.

Liquidity is a primary concern for both of them, and they say that for the next year they want to be able to access their savings on relatively short notice. This is because they anticipate purchasing a home in the near future, and the local housing market is fairly hot. If they see an opportunity they may need to move quickly.

Wills and Powers of Attorney

Shortly after Shabnam was born, Shakir and Watjarna purchased a will planning package from a Canadian software company. They filled out the forms on their computer, printed off the wills, and had two of their friends from school witness the documents. They have named Shakir's sister, Jill, as the executor, and they have named Watjarna's brother, Charles, as Shabnam's guardian.

Goals and Objectives

Besides home ownership, Shakir and Watjarna say that their first priority is making certain that Shabnam has enough money so that she can go to university. Since they work in education themselves, they know how much the cost of tuition has increased over the last decade and they expect the trend to continue in the future. They read that the cost of a post-secondary education is expected to rise to about $100,000 by the time Shabnam attends university and they want to try to have this amount on hand by the time she finishes high school.

Shakir and Watjarna say that their primary focus is on saving for Shabnam's education instead of their retirement, since they already have very good pension plans and many years to earn income to fund retirement.

Shakir and Watjarna Nagi
Statement of Net Worth at January 1, 2009

	Shakir	Watjarna	Total
ASSETS			
Liquid Assets			
Joint Chequing Account	$ 1,500	$ 1,500	$ 3,000
Canada Savings Bonds	1,000		1,000
Savings Account (for daughter)	2,000	2,000	4,000
Total Liquid Assets	**$ 4,500**	**$ 3,500**	**$ 8,000**
Investment Assets			
Registered Assets	4,000	4,500	8,500
Total Investment Assets	**$ 4,000**	**$ 4,500**	**$ 8,500**
Personal-Use Assets			
Automobile	5,000	5,000	10,000
Personal Effects (owned jointly)	2,000	2,000	4,000
Artwork		10,000	10,000
Total Personal-Use Assets	**$ 7,000**	**$ 17,000**	**$ 24,000**
TOTAL ASSETS	**$ 15,500**	**$ 25,000**	**$ 40,500**
LIABILITIES			
Student Debt	5,000		5,000
Credit Card	1,000		1,000
TOTAL LIABILITIES	**$ 6,000**	**$ 0**	**$ 6,000**
NET WORTH	**$ 9,500**	**$ 25,000**	**$ 34,500**

Shakir and Watjarna Nagi
Monthly and Annual Cash Flow as of January 1, 2009

	Monthly	Annually
INCOME		
Shakir's Employment Income	$ 3,750	$ 45,000
Shakir's Business Income	1,000	12,000
Watjarna's Employment Income	4,500	54,000
Interest Income		
Shakir	12	144
Watjarna	8	96
Total Income	**$9,270**	**$111,240**
EXPENSES		
Withholdings at Source — Shakir		
Taxes, CPP and EI	1,000	12,000
Withholdings at Source — Watjarna		
Taxes, CPP and EI	1,167	14,004
Loan and Credit Card Payments	100	1,200
Rent	250	3,000
Home Insurance	30	360
Automobile		
Lease	300	3,600
Insurance	90	1,080
Gas and Operating Expenses	75	900
Repairs and Maintenance	45	540
Telephone	50	600
Internet and Cable TV	80	960
Food	300	3,600
Clothing	300	3,600
Personal Care	75	900
Childcare (for Shabnam)	1,000	12,000
Entertainment	250	3,000
RRSP Contribution — Shakir	84	1,008
RRSP Contribution — Watjarna	125	1,500
TOTAL EXPENSES	**$5,321**	**$ 63,852**
SURPLUS	**$3,949**	**$ 47,388**

QUESTIONS

Question 1

How much of his automobile costs may Shakir deduct from his tutoring income as a business expense?

    a. $756

    b. $1,080

    c. $1,836

    d. $6,120

Answer: c

Question 2

If Shakir withdraws all the money from his RRSPs under the Home Buyers Plan tomorrow, how much of this year's $1,000 contribution will he be able to claim as a deduction on his tax return?

    a. 0

    b. $1,000

    c. $3,000

    d. $4,000

Question 3

If Shakir and Watjarna deposit their earmarked savings for Shabnam into a registered education savings plan (RESP) in 2009 for Shabnam who is two years old, how much will they receive under the Canada Education Savings Grant (CESG) program?

    a. $400

    b. $1,000

    c. $2,000

    d. $4,000

Question 4

How much of a federal tax credit did Shakir receive on the interest he paid on his $5,000 student loan in 2008?

    a. 0%

    b. 15%

    c. 15.25%

    d. 23%

Question 5

Watjarna's GICs are protected by (the):

    a. CDIC

    b. CUIC

    c. CUDIC

    d. Assuris

Question 6

Based only on their stated additional income requirement, and ignoring any insurance currently owned, what is the total amount of new life insurance that Shakir and Watjarna require? Assume a 5% rate of return, with annual payments made at the end of the year and a complete depletion of capital.

    a. $817,891

    b. $858,785

    c. $1,361,221

    d. $1,472,432

Question 7

If Shakir and Watjarna were to take out mortgage insurance through the bank, which of the following statements is/are true?

1. The cash surrender value of the policy would increase as the mortgage decreased.

2. The bank would be the beneficiary of the policy.

3. They would not be required to re-apply for new coverage if they changed lenders.

    a. 1 only

    b. 1 and 2 only

    c. 2 only

    d. 3 only

Question 8

If Watjarna were to sell her painting, how much would she have to include on her tax return as income for the year?

    a. $0

    b. $4,500

    c. $4,750

    d. $9,500

Question 9

Which of the following statements is true?

    a. Shakir may claim $12,000 for the childcare deduction (line 214)

    b. Watjarna may claim $12,000 for the childcare deduction (line 214)

    c. Shakir may claim $4,000 for the childcare deduction (line 214)

    d. Watjarna may claim $7,000 for the childcare deduction (line 214)

Question 10

Which of the following best describes your fee structure? You are a:

    a. Commission-only financial planner

    b. Fee plus commission financial planner

    c. Fee-only financial planner

    d. Salary plus bonus financial planner

Question 11

If Watjarna were to withdraw all of her RRSP funds under the Home Buyers Plan, what amount would she be required to repay annually, starting the second year following the year she made the withdrawal?

    a. $225

    b. $300

    c. $375

    d. $450

Question 12

Under the CMHC mortgage loan insurance program, what is the minimum down payment that Shakir and Watjarna would be required to make on the single family home they are currently considering assuming they do not qualify for the 0% down CMHC program?

    a. $52,500

    b. $35,000

    c. $17,500

    d. $5,000

Question 13

Which of the following would be the best use of Shakir's Canada Savings Bonds?

    a. Use towards a down payment on their home

    b. Use to pay off his credit card debt

    c. Use to contribute to Shabnam's RESP

    d. Use to contribute to a spousal RRSP

Question 14

Which of the following would be the most suitable form of life insurance coverage for Shakir and Watjarna to offset the mortgage on their first home?

    a. Two 10-year term insurance policies, one on each of their lives, each with a face value of $125,000.

    b. A joint first-to-die 10-year term life insurance policy for $350,000.

    c. A joint last-to-die T-100 life insurance policy for $350,000.

    d. A joint first-to-die whole life insurance policy for $350,000.

Question 15

How much money will Shabnam have in her RESP by 2024 if Shakir and Watjarna contribute the $4,000 they have already saved, and then add $2,000 to her account at the end of 2010 and at the end of every year thereafter? Assume an 8% rate of return.

    a. $89,514

    b. $92,255

    c. $92,940

    d. $98,760

DISCUSSION QUESTIONS

Question 16

Why was it important to discuss the products you are licensed to offer and how you are compensated during the first meeting?

Question 17

What additional information would you request from Shakir and Watjarna?

Question 18

Summarize and prioritize what you see as the Nagi's priorities, personal and financial goals, and main needs.

Question 19

Discuss the major problems areas or opportunities that you have identified.

Question 20

Would the Nagis be able to qualify for a mortgage on the new house?

Question 21

Should they purchase mortgage insurance from Massive Bank? Is mortgage insurance the same thing as CMHC insurance?

Question 22

Explain the main features of RESP plans. Would you recommend they invest in the pooled scholarship trust fund?

Question 23

Comment on their investment portfolio. Would you recommend any changes given their priorities and financial goals?

Question 24

Explain the main characteristics of the Home Buyers' Plan (HBP) to the Nagis. Would you recommend they participate in the HBP?

Question 25

Discuss any financial management issues you have identified and propose recommendations to assist the Nagis.

QUESTIONS & SOLUTIONS

Question 1

How much of his automobile costs may Shakir deduct from his tutoring income as a business expense?

     a. $756

     b. $1,080

     c. $1,836

     d. $6,120

Answer: c

     ⇨   Shakir drives the car for business purposes 30% of the time. The combined annual cost, including lease, insurance, maintenance and operating expenses is $6,120. Thirty per cent of this amount is $1,836.

Question 2

If Shakir withdraws all the money from his RRSPs under the Home Buyers Plan tomorrow, how much of this year's $1,000 contribution will he be able to claim as a deduction on his tax return?

     a. 0

     b. $1,000

     c. $3,000

     d. $4,000

Answer: a

     ⇨   The case study indicates that Shakir deposited $1,000 into his RRSP just last week. Contributions must remain inside the RRSP for a minimum of 90 days before being withdrawn under the Home Buyers Plan, or the taxpayer will not be allowed to claim the deduction.

Question 3

If Shakir and Watjarna deposit their earmarked savings for Shabnam into a registered education savings plan (RESP) in 2009 for Shabnam who is two years old, how much will they receive under the Canada Education Savings Grant (CESG) program?

     a. $400

     b. $1,000

     c. $2,000

     d. $4,000

Answer: b

     ⇨   The federal Budget of March 19, 2007 eliminated the annual limit and increased the lifetime limit to $50,000. While the CESG is calculated as 20% based on a maximum contribution of $2,000 per year, it is possible to carry forward grant room to future years. Each child accumulates grant room of $500 per year, up to and including the year in which they attain age 17 to a lifetime maximum of $7,200.

     ⇨   Since Shabnam was born last year, she is eligible for a CESG for both 2008 and 2009 — for a total of $1,000.

Question 4

How much of a federal tax credit did Shakir receive on the interest he paid on his $5,000 student loan?

 a. 0%

 b. 15%

 c. 15.25%

 d. 23%

Answer: b

⇨ Shakir will receive a federal tax credit of 15% of the interest he has paid each year on his student loan.

Question 5

Watjarna's GICs are protected by (the):

 a. CDIC

 b. CUIC

 c. CUDIC

 d. Assuris

Answer: c

⇨ Watjarna banks with a credit union. Her deposits are guaranteed by the Credit Union Deposit Insurance Corporation (CUDIC). Deposits made with the banks are protected by the Canadian Deposit Insurance Corporation (CDIC) and assets invested with life insurance companies are protected by Assuris.

Question 6

Based only on their stated additional income requirement, and ignoring any insurance currently owned, what is the total amount of new life insurance that Shakir and Watjarna require? Assume a 5% rate of return, with annual payments made at the end of the year and a complete depletion of capital.

 a. $817,891

 b. $858,785

 c. $1,361,221

 d. $1,472,432

Answer: a

⇨ Shakir and Watjarna say that the survivor would require additional income of 45% of their current combined gross earned income of $111,000 ($240/year is investment income), which is $49,950. In order to generate $49,950 every year for 35 years, a lump sum of $817,891 would be required. The steps on a financial calculator are as follows:

⇨ Set mode to END

⇨ P/YR = 1

⇨ XP/YR = 35

⇨ I/YR = 5

⇨ PMT = -49,950

SOLVE FOR PV, which equals $817,891

Question 7

If Shakir and Watjarna were to take out mortgage insurance through the bank, which of the following statements is/are true?

1. The cash surrender value of the policy would increase as the mortgage decreased.

2. The bank would be the beneficiary of the policy.

3. They would not be required to re-apply for new coverage if they changed lenders.

    a. 1 only

    b. 1 and 2 only

    c. 2 only

    d. 3 only

Answer: c

⇨ Creditor's group mortgage insurance is a term insurance product, and has no cash surrender value. The lender is named as beneficiary under the policy. If Shakir and Watjarna were to change banks at a later date, they would have to re-apply for mortgage insurance, and submit current medical evidence to their new lender.

Question 8

If Watjarna were to sell her painting, how much would she have to include on her tax return as income for the year?

    a. $0

    b. $4,500

    c. $4,750

    d. $9,500

Answer: b

⇨ The painting is listed personal property. The personal property rules state that if the adjusted cost base (ACB) of the item is less than $1,000, its ACB is considered to be $1,000 so even though Watjarna purchased the painting for $500 the gain is calculated as if she paid $1,000. Only 50% of a capital gain — in this case $4,500 ($10,000 - $1,000) × 50% — must be reported as income.

Question 9

Which of the following statements is true?

    a. Shakir may claim $12,000 for the childcare deduction (line 214)

    b. Watjarna may claim $12,000 for the childcare deduction (line 214)

    c. Shakir may claim $4,000 for the childcare deduction (line 214)

    d. Watjarna may claim $7,000 for the childcare deduction (line 214)

Answer: d

⇨ The maximum amount of the deduction for daycare expenses is the least of: the amount paid, the sum of $4,000 per child seven and older plus $7,000 per child under age 7 plus $10,000 for each child under 17 who is eligible for the disability credit, or two-thirds (⅔) of the earned income of the taxpayer. The lower-income parent, who is Watjarna, must normally claim the deduction.

Question 10

Which of the following best describes your fee structure? You are a:

    a. Commission-only financial planner

    b. Fee plus commission financial planner

    c. Fee-only financial planner

    d. Salary plus bonus financial planner

Answer: b

    ⇨ While you charge a flat fee for the preparation of a financial plan, the case study indicates that you also sell insurance products, which generate a commission payable to you by the insurance company. While you only sell no-load funds, there may also be trailing commissions payable to you.

Question 11

If Watjarna were to withdraw all of her RRSP funds under the Home Buyers Plan, what amount would she be required to repay annually, starting the second year following the year she made the withdrawal?

    a. $225

    b. $300

    c. $375

    d. $450

Answer: b

    ⇨ Watjarna has $4,500 in her RRSP. If she makes a withdrawal under the Home Buyers Plan, she will be required to repay $1/15$ of that amount every year, starting the second year following the year she made the withdrawal; $4,500 divided by 15 is $300. If she fails to make the annual repayment, that amount of withdrawal must be included in her income for that year.

Question 12

Under the CMHC mortgage loan insurance program, what is the minimum down payment that Shakir and Watjarna would be required to make on the single family home they are currently considering assuming they do not qualify for the 0% down CMHC program?

    a. $52,500

    b. $35,000

    c. $17,500

    d. $5,000

Answer: c

    ⇨ The Canadian Mortgage and Housing Corporation (CMHC) allows homebuyers to finance up to 95% of the purchase price of a home. The home they are considering is priced at $350,000, so Shakir and Watjarna would have to make a minimum down payment of 5%, or $17,500. With a proven track record of meeting debt requirements and sufficient income to support mortgage loan payments, their lender may be able to provide Shakir and Watjarna with CMHC's Flex Down product which would allow $0 down payment.

Question 13

Which of the following would be the best use of Shakir's Canada Savings Bonds?

    a. Use towards a down payment on their home

    b. Use to pay off his credit card debt

    c. Use to contribute to Shabnam's RESP

    d. Use to contribute to a spousal RRSP

Answer: b

    ⇨ The case study states that Shakir is currently paying 22% interest on his $1,000 credit card debt. Watjarna already has more RRSP funds than he does. It is highly unlikely that the rate of return earned by the RRSP or RESP contribution would match the interest he is currently paying on the credit card.

Question 14

Which of the following would be the most suitable form of life insurance coverage for Shakir and Watjarna to offset the mortgage on their first home?

    a. Two 10-year term insurance policies, one on each of their lives, each with a face value of $125,000.

    b. A joint first-to-die 10-year term life insurance policy for $350,000.

    c. A joint last-to-die T-100 life insurance policy for $350,000.

    d. A joint first-to-die whole life insurance policy for $350,000.

Answer: b

    ⇨ The case study says that Shakir and Watjarna wish to have the mortgage completely paid off should one of them die. Buying two policies for $125,000 would not accomplish this, and neither would a joint last-to-die T-100 policy (since it would only pay the insurance on the second death). A whole life insurance policy would be quite expensive for Shakir and Watjarna, and it would require funds that they have indicated they would prefer to spend on other priorities (i.e., home ownership and education savings). A 10-year term policy with a convertible option could be converted to a permanent insurance contract at a later date if they decided they required longer-term protection without requiring evidence of insurability.

Question 15

How much money will Shabnam have in her RESP by 2024 if Shakir and Watjarna contribute the $4,000 they have already saved, and then add $2,000 to her account at the end of 2010 and at the end of every year thereafter? Assume an 8% rate of return.

    a. $89,514

    b. $92,255

    c. $92,940

    d. $98,760

Answer: d

  ⇨ Shakir and Watjarna have already saved $4,000, which will attract a CESG of $800 in 2009 for a total present value of $4,800. Each subsequent RESP contribution of $2,000 will attract a CESG of $400 for the next 16 years (2024 – 2009), for a total annual payment of $2,400. Earning a return of 8% a year, the value of the RESP will grow to $98,760.63 by 2024.

  ⇨ The steps on a financial calculator are as follows:

  ⇨ Set mode to END

  ⇨ P/YR = 1

  ⇨ XP/YR = 17

  ⇨ I/YR = 8

  ⇨ PMT = (2,400)

  ⇨ PV = (4,800)

SOLVE FOR FV, which equals $98,760.63

CASE STUDY 3 — HENRY AND JUNE PICKARD

Background

Henry and June have been referred to you by one of your clients. While they have done all of their own financial planning in the past and tell you that they are happy with the results, they have recently decided that it would be a good idea to get another opinion of their financial circumstances. Henry's brother, Carl, died recently, and Henry is acting as the executor of the estate. Henry says that he was surprised at what a mess Carl's finances were in, and he wants to make sure that his affairs are better organized.

In your initial meeting on February 1, 2010, Henry expressed concern that some of June's investments are too aggressive, and is worried about her losing too much of her retirement savings in the market.

Henry has prepared net worth and cash flow statements to give you a better idea of their situation (see Tables).

Personal Information

Henry (age 58) and June (age 59) live in Vancouver, British Columbia. They have been married for 30 years. While neither of them is seriously ill, they do report having some minor physical ailments. Both of them have also been diagnosed with borderline diabetes. June is a non-smoker, but Henry says that he likes to have a cigar once in a while.

June and Henry have two children. The eldest, named David (age 27), is unmarried and lives in his own apartment in the city. Their younger son, John (age 20) is a university student, currently studying medieval history in France.

June runs a successful advertising and public relations firm. Up until just a little while ago, she had been operating the business almost entirely on her own. Last year, however, David began working with her and is learning the business.

When she retires, June says wants to leave the business in David's hands, because she says that John has neither the interest nor the ability to run it successfully.

Employment Information

Details of June's Business

June has been running ABC Communications since 1980. Over the years, she has gained many corporate and government contracts. The company now brings in gross revenue of about $170,000 every year. She says that if she and Henry decide to move to a smaller condo, she will have more money on hand than she really needs. She says she hates seeing so much of her income lost in income taxes. She wants to know if there is some way she can invest money through the business and avoid taxation.

She has one full-time employee, Frank, who handles day-to-day tasks and answers customer inquiries. She hires freelance copywriters and graphic designers as needed to create the advertisements. When David started working for the firm, she put him on a flat salary of $30,000.

June says that she would like to start cutting back on her work hours next year, but isn't quite ready to leave work entirely. She says she'd also like to find a way to provide insurance benefits for David. She hasn't bothered looking into the matter until now, since she has coverage under Henry's health care plan.

Details of Henry's Employment

Henry is an architect with a local firm. He has worked in this field since he graduated from university more than 27 years ago, although he has only been with his current employer for the last 15 years. He earns $90,000 a year. Now that he is approaching retirement, he is trying to decide what he would like to do. He thinks he may work as a part-time consultant for a few years until June is ready to leave her job completely.

Henry has been contributing into the pension plan at work, and his contributions are matched 100% by his employer. He is now paying $5,000 into the plan every year.

Financial Position

Real Estate

Henry and June own a large home in Vancouver. They purchased it 10 years ago for $300,000. It is now worth about $500,000.

While Henry and June are very happy with their home in the city, they are especially proud of their luxury summer home in Washington State, which they also own jointly. After he paid off his debts, Henry used what was left of an inheritance he received from his father three years ago to purchase the summer home, and the couple spends all of their holidays there. The Washington property cost C$1 million, and is currently valued at about C$1.1 million.

They are thinking about downsizing in the near future, and say they would probably just buy a small condo in Vancouver and keep the summer home.

June's Investments, Registered

June holds the following investments inside her self-directed RRSP account:

- $45,000 in the ABC Precious Metals Fund
- $16,000 in the Solidarity Labour-Sponsored Fund
- $87,000 in the USA American Growth Clone Fund
- $194,000 in the XYZ Long-Term Bond Fund
- $76,000 in the XYZ Short-Term Bond Fund

June says that she has been a very conservative investor until recently. She began following the precious metals market about five years ago, and experienced some very high rates of return — in 2003, she earned more than 40%. Last year, however, she lost about 20%. She says that she is comfortable with a certain amount of volatility, and never invests more than 20% of her portfolio in this category. She also says that she has no unused RRSP contribution room.

June's Investments, Non-Registered

June also holds the following in a non-registered trading account at a discount brokerage:

- $45,000 Acme Corporation Bond, 4% maturing on January 1, 2011
- $45,000 ABC Canadian Blue Chip Fund

Henry's Investments, Registered

Henry has opened two separate RRSP accounts.

Account 1 holds:

- $139,000 in the SuperDuper Canadian Diversified Fund

Account 2 holds:

- $30,000 Wonderfund Canadian T-Bill Fund
- $9,000 Wonderfund European Blue Chip Fund

Henry says that he opened up the second account just a few weeks ago.

Besides his personal RRSPs, Henry also has a defined contribution pension plan at work, managed by Mountain Financial. It holds the following investments:

- $110,000 Mountain Canadian Income Fund
- $53,000 Mountain Canadian Real Estate Fund
- $47,000 Mountain Canadian Mortgage Fund

Henry says that his estate is named as beneficiary of the pension funds.

Henry's Investments, Non-Registered

Henry has the following investments in an investment account with the Smith & Brown Insurance Company:

- $64,000 S&B Canadian Bond Segregated Fund
- $19,000 S&B Canadian T-Bill Segregated Fund

Henry's friend, Larry, works for a local securities dealer, and was the one who sold him these investments. Larry told him that there are specific advantages to holding investments like these. Larry said he is a "financial planner", but Henry knows that Larry only started working in the financial services industry a few months ago. He wants to know if what Larry said is true.

Henry also holds $9,000 in Canada Savings Bonds, currently earning 3%.

Liabilities

Henry and June used the inheritance Henry received to pay off their mortgage and have no debts. They are, however, worried about the cost of looking after June's mother Gertrude, who is 79 years old. They currently contribute $30,000 annually to help her meet her expenses, and they believe this cost will rise with inflation.

The couple is also helping their son John, giving him $2,000 a month to support him while he is in school.

Insurance Information

Henry has life insurance worth twice his salary through work, and his employer also provides him with health, dental and long-term disability insurance. The disability insurance offers "own occupation" coverage for the first two years, and then "any occupation" coverage to age 65 at 66% of regular income. The health and dental coverage is only available to himself, June, and to John for as long as he is a student and under the age of 25.

Henry and June have a joint first-to-die 10-year renewable term insurance policy with a face value of $1 million. They are concerned that when the policy renews next year, the rate may be quite high.

June also has a T-100 life insurance policy, with a face value of $100,000 that she purchased 20 years ago. She says she's not sure she really needs the coverage any more, and wants to know if there's a way she can give the policy to her favourite charity.

Children

Henry and June think it unlikely that John will return to North America, and believe he will go on to do graduate work in Europe and probably become a professor. They have indicated that John and David do not get along very well, and are worried the two may quarrel over the estate after their deaths.

Risk Profile

Henry describes himself as a very conservative investor. He says that he would rather have a lower, guaranteed return rather than face the extreme volatility of the equity markets. He has also said that he is worried that he is not getting enough exposure to foreign markets.

Goals and Objectives

Both Henry and June say that their top priority is to make sure that their estate is divided equitably between their two sons. They also want to make sure that John is able to continue at university for as long as he wishes, ideally all the way to post-graduate work.

June has said that she would like to know if there is a way she could reduce the income tax she pays. She also wants to know how to structure her business so that it can eventually be taken over by David.

Henry would like to know how best to approach his own semi-retirement, and whether it would be better to work as a part-time employee or freelance consultant.

Wills and Powers of Attorney

Henry and June purchased a book about estate planning five years ago, and used the information they found there to write out their own wills by hand. They have appointed June's sister, Agatha, as executor, and named each other as beneficiaries. Their estate is to be divided equally between David and John upon their deaths.

Henry and June Pickard
Statement of Net Worth at January 8, 2010

ASSETS	June	Henry	Total
Liquid Assets			
Joint Chequing Account	$ 1,500	$ 1,500	$ 3,000
Business Chequing Account	6,000		7,000
Canada Savings Bonds		9,000	9,000
Cash Surrender Value of Insurance	1,000		
Total Liquid Assets	**$ 8,500**	**$ 10,500**	**$ 19,000**
Investment Assets			
Non-Registered Assets	90,000	83,000	173,000
Registered Assets	418,000	388,000	806,000
Total Investment Assets	**$ 508,000**	**$ 471,000**	**$ 979,000**
Personal Use Assets			
Residence (Vancouver)	250,000	250,000	500,000
Residence (Washington)	550,000	550,000	1,100,000
Automobile	7,000	7,000	14,000
Personal Effects (owned jointly)	15,000	15,000	30,000
Total Personal-Use Assets	**$ 822,000**	**$ 822,000**	**$ 1,644,000**
TOTAL ASSETS	**$ 1,338,500**	**$ 1,303,500**	**$ 2,642,000**
LIABILITIES			
None			
TOTAL LIABILITIES	**$ 0**	**$ 0**	**$ 0**
NET WORTH	**$ 1,338,500**	**$ 1,303,500**	**$ 2,642,000**

Henry and June Pickard
Monthly and Annual Cash Flow as of January 8, 2010

	Monthly	Annually
INCOME		
June's Net Business Income	$ 9,000	$ 108,000
Henry's Employment Income	7,500	90,000
Investment Interest Income		
June	225	2,700
Henry	200	2,400
Total Income	**$ 16,925**	**$ 203,100**
EXPENSES		
Tax Instalments — June	3,000	36,000
Withholdings at Source — Henry		
Taxes, CPP and EI	2,500	30,000
Royal Architectural Institute of Canada		
Member Fees — Henry	23	276
Maintenance, Repairs		
Vancouver House	200	2,400
Washington House	250	3,000
Home Insurance		
Vancouver House	300	3,600
Washington House	530	6,360
Heating, Water and Electricity		
Vancouver House	275	3,300
Washington House	190	2,280
Property Taxes		
Vancouver House	420	5,040
Washington House	917	11,004
Automobile		
Insurance	88	1,056
Operating Expenses	265	3,180
Repairs and Maintenance	57	684
Life Insurance Premiums		
Joint Policy	525	6,300
June's Policy	130	1,560
Telephone	60	720
Food	420	5,040
Clothing	300	3,600
Personal Care	80	960
Entertainment	250	3,000
RRSP Contribution — June	1,125	13,500
RRSP Contribution — Henry	417	5,004
Payments to Gertrude	2,500	30,000
Payments to John	2,000	24,000
TOTAL EXPENSES	**$ 16,822**	**$ 201,864**
SURPLUS	**$ 103**	**$ 1,236**

QUESTIONS

Question 1

Given June's current situation and her plans for the future, which of the following business structures would be best suited to her needs?

    a. sole proprietor

    b. partnership

    c. corporation

    d. co-operative

Question 2

How much is Henry able to deduct as an "annual union, professional, or like due" on line 212 of his income tax return?

    a. $276.00

    b. $138.00

    c. $46.92

    d. $0

Question 3

If Henry were to become totally disabled next month, which of the following amounts would he most likely receive as a monthly payment from the disability insurance coverage offered by his employer?

    a. $2,250

    b. $3,750

    c. $4,950

    d. $6,000

Question 4

If June were to set up a Personal Health Services Plan (PHSP) at her place of work, to whom would she be required to provide insurance coverage in order to ensure that the premiums would qualify as a fully deductible business expense?

    a. June

    b. David

    c. June and David

    d. June, David and Frank

Question 5

If June were to absolutely assign her T-100 life insurance policy to a charity and name them as beneficiary, but continue paying the annual premiums herself, which of the following scenarios would be true?

1. She would receive a tax credit for the cash surrender value of the policy at the time of the initial assignment.

2. She would receive a tax credit every year, based on the annual premium she pays.

3. Her estate would receive a tax credit for a $100,000 donation in the year of her death.

    a. 1 only

    b. 1 and 2 only

    c. 2 and 3 only

    d. 3 only

Question 6

If Henry were to sell today all the units in his first RRSP account and transfer all of the money into the second, how much more money could he invest in foreign property (i.e., in addition to what he already has in the European fund)?

    a. $26,600

    b. $35,600

    c. $44,440

    d. 139,000

Question 7

With respect to the investments sold to Henry by his friend Larry, which of the following statements is false?

    a. Larry must hold an insurance license in order to offer these funds.

    b. With a named beneficiary, the funds may bypass probate fees in the event of Henry's death.

    c. The investment may be protected from creditors provided that Henry names June as beneficiary on the contract.

    d. A minimum of 65% of Henry's initial investment is guaranteed, provided Henry holds the funds until the contract's maturity date.

Question 8

Henry holds nine Canada Savings Bonds ($1,000 denomination bonds). Each bond pays 3%. Today comparable bonds are now paying 4.5%. What is the approximate profit or loss you would realize if you sold one bond?

    a. $333.33 loss

    b. $666.67 loss

    c. $666.67 profit

    d. $333.33 profit

Question 9

If both Henry and June were to die next week, how much of their estate would be subject to U.S. estate tax?

    a. $1.1 million

    b. $1 million

    c. $500,000

    d. $0

Question 10

What is the maximum amount that June could contribute to her RRSP for the coming (i.e., 2008) tax year?

    a. $20,000

    b. $19,000

    c. $18,000

    d. $14,500

Question 11

Henry and June have mentioned that they are both considering what they would like to do since they are approaching retirement. He is expecting to live to 80 years of age. Henry's Investments are consistently earning 6%. He believes that we will need to receive a before-tax income of $60,000 at the beginning of each year during his retirement if he draws on his capital. He had originally planned to retire at the age of 60 years. However, he is enjoying his work and is wondering the impact if he continues working until age 65.

If Henry does change his retirement from age 60 to age 65, how much less will he need in savings to meet his retirement objectives?

    a. $267,906

    b. $171,917

    c. $111,788

    d. $102, 917

Question 12

How much money should Henry and June set aside if they want to keep providing June's mother Gertrude with her usual income, paid at the end of each month, assuming she lives to be 89 and the investment earns 5% a year?

    a. $265,897

    b. $235,703

    c. $231,876

    d. $229,452

Question 13

If Henry and June decide to downsize and purchase a condo, how much of a capital gain will they each have to include as income after they sell their house in Vancouver:

    a. $0

    b. $50,000

    c. $100,000

    d. $200,000

Question 14

What portion of June's registered retirement savings would be most adversely affected by an increase in interest rates?

    a. $16,000

    b. $45,000

    c. $87,000

    d. $270,000

Question 15

If June were to swap her Acme bond for her ABC Precious Metals Fund, which of the following is/are true?

1. She would be able to apply any future capital losses in the Precious Metals Fund against capital gains in other investments, reducing taxes.

2. She might face a capital gain or loss on the bond if the current market price has changed, since the transfer would result in a deemed disposition.

3. She would be able to deduct $45,000 from her income that year as an RRSP contribution.

    a. 1 only

    b. 1 and 2 only

    c. 2 only

    d. 3 only

DISCUSSION QUESTIONS

Question 16

What do you see as your responsibilities to the Pickards as a financial planner?

Question 17

Gathering client information can be done thorough interviews or questionnaires. Discuss the benefits and drawbacks of using questionnaires compared to personally interviewing the Picards.

Question 18

Why is important for Henry and June to provide all of the information you have requested during the early phases of the engagement?

Question 19

What recommendations do you have for June in regards to transferring the business to David?

Question 20

Address Henry's question about his segregated funds.

Question 21

What are the financial planning implications of June donating her T-100 life insurance policy to her favourite charity?

Question 22

Discuss the estate planning issues you have identified and make recommendations to the Pickards.

Question 23

Assess Henry and June's current investment strategy and make recommendations.

QUESTIONS & SOLUTIONS

Question 1

Given June's current situation and her plans for the future, which of the following business structures would be best suited to her needs?

    a. sole proprietor

    b. partnership

    c. corporation

    d. co-operative

Answer: c

    ⇨ June is already operating the business as a sole proprietor. She has indicated that she would like to leave more money inside the firm. Neither a partnership nor a co-operative would allow her to shelter income to the extent she should under the favourable small business rate available to Canadian corporations. A corporation would also provide greater flexibility in succession planning (e.g., the ability to issue shares).

Question 2

How much is Henry able to deduct as an "annual union, professional, or like due" on line 212 of his income tax return?

    a. $276.00

    b. $138.00

    c. $46.92

    d. $0

Answer: a

    ⇨ Henry is an architect and pays a $276 membership fee for the Royal Architectural Institute of Canada out of his own salary. Dues paid to a trade union or a professional association are fully deductible.

Question 3

If Henry were to become totally disabled next month, which of the following amounts would he most likely receive as a monthly payment from the disability insurance coverage offered by his employer?

    a. $2,250

    b. $3,750

    c. $4,950

    d. $6,000

Answer: c

    ⇨ Disability benefits are typically set at 66% of the employee's after-tax income. Insurers deliberately set the benefit level at this lower level in order to account for potentially lower tax treatment and to prevent the insured from misrepresenting the claim. In addition, the carrier often applies an overall dollar maximum.

Question 4

If June were to set up a Personal Health Services Plan (PHSP) at her place of work, to whom would she be required to provide insurance coverage in order to ensure that the premiums would qualify as a fully deductible business expense?

  a. June

  b. David

  c. June and David

  d. June, David and Frank

Answer: d

⇨ Changes introduced in the 1998 federal Budget made health care insurance premiums paid for a PHSP fully deductible business expenses for unincorporated business owners, under the condition that benefits must be offered to all employees.

Question 5

If June were to absolutely assign her T-100 life insurance policy to a charity and name them as beneficiary, but continue paying the annual premiums herself, which of the following scenarios would be true?

1. She would receive a tax credit for the cash surrender value of the policy at the time of the initial assignment.

2. She would receive a tax credit every year, based on the annual premium she pays.

3. Her estate would receive a tax credit for a $100,000 donation in the year of her death.

  a. 1 only

  b. 1 and 2 only

  c. 2 and 3 only

  d. 3 only

Answer: b

⇨ The absolute assignment of a life insurance policy provides income tax relief during the donor's lifetime. The initial gift will generate a tax credit for the donor based on the current cash surrender value of the policy. The donor will then receive a tax credit for each subsequent premium he or she pays. The charity, however, is the beneficiary of the policy — no money will flow to the donor's estate.

Question 6

If Henry were to sell today all the units in his first RRSP account and transfer all of the money into the second, how much more money could he invest in foreign property (i.e., in addition to what he already has in the European fund)?

  a. $26,600

  b. $35,600

  c. $44,440

  d. 139,000

Answer: d

⇨ The 2005 federal Budget eliminated the limitation on foreign property.

Question 7

With respect to the investments sold to Henry by his friend Larry, which of the following statements is false?

   a. Larry must hold an insurance license in order to offer these funds.

   b. With a named beneficiary, the funds may bypass probate fees in the event of Henry's death.

   c. The investment may be protected from creditors provided that Henry names June as beneficiary on the contract.

   d. A minimum of 65% of Henry's initial investment is guaranteed, provided Henry holds the funds until the contract's maturity date.

Answer: d

   ⇨   Because segregated funds are technically insurance products, advisors who offer them must be insurance licensed. The insurance classification also provides potential protection against creditors under provincial insurance law. Segregated funds allow for the naming of a preferred beneficiary — meaning funds can bypass probate. Segregated funds guarantee a minimum of 75% of the investor's capital, provided he or she holds the investment until the maturity date.

Question 8

Henry holds nine Canada Savings Bonds ($1,000 denomination bonds). Each bond pays 3%. Today comparable bonds are now paying 4.5%. What is the approximate profit or loss you would realize if you sold one bond?

   a. $333.33 loss

   b. $666.67 loss

   c. $666.67 profit

   d. $333.33 profit

Answer: a

   ⇨   ($1,000 × 0.03) ÷ 0.045 - $1,000 = $333.33

Question 9

If both Henry and June were to die next week, how much of their estate would be subject to U.S. estate tax?

   a. $1.1 million

   b. $1 million

   c. $500,000

   d. $0

Answer: d

   ⇨   The U.S. estate tax is being phased out and will be ultimately repealed in 2010. For 2009, an estate credit based on US$3.5 million of assets applies — meaning that Henry and June would not be liable for estate taxes on their home in Washington.

Question 10

What is the maximum amount that June could contribute to her RRSP for the coming (i.e., 2009) tax year?

    a. $21,000

    b. $20,000

    c. $19,000

    d. $14,500

Answer: a

    ⇨ For 2009 the maximum RRSP contribution limit to $21,000 for 2009. June has indicated that she has no unused contribution room.

Question 11

Henry and June have mentioned that they are both considering what they would like to do since they are approaching retirement. He is expecting to live to 80 years of age. Henry's Investments are consistently earning 6%. He believes that we will need to receive a before-tax income of $60,000 at the beginning of each year during his retirement if he draws on his capital. He had originally planned to retire at the age of 60 years. However, he is enjoying his work and is wondering the impact if he continues working until age 65.

If Henry does change his retirement from age 60 to age 65, how much less will he need in savings to meet his retirement objectives?

    a. $267,906

    b. $171,917

    c. $111,788

    d. $102, 917

Answer: c

    ⇨ At the beginning of Henry's retirement, he would require $729,486.99 in savings to fund his 20 years of retirement. By reducing the number of years he will be retired by 5 years, we reduce his needs to $617,699.04. This produces the reduction in amount of required savings of $111, 790.95. Calculator keystrokes below.

    ⇨ Set mode to BEGIN

    ⇨ P/YR = 1

    ⇨ xP/YR = 80 - 60 = 20 (Change xP/YR = 80 - 65 = 15)

    ⇨ I/YR = 6

    ⇨ PMT = 60,000

    ⇨ FV = 0

SOLVE FOR PV, which equals -729,486.99 (PV = -617,699.04)

729,486.99 - 617,699.04 = $111,787.96

Question 12

How much money should Henry and June set aside if they want to keep providing June's mother Gertrude with her usual income, paid at the end of each month, assuming she lives to be 89 and the investment earns 5% a year?

    a. $265,897

    b. $235,703

    c. $231,876

    d. $229,452

Answer: b

    ⇨ If Gertrude is to receive $2,500 a month for the next 10 years, Henry and June will need to set aside $235,703 at 5% in order to fund that need. The steps on a business calculator are as follows:

    ⇨ Set mode to END

    ⇨ P/YR = 12

    ⇨ xP/YR = 10

    ⇨ I/YR = 5

    ⇨ PMT = -2,500

    ⇨ FV = 0

SOLVE FOR PV, which equals $235,703

Question 13

If Henry and June decide to downsize and purchase a condo, how much of a capital gain will they each have to include as income after they sell their house in Vancouver:

    a. $0

    b. $50,000

    c. $100,000

    d. $200,000

Answer: a

    ⇨ In Canada, a taxpayer's principal residence is exempt from capital gains taxation.

Question 14

What portion of June's registered retirement savings would be most adversely affected by an increase in interest rates?

    a. $16,000

    b. $45,000

    c. $87,000

    d. $270,000

Answer: d

    ⇨ June holds $194,000 in the XYZ Long-Term Bond Fund and $76,000 in the XYZ Short-Term Bond Fund, for a combined total of $270,000. Of all asset classes, bonds are most sensitive to changes in interest rates — as interest rates rise, bond prices fall.

Question 15

If June were to swap her Acme bond for her ABC Precious Metals Fund, which of the following is/are true?

1. She would be able to apply any future capital losses in the Precious Metals Fund against capital gains in other investments, reducing taxes.

2. She might face a capital gain or loss on the bond if the current market price has changed, since the transfer would result in a deemed disposition.

3. She would be able to deduct $45,000 from her income that year as an RRSP contribution.

    a. 1 only

    b. 1 and 2 only

    c. 2 only

    d. 3 only

Answer: b

⇨ An RRSP swap allows the investor to exchange one investment held outside the RRSP for another held inside the RRSP. Because the Precious Metals Fund is more volatile, and because it earns capital gains rather than interest income, swapping it for the interest paying bond would allow June to write off future losses — something she cannot do inside of an RRSP. An RRSP swap will result in a deemed disposition. While a bond primarily generates interest income, if it is sold at a profit or a loss it will generate a capital loss or gain. An RRSP swap does not count as a new contribution.

CASE STUDY 4 — CHARLES AND ANN GUPTA

Background

Charles and Ann saw your advertisement in the local newspaper and have booked an appointment with you on May 1, 2010 to review their retirement plan and their investment portfolio. They say that they already have a financial advisor who is a Certified Financial Planner (as you are), but they have decided that they would like a second opinion about some of his recommendations. They are concerned that their investments are not performing as well as they had expected, and are worried that they may not be on track to reach their early retirement goal.

Ann tells you that she is the one who keeps track of the family finances, and she has prepared a net worth statement and a cash flow statement so that you can have a better idea of their financial position.

Both Charles and Ann are surprised when you provide them with your letter of engagement and fee schedule. They say that their other advisor has never provided them with a written letter of engagement.

Personal Information

Charles (age 48) and Ann (age 27) live in Kingston, Ontario. They have been living together for four years. Both are in good health. They used to be fairly heavy smokers, but they tell you that they have cut back to almost nothing now. They say they now only smoke a cigarette one or two times a week when they are out with friends.

This is Charles's second marriage, and Ann's first. Charles is making regular support payments to his first wife, Mary, under an agreement signed in June 1998. Charles and Mary did not have any children.

Charles and Ann have a child, Isabel, who is two years old. They are paying $680 a month to send her to a nearby day care program.

Employment Information

Details of Charles's Employment

Charles is a professor at a nearby community college, and earns $81,000 a year. He says that while he enjoys his research work there, the day-to-day grind of teaching students is starting to get to him. He would like to retire in the next five to ten years. He thinks that, in addition to the pension funds provided by the university, he has enough money set aside to provide him with the sort of lifestyle he wants.

Besides his regular employment income, Charles has published several books on media history and popular culture. He receives royalties from his publisher, and is often asked to contribute articles to the national newspapers. This usually makes him an extra $650 a month. He says that when he retires from teaching, he hopes to spend more time doing this sort of work. He says that, between writing and appearing as an expert on TV and radio, he should be able to earn $40,000 a year.

Details of Ann's Employment

Ann works for the local newspaper as a commissioned employee, selling advertisements to businesses in the area. Instead of working at the newspaper, she meets with clients at their offices or at her own home. She uses her own car to travel to and from appointments, and has converted one of the rooms in their house into an office, where she has installed a separate phone line.

Ann's income varies a little bit from year to year, but as a rule she earns $40,000 annually. Of that $40,000, she says $30,000 is the base salary paid by her employer, and $10,000 is commission income. She is quite happy with her job, and says that the newspaper offers all of their salespeople perks, including a laptop computer to use, subsidized meals in their cafeteria, sales training courses every year, as well as use of the company gym.

Financial Position

Real Estate

Charles and Ann live in a house that they purchased four years ago. It is a large Victorian era home with 12 rooms and cost them $250,000 at the time. He says that, after the renovations and improvements the two have made over the last couple of years, he believes its current value should be around $300,000. They are currently making mortgage payments of $950 a month, $500 of which is interest. Last year, the house adjacent to them went up for sale for a very low price — just $160,000. While it was (and still is) a little run down, the couple decided to purchase the home as an investment, and they are now renting it out to students. They tell you that, because of the shortage of housing in the area, they are able to demand a fairly high rent despite the house's ramshackle condition. They are making monthly mortgage payments of $1,200 for the house ($800 of which is interest), but are bringing in $1,000 more than that in rental income every month. They think the property is currently worth about $180,000.

Charles's Investments, Registered

The community college has a defined contribution pension plan, managed by the Super Insurance Company, and the balance in Charles's account is as follows:

- $78,000 in the Super Canadian Balanced Fund
- $52,000 in the Super Canadian Small Cap Fund
- $44,000 in the Super Canadian Blue Chip Fund

Charles's Investments, Non-Registered

Charles owns the stock of two firms listed on the TSX.

- 800 shares of JKL Communications, currently trading at $10 a share
- 450 shares of QRS Manufacturing, currently trading at $12 a share

He says that he purchased JKL at $8 a share two years ago, and picked up QRS at just $4 a share last year. Both of these purchases were made on advice he received from his brother-in-law, Dan, who spends a great deal of time researching the stock markets. JKL last reported earnings per share of $0.40, while QRS posted earnings per share of $0.85.

Ann's Investments, Registered

Charles has contributed $5,000 to a spousal RRSP for Ann each year for the last two years. The funds are in an account with High Street Investment Management and they are invested as follows:

- $5,000 in the High Street Canadian Tactical Asset Allocation Fund
- $5,000 in the High Street Long-Term Bond Fund

Ann's Investments, Non-Registered

Ann was very close to her great aunt, Beatrice, and lived with her for a year while she was on a student exchange in the Netherlands. When Beatrice died late last year, she left Ann an amount equivalent to C$75,000 in her will. Ann travelled to Amsterdam last summer and received the money from her aunt's solicitor, which she then deposited into a savings account at a bank in Holland.

Insurance Information

Charles has life insurance for three times his salary from the college, and Ann has life insurance through her employer for twice her salary. Charles and Ann each purchased five-year term individual insurance policies from a local insurance broker when they purchased the house, with a face value of $250,000.

Charles and Ann also took out life insurance when Isabel was born — a joint first-to-die T-100 policy for $300,000.

Charles says that if something were to happen to him, he would want Ann to have a regular income of at least $35,000 a year until she reaches the age of 65.

Children

Charles and Ann said that they have heard they can shelter funds for Isabel's education by purchasing a life insurance policy for her, but are not sure what face value to purchase or what riders to consider. They would like your advice on whether this is really the best way to set aside education savings.

Risk Profile

Charles and Ann describe themselves as low to moderate risk-takers, and are prepared to accept a little risk in exchange for better returns — especially inside of their RRSPs, where they have a longer time horizon. Charles says that he has been very fortunate in the stock market recently, but through no effort of his own — he has taken a couple tips from Ann's brother-in-law. He says he's started to feel a bit uncomfortable investing in individual securities, and would like to "get out while the going is good".

Ann says that, because she is younger than Charles, she thinks she is prepared to accept a little more volatility — although she is not prepared to risk all of her capital. At most, she says she could tolerate a decline of 20% in one year.

Goals and Objectives

Charles says he looks forward not to retirement, but to semi-retirement, and plans to stay active and earning for quite a while — he is happy to let his money sit inside his registered portfolio while he earns income from his writing. He says his primary concern is making sure that Ann and Isabel will be provided for no matter what. This is one of the reasons he was anxious to purchase the rental property — to provide a steady source of income regardless of what the future may hold.

Ann says that she worries about the cost of education, and wants to make certain that Isabel can stay in school for as long as she wishes.

Wills and Powers of Attorney

Charles and Ann had wills and powers of attorney drawn up by their lawyer shortly after Isabel was born. They have named each other as beneficiaries and her brother, Dan, as executor. He is also named as Isabel's guardian and trustee in the event of common disaster.

Charles and Ann Gupta
Statement of Net Worth at December 31, 2009

ASSETS	Charles	Ann	Total
Liquid Assets			
Joint Chequing Account	$ 400	$ 400	$ 800
Savings Account		75,000	75,000
Total Liquid Assets	**$ 400**	**$ 75,400**	**$ 75,800**
Investment Assets			
Non-Registered Assets	13,400		13,400
Registered Assets	174,000	10,000	184,000
Rental Property	90,000	90,000	180,000
Total Investment Assets	**$ 277,400**	**$ 100,000**	**$ 377,400**
Personal-Use Assets			
Residence	150,000	150,000	300,000
Automobiles	8,000	11,000	19,000
Personal Effects (owned jointly)	9,000	9,000	18,000
Total Personal-Use Assets	**$ 167,000**	**$ 170,000**	**$ 337,000**
TOTAL ASSETS	**$ 444,800**	**$ 345,400**	**$ 790,200**
LIABILITIES			
Short-Term Liabilities			
Car Loan		5,000	5,000
Long-Term Liabilities			
Mortgage (Home)	61,000	61,000	122,000
Mortgage (Rental Property)	50,000	50,000	100,000
TOTAL LIABILITIES	**$ 111,000**	**$ 116,000**	**$ 227,000**
NET WORTH	**$ 333,800**	**$ 229,400**	**$ 563,200**

Charles and Ann Gupta
Monthly and Annual Cash Flow as of December 31, 2009

	Monthly	Annually
INCOME		
Charles's Employment Income	$ 6,750	$ 81,000
Charles's Self-Employment Income	650	7,800
Ann's Employment Income	3,333	39,996
Ann's Interest Income	187	2,244
Rental Income	2,200	26,400
Total Income	**$ 13,120**	**$ 157,440**
EXPENSES		
Taxes, CPP and EI Withholdings at Source — Charles	1,900	22,800
Taxes, CPP and EI Withholdings at Source — Ann	700	8,400
Taxes, Instalments	675	8,100
Mortgage Payments		
Home	950	11,400
Rental House	1,200	14,400
Maintenance, Repairs		
Home	175	2,100
Rental House	280	3,360
Home Insurance		
Home	120	1,440
Rental House	233	2,796
Heating, Water and Electricity		
Home	489	5,868
Property Taxes		
Home	310	3,720
Rental House	186	2,232
Automobile — Charles		
Insurance	78	936
Gas and Operating Expenses	131	1,572
Repairs and Maintenance	85	1,020
Automobile — Ann		
Insurance	110	1,320
Gas and Operating Expenses	241	2,892
Repairs and Maintenance	45	540
Life Insurance Premiums		
Charles's 5 YRT Policy	71	852
Ann's 5 YRT Policy	29	348
Joint Policy	350	4,200
Telephone	40	480
Telephone — Ann	55	660
Food	580	6,960
Clothing	420	5,040
Personal Care	180	2,160
Entertainment	195	2,340
Daycare	680	8,160
Support Payments to Mary	600	7,200
RRSP — Charles	1,000	12,000
RRSP — Ann	600	7,200
TOTAL EXPENSES	**$ 12,708**	**$ 152,496**
SURPLUS	**$ 412**	**$ 4,944**

QUESTIONS

Question 1

Of the amount Charles and Ann are paying for Isabel's day care, what portion should they claim as a child care expense deduction?

    a. Charles should claim $8,160

    b. Ann should claim $7,000

    c. Ann should claim $4,080

    d. Ann and Charles should each claim $3,500

Question 2

What is the net income (or loss) the Guptas will earn from the rental property for the year?

    a. $19,500

    b. $3,372

    c. $5,844

    d. $8,412

Question 3

Based on Charles' desire to purchase enough life insurance that Ann would have a regular income of at least $35,000 per year until the age of 65, what is the total amount of life insurance that is required? Assume a 5% rate of return, with annual payments made at the end of the year and a complete depletion of capital.

    a. $584,450

    b. $590,376

    c. $595,596

    d. $679,132

Question 4

With respect to the High Street RRSP account, which of the following is/are true?

1. Charles is the owner.

2. Charles is the contributor.

3. Ann is the annuitant.

    a. 1 only

    b. 1 and 3 only

    c. 2 only

    d. 2 and 3 only

Question 5

If all of the funds were withdrawn from the High Street RRSP account:

    a. Ann would have to declare $5,000 as income for that year

    b. Ann would have to declare $10,000 as income for that year

    c. Charles would have to declare $5,000 as income for that year

    d. Charles would have to declare $10,000 as income for that year

Question 6

If Ann and Charles wish to qualify for lower life insurance premiums, they must:

    a. not smoke for 30 days

    b. not smoke for 6 months

    c. not smoke for 1 year

    d. inform their insurer that they have already cut back to less than 10 cigarettes a month

Question 7

With respect to the money Ann inherited from her great aunt, which of the following is/are true?

1. Ann must report any interest she earns on her income tax return.

2. Ann must file a separate T1135, "Foreign Income Verification Statement".

3. Ann must pay a 20% penalty tax on any interest she earns in her foreign account.

    a. 1 only

    b. 1 and 2 only

    c. 2 only

    d. 2 and 3 only

Question 8

Charles is making support payments to his first wife, Mary. How much of the total annual amount paid may he claim as a deduction?

    a. $0

    b. $3,600

    c. $5,000

    d. $7,200

Question 9

What amount of the annual mortgage payments should Ann deduct as a home office expense?

    a. $0

    b. $500

    c. $950

    d. $1,368

Question 10

If Charles decided to leave his teaching job to focus on his writing, he may transfer his pension assets to a:

    a. RRSP

    b. LIF

    c. LRIF

    d. LIRA

Question 11

You are concerned about the conduct of Charles and Ann's other advisor, specifically with his failure to provide them with a letter of engagement. Your first action should be to:

    a. contact his or her supervisor to report the omission

    b. submit your criticism to him in writing for an explanation

    c. report him to the provincial securities regulator

    d. report him to the provincial insurance regulator

Question 12

Of the four "perks" Ann says she receives, which would be considered a non-taxable benefit?

1. Use of the gym
2. Subsidized meals
3. Sales training courses
4. Home computer

    a. 1 and 2 only

    b. 3 only

    c. 3 and 4 only

    d. 1, 2, 3 and 4

Question 13

Calculate the PE Ratio for JKL Communications. It is:

    a. 10

    b. 20

    c. 25

    d. 30

Question 14

If Charles were to give his shares in QRS Manufacturing to a registered Canadian charity tomorrow, what amount would he have to include in his income as a taxable capital gain?

    a. $0

    b. $900

    c. $1,800

    d. $3,600

Question 15

If Charles were to give his shares in QRS Manufacturing to a registered Canadian charity tomorrow, he would receive a tax receipt for a gift of:

    a. $5,400

    b. $3,600

    c. $1,800

    d. $900

DISCUSSION QUESTIONS

Question 16

The Guptas came to you to obtain a second opinion on the recommendations of their current Certified Financial Planner. Are there any professional standards you need to follow in this case?

Question 17

Why should a financial planner provide clients with a letter of engagement?

Question 18

What risks do they face in terms of their overall financial plan?

Question 19

Do the Guptas have an adequate amount of insurance should Charles die?

Question 20

Discuss the tax implications of the Gupta's selling the rental property. The Gupta's would like to minimize the amount of tax they have to pay. Provide qualitative and quantitative support for your response.

Question 21

Comment on the couple's overall financial position based on the net worth statement and cash flow statement.

QUESTIONS & SOLUTIONS

Question 1

Of the amount Charles and Ann are paying for Isabel's day care, what portion should they claim as a child care expense deduction?

    a. Charles should claim $8,160

    b. Ann should claim $7,000

    c. Ann should claim $4,080

    d. Ann and Charles should each claim $3,500

Answer: b

    ⇨ Child care expenses are claimed by the spouse with lower income, under the assumption that he or she would otherwise be the one to stay home with the child. Eligible expenses are limited to the lower of (1) $7,000 per child under the age of 7; (2) the amount actually paid; or (3) two thirds of earned income. Charles and Ann say they pay $8,000 a year, and two thirds of Ann's income would be $10,000, so the lowest of the three amounts is $7,000.

Question 2

What is the net income (or loss) the Guptas will earn from the rental property for the year?

    a. $19,500

    b. $3,372

    c. $5,844

    d. $8,412

Answer: d

    ⇨ The net income is $8,412 - the revenue of $26,400 less expenses of 17,988. Expenses include the interest portion of mortgage ($800 × 12 = 9,600), maintenance $3,360, insurance $2,796 and property taxes $2,232. The principle portion of the mortgage payment ($400) is not tax deductible.

Question 3

Based on Charles' desire to purchase enough life insurance that Ann would have a regular income of at least $35,000 per year until the age of 65, what is the total amount of life insurance that is required? Assume a 5% rate of return, with annual payments made at the end of the year and a complete depletion of capital.

    a. $584,450

    b. $590,376

    c. $595,596

    d. $679,132

Answer: c

    ⇨ The steps on a financial calculator are as follows:

    ⇨ Set mode to END

    ⇨ P/YR = 1

    ⇨ xP/YR = 39 (65 - 27 + 1)

    ⇨ I/YR = 5

    ⇨ PMT = -35,000

SOLVE FOR PV, which equals $595,596

Question 4

With respect to the High Street RRSP account, which of the following is/are true?

1. Charles is the owner.

2. Charles is the contributor.

3. Ann is the annuitant.

    a. 1 only

    b. 1 and 3 only

    c. 2 only

    d. 2 and 3 only

Answer: d

    ⇨ The High Street RRSP is a spousal RRSP, meaning that Ann is the annuitant under the contract. Charles is the contributor and will receive the tax deduction, but once the funds have been deposited they belong to Ann, not to Charles.

Question 5

If all of the funds were withdrawn from the High Street RRSP account:

    a. Ann would have to declare $5,000 as income for that year

    b. Ann would have to declare $10,000 as income for that year

    c. Charles would have to declare $5,000 as income for that year

    d. Charles would have to declare $10,000 as income for that year

Answer: d

    ⇨ Since the High Street account is a spousal RRSP, the funds are subject to the three-year attribution rules. The case study indicates that Charles made both $5,000 contributions within the last two years. If Ann were to withdraw all of the funds, Charles would be required to add the full amount withdrawn — $10,000 — to his income for that year.

Question 6

If Ann and Charles wish to qualify for lower life insurance premiums, they must:

    a. not smoke for 30 days

    b. not smoke for 6 months

    c. not smoke for 1 year

    d. inform their insurer that they have already cut back to less than 10 cigarettes a month

Answer: c

    ⇨ In order for smokers to qualify for non-smoker rates on their life insurance policies, they must sign a declaration stating that they not have smoked for the previous twelve months. The fact they are smoking less than they were previously will not allow them to qualify for reduced premiums.

Question 7

With respect to the money Ann inherited from her great aunt, which of the following is/are true?

1. Ann must report any interest she earns on her income tax return.

2. Ann must file a separate T1135, "Foreign Income Verification Statement".

3. Ann must pay a 20% penalty tax on any interest she earns in her foreign account.

     a. 1 only

     b. 1 and 2 only

     c. 2 only

     d. 2 and 3 only

Answer: a

     ⇨   Ann is required to report any interest she earns on her income tax return, even if it is earned in a foreign bank account. She does not have to pay a foreign penalty tax. Ann's aunt left her the equivalent of $75,000 — she would only be required to file a T1135, "Foreign Income Verification Statement", if she had acquired foreign property valued at $100,000 or more.

Question 8

Charles is making support payments to his first wife, Mary. How much of the total annual amount paid may he claim as a deduction?

     a. $0

     b. $3,600

     c. $5,000

     d. $7,200

Answer: d

     ⇨   Support payments made to a spouse are deductible to the payer and taxable to the recipient regardless of the date the agreement was signed. If the agreement was for child support and signed after April 30, 1997, those payments would not be deductible for Charles or taxable to Mary, but the case study states that they have no children.

Question 9

What amount of the annual mortgage payments should Ann deduct as a home office expense?

     a. $0

     b. $500

     c. $950

     d. $1,368

Answer: a

     ⇨   Ann is not self-employed, but rather a commissioned employee. She may not deduct any of her mortgage interest as a business expense, although she may write off other items such as heating, electricity and home insurance premiums.

Question 10

If Charles decided to leave his teaching job to focus on his writing, he may transfer his pension assets to a:

    a. RRSP

    b. LIF

    c. LRIF

    d. LIRA

Answer: d

    ⇨   Charles pension assets are locked-in funds, meaning that he may not transfer them to a traditional RRSP, but must instead move them into a Locked-In Retirement Account (LIRA) should he leave his employer. Charles has indicated that he wishes to keep working and earn income, so he would not transfer the funds to a Locked-In Retirement Income Fund (LRIF) or a Life Income Fund (LIF) until a later date when he wanted to start receiving regular retirement income.

Question 11

You are concerned about the conduct of Charles and Ann's other advisor, specifically with his failure to provide them with a letter of engagement. Your first action should be to:

    a. contact his or her supervisor to report the omission

    b. submit your criticism to him in writing for an explanation

    c. report him to the provincial securities regulator

    d. report him to the provincial insurance regulator

Answer: b

    ⇨   The failure to provide a letter of engagement may be unprofessional, but it is not criminal or fraudulent, so you are not under an obligation to contact either of the provincial authorities or his manager. Rule 603 of the Financial Planners Standards Council (FPSC) Code of Ethics states that a CFP professional shall not criticize another CFP professional without first submitting this criticism to the CFP professional for explanation. Where the criticism may result in a complaint being lodged with FPSC, the CFP professional must, where required, first submit that criticism in writing to the other CFP professional for explanation.

Question 12

Of the four "perks" Ann says she receives, which would be considered a non-taxable benefit?

1. Use of the gym

2. Subsidized meals

3. Sales training courses

4. Home computer

    a. 1 and 2 only

    b. 3 only

    c. 3 and 4 only

    d. 1, 2, 3 and 4

Answer: d

    ⇨   Use of recreational facilities, subsidized meals and business-related courses are all non-taxable benefits. Ann's home computer is also a non-taxable benefit, since she uses it for work and she says that laptops are made available to all salespeople employed by the newspaper.

Question 13

Calculate the PE Ratio for JKL Communications. It is:

    a. 10

    b. 20

    c. 25

    d. 30

Answer: c

⇨ The Price Earnings Ratio, or PE Ratio, is calculated by dividing the current stock price by the company's earnings per share. JKL is valued at $10 a share, and reported earnings of 40 cents a share, so JKL has a PE Ratio of 25.

Question 14

If Charles were to give his shares in QRS Manufacturing to a registered Canadian charity tomorrow, what amount would he have to include in his income as a taxable capital gain?

    a. $0

    b. $900

    c. $1,800

    d. $3,600

Answer: a

⇨ The case says that Charles purchased 450 shares at $4, and that they are currently valued at $12 a share. The difference between the purchase price of $1,800 and the current price of $5,400 is $3,600. The 2006 Budget eliminated capital gains on publicly-listed securities donated to charity.

Question 15

If Charles were to give his shares in QRS Manufacturing to a registered Canadian charity tomorrow, he would receive a tax receipt for a gift of:

    a. $5,400

    b. $3,600

    c. $1,800

    d. $900

Answer: a

⇨ Those who make a gift of securities will receive a tax receipt from the charity based on the market price of the shares.

CASE STUDY 5 — LAURA AND WILLIAM ROGERS

Background

It is December 2009, and Laura and William Rogers have made an appointment with you to review their finances.

Personal Information

Laura (59) and William (65) have been married for 15 years. Both were previously divorced, and both have children from their prior marriages.

Laura's son, John, is single and 38 years old. He had been working as a newspaper reporter, but lost his job when his employer was bought out two months ago. He has moved into Laura's family cottage while he looks for other work. They confide in you that they think John may have a drinking problem, and they don't believe he has any savings.

William has a daughter named Jean, who is 34 years old. She works with him in his leather business. She is married to Howard (age 34), and they have a two-year-old daughter named Fran.

Employment Information

Details of Laura's Employment

Laura is a television news producer at the local station. She has worked there for 30 years. While she says her job used to be interesting and fulfilling, she is dissatisfied with the way things have changed at her workplace in the last few years. She is thinking about taking early retirement. JunkTV Broadcasting is offering early retirement packages to older employees, and she is considering accepting. In addition to her regular pension, JunkTV will provide her with a lump-sum retiring allowance equal to one year's pay, plus an additional payment of $2,000 for unused sick leave credits.

Her 60th birthday is in February of next year, and she has heard that she might be able to start receiving her Canada Pension Plan (CPP) retirement benefits then.

Details of William's Business

William is the sole shareholder and manager of Big Bill's Leatherworks, a small factory that produces leather bags and coats. He started the company 30 years ago with a $10,000 inheritance he received from his grandmother. The firm has grown since then, and William now employs five people, including his son-in-law, Howard, who has shown a great deal of aptitude in the business. The company is incorporated and is valued at $1 million.

William says he expects the company to do very well in future, but he is worried about the tax implications of this future growth — he says he doesn't want to face a huge tax bill when he hands the business over to Jean and Howard. For the time being, he would like to keep control over the company and keep receiving income. He says he'd be happy if he could sell out to his daughter and son-in-law for $1 million — but only when he's ready.

Financial Position

Real Estate

William and Laura own a 10-acre hobby farm outside of town. They bought it for $80,000 15 years ago. They have made significant improvements to the four-bedroom house, and now believe the property would sell for $300,000. They paid off their mortgage several years ago.

William and Laura also have a cottage on a small lake about 15 minutes away. Laura inherited the property from her mother 10 years ago when it was worth $50,000, and is now valued at $150,000. The value of recreational real estate in that area has been increasing at a rate of about 5% a year, and they expect the value of this property to continue to rise at that rate indefinitely. In the event of her death, Laura wants to make sure that William will be able to enjoy the property for as long as he is alive, but she wants the cottage to go to John eventually.

Laura's Investments, Registered

Since there was no pension plan or deferred profit sharing plan at her work, Laura has contributed the maximum to her own RRSPs at Savealot Bank every year, and has no unused RRSP contribution room.

- $25,000 Savealot money market fund
- $134,000 Savealot long-term bond fund
- $100,000 Savealot short-term bond fund
- $80,000 Savealot T-Bill fund

Laura's Investments, Non-Registered

Laura inherited money from a wealthy uncle nine years ago, and invested these funds in three index funds:

- $50,000 Canadian Equity Index Fund, book value $20,000
- $100,000 Canadian Bond Index Fund, book value $65,000

William's Investments, Registered

William has contributed relatively little to his RRSP, and still has more than $100,000 of unused RRSP contribution room left. He recently cashed in some of his investments, and the money is sitting in a short-term savings account.

- $120,000 at the Savealot Bank at 4% interest

William's Investments, Non-Registered

Several years ago, William bought $20,000 worth of shares in his brother Steve's business, Slaphead Enterprises — a Canadian-controlled, private corporation that manufactured battery-powered, dancing Santa Claus figures. William says that Steve couldn't manage his way out of a wet paper bag, and earlier this year, Slaphead Enterprises went bankrupt.

William is interested in the mining and precious metals sector, and has made several successful investments over the years.

- $20,000 ABC Mines, purchased at $5,000
- $30,000 DEF Mines, purchased at $7,000
- $10,000 GHI Mines, purchased at $9,000
- $20,000 JKL Mines, purchased at $3,000
- $10,000 MNO Mines, purchased at $8,000

William says that, if he were to die, he would like Laura to keep receiving the income from these investments, but that he ultimately wants the money to pass to his daughter, Jean. He tells you privately that he is afraid that if he were to die and leave all of this money to Laura outright, she would end up giving everything to John instead. He says he didn't work all these years to see his investments converted to liquor and poured down John's throat.

Liabilities

William took out a loan to purchase some of his mining shares. He owes $10,000, and is paying 7% interest.

Insurance Information

Neither William nor Laura have any life or disability insurance. They have drug, vision and dental insurance coverage through a Personal Health Services Plan paid for by William's company.

Risk Profile

William is a very aggressive, speculative investor and doesn't mind taking risks in the hopes of obtaining a higher return.

Laura is a moderately conservative investor. She says that she was once prepared to accept more volatility, but she believes she should be more careful now that her retirement is approaching.

Goals

Laura's most concerned about whether or not she can afford to take early retirement. She also wants to make certain that her cottage will remain on her side of the family.

William wants to make sure that the business he has worked so hard to build can be passed on to his children, but is worried about the eventual tax consequences.

Wills and Powers of Attorney

Both William and Laura have wills. They tell you that the documents were drawn up after they divorced from their ex-spouses, but before they were married.

When discussing estates, William mentions that another of his brothers, Charles, passed away last month and he is acting as executor of the will. Charles was quite wealthy, but his other siblings are not as well off. They would like William to distribute some of the funds from the estate immediately. William says that the estate seems fairly complex, and is worried that Charles may actually owe quite a bit of money to the Canada Revenue Agency.

Laura and William Rogers
Statement of Net Worth at November 1, 2009

ASSETS	Laura	William	Total
Liquid Assets			
Joint Chequing Account	$ 1,500	$ 1,500	$ 3,000
Total Liquid Assets	**$ 1,500**	**$ 1,500**	**$ 3,000**
Investment Assets			
Registered Assets	339,000	120,000	459,000
Non-Registered Assets	150,000	90,000	240,000
Total Investment Assets	**$ 489,000**	**$ 210,000**	**$ 699,000**
Personal-Use Assets			
Residence	150,000	150,000	300,000
Cottage	150,000	N/A	150,000
Automobile	10,000	10,000	20,000
Personal Effects (owned jointly)	5,000	5,000	10,000
Business Assets			
Big Bill's Leatherworks	N/A	1,000,000	1,000,000
Total Personal and Business Assets	**$ 315,000**	**$ 1,165,000**	**$ 1,480,000**
TOTAL ASSETS	**$ 805,500**	**$ 1,376,500**	**$ 2,182,000**
LIABILITIES			
Short-Term Liabilities			
Loan	N/A	10,000	10,000
TOTAL LIABILITIES	**$ N/A**	**$ 10,000**	**$ 10,000**
NET WORTH	**$ 805,500**	**$ 1,366,500**	**$ 2,172,000**

Laura and William Rogers
Monthly and Annual Cash Flow as of November 1, 2009

	Monthly	Annually
INCOME		
Laura's Income	$ 4,833	$ 58,000
William's Income	6,000	72,000
Total Income	**$ 10,833**	**$ 130,000**
EXPENSES		
Taxes, CPP and EI Deductions		
Laura	1,275	15,300
William	1,700	20,400
Maintenance and Repairs		
Home	300	3,600
Cottage	100	1,200
Property Insurance		
Home	150	1,800
Cottage	90	
Home Heating, Water and Electricity	575	6,900
Property Taxes		
Home	250	3,000
Cottage	80	960
Automobiles		
Insurance	350	4,200
Gas and Operating Expenses	270	3,240
Repairs and Maintenance	200	2,400
Telephone	120	1,440
Food	500	6,000
Clothing	400	4,800
Personal Care	150	1,800
Entertainment	700	8,400
Loan Payments	200	2,400
RRSP Savings — Laura	870	10,440
RRSP Savings — William	650	7,800
Non-Registered Savings	1,000	12,000
TOTAL EXPENSES	**$ 9,930**	**$ 119,160**
SURPLUS	**$ 903**	**$ 10,840**

QUESTIONS

Question 1

If Laura decides to start receiving the Canada Pension Plan next year, by what per cent will her benefits be reduced?

    a. 5%

    b. 15%

    c. 25%

    d. 30

Question 2

If Laura wants to start receiving her Canada Pension Plan retirement benefits in March, she

    a. must stop working at the end of February, and may not work during the month of March

    b. must stop working at the end of February, but may begin again on March 1

    c. may work until March 15

    d. may work until March 30

Question 3

If Laura decides to take the early retirement package from JunkTV, how much money will she be able to roll-over into her RRSP?

    a. $60,000

    b. $52,500

    c. $36,000

    d. $0

Question 4

With regard to the investment in Slaphead Enterprises, William can

    a. not write off the loss, since he has no capital gains to offset

    b. use the loss to reduce his investment income by $20,000

    c. use the loss to reduce his business income by $20,000

    d. use the loss to reduce his business income by $10,000

Question 5

Given William's feelings about how his non-registered assets should be distributed, which of the following would be most appropriate?

    a. an *inter vivos* trust

    b. a joint partner trust

    c. an outright gift to Jean

    d. an outright gift to Laura

Question 6

If William wanted to make sure that any future growth of Big Bill Leatherworks accrued to Jean and Howard, they should subscribe to new 10 common shares and he should exchange his shares for

    a. 100 preferred, voting shares

    b. 100 preferred, non-voting shares

    c. 100 preferred, retractable shares

    d. 100 preferred, voting, retractable shares

Question 7

With regard to the cottage, what kind of clause should Laura include in her will?

    a. A life interest clause

    b. A guardianship clause

    c. An encroachment clause

    d. An election clause

Question 8

Assuming Laura lives to age 85 and is pre-deceased by William, how large a tax liability would her estate face on the cottage? Use a 47% marginal tax rate.

    a. $184,652

    b. $113,587

    c. $100,000

    d. $ 0

Question 9

With regards to his brother's estate, which of the following is/are true? William

1. should advertise for creditors and pay off all of the estate's valid debts, or he could be held personally liable

2. is entitled to charge a fee and be reimbursed for expenses incurred while looking after the estate

3. does not need to obtain a clearance certificate before distributing funds to his siblings

    a. 1 only

    b. 2 only

    c. 1 and 2 only

    d. 3 only

Question 10

How much of William's annual interest payment is tax deductible?

    a. $0

    b. $350

    c. $525

    d. $700

Question 11

Which portion of Laura's registered portfolio is most volatile?

    a. $134,000

    b. $100,000

    c. $ 80,000

    d. $ 25,000

Question 12

The generally accepted principles for accessing capital lead to integrated strategies to minimize taxes and maximize overall income for the family unit. According to these strategies, When Laura and William are retired, which of the following would be the last source of capital to access?

　　a. Higher-income spouse's non-registered investments

　　b. Lower-income spouse's non-registered investments

　　c. Lower-income spouse's registered investments

　　d. Higher-income spouse's registered investments

Question 13

Which of the following CPP factors are relevant in calculating Laura's CPP pension benefits?

1. The later the application, the better because of the increase in the amount of pension available at later ages.

2. The length of time during which the contributor was a plan member.

3. The level of contributory earnings.

4. Other sources of retirement income.

5. The health of the contributor.

　　a. 1, 2, 3, 4 and 5

　　b. 2, 3, 4 and 5 only

　　c. 2 and 3 only

　　d. 2, 3 and 4 only

Question 14

Laura heard about the Guaranteed Income Supplement (GIS) program. Which of the following statements about eligibility requirements for the GIS are correct?

1. The recipient must be age 65 or older.

2. The recipient must be single or the survivor of a marriage or common law partnership.

3. The recipient must be in receipt of the Old Age Security pension.

4. The recipient must be a resident in Canada or an expatriate who qualifies for an OAS pension for life.

5. The recipient must meet certain income requirements.

　　a. 1, 2, 3, 4 and 5

　　b. 1, 3 and 5 only

　　c. 2 and 3 only

　　d. 1 and 2 only

Question 15

In addition to retirement pensions, the CPP provides a number of other benefits. Which of the following comments regarding these other benefits is correct?

 a. The one-time death benefit payment under the CPP is $2,500.

 b. A pension is payable to the deceased contributor if the surviving spouse is age 35 or older, or if she has dependent children, or is disabled.

 c. Children of a deceased CPP contributor are entitled to a child benefit up to age 19.

 d. After age 65, the surviving spouse is entitled to a pension equal to 60% of the pension entitlement of the deceased, if the surviving spouse is not receiving other CPP benefits.

DISCUSSION QUESTIONS

Question 16

Advise Laura on her plan to retire early.

Question 17

Create strategy/recommendations on how William should structure the transfer of the business to Howard.

Question 18

Discuss the best way for Laura to ensure her wishes regarding the cottage are followed.

Question 19

Recommend retirement planning strategies for the Rogers.

Question 20

Discuss the tax implications of William's investment in Slaphead Enterprises.

Question 21

What would be the tax implications if William were to sell all of his non-registered investments this year?

Question 22

What are William's responsibilities as Charles's executor. Would you recommend William distribute some of Charles' estate to his siblings?

QUESTIONS & SOLUTIONS

Question 1

If Laura decides to start receiving the Canada Pension Plan next year, by what per cent will her benefits be reduced?

    a. 5%

    b. 15%

    c. 25%

    d. 30

Answer: d

    ⇨   The CPP adjusts the amount of a pension by 0.5% for each month before or after the 65th birthday from the time the pension starts to be received. The case states that Laura wants to retire at 60, so her monthly payment will be 30% lower than if she had waited until age 65.

Question 2

If Laura wants to start receiving her Canada Pension Plan retirement benefits in March, she

    a. must stop working at the end of February, and may not work during the month of March

    b. must stop working at the end of February, but may begin again on March 1

    c. may work until March 15

    d. may work until March 30

Answer: a

    ⇨   Those between the ages of 60 and 64 must have "stopped working" when they receive their CPP retirement pension. This means the person is not working by the end of the month before the CPP retirement pension begins and during the month in which it begins. Once a person starts receiving the CPP pension, he or she can work as much as desired without affecting the pension amount.

Question 3

If Laura decides to take the early retirement package from JunkTV, how much money will she be able to roll-over into her RRSP?

    a. $60,000

    b. $52,500

    c. $36,000

    d. $0

Answer: b

⇨ The case states that Laura has worked at JunkTV since 1978, and that there is no pension plan or DPSP. The retirement package consists of a lump-sum payment of $58,000 (one times salary), plus $2,000 for unused sick leave, all of which qualifies as a "retiring allowance". The portion of a retiring allowance that Laura may transfer to her RRSP is not determined by her contribution room, but is computed as $2,000 for every year prior to 1996, plus $1,500 for the number of years before 1989 during which there was no company pension plan or DPSP. The calculations are therefore as follows:

⇨ Lump sum (1 x salary) — $58,000

⇨ Sick leave credit — $2,000

⇨ Retiring allowance — $60,000

⇨ 18 years before 1996 at $2,000 per year = $36,000

⇨ *plus*

⇨ 11 years (1978 to 1988)

⇨ at $1,500 per year = $16,500

The total eligible for rollover is $52,500

Question 4

With regard to the investment in Slaphead Enterprises, William can

    a. not write off the loss, since he has no capital gains to offset

    b. use the loss to reduce his investment income by $20,000

    c. use the loss to reduce his business income by $20,000

    d. use the loss to reduce his business income by $10,000

Answer: d

⇨ One-half of the money lost on the shares of a private, Canadian-controlled small business corporation can be claimed as an "allowable business investment loss" (ABIL). The deduction can be used against employment, business or investment income. The case states that William invested $20,000 in Slaphead Enterprises, so his ABIL is $10,000.

Question 5

Given William's feelings about how his non-registered assets should be distributed, which of the following would be most appropriate?

    a. an *inter vivos* trust

    b. a joint partner trust

    c. an outright gift to Jean

    d. an outright gift to Laura

Answer: b

    ⇨ The case states that William is 65 years old and wants the income from his non-registered investments to be available to Laura for as long as she is alive, but wants to make certain that the capital will ultimately pass on to his daughter, Jean. He does not want John to inherit any of these funds. The best tool to accomplish this is a joint partner trust. This would allow him to transfer his assets to a trust without incurring a deemed disposition. Both he and Laura draw could draw income from the trust until the death of the surviving partner, at which point the capital would go to Jean. Joint partner trusts may only be established by those who are 65 years old and older.

Question 6

If William wanted to make sure that any future growth of Big Bill Leatherworks accrued to Jean and Howard, they should subscribe to new 10 common shares and he should exchange his shares for

    a. 100 preferred, voting shares

    b. 100 preferred, non-voting shares

    c. 100 preferred, retractable shares

    d. 100 preferred, voting, retractable shares

Answer: d

    ⇨ William should exchange his common shares for preferred, voting, retractable shares. Future growth will accrue to the common shares, while his voting preferred shares will allow him to retain control of the firm and receive dividend income. Since they are retractable, William can require the corporation to buy him out at a fixed price when he is ready to retire.

Question 7

With regard to the cottage, what kind of clause should Laura include in her will?

    a. A life interest clause

    b. A guardianship clause

    c. An encroachment clause

    d. An election clause

Answer: a

    ⇨ The case states that, in the event of her death, Laura will allow William to use the cottage for as long as he is alive, but wants ownership to pass to her son. By leaving a "life interest" in something, the testator can allow one person to use and enjoy an asset while another beneficiary will receive ownership at his or her death. "Guardianship" would deal with the care of minors, "encroachment" with the responsibilities of trustees managing capital, and "election" with the executor's duty to pay taxes.

Question 8

Assuming Laura lives to age 85 and is pre-deceased by William, how large a tax liability would her estate face on the cottage? Use a 47% marginal tax rate.

    a. $184,652

    b. $113,587

    c. $100,000

    d. $ 0

Answer: b

    ⇨ The case states that real estate in the cottage area has been appreciating at a rate of 5% a year. The original value of the property was $50,000 and it is currently valued at $150,000. Laura is 59 years old, meaning there are 26 years before she reaches 85. Half of any capital gain will have to be included as income on in her terminal tax return. The calculation is therefore as follows:

    ⇨ Set to 1 P/YR since assuming 5% annual growth

    ⇨ PV = 150,000

    ⇨ XP/YR = 26

    ⇨ I/YR = 5

    ⇨ PMT = 0

SOLVE FOR FV, which equals $533,351

$533,351 minus original value of $50,000 = $483,351. Half of the $483,351 gain must be included as income = $241,675, and 47% tax on $241,675 is $113,587.

Question 9

With regards to his brother's estate, which of the following is/are true? William

1. should advertise for creditors and pay off all of the estate's valid debts, or he could be held personally liable

2. is entitled to charge a fee and be reimbursed for expenses incurred while looking after the estate

3. does not need to obtain a clearance certificate before distributing funds to his siblings

    a. 1 only

    b. 2 only

    c. 1 and 2 only

    d. 3 only

Answer: c

    ⇨ The case text states that Charles' estate is fairly complex, and William is worried that Charles may have owed quite a bit of money in taxes. William should certainly obtain a clearance certificate from the Canada Revenue Agency before distributing assets to his siblings, or he could be held liable for any amount owed by the estate.

Question 10

How much of William's annual interest payment is tax deductible?

    a. $0

    b. $350

    c. $525

    d. $700

Answer: d

    ⇨ The case study states that William has a $10,000 loan that he took out to purchase mining shares for his non-registered account. The loan is at 7%, so he is paying $700 a year. All of this amount may be deducted, since the loan was taken out for the purpose of earning investment income.

Question 11

Which portion of Laura's registered portfolio is most volatile?

    a. $134,000

    b. $100,000

    c. $ 80,000

    d. $ 25,000

Answer: a

    ⇨ The case states that Laura's RRSPs consists of $25,000 in a money market fund, $134,000 in a long-term bond fund, $100,000 in a short-term bond fund and $80,000 in a T-Bill fund. Of these four, the long-term bond fund will be the most volatile.

Question 12

The generally accepted principles for accessing capital lead to integrated strategies to minimize taxes and maximize overall income for the family unit. According to these strategies, When Laura and William are retired, which of the following would be the last source of capital to access?

    a. Higher-income spouse's non-registered investments

    b. Lower-income spouse's non-registered investments

    c. Lower-income spouse's registered investments

    d. Higher-income spouse's registered investments

Answer: d

    ⇨ The recommended use of assets is: the higher-income spouse's non-registered investments, the lower-income spouse's non-registered investments, the lower-income spouse's registered investments and finally, the higher-income spouse's registered investments.

Question 13

Which of the following CPP factors are relevant in calculating Laura's CPP pension benefits?

1. The later the application, the better because of the increase in the amount of pension available at later ages.

2. The length of time during which the contributor was a plan member.

3. The level of contributory earnings.

4. Other sources of retirement income.

5. The health of the contributor.

    a. 1, 2, 3, 4 and 5

    b. 2, 3, 4 and 5 only

    c. 2 and 3 only

    d. 2, 3 and 4 only

Answer: c

    ⇨ An individual's retirement benefit is a function of his or her CPP contributions over the course of his or her contributory period. The CPP is not reduced by other income sources.

    ⇨ The contributor's health has no bearing on the amount of pension payable.

    ⇨ It is not necessarily true that deferring receipt of the CPP results in a larger amount of pension since the CPP ceases at the contributor's death or age 70.

Question 14

Laura heard about the Guaranteed Income Supplement (GIS) program. Which of the following statements about eligibility requirements for the GIS are correct?

1. The recipient must be age 65 or older.

2. The recipient must be single or the survivor of a marriage or common law partnership.

3. The recipient must be in receipt of the Old Age Security pension.

4. The recipient must be a resident in Canada or an expatriate who qualifies for an OAS pension for life.

5. The recipient must meet certain income requirements.

    a. 1, 2, 3, 4 and 5

    b. 1, 3 and 5 only

    c. 2 and 3 only

    d. 1 and 2 only

Answer: b

    ⇨ To be eligible for the GIS, the recipient must be age 65 or older, in receipt of OAS, and a resident in Canada. If the recipient leaves Canada, benefits will cease after six months. GIS benefits are subject to a means test. The benefit is reduced proportionately as an individual's base income increases.

Question 15

In addition to retirement pensions, the CPP provides a number of other benefits. Which of the following comments regarding these other benefits is correct?

    a. The one-time death benefit payment under the CPP is $2,500.

    b. A pension is payable to the deceased contributor if the surviving spouse is age 35 or older, or if she has dependent children, or is disabled.

    c. Children of a deceased CPP contributor are entitled to a child benefit up to age 19.

    d. After age 65, the surviving spouse is entitled to a pension equal to 60% of the pension entitlement of the deceased, if the surviving spouse is not receiving other CPP benefits.

Answer: d

    ⇨ With CPP Benefits for Survivors, the death benefit is the *lesser* of: six times the contributor's normal age 65 monthly retirement pension; or 10% of the contributor's maximum pensionable earnings; or $2,500.

    ⇨ CPP is paid to a surviving spouse not the deceased contributing spouse. A survivor's pension is based on, among other things, whether or not the survivor is supporting any of the deceased's dependent children.

    ⇨ A children's benefit is payable for each dependent child of a deceased contributor who is under 18, or under 25 if attending school full-time.

CASE STUDY 6 — LOUISE AND PHIL XIU

Background

It is December 2009. Louise and Phil are a young couple with three children. They have booked an appointment with you to review their own financial position, and are particularly interested in learning how they should invest for their children's education.

Personal Information

Louise (36), Phil (36), Morgan (5), Amy (6), and Evan (7) live together on a farm outside of the town in which you live. Louise and Phil are both non-smokers and are in good health.

Phil's mother died of cancer when he was in high school, and his father passed away suddenly from a heart attack five years ago. Louise's mother, Gail, lives down the road, and looks after the children when Phil is not able to do so.

Employment Information

Details of Louise's Employment

Louise says she would prefer to work on the farm with Phil, but in order to bring in some more money and obtain insurance benefits for the family, she has taken a job in town. She did graduate work in chemistry, so had no trouble finding employment as a laboratory technician at a nearby pharmaceutical company. Her employer does not offer a company pension plan.

Details of the Farm and Phil's Income

Phil decided to quit his job at the automotive plant and take over his father's farm. He is making the switch to organic farming. Phil says that the transition has not been easy (he lost $20,000 last year), but in the long term he thinks he is doing the right thing — he is happy to be home and with his young children, and believes that going organic will work out well both for the environment, and from a business point of view. While he is still quite young, Evan has shown a real interest in farming, and Phil and Louise hope he might take over the entire operation one day.

Phil has now set up a community supported agriculture (CSA) program, and is gradually building up a base of clients who pay him an annual lump sum in return for a share of his seasonal produce. He uses the family pickup truck to make deliveries, and to get supplies for the farm.

For the first time since he took over the farm, Phil expects to generate a decent profit this year. By "decent" he means more than $10,000. In previous years, they tell you that they barely managed to scrape by on what they had earned.

Financial Position

Real Estate

Phil and Louise's five bedroom brick farmhouse dates from the late 1800s. Phil's father purchased the farm for $10,000 in 1945. Phil's father gave the farm to him shortly before he passed away. Both the house and the 100-acre farm were in a terrible state of disrepair, and the entire property was only valued at $150,000 when it came into their possession.

Phil and Louise are gradually renovating the home, barn, and outbuildings in order to bring the farm back to good order. They believe they could sell the property to developers for $350,000 today. Phil thinks the property will be worth $1 million by the time he is 65. They say they have considered taking out a home equity line of credit to help make ends meet, but so far they have resisted the temptation. They say they would prefer not to take on debts that they cannot pay off.

Louise's Investments, Registered

Louise opened an RRSP at Right Save, the local credit union, shortly after she got her job at the pharmaceutical company. She has invested her savings in three mutual funds.

- $500 Canadian Dividend Fund
- $500 Canadian Blue Chip Fund
- $500 Japan Equity Fund

Louise has $25,000 of unused RRSP contribution room.

Louise's Investments, Non-Registered

Louise has a 3-year, $500 C-Series Canada Savings Bond. It is currently paying 3% interest.

Phil's Investments, Registered

Having earned relatively little money to date, Phil says he has not bothered to set up his own registered retirement savings plan (RRSP). He does, however, have a locked-in retirement account (LIRA) from his employment at the automotive plant.

- $15,000 Global Growth Fund
- $50,000 Canadian Precious Metals Fund

He brought his most recent letter of assessment from the Canada Revenue Agency and you see that Phil has $50,000 of unused RRSP contribution room available.

Phil's Investments, Non-Registered

Phil has a $500 Canada Savings Bond. It is currently paying 3% interest.

Liabilities

Phil and Louise purchased a new truck two years ago, and owe $5,000. They are paying 7% interest on the loan.

Insurance Information

Louise has life insurance equal to twice her salary through her group plan at work, and the premiums are a taxable employee benefit. Phil is named as beneficiary. Phil and Louise mention they also have supplementary accidental death and dismemberment (AD&D) insurance coverage they purchased through Louise's group plan; each of them is covered for $500,000.

Risk Profile

Phil and Louise say that, since they are not able to set aside much money every month, they have come to realize that they will have to accept a higher level of risk in their investment portfolios in order to generate a potentially higher return.

Goals

Phil and Louise are concerned about how much university tuition will cost them by the time their three children are finished high school, and would like to start saving now. They are not sure if all of their children will go on to higher education, but they would like to start preparing, just in case. The local university is currently charging $8,000 a year for an undergraduate degree. They have heard about registered education savings plans (RESPs) and would like to know more. Phil and Louise indicate that Louise's mother, Gail, would also like to help to set aside money for her grandchildren's education.

Phil says that before winter sets in he plans to spend some of his earnings on improving the land — specifically, $5,000 to clear and level several acres of land that his father had allowed to go to bush. He says that having this extra land available for cultivation will allow him to grow more produce and therefore earn some more money. He has been setting aside these funds in a high-interest savings account.

Wills and Powers of Attorney

Louise and Phil do not have wills or powers of attorney.

Louise and Phil Xiu
Statement of Net Worth at December 31, 2009

ASSETS	Louise	Phil	Total
Liquid Assets			
Joint Chequing Account	$ 500	$ 500	$ 1,000
Cash (CSBs)		5,000	5,000
Canada Savings Bonds	500	500	1,000
Total Liquid Assets	**$ 1,000**	**$ 6,000**	**$ 7,000**
Investment Assets			
Registered Assets	1,500	65,000	66,500
Total Investment Assets	**$ 1,500**	**$ 65,000**	**$ 66,500**
Personal-Use Assets			
Farm	175,000	175,000	350,000
Automobile	7,000	7,000	14,000
Personal Effects (owned jointly)	2,000	2,000	4,000
Total Personal Assets	**$ 184,000**	**$ 184,000**	**$ 368,000**
TOTAL ASSETS	**$ 186,500**	**$ 255,000**	**$ 441,500**
LIABILITIES			
Short-Term Liabilities			
Auto Loan	2,500	2,500	5,000
TOTAL LIABILITIES	**$ 2,500**	**$ 2,500**	**$ 5,000**
NET WORTH	**$ 184,000**	**$ 252,500**	**$ 436,500**

Louise and Phil Xiu
Monthly and Annual Cash Flow as of December 31, 2009

	Monthly	Annually
INCOME		
Louise's Income	$ 1,625	$ 19,500
Phil's Income	1,250	15,000
Total Income	**$ 2,875**	**$ 34,500**
EXPENSES		
Taxes, EI and CPP		
Louise	265	3,180
Phil	185	2,220
Maintenance and Repairs		
Home	400	4,800
Home Insurance	100	1,200
Heating and Electricity	100	1,200
Property Taxes	70	840
Automobile		
Loan Payment (Principal and Interest)	150	1,800
Insurance	120	1,440
Gas	150	1,800
Repairs and Maintenance	50	600
Life Insurance Premiums		
AD&D Policy	20	240
Telephone	60	720
Food	200	2,400
Clothing	250	3,000
Personal Care	100	1,200
Entertainment	75	900
RRSP Savings — Louise	100	1,200
Non-Registered Savings — Phil	400	4,800
TOTAL EXPENSES	**$ 2,795**	**$ 33,540**
SURPLUS	**$ 80**	**$ 960**

QUESTIONS

Question 1

Which of the following statements is/are true?

    a. None of the money Phil plans to spend on clearing and leveling the land can be deducted since it is a capital expense.

    b. Phil can only claim half of the allowable Capital Cost Allowance for the year.

    c. Phil can deduct $2,500 of the money he plans to spend on clearing and leveling the land this year.

    d. Phil can claim all of the money he plans to spend on clearing and leveling the land this year as a deductible expense.

Question 2

If Phil and Louise were to open a registered education savings plan (RESP) tomorrow and deposit $2,000 for each child, what is the combined total amount of money they would receive this year under the government's Canada Education Savings Grant (CESG) program?

    a. $ 400

    b. $1,200

    c. $1,500

    d. $1,800

Question 3

If Phil and Louise were to open a RESP tomorrow and deposit $2,000 for each child, what is the combined, total amount of extra money they would receive this year under the government's Canada Learning Bond program?

    a. $0

    b. $75

    c. $1,500

    d. $1,575

Question 4

If Phil and Louise were to have a fourth child in 2008 and open a RESP in his or her name, depositing only $100 for the year, what is the amount of money that child would receive that year under the government's Canada Learning Bond program?

    a. $525

    b. $500

    c. $100

    d. $0

Question 5

Assuming that education costs rise at the rate of 5% a year, what can Phil and Louise expect to pay for Evan's first year tuition when he goes to university at age 18?

    a. $13,683

    b. $12,853

    c. $10,462

    d. $8,374

Question 6

Which of the following statements is/are true? If Phil were to obtain critical illness insurance, his premium would be

1. that of a standard, non-smoking risk
2. higher than that of a standard, non-smoking risk
3. a tax deductible business expense

   a. 1 only
   b. 1 and 3 only
   c. 2 only
   d. 2 and 3 only

Question 7

How many years can Phil carry forward his loss from last year?

   a. 10 years
   b. 7 years
   c. 3 years
   d. Phil cannot carry forward his loss

Question 8

If Louise were to set up in-trust investment accounts for each of their three children,

1. dividends would be taxed in the child's hands
2. interest would be taxed in the child's hands
3. capital gains would be taxed in the child's hands

   a. 1 only
   b. 1 and 3 only
   c. 2 only
   d. 3 only

Question 9

Which of the following statements is/are true? If Phil were to set up a family RESP,

1. he could not contribute any more money to the plan after Morgan's 26th birthday
2. it would have to be wound up and all of the funds would have to be distributed by the time Morgan is 31 years old
3. it would have to be wound up and all of the funds would have to be distributed by the time Evan is 21 years old

   a. 1 only
   b. 1 and 2 only
   c. 2 only
   d. 3 only

Question 10

Concerning Louise's RRSP, which of the following statements is/are true?

1. It is protected by the CUDIC
2. It is above the foreign content limit

   a. 1 only
   b. 2 only
   c. both 1 and 2
   d. neither 1 nor 2

Question 11

Which of the following statements is true? If Phil were to establish a RESP, but none of the children were to go on to post-secondary education,

    a. he would not have to repay the CESG.

    b. he would have to repay both the CESG as well as all the money that had been earned on the CESG.

    c. he could roll over up to $50,000 of the accumulated earnings to a spousal RRSP, without penalty, provided he had sufficient contribution room available.

    d. he could roll over up to $50,000 of the accumulated earnings to his own RRSP, subject to a 20% penalty tax, provided he had sufficient contribution room available.

Question 12

If Louise were to die of cancer one year from now, how much money would Phil receive after taxes?

    a. $19,500

    b. $39,000

    c. $500,000

    d. $539,000

Question 13

Assuming that Phil's father is not going to use his capital gains exemption for the transfer, Phil is deemed to have acquired the farm at a cost of

    a. $0

    b. $10,000

    c. $75,000

    d. $150,000

Question 14

During the year, Louise purchased a Canada Savings Bonds (CSB) on October 20, 2009. Which of the following statements is/are true?

1. The CSBs are eligible investments for an RRSP.

2. Interest on the bonds will be paid upon maturity and will be reported in 2010 for tax purposes.

3 CSB are good investments since they protect Phil and Louise from inflation risk.

4. If Phil redeems the CSB on January 5, 2010, he will receive $500 and accrued interest up to end of the month prior to redemption.

    a. 1 and 2

    b. 1 and 3

    c. 1 and 4

    d. 1 only

Question 15

Phil and Louise realized that they may have to accept a higher level of risk in their investment portfolios to generate potentially higher returns. On a Risk-Return scale, place the following types of mutual funds in order starting with the safest alternative and ending with the riskiest:

1. Bond Fund

2. Global Fund

3. Money Market Fund

4. Equity Fund

    a. 1, 2, 3, 4

    b. 4, 3, 1, 2

    c. 3, 1, 4, 2

    d. 1, 3, 4, 2

DISCUSSION QUESTIONS

Question 16

Summarize and prioritize what you see as the Xiu's priorities, personal and financial goals, and needs.

Question 17

Explain to the Xius how RESPs work and establish a strategy for the Xiu's how they should save for their children's education.

Question 18

What are the financial planning implications of Phil passing on the farm to his son in the future?

Question 19

What are your professional responsibilities if you recommend Phil speaks to an accountant about transferring the farm to his son?

Question 20

Provide retirement planning recommendations for the Xius.

Question 21

Discuss financial management recommendations for the couple.

Question 22

How often should you and the Xiu's review the financial plan you have prepared? How would you propose measuring the progress towards the achievement of the objectives of the financial plan?

QUESTIONS & SOLUTIONS

Question 1

Which of the following statements is/are true?

 a. None of the money Phil plans to spend on clearing and leveling the land can be deducted since it is a capital expense.

 b. Phil can only claim half of the allowable Capital Cost Allowance for the year.

 c. Phil can deduct $2,500 of the money he plans to spend on clearing and leveling the land this year.

 d. Phil can claim all of the money he plans to spend on clearing and leveling the land this year as a deductible expense.

Answer: d

 ⇨ All of the money farmers spend to improve land (such as leveling or clearing bush, for example) can be claimed as a deductible expense.

Question 2

If Phil and Louise were to open a registered education savings plan (RESP) tomorrow and deposit $2,000 for each child, what is the combined total amount of money they would receive this year under the government's Canada Education Savings Grant (CESG) program?

 a. $ 400

 b. $1,200

 c. $1,500

 d. $1,800

Answer: c

 ⇨ The case study states that Phil and Louise have a combined income of less than $38,832 (2009). This means that they would qualify for the enhanced Canada Education Savings Grant rate of 40% on the first $500 of contributions, and that they would receive the standard 20% CESG on the remaining $1,500 contribution. The calculations are as follows.

 ⇨ Enhanced 40% CESG on first $500 contribution = $200

 ⇨ Standard 20% CESG on next $1500 contribution = $300

 ⇨ $500 × three children = $1,500

Question 3

If Phil and Louise were to open a RESP tomorrow and deposit $2,000 for each child, what is the combined, total amount of extra money they would receive this year under the government's Canada Learning Bond program?

 a. $0

 b. $75

 c. $1,500

 d. $1,575

Answer: a

 ⇨ The Canada Learning Bond is a special payment available to lower income families whose Canada Child Tax Benefit payment (commonly known as "baby bonus" or "family allowance") includes the National Child Benefit Supplement. Generally speaking, these are families with a net annual income below $38,832.

 ⇨ Although Phil and Louise's combined incomes add up to just $34,500 — meaning they would meet the income requirements — the Canada Learning Bond is only available to children who were born after December 31, 2003. All of their children are over the age of 5, so none of them would qualify for the Canada Learning Bond.

Question 4

If Phil and Louise were to have a fourth child in 2010 and open a RESP in his or her name, depositing only $100 for the year, what is the amount of money that child would receive that year under the government's Canada Learning Bond program?

    a. $525

    b. $500

    c. $100

    d. $0

Answer: a

    ⇨ For families that qualify, the government will make an initial payment of $525 to a child's RESP under the Canada Learning Bond program — a $500 bond and an additional $25 to help cover the cost of opening a RESP. There is no minimum contributory requirement — even if there is no money in a RESP, the Government of Canada will deposit the CLB into the child's RESP.

Question 5

Assuming that education costs rise at the rate of 5% a year, what can Phil and Louise expect to pay for Evan's first year tuition when he goes to university at age 18?

    a. $13,683

    b. $12,853

    c. $10,462

    d. $8,374

Answer: a

    ⇨ The case states that university tuition currently costs $8,000 a year. Evan is 7 years old, so he will attend university in 11 years. The steps on a financial calculator are as follows:

    ⇨ Set to 1 P/YR since it is an annual increase in the cost of tuition

    ⇨ xP/YR = 11

    ⇨ I/YR = 5

    ⇨ PV = $8,000

    ⇨ PMT = 0

SOLVE FOR FV, which equals $13,683

Question 6

Which of the following statements is/are true? If Phil were to obtain critical illness insurance, his premium would be

1. that of a standard, non-smoking risk

2. higher than that of a standard, non-smoking risk

3. a tax deductible business expense

    a. 1 only

    b. 1 and 3 only

    c. 2 only

    d. 2 and 3 only

Answer: c

⇨   The case study states that Phil's mother died of cancer when he was in high school, and his father passed away suddenly from a heart attack five years ago. Critical illness insurance considers family medical history when pricing coverage, so with his background, Phil should expect to pay higher than standard risk premiums. Any premiums paid for critical illness insurance coverage could not be deducted as a business expense.

Question 7

How many years can Phil carry forward his loss from last year?

    a. 10 years

    b. 7 years

    c. 3 years

    d. Phil cannot carry forward his loss

Answer: a

⇨   The case indicates that Phil lost $20,000 on the farm last year. Farm losses can be carried forward and used against income for 10 years.

Question 8

If Louise were to set up in-trust investment accounts for each of their three children,

1. dividends would be taxed in the child's hands

2. interest would be taxed in the child's hands

3. capital gains would be taxed in the child's hands

    a. 1 only

    b. 1 and 3 only

    c. 2 only

    d. 3 only

Answer: d

⇨   With an in-trust account, only capital gains are taxed in the hands of the child. Dividends and interest would be attributed back to Louise.

Question 9

Which of the following statements is/are true? If Phil were to set up a family RESP,

1. he could not contribute any more money to the plan after Morgan's 26th birthday

2. it would have to be wound up and all of the funds would have to be distributed by the time Morgan is 41 years old

3. it would have to be wound up and all of the funds would have to be distributed by the time Evan is 21 years old

    a. 1 only

    b. 1 and 2 only

    c. 2 only

    d. 3 only

Answer: b

    ⇨   The case states that Morgan is 5 years old. Contributions to a RESP must cease after the plan has been in existence for 21 years, and must be wound up after 36 years, so Phil's plan must be closed to contributions by the time Morgan is 26 and terminated by the time she is 41.

Question 10

Concerning Louise's RRSP, which of the following statements is/are true?

1. It is protected by the CUDIC

2. It is above the foreign content limit

    a. 1 only

    b. 2 only

    c. both 1 and 2

    d. neither 1 nor 2

Answer: d

    ⇨   The case indicates that Louise's RRSP is invested in mutual funds, not in term deposits, so her money is not covered by the Credit Union Deposit Insurance Corporation (CUDIC). The 30% cap on foreign content in RRSPs was eliminated by the 2005 federal Budget.

Question 11

Which of the following statements is true? If Phil were to establish a RESP, but none of the children were to go on to post-secondary education,

    a. he would not have to repay the CESG.

    b. he would have to repay both the CESG as well as all the money that had been earned on the CESG.

    c. he could roll over up to $50,000 of the accumulated earnings to a spousal RRSP, without penalty, provided he had sufficient contribution room available.

    d. he could roll over up to $50,000 of the accumulated earnings to his own RRSP, subject to a 20% penalty tax, provided he had sufficient contribution room available.

Answer: c

    ⇨   If beneficiaries do not go on to higher education, the CESG must be repaid, but the money earned on the CESG does not. Provided the contributor has contribution room available, up to $50,000 of the accumulated earnings can be rolled into the contributor's RRSP or to a spousal RRSP without penalty.

Question 12

If Louise were to die of cancer one year from now, how much money would Phil receive after taxes?

     a. $19,500

     b. $39,000

     c. $500,000

     d. $539,000

Answer: b

     ⇨ The case states that Louise has life insurance equal to twice her salary through her group plan at work and that Phil is named as beneficiary. The accidental death and dismemberment insurance coverage they have would not pay out in the event of death from cancer. Life insurance premiums paid by an employer are treated as a taxable employee benefit, so any benefit paid under the plan would not be subject to tax.

Question 13

Assuming that Phil's father is not going to use his capital gains exemption for the transfer, Phil is deemed to have acquired the farm at a cost of

     a. $0

     b. $10,000

     c. $75,000

     d. $150,000

Answer: b

     ⇨ Qualifying farm property can be rolled over to children or grandchildren at the original cost base, provided the child or grandchild is also using the property principally as a farming business. The case indicates that Phil's father acquired the farm for $10,000, so assuming his father did not use his $500,000 "qualified farm property" capital gains exemption to give Phil a higher cost base, Phil is deemed to have acquired the farm for $10,000.

Question 14

During the year, Louise purchased a Canada Savings Bonds (CSB) on October 20, 2009. Which of the following statements is/are true?

1. The CSBs are eligible investments for an RRSP.

2. Interest on the bonds will be paid upon maturity and will be reported in 2010 for tax purposes.

3 CSB are good investments since they protect Phil and Louise from inflation risk.

4. If Phil redeems the CSB on January 5, 2010, he will receive $500 and accrued interest up to end of the month prior to redemption.

     a. 1 and 2

     b. 1 and 3

     c. 1 and 4

     d. 1 only

Answer: d

     ⇨ CSB is eligible investments for RRSP purposes. Phil's R-series bond pays interest on the anniversary date every year and not upon maturity. Louise's C-series bond accrues interest each year and pays the interest upon maturity. CSB are poor investments since they expose the investor to inflation and reinvestment risk. If Phil redeems his CSB prior to 90 days, he only receives the face value of the bond and does not receive any accrued interest.

Question 15

Phil and Louise realized that they may have to accept a higher level of risk in their investment portfolios to generate potentially higher returns. On a Risk-Return scale, place the following types of mutual funds in order starting with the safest alternative and ending with the riskiest:

1. Bond Fund

2. Global Fund

3. Money Market Fund

4. Equity Fund

   a. 1, 2, 3, 4

   b. 4, 3, 1, 2

   c. 3, 1, 4, 2

   d. 1, 3, 4, 2

Answer: c

   ⇨ In order, from the least risky/lowest return to highest risk/return tradeoff is money market funds, bond funds, equity funds and then global funds.

Topical Index — Capstone Course